CAREER
OPPORTUNITIES
in

ANIMATION

CAREER

OPPORTUNITIES
in
ANIMATION

JEFF LENBURG

Foreword by
BOB KURTZ

Ferguson's
An Infobase Learning Company

Career Opportunities in Animation

Copyright © 2012 by Jeff Lenburg

Ferguson's
An imprint of Infobase Learning
132 West 31st Street
New York NY 10001

Library of Congress Cataloging-in-Publication Data
Lenburg, Jeff.
   Career opportunities in animation / Jeff Lenburg ; foreword by Bob Kurtz. — 1st ed.
      p. cm.— (Career opportunities)
   Includes bibliographical references and index.
   ISBN-13: 978-0-8160-8182-0 (hardcover : alk. paper)
   ISBN-10: 0-8160-8182-4 (hardcover : alk. paper)
1. Animated films—Vocational guidance—Juvenile literature. 2. Animation (Cinematography)—Vocational guidance—Juvenile literature. I. Title.
   NC1765.L355 2011
   791.43'34023—dc22   2011013031

Ferguson's books are available at special discounts when purchased in bulk quantities for businesses, associations, institutions, or sales promotions. Please call our Special Sales Department in New York at (212) 967-8800 or (800) 322-8755.

You can find Ferguson's on the World Wide Web at http://www.infobaselearning.com

Text design by Kerry Casey
Composition by Hermitage Publishing Services
Cover printed by Sheridan Books, Ann Arbor, Mich.
Book printed and bound by Sheridan Books, Ann Arbor, Mich.
Date printed: December 2011
Printed in the United States of America

10 9 8 7 6 5 4 3 2 1

This book is printed on acid-free paper.

In loving memory of Pat and Betty Grenis

CONTENTS

FOREWORD

If you love animation, this is the book for you. Technologically, the animation field is one of the fastest changing arts today and can offer some of the most rewarding career experiences.

Animation contributes not only to television and theatrical releases but also to the Internet, video games, live-action visual effects, mobile phones, rock concerts, electronic billboards, Blu-Ray extras, 3-D, special venues, and on and on. This art form is expanding rapidly. Changes in animation are happening as you read this foreword. Nearly every year, the Academy of Motion Picture Arts and Sciences redefines animation in its rules book.

If you have a passion for this dynamic art form, jump right in! It can even help to be a bit of an outsider. Like a magnet, animation pulls in people who think and draw differently to work collectively to make animation dreams a reality. By the way, did I mention *drawing,* that old, antiquated art form? While it is true that, increasingly, you need to have computer skills in today's animation environment, those with the ability to draw well have a distinct advantage over those who rely exclusively on technological aids. Many of today's top directors, animators, and designers carry sketchbooks that they fill with drawings.

Animation is a constant learning process. One director I know even likes to create flipbooks. But just wait (or don't wait), there are more innovative animation programs, systems, and drawing tools on the horizon. Many working professionals are going back to school to learn new computer graphics (CG) programs in order to keep up with the changing technological landscape.

Coming straight out of Chouinard Art Institute, my first job in animation was designing experimen-

tal films—white-on-white modeled paper sculpture films—for Walt Disney Studios. My instructor at Chouinard, T. Hee (yes, that was his name), asked me to come and work alongside him. Hee became my mentor, along with Marc Davis, one of Walt's legendary "Nine Old Men." I had studied life drawing at Chouinard with Marc, so he knew me well. Later, at another studio, Cal Howard, the great animation gag man, became my third mentor. These three men are legends in animation, and I am so privileged and honored to have had those three amazing talents adopt me.

So there I was, my first job, very young, working on the third floor with Walt Disney and his astonishingly talented crew. I was having story meetings with Walt, working on new techniques. How's that for a start in the animation biz?

One day, on entering the crowded studio elevator, one fellow who I had not seen before asked me, "So how long have you been working here at Disney?" At the time, I looked about 15 years old and proudly replied, "Oh, a long time, six months!" I still remember vividly the loud laughter that filled that small, crowded space and echoed up the elevator shaft. It was a time when people in animation worked and stayed 10 to 20 years at one studio. That was the norm. Today, if you answered that same question with "six months," the response would probably be "good for you!" When I left Disney after one year, the animation workplace was already going through a transformation. Artists were moving from studio to studio far more frequently. The idea of staying at one studio for the duration of your career was becoming a thing of the past.

As for me, I also traveled from studio to studio. I worked on TV commercials as a storyboard artist and character designer. At the time, TV commercials were one of the most innovative and creative areas in animation. The talents who worked in TV commercials were the best in the business. I also worked on the animated TV shows *Alvin and the Chipmunks* and *Linus the Lionhearted* as a writer, character designer, and storyboard artist. I was a writer on the first year of the *Pink Panther* theatrical shorts, in addition to other projects for DePatie-Freleng. Along the way, I picked up some layout skills. While doing a freelance layout job for Pantomime Pictures, Fred Crippen, the owner and a talent in his own right, said to me, "You are too good to do layout, how would you like to direct for me?" That's how I became a director. He just asked me. I learned on the job. I directed more than 70 four-minute *Roger Ramjet* episodes for television. It was a great time! It was a learning time!

For the next four years, I was known as a designer/director until I did something I never thought I would do. I started my own animation production company, Kurtz & Friends. I had run out of companies I wanted to work for. I never thought I would be a producer. I didn't want to be a producer. Most producers I worked for were *crazy.* So now my complete job title was writer, designer, director, and, yes, producer. At Kurtz & Friends, we work on a diverse range of projects, including animated television specials, feature film segments, animated opening titles, animated shorts, public-service spots, an animation/live action/interactive show for a 3-D multiscreen venue, animation for a Las Vegas show in which animation interacts with live actors, an animated simulator theme park ride, animation for sports Jumbotrons, animated pilots, video games, Blu-Ray extras, the Internet, and more.

I am so proud of the mastery and brilliance of my multitalented team. Most of our work is done in 2-D with CG (computer graphic) assists combined with digital ink and paint. As a group, we have adapted to new technology. Gone are the clacking double-head moviolas, the animation camera services, film splicers, rewinds, mag-tracks, and film bins. Gone is the smell of painted cels stacked three feet high drying on shelves. No more telecine, paint labs, and scratched film. No more waiting until the next day to view our dailies. But, personally, I like the magic you can still achieve with a pencil. That magic is hard to replace.

What are the differences in job titles from when I first came into the business? The job titles were fewer and actually described what you did: director, storyboard artist, designer, layout artist, animator, assistant animator, animation clean-up, background painter, and so on. From studio to studio, the job titles were the same, and the functions were the same. Today, the titles can be somewhat confusing. Sometimes directors are called sheet timers. Then there are technical directors, character TDs, riggers, lead lighters, 3-D modelers, previsual development, texture painters, look development, design clean-up, character layout, rough layout, background layout, model designers, character designers, prop designers, compositors, and a title that makes me laugh every time I hear it: storyboard revisionist. These job titles and their functions often vary from studio to studio and from country to country. In the future, these job titles will evolve and become even more specialized.

There's an old saying, "If you love your job, you will never work a day in your life." Come and join us in the animation sand pile.

—Bob Kurtz

INDUSTRY OUTLOOK

The business of animation, like the entertainment industry generally, is highly cyclical and has experienced numerous highs and lows over the years. Yet its ability to create new paths and make technological inroads has kept the art form thriving in one form or another. Numerous changes and technological innovations in its methods and processes have only enhanced its prestige since its inception in the late 1890s. It was then that the lightning-fast sketch pad cartoonists Tom Merry (William Machin) and James Stuart Blackton produced the first three- to four-minute kinetoscopes of them simply "sketching" in live action a myriad of cartoon drawings, one right after another, before audiences' very eyes. Blackton first achieved success with this crude practice in the live-action Edison film short *The Enchanted Drawing,* based on his "chalk-talk" vaudeville act, made up of a series of scenes featuring letters, words, and faces created by his unseen hand. Since those days, many technological trends, far removed from the archaic roots when animators laboriously drew every drawing to animate a single cartoon—including the introduction of computer-generated animation, or CGI, Flash and Web animation, motion-picture capture animation, and digital 3-D—have once again taken the industry to breathtaking new heights in terms of creativity, artistry, and production.

Animated cartoons first took root in America in 1906, when Blackton produced the country's first animated cartoon, *Humorous Phases of Funny Faces,* for Vitagraph. His earliest example of motion picture "cartooning" demonstrated the tremendous promise of the medium. In 1908, the French cartoonist Emil Cohl applied the principles of stick-figure animation in a series of comic vignettes,

titled *Drame chez les Fantoches* (1908). The newspaper cartoonist Winsor McCay took animation to the next level, introducing the first fully animated cartoon, *Little Nemo* (1911), based on his popular *New York Herald* strip, *Little Nemo in Slumberland,* which took him four years to animate. Three years later, he unveiled the first genuine American cartoon star, *Gertie the Dinosaur* (1914), the first frame-by-frame animated film, created from approximately 10,000 individual pencil drawings.

Many more important technological breakthroughs aided animation's proliferation. In 1913, pioneer animator Earl Hurd patented the first cel animation method, or celluloid sheet, layering elements on top of one another so that static drawings, including backgrounds, were drawn only once, with characters animated over the top on clear acetate cels. This technique saved an enormous amount of time and cost, as previously each animated frame had to be entirely hand drawn. In 1914, America's most prolific cartoon producer, John Randolph ("J.R.") Bray, invented the labor-saving animation process of printing backgrounds on translucent paper to facilitate the positioning of moving objects in successive drawings, thus requiring only a few more than a hundred basic arrangements of cels in 1,600 frames of footage. That year, he also pioneered the idea of the animation assembly line, in which artists are assigned to handle specific jobs—to write the story, design the characters, animate the key drawings, assist or clean-up key drawings, do in-between drawings to complete the action of the animation, paint background landscapes, and photograph the drawings onto film—a process still largely in use today. In 1915, pioneer animator Max Fleischer demonstrated his patented process,

Rotoscope, in his famed *Out of the Inkwell* series, enabling animators to trace live-action figures seen on projected film and redraw them as a cartoon.

Putting sound to nontalking moving images took animation down an exciting new path. In 1924, Fleischer produced the first sound cartoons, *Song Car-Tunes,* a series of "bouncing ball sing-a-longs" synchronized to popular music by the then-revolutionary DeForest Phonofilm system. In 1928, a year after the first "talking" motion picture, Al Jolson's Warner Bros. musical feature *The Jazz Singer,* animator Walt Disney produced the first successful cartoon that used synchronized sound, Mickey Mouse's *Steamboat Willie.*

During the 1930s and 1940s, the U.S. animation industry dominated the worldwide market with its artistry and innovation. In 1932, Disney accomplished another historic milestone by producing the first true Technicolor cartoon, a *Silly Symphony* called *Flowers and Trees;* he exclusively owned the rights to the process for five years. In 1934, Max Fleischer created the illusion of greater depth in animation with his revolutionary method of table-top animation, which was employed in the Betty Boop cartoon *Poor Cinderella.* Meanwhile, Ub Iwerks and Disney achieved greater results in 3-D animation using a technique known as multiplane animation, whereby animation was shot in layers over movable backgrounds using a special camera to give each shot more depth and movement. Three years later, Disney again made history by releasing the first commercially successful full-length animated feature in full Technicolor, *Snow White and the Seven Dwarfs,* which significantly advanced the art of "personality animation" in movies and short subjects (films one to two reels in length). In 1940, he then demonstrated in six movie theaters the first multichannel stereo system, known as "Fantasound," with the release of his animated classic *Fantasia.*

By the mid-1940s, United Productions of America (UPA), a small, independent studio (producers of the Oscar-winning *Gerald McBoing Boing* and *Mister Magoo* theatrical shorts), introduced an innovative, more cost-effective style of animation: limited animation. The new system, a stark contrast to the more expensive and more elaborately detailed full animation, used comparably fewer cels per second to create the illusion of movement. In the late 1940s, as costs became prohibitive after the U.S. Supreme Court's decision to ban the studio practice of "block bookings" effectively reduced the percentage of rental fees they received from packaging cartoons, newsreels, and live-action shorts with feature films to movie theaters, many would adopt this economical method of producing cartoons that were mostly profitable and still achieved a wide range of motion and believability on screen by the late 1950s.

****

Television, a live and rather unsophisticated medium transmitted over free public airwaves to millions of television sets across the country, impacted the film and animation industry much more than had been imagined. Most major animation studios, except for Walt Disney and Walter Lantz, which struggled to remain profitable, closed their doors in the late 1950s and early 1960s as the market for short subjects was "virtually dead." However, the small-box medium eventually became a boon to the industry. In 1957, Academy Award–winning animators William Hanna and Joseph Barbera (creators of Tom and Jerry) premiered the first hosted cartoon series for Saturday mornings on NBC, *The Ruff and Reddy Show.* Made six years after Jay Ward (later of Rocky and Bullwinkle fame) and producer Jerry Fairbanks' trailblazing first-made-for-television, cliff-hanging cartoon series, *Crusader Rabbit,* the traditional ink-and-paint trained duo applied their innovative, budget-conscious system of "planned animation," a variation of UPA's limited animation, that effectively cut down on much of the repetitive work in redrawing entire characters for each frame and kept character bodies static (like backgrounds) wherever possible. They simply animated only the moving body parts on a separate level. Hanna and Barbera single-handedly transformed the industry, proving that low-cost cartoons could be made for television for a profit, including the first half-hour all-cartoon program, *The Huckleberry Hound Show,* and first prime-time animated series, *The Flintstones.*

Throughout the 1960s, demand for new and original cartoons for television skyrocketed. Hanna-Barbera and many other independent studios, including Filmation Studios, DePatie-Freleng, and Jay Ward, produced many successful limited-style cartoons for network television, resulting in large audience shares and advertising revenue, along with intensely competitive bidding wars for programming, for their respective prime-time and Saturday morning lineups. That same decade, Disney, still the leading producer of full-length animated features, demonstrated new advances in cutting-edge technology. In 1960, the studio was the first to use a Xerox process to ink cels in the theatrical cartoon short *Goliath II* and, a year later, released the first full-length feature to use the process, *101 Dalmatians*. In 1961, in the full-length live-action/animated feature *Mary Poppins,* the studio became the first to use a revolutionary sodium-loss process to produce special-effects mattes.

The seeds of another trend, which would forever change the landscape of the industry, gained momentum during the 1970s and 1980s. Known as CGI, or computer-generated imagery, this technology, an outgrowth of experimentation done during the 1960s in laboratories, proved it was capable of producing animation and special effects that were not cold or lifeless, and it consequently had a widespread effect on the industry. In 1971, animator Peter Foldes produced the first experimental 2-D animated short, *Metadata,* drawn on a data table, using the world's first keyframe animation software, invented by Nestor Burtnyk and Marceli Wein. In 1973, MGM's futuristic western *Westworld* became the first to significantly use 2-D computer animation in a feature film, showing audiences the world viewed by the eye circuitry of a synthetic human/gunslinger (played by Yul Brynner) in a western theme park. A year later, the 1974 sequel, *Futureworld,* was the first to demonstrate 3-D computer graphics of an animated hand and face using 2-D digital compositing to materialize characters over a background. Then, in 1977, *Star Wars* became the first film to use an animated 3-D wire-frame graphic, and, in 1979, in *The Black Hole* and *Alien,* the use of raster wire-frame model rendering was introduced.

Extensive use of CGI seemed like a far-flung fantasy until the 1980s—dubbed the "start up decade for CGI"—when animated images generated by computer gained popularity, including traditional effects made in the digital realm. In 1981, the film *Looker* featured the first CGI human character, Cindy, and first use of shaded 3-D computer-generated animation. Two years later, Industrial Light & Magic's graphics division demonstrated the first use of a fractal-generated landscape in a film, in addition to creating a new graphics technique called Particle Systems, and Walt Disney's science fiction feature *TRON* incorporated the most extensive use of 3-D CGI—15 minutes of fully computer-generated animation—and early use of facial animation. In 1984, Lucasfilm's computer animation division created the first all-CGI animated short, *The Adventures of André and Wally B,* and Robert Abel & Associates produced television's first entirely CGI 3-D character animated commercial, "Sexy Robot." Throughout the decade, CGI and effects in film enhanced the commercial success of many other features, including *Star Trek II: The Wrath of Khan* (1982); *Star Wars: Return of the Jedi* (1983), which originally was to become the first full-length CGI film but was never completed; and *The Abyss* (1989). In 1985, Lucasfilm unveiled the first photorealistic CGI character, Stained Glass Knight, in the feature film *Young Sherlock Holmes,* and *Dire Straits—Money for Nothing* became the first computer-generated music video. In 1986, Pixar Animation became the first to use shadows in CGI, made with their exclusively developed software, Renderman, in the animated short *Luxo Jr*—also the first CGI film to be nominated for an Academy Award.

In 1988, following a period of artistic and financial failures produced by a growing number of independent studios, the enormous commercial success of one film totally revived the theatrical cartoon feature industry. Walt Disney's elaborate live-action/animated *Who Framed Roger Rabbit* (1988) had success that fueled one of the biggest booms in the industry since Hollywood's so-called golden age of animation in the 1940s, with Disney producing one big-budget animated feature per year, along with theatrical shorts and featurettes. The studio also opened and re-opened four animation studios to start production of new theatrical features and cartoon shorts.

In the late 1980s, the largest step toward the evolution of CGI came with the introduction of digital ink-and-paint software for 2-D studios, codeveloped by Walt Disney Studios with Pixar, to computerize the ink and paint and postproduction processes of traditionally animated feature films produced by Disney. By 1990, the studio's Computer Animation Production System (CAPS), a proprietary collection of software programs, replaced the traditional ink-and-paint method, which animators first used in the animated feature *The Rescuers Down Under.* Mixing 2-D computer animation with limited 3-D special effects became a popular method in many full-length cartoons produced during the 1990s, including *Aladdin* and *The Prince of Egypt,* since 3-D imagery was still expensive to produce.

By the mid-1990s, 3-D computer animation fully exploded onto the scene. Entire films were produced in the genre, starting with the first fully computer-animated feature, Pixar's *Toy Story* (1995), which opened a floodgate of high-quality 3-D computer features that followed. The popular films set box-office records and marked the end of old-fashioned ink-and-paint features, which were far more expensive to produce and had largely become unprofitable. With increased computer speeds and more technologically advanced software, the application of 3-D computer graphics to special effects in films, television programs, commercials, and video games only became more vivid, realistic, and seamless. Advances included the use of motion capture for CGI characters, CGI for digitally manipulated matte painting and creation of major 3-D effects in movies, and real-time computer graphics, or "digital puppetry," to create a character in a motion picture. Other advances included the rendering of thousands of shots in feature films, including backgrounds, environmental effects, vehicles, and crowds.

Beginning in 1997, yet another software-driven form of animation exploded onto the scene. Flash animation was first prominently used that October by *Ren & Stimpy* creator John Kricfalusi when he launched *The Goddamn George Liquor Program,* the first cartoon series produced specifically for the Internet. Since then, countless Flash-animated television series (including Flash "Webisodes," such as Showtime's milestone Web series, *WhirlGirl*), commercials, and award-winning shorts have appeared on the Web, enjoying widespread success. Advances in computer technology, including the convergence of high technology and art, have become commonplace. In 2001, *Final Fantasy: The Spirits Within,* inspired by the best-selling video game series, became the first photorealistic, computer-generated feature film to be released. In 2004, *The Polar Express* became the first CGI film to use motion capture animation for all of its actors.

With traditional hand-made animation waning yet still in use today by a few studios, mostly in producing made-for-television cartoon series, between 2003 and 2006, studios such as DreamWorks, 20th Century Fox, Walt Disney, and Warner Bros. closed their hand-drawn animation departments, thereafter going completely digital. Universal's *Curious George* (2006) became the last traditional animated feature made until Disney's return to producing 2-D animated films in 2009 with release of *The Princess and the Frog.*

****

Every animated production, from animated films and television shows to video games, operates under a specific structure or hierarchy that has been in existence for decades. It has since been streamlined in some areas to ensure the production runs smoothly and delivers the product on time with the highest quality possible. In each case, a number of highly skilled and talented artists, technicians, and production crew members are involved in every step of the creative process.

Animation is commonly applied in many areas these days, including feature films, short subjects, educational films, experimental films, medical and industrial films, television series and specials, television bumpers (introductions/endings of program segments only a few seconds long), original direct-to-video productions, music videos, video games, mobile phones, and Web animation and Web advertising, as well as visual and special effects. Different hybrids, or a mixing, of different methods, such as 2-D drawn animation combined with 3-D elements or vice versa or with live-action footage, is also common.

The process of bringing animated images to life from the esoteric level to physical reality is commonly divided into four stages: development, preproduction, production, and postproduction. Four of the most popular categories of animation today are 2-D drawn animation (examples: *The Simpsons* and *Family Guy*), 3-D computer animation (examples: *The Incredibles* and *Toy Story*), 3-D stop-motion animation (examples: *Wallace & Gromit: Curse of the Were-Rabbit, Fantastic Mr. Fox,* and *Coraline*), and Flash animation (examples: *Foster's Home for Imaginary Friends,* Disney's *Little Einsteins,* and *The Mr. Men Show*).

Though less favored today than computer animation, several major and smaller studios from coast to coast, including Walt Disney, Nickelodeon, Bill Melendez Productions, Calabash Animation, Film Roman, Rough Draft Studios, and Starz! Animation, are among those actively producing traditional ink-and-paint animation, mostly for television. Animation in this form is almost entirely hand drawn and includes storyboards, character model sheets, character animation, and backgrounds that, in most cases, are individually inked and painted before being filmed one frame at a time. Most studios are similarly staffed with a full range of professionals involved in creating this kind of animation, including animators, assistant animators, character animators, background artists, inbetweeners, clean-up artists, inkers and painters, animation checkers, and supervisory personnel, such as lead animators and supervising animators, along with writers, directors, producers, camera operators, and editors. Many of the shows they produce are made specifically for network television, including Saturday morning and prime-time television, and first-run syndication, including educational programming blocks for network affiliates, throughout the country.

Most major motion picture studios on both coasts, with Pixar Animation, Blue Sky Studios, and DreamWorks Animation considered the leaders in their field, are behind the production of 3-D CGI, popularized in many animated movies that audiences have embraced around the world, from *Toy Story* (1995) to *Shrek 3* (2010). Unlike its ink-and-paint counterpart, productions are created and rendered from flat, primitive stick-figure or wire-framed skeletal characters in fully fleshed humanistic, movable, and talking creations entirely on powerful and expensive supercomputers using robust proprietary design and editing software to achieve impressive lifelike and realistic results. Everyone, from art directors and production designers to storyboard artists and story artists to concept artists, is responsible for readying the design, visual look, and story for production. The overall production team responsible for working their magic in producing the animated characters, backgrounds, and effects and giving them their lifelike appearance includes 3-D animators, modelers, texturers, rigging artists, and lighters or lighting artists. Films these studios produce are usually released directly to movie theaters through their own distribution arms or other studios that act as their distributors.

Well-established studios and independent animators produce both large- and small-scale stop-motion animated features, such as films, short subjects, and occasional television programs and commercials. The process differs greatly from CGI or computer animation. Actual working physical models or puppets of the characters, meticulously built on a flexible wire skeleton called an armature, are made from clay, foam rubber, or hard plastic (known as plasticine) with interchangeable lips so lip syncing of the actors' voices can be done in small increments as they are photographed to create the illusion of continuous movement. Various professionals, besides the director and producer, play an important role in the characters' creation and execution. Miniature sets and scenic backdrops are also involved. All of this work requires the expertise of art directors, production designers, character designers, set designers, storyboard artists, modelers or model makers, animators, key animators, set builders, scenic artists, and lighting artists. Major feature-length films are advertised, marketed, and distributed to mainstream movie theaters, while short subjects often play in special animation festivals in the United States and abroad.

Flash animation has evolved from Macromedia's introduction of this first-of-its-kind software in the late 1990s as a tool to create and distribute Flash-animated online cartoons, or "Webtoons," and advertisements. It has become the method of choice among many major and independent animation studios, online game manufacturers, Web hosting companies, and advertising and marketing companies. Many highly rated animated television series for Cartoon Network, Comedy Central, Disney Channel, and Nickelodeon, as well as original online series, top-selling games, and experimental music videos, have been made using this comparatively low-cost alternative to computer animation and traditional hand-drawn animation. Various companies experienced in creating and using this type of animation employ a wide range of practitioners in the field. These professionals possess both artistic and technical knowledge and include directors or creative directors, art directors, lead animators, and Flash animators to produce the designs, backgrounds, and character animation entirely with this and other design software.

Video game publishers produce and manufacture 3-D video games using real-time computer graphics, including some prerendered scenes typical of CGI applications, either developed internally or by a video game developer. Besides handling the product's manufacturing and marketing, most large companies also distribute their games, while smaller companies contact distributors or larger video game publishers to distribute their games. Most handle layout, design, and creation of the games along with box design and possibly the content of the accompanying user manuals. Larger publishers boast internal and external creative staffs, including producers or project managers, creative directors, game designers, animators, concept artists, environment artists, technical artists, and others to create and produce a fully functional and interactive 3-D game.

Most major studios with established in-house special effects departments and independently owned effects houses in major urban centers throughout the United States, the largest concentration of which is in cities such as Los Angeles and New York, produce stunning special effects or backdrops for use in feature-length motion pictures, television shows, music videos, and games. Job opportunities generally include such specialties as software engineer, CG supervisor, effects animator, compositor, and special effects technician. These professionals rely on CGI and a wide set of tools and technology, including state-of-the-art digital rendering, blue-screen technology, motion capture, morphing, matte painting, and Rotoscoping that often "make or break" a project in creating worlds unseen by the human eye or ones too difficult to photograph.

Many visual effects (commonly referred to as VFX) companies are responsible for producing realistic and dangerous-looking elements, integrating CGI and live action, in big-budget films; these would be simply too costly or impossible to capture on film. At such production facilities, a skilled group involved in the creation of these effects includes compositors, digital effects artists, matte painters, model builders, and visual effects technicians. These professionals create digital animation, computer 3-D characters, sets and backgrounds, texturing, painting, and rigging—like most computer-animated and stop-motion animated movies—and composite the live actors and live action with the effects in various scenes throughout each production.

****

Now and in the future, the top four sectors for employment for animators, artists, and technicians include computer and video games, feature film character animation, advertising/commercials, and television shows. Many applications and specialties in the field of animation require the top-notch skills necessary to create character animation and special and visual effects. In addition, opportunities will be available in a variety of other specialty jobs within each category, such as lighting, rigging, rendering, storyboarding, technical directing, and pre- and postproduction areas.

Today's animators and animation professionals have to surmount many challenges—competitive personalities and other sources of stress—in otherwise creative and fulfilling jobs to become and stay successfully employed. These jobs require teamwork skills, maturity, and professionalism to see projects through from inception to completion. The most successful are those who perform their jobs reliably and consistently, demonstrating not only tremendous talent and skill but also great flexibility in working with all members of the design and production staff.

Depending on your role, along with developing a solid reputation and exceeding the expectations of the job, remaining up to speed on the latest advancements, changes, and trends—including commonly used 3-D design, animation, and editing software—attending refresher courses and certification classes, and obtaining additional or specialized training will aid in advancing your career. In the coming decades, the animation industry is expected to undergo an even greater transformation, making it important to understand the use and functionality of new high-tech innovations and rapidly developing technology that will help drive the industry. Among these developments will be the proliferation of digital 3-D, further integration of the Internet with mobile devices and PDAs, and strong growth of emerging technology such as motion capture (rendering every action and gesture of live humans and animals in cartoon form) and stereoscopic production. These advances will result in higher-quality, character-driven animation in computer and video games and will require qualified personnel to produce the work for studios, companies, and other corporate entities.

In the United States, the hot spots for employment in the animation film and television industry will remain most major urban centers, such as Los Angeles and New York, as well as other cities throughout the country with smaller studios and companies that produce animation for television, film, visual effects, gaming, and the Web. Industry jobs will grow overseas, where animation industries are expanding at a fast pace to create, as reported by AnimatorMentor.com, "culturally themed animated movies and TV shows in their native languages." Demand will be high for animators and artists willing to relocate to countries with the highest concentration of animation studios, such as Canada, Japan, and India. In the latter, the animation, gaming, and visual effects industry grew by almost 27 percent in 2007 to $325 billion, and

business is projected to reach $1 trillion by 2012, thereafter growing at a compound annual rate of 25 percent.

Expansion to regions in the world where the cost of animation production is far less—and in new state-of-the-art facilities, no less—as has already been the case in studios in cities such as London, Sydney, and Wellington, will remain high as U.S. studios will continue to outsource some of their animation to low-cost studios in India and Singapore. Project-based opportunities around the globe may become the norm, with animators enticed to live or work abroad, potentially changing the face of the job landscape for many in the industry.

In addition, jobs in other sectors, such advertising and e-learning, will continue to rise. The Internet will continue to expand at a mind-boggling rate. Animators and digital artists will be needed to produce animated advertisements and Web sites. Likewise, opportunities will continue to grow for visual and special effects artists due to the flourish of special effects and visual effects–driven live-action movies. On a much narrower scale, artists experienced in texture mapping, lighting effects, and special effects will be in greater demand.

3-D computer animation will remain a major, driving influence. It will continue to rival hand-drawn 2-D animation and push the art form to new heights, which could possibly result in a new style of animation yet to be seen. Trends toward more stylized, abstract mixed media and photorealism in animation, or motion graphics, will push the industry forward as well. Artists will continue to break free from major studios to create their own animated shorts, games, Webisodes, and other art forms, and it is becoming increasingly easier for much smaller entities to produce animation as technology improves and Internet bandwidth increases.

ACKNOWLEDGMENTS

First, I want to sincerely thank my editor, James Chambers, for his guidance, patience, enthusiasm, and support from the seedlings to the completion of this much-need resource. In addition, my thanks to my friend, the legendary Bob Kurtz, for his wonderfully insightful foreword to this book.

I also wish to thank the following industry professionals for their kind assistance and contributions of information and material throughout this volume: Holli Alvarado, Hydraulx; Thomas Baker, Walt Disney Feature Animation; Michael Borkowski; Aharon Charnov, Jim Henson Company; Ben Jammin Chow, Calabash Animation; Shavonne Cherry, Producto Studios; Wallace Colvard, DreamWorks Animation; Gary Conrad, Nickelodeon Animation Studios; Matt Corcoran, Cinematico Inc.; Christina DeSilva Rowell; Kristen Drewski, Blue Sky Studios; Daniel Driscoll, Shadow Animation; Charles Ellison, Dreamworks Animation; Joe Elwood, Warner Bros. Animation; Eric Freeman, Deluxe Digital Studios; Quentin Frost, Walt Disney Feature Animation; Kevin Gallegly; Carolyn Guske; Amy Hay; Brett Hoffman, Illumination Entertainment; John Hurst, Blue Sky Studios; Jon Hooper, Rough Draft Studios; Marty Isenberg, Cartoon Network; Chris Jolly, Walt Disney Animation Studios; Jason Jones; Tom Kane; Thomas Kernan, Digital Domain; Apollo Kim, ScanLineVFX LA and Café FX; Tom Kane; Owen Klatte, Rising Sun Pictures; Dan Krall, Warner Bros. Animation; and Piet Kroon, Blue Sky Studios.

I would further like to thank Mark Lewis; Christian Lignan, Disney Toon Studios; Luis Lu, Monolith Productions; Michael Lubuguin; Rosanna Lyons, Film Roman; Teri McDonald, Walt Disney Animation Studios; Gene McGuckin, Renegade Animation, Inc.; Chad Moore and Brad Clark, Rigging Dojo; Jennifer Nelson, Nick Jr.; Nollan Obena, Cartoon Network; Celine O'Sullivan; Gary Owens; Van Partible, Cartoon Network; Craig Paulsen, Warner Bros. Animation; Philip Pignotti, Nickelodeon Animation Studios; Andrew R. Robinson; Christian Roman, Pixar Animation Studios; Sarah Satrun; Stephen Silver; Brian Smith, Warner Bros. Animation; Brock Stearn, DreamWorks Animation; Dean Stefan, The Walt Disney Company; Joslin Torrano, Nickelodeon Animation Studios; Nancy Ulene, Walt Disney Television Animation; Jeffrey Varab, N4D/3DH Entertainment, 3D Eye Solutions, INV3; Ted Warnock, Flying Lab Software; Nicolas Weis, DreamWorks Animation; Rich Wolf; Carol Wyatt, 20th Century Fox; Michael Yank, Cartoon Network; and Gregory Yepes, DreamWorks Animation.

Specials thank as well to the following organizations for additional resources used in making this book a reality: ACM SIGGRAPH; Activision; Adobe Systems Inc.; All Star Directories, Inc.; American Institute of Graphics Artists (AIGA); Animated Jobs; Animation Arena; Animation Mentor; Animation World News; The Animation Guild, Local 839; The Art Institute; ASIFA; BBC; Blue Sky Studios; CalArts; Cartoon Network; Cartoonists Association; Computer Game Developers' Association; Creative Talent Network; Education-Portal.com; EntertainmentCareers.Net; Entertainment Partners; Employment Development Departments, State of California; Graphic Artists Guild; GuideToArtSchools.com; Institute of Electrical and Electronics Engineers (IEEE): International Game Developers Association (IGDA); Macromedia; Multimedia Development Group (MDG); Nickelodeon Animation

Studios; Payscale, Inc.; Pixar Animation Studios; Pratt Institute; Princeton University; Rainmaker Entertainment; Salary.com, Inc.; Skillset; Society of Motion Picture & Television Engineers (SMPTE); Softimage XSI; Sony Pictures Animation; The 13th Grade, LLC; Tutorialboard; U.S. Bureau of Labor Statistics; and The Walt Disney Company.

HOW TO USE THIS BOOK

Purpose

Featuring career descriptions of approximately 60 jobs, *Career Opportunities in Animation* is the most comprehensive and up-to-date guide of animation jobs in major areas of employment. Unprecedented expansion has fueled widespread growth of animation jobs in virtually every field and industry, including film and television animation, visual and specials effects, online and video games, mobile gaming, digital media, and much more, all of which rely on animation. With high demand for qualified individuals to work in these industries, there has never been a better time to start or advance your career in the field of animation.

Whether you are seeking to start an exciting career in this challenging and diverse industry or move up from your current position, this book provides everything you need to know to break into the animation industry or change paths in your current career.

Whether you want to ply your trade as a film and television animator, director, producer, editor, character designer, layout artist, painter, production designer, storyboard artist, modeler or rigger; a computer, video or online game animator or artist and designer; or a writer, screenwriter, or voice talent for film, television, and video productions, *Career Opportunities in Animation* will put you on the right track toward a rewarding career in one of the fastest-growing industries in the world.

Sources of Information

Information contained in this book was derived from more than 225 credible sources, including interviews with 75 animation professionals in assorted positions in the film, television, and games industry; books and factual articles; and reports and surveys from various national job data banks, professional associations, unions/guilds, and the federal government.

The job descriptions featured are based on actual job posts, employment documents, salary surveys, and many other sources, including the personal testimony of many individuals spotlighted in this volume and various studios and production houses within the animation industry throughout the United States. As a result, each career description is thoroughly detailed and reflects the current practice and structure of jobs in the industry.

Organization of Material

The jobs profiled in *Career Opportunities in Animation* are divided into 12 sections covering every key area of the industry: Animation (Film and Television), Art, Backgrounds and Layouts, Design, Engineering, Directing, Game Animation and Design, Painting and Texturing, Performing, Producing, Technical Production (Camera, Editing, Production Management, Sound, Special Effects, Visual Effects), and Writing.

A complete and thoroughly researched and written Industry Outlook discusses at length career opportunities in the animation industry, with an overview of how the field has changed over the years to the current status.

This book also discusses the most sought-after positions within the animation industry in all fields. While job titles and summaries of responsibilities may vary from one company to the next, this book uses the most universal job titles and most common definitions and descriptions for such positions. Moreover, the full scope and responsibilities of jobs listed by section are further divided into specific components or subcategories for ease of locating information for particular jobs in that area.

The Job Profile

Each job has a fully detailed Career Profile for quick reference that summarizes notable features of the job, including job title, duties, alternate title, salary range, employment prospects, advancement prospects, best geographical location(s), and prerequisites for the job; a Career Ladder highlighting frequent routes to and from the position described; and a comprehensive text discussing the level of education, training, experience, special skills, personality traits, special requirements, and various unions and associations relevant to each job. Additionally, each profile features an expanded narrative that provides explicit details and information about each job, including the following.

- position description, highlighting key responsibilities and duties, working hours and conditions, and additional duties as required
- salary ranges from average minimum to maximum salaries, including established union scales and wages and entry-level, median, and top hourly and yearly earnings
- employment prospects and forecasts, including discussion of current and projected trends of hiring and difficulties landing jobs in the respective fields
- advancement expectations on the job, including a review of possibilities for progression and promotion within the industry and inherent obstacles or difficulties to expect

- general required experience, skills, and personal attributes of each job and key points on how to improve the chances of hiring and success in the position
- related unions/guilds and professional associations by position and access to employment information, requirements, wages, benefits, and other useful resources for a particular career or position
- practical tips and suggestions on preparations for obtaining a specific job or career in each category

The Appendixes

For fast and easy reference, *Career Opportunities in Animation* features additional resources to aid job seekers. Five appendixes follow the 60-plus job profiles in this book.

Appendix I, "Animation Schools and Educational Institutions," features the most comprehensive listing available of accredited colleges, universities, animation and trade schools, and other educational institutions by state that offer undergraduate degrees. Included are two-year and four-year degree and certificate programs in animation and related disciplines, including such specialties as cartooning, character animation, computer animation/digital art, computer engineering, experimental animation, film/video arts, fine arts, graphics/design, multimedia/games, playwriting/screenwriting, voice acting, and Web animation. Each listing provides, when available, the institution's address, telephone number, fax number, e-mail address, and Web site, as well as academic programs and courses offered. Not listed are nonaccredited schools and workshops that do not offer certificates or degrees.

Appendix II, "Major Trade Periodicals, Newsletters, and Other Publications," offers the most complete list available of journals, consumer and trade magazines, and industry and association publications that cover all relevant industries, including film, television, and gaming.

Appendix III, "Industry and Trade Associations, Guilds, and Unions," provides an A-to-Z listing of notable industry and trade associations and professional guilds and unions in the industry. Each entry includes key contact information, when available, including the address, telephone number, fax number, e-mail address, and Web site.

Appendix IV, "Recommended Animation Industry Web Sites" offers a useful guide to important Web resources for searching and locating information on employment, history, organizations, and the latest news in the industry.

Appendix V, "U.S. Film, Television, Game, and Web Animation Companies," features information on and Web links to thousands of potential employers, including studios, production companies, visual effects houses and more, by specialty, in all fields in the industry.

A Glossary includes keywords and definitions of relevant terms used frequently in the industry, followed by a Bibliography of sources used in researching this volume. Included are an expansive list of books and many other resources on careers in animation, including relevant labor, statistical, and wage information on jobs within the industry.

ANIMATION (FILM AND TELEVISION)

2-D ANIMATOR

CAREER PROFILE

Duties: Animate scenes that fit into various styles at an animation studio or production facility

Alternate Title(s): Cel Animator; 2-D Digital Animator

Salary Range: $20,000 to $90,000

Employment Prospects: Fair

Advancement Prospects: Excellent

Best Geographical Location(s): Atlanta, Chicago, Los Angeles, New York, Orlando, San Francisco, Seattle

Prerequisites:

Education and Training—Bachelor's degree or higher or certificate in traditional animation, film, or related field or equivalent production animation experience is preferred

Experience—Considerable film, television, or work-related experience at a studio recommended

CAREER LADDER

Supervising Animator; Lead Animator

2-D Animator; Character Animator

Assistant Animator

Special Skills and Personality Traits—Creativity; excellent drawing skills; ability to take orders and follow directions; cooperative; adaptable/flexible; dependable; organized; persistent; resourceful; innovative; work long hours

Position Description

Whether on paper, computers or the big and small screens, animators are appropriately dubbed "creators of life." They are responsible for creating realistic movement and motion and believable 2-D and 3-D characters that bring laughter and entertainment in all forms. Embarking on a career as an animator can lead to working in a variety of exciting fields, including film, television, video gaming, and the Internet.

Whether working in 2-D or 3-D animation, animators typically report to and work under the supervising animator, who assigns them the scenes they are to animate. Animators also work in groups, or "units," under the direction of a lead animator. The animator is routinely responsible for planning and timing scenes assigned to his or her team. Animators must conform to the style of the production and with the work done by their animation supervisor, who assigns them the scenes to animate and provides the overall direction of the animation.

2-D Animators, also known as traditional cel animators, usually have worked up the ranks from such areas of animation as character, cleanup, modeling, and storyboarding and developed their skills from studying from proportion, line of action, structure, and basic anatomy. They create animation that is 2-D in nature using the most traditional form of animation, called cel animation, a process wherein cels and backgrounds are hand drawn and inked in color, mounted on an animation stand, and then photographed in sequence.

Animation performed by the 2-D Animator must work appropriately within the context of the story and style of the project. Such work can apply to story development, directing, cinematography, and editing to create storyboards that show the flow of the animation and map out key scenes and characters. Creating basic designs and drawings and planning creative narrative sequences under tight deadlines using hand-drawing techniques or computer animation is another part of the job.

For the Atlanta-based traditionally trained 2-D Animator Danielle Paulet, who has been fascinated by animation since she was a child, nothing beats using a pencil and flipping a couple of sheets of paper back and forth to create the illusion of movement in animation. As she noted, "I live to make drawings come to life, whether it be on a Web site or on television."

2-D Animators work many long hours and nights. In most structured studio environments, they work as part of a team, or "unit," of other animators required to produce a certain quota of drawings within a specified period of time and to animate each individual scene or character for the production, often under the direction of the unit supervisor or director. The requirements of the position involve long periods of sitting at a drawing table and quickly producing drawings that can be quite complex. As a result, tremendous hand-eye coordination, patience, and skill are necessary to perform their duties under circumstances that can be stressful and less than ideal. Paulet once had a project manager tell her she needed to create an animated sales demo that was five minutes long in one week. She proceeded to tell her, "If Pixar and Disney can make a movie in a year, you can make this in a week," with their conversation becoming a "one-sided yelling match on my part."

The position requires a tremendous desire to succeed no matter what the outcome and is "not for the faint of heart." From Paulet's experiences, it takes a lot of hard work, dedication, and sleepless nights. In college, she would go down to the animation building at 10 A.M. and be there until 6 P.M. the next day, with two hours of sleep that, as she added, "I got under my light table or computer."

Despite such hurdles and obstacles, the idea of creating something new and giving it life somehow make it all worthwhile. "The people, bringing life to art, and the incredible feeling of seeing what you have worked on being completed are what make [the job] fun," Paulet added.

2-D Animators mostly work for a studio or production company that produces animation; sometimes work affords them the opportunity to work independently in their own home studios. The physical demands of the job involve long periods of sitting behind a drafting table, usually well lit. The hours they work vary from a standard 40-hour work week or more, depending the needs of the production.

Salaries

Wages for 2-D Animators tend to vary depending on the size of the company, duties, area of specialty, and geographical location. In May 2009, the national median wage for multimedia artists and animators, according to the Bureau of Labor Statistics, was $28.01 per hour, or $58,250 annually. The lowest paid 10 percent earned an hourly wage of $15.56, or $32,360 annually. The highest paid 10 percent earned $47.66 per hour, or $99,130 annually. As of October 2009, based on human resources data, Salary.com reported earnings for the middle 50 percent of cartoonists and animators between $44,631 and $60,745. Nationally, PayScale.com, in its most recent salary data, breaks down earnings based on years served in the industry. Multimedia artists or animators with one to four years of experience can expect to earn from $30,578 to $43,867; with three

to nine years, from $45,057 to $65,356; and with 10 to 19 years or more, $47,917 to $80,000 per year.

According to The Animation Guild, Local 838, of the IATSE, as of July 31, 2011, traditional 2-D Animators made $38.375 an hour, or $1,535.00 weekly for the first six months of employment; for the next six months and thereafter, $39.25 an hour, or $1,570.04 weekly. Meanwhile, journey animators with years of experience draw comparably higher pay—$40.71 an hour, or $1,628.56 a week. Under the union's current collective bargaining agreement with signatory studios, Cartoon Network Studios, for example, pays 2-D digital animators 1, as they are classified, the same hourly and weekly wages as those listed above for 2-D Animators.

Employment Prospects

The U.S. Bureau of Labor Statistics, which lumps multimedia artists and animators into the same occupational category, projects a much faster than average job growth (21 percent) from 2006 through 2016, with the need for 43,000 additional employees during that period. However, prospects for 2-D Animators are only fair. Jobs that exist are limited to major cities such as Atlanta, Chicago, Los Angeles, San Francisco, and New York, which are home to studios and production facilities that still produce traditional hand-drawn animation, and are hard to get into, as qualified applicants usually exceed the number of positions available.

Animation is a very hard field to break into. Paulet, a 2007 graduate of Savannah College of Art and Design who, in addition to being an animator, is experienced in graphic and Web design as well as video compositing and editing, wishes she had known the condition of the economy when she graduated and just how much work is outsourced to places such as Korea and India. Most entry-level positions animators used to get to break into the industry are now outsourced to other countries. "This is part of why it has become so hard to get into it," she explained.

Advancement Prospects

Advancement opportunities for 2-D Animators to similar positions or positions higher up the ladder are excellent. Most artists advance professionally as they establish a reputation for a particular style. The most successful are those who continually develop news ideas and whose work evolves over time. Many with years of experience under their belts become character animators. Those demonstrating leadership abilities move up the scale to lead animator and eventually the higher echelon of supervising animator. "The great thing about animation is that if you're good, you will go far," Paulet stated. "Once you break into the industry, if you prove you have the chops, moving up isn't as hard as in other industries."

Most 2-D Animators begin their careers working at small, independent studios and companies. Depending on the type of 2-D animation they do, many follow the traditional career ladder, working their way up to assistant animator and then animator. Some start off as in-betweeners and go on to become clean-up artists, color stylists, or key animators and then character designers and lead animators or switch to work as background artists or storyboard artists. As Paulet said, "It all depends on what you are actually interested in and what the structure of the studio is like."

After becoming more experienced, some have been able to move to larger and more prestigious studios doing 2-D animation. Others have successfully retrained and crossed over to doing 3-D computer animation. In other cases, some animators take on different positions altogether in the areas of film, game design, television, and others as character riggers, colorists, conceptual artists, digital artists, film modelers, illustrators, layout artists, lighting artists, motion capture animators, special effects animators, and storyboard artists. Many 2-D Animators are hired on a freelance or contractual basis and work independently as subcontractors or for themselves. Others work for small and large companies, including advertising agencies, gaming firms, and publishing companies.

Education and Training

A certificate from a certified trade school of animation or an associate's degree in animation from a two-year college is a minimum requirement. Most large commercial film and television studios prefer a candidate to have a college degree, preferably a bachelor's, in traditional animation, film, or a related area. The U.S. Bureau of Labor Statistics (BLS) reports that most companies today are looking for animators who possess either an associate's or bachelor's degree in animation, computer animation, graphic design, or media arts. In fact, in its annual Occupation Employment, Training and Earnings report, the BLS notes that 58% of all multimedia artists and animators hold at least a bachelor's degree and that this number is "expected to increase as technology advances and the significance of education becomes more and more essential."

Besides providing entry into the film and television industry, a degree in animation also qualifies undergraduates to work in fields outside the entertainment industry, including computer specialization, network system and data communication, graphic design, and computer information science. For those wanting to work in Web development, acquiring certification in computer programming and Web design is recommended. Depending on the major or career objective, most schools require undergraduates to complete course work in animation principles, animation history and theory, character development and design, computer animation, graphic design, life drawing, modeling, storyboarding, traditional 2-D animation, and video and film production.

Paulet recommends getting a degree in animation that focuses on traditional 2-D animation. Most schools automatically gear undergraduates to 3-D (computer animation) because there are more jobs in that field. "You can learn software anytime, but the key is learning to animate and the best way to learn is using good ol' pencil and paper," she remarked.

Established animation schools, such as CalArts, Ringling College of Art and Design, and Savannah College of Art and Design, offer the best education for would-be animators since their professors on staff are actually industry professionals with years of experience in the field. These schools also have the connections to get your foot in the door, and having a recommendation from a seasoned Disney animator will help when you apply for jobs.

In order to get the most out of your education, most animators already working in the industry suggest developing good relationships with your professors and tapping into their knowledge base. As Paulet said, do not be afraid to ask your professors to show you things you do not understand and need to know. She had a professor give her an extra hour each week to help her work on a variety of things. Not only did this help her learn more, she also built a strong friendship with him.

The bottom line: Don't get into animation for money. Instead, as Paulet said, get into the industry because "you love to draw a lot and all the time."

Experience, Skills, and Personality Traits

Most animation studios and production houses require minimum experience for the position of 2-D Animator, but animators must have a high level of proficiency on the job. A strong foundation in traditional or 3-D art and design skills is a plus. An understanding of form, structure, figure drawing, light, shade and color, details and character design, and landscape painting and illustration are helpful. Skills in other areas of animation, such as storyboarding and computer graphics, are helpful.

Potential employers seek highly motivated and diligent workers who are team players, self-motivated, reliable, responsible, and dependable in fulfilling their obligations. 2-D Animators must work well under deadlines, and they should demonstrate good problem-solving, analytical, and communication skills. They should be open to change (positive or negative) in the workplace and be able to accept criticism effectively in high-stress situations. Also, employers look for a willingness to take on responsibilities and think creatively to develop new ideas for answers to work-related problems.

Acclaimed animator/director Brad Bird of *The Incredibles, The Iron Giant,* and *Family Dog* fame once said animation is about creating the illusion of life, and "you can't create it if you don't have one." As a result, the most successful 2-D Animators are those not only with the essential artistic and professional skills, but who have experienced life and the things they draw, using them as a point of reference to make their creations more lifelike and realistic. To be a successful animator, you need to be a social person who likes to do all sorts of stuff and social in the sense that you like to explore and are open to doing new things. Paulet believes animation is all about observing and creating life. "If you need to animate a guy hiking, and you've never been hiking," she says, "you're going to have a problem." In her opinion, watching reference videos will only bridge part of the gap. Someone animating a hiker who has actually been hiking will know that it's all about being with nature, observing nature, and enjoying nature. He or she will know how it "feels" to go hiking and not just how it "looks" to go hiking. As a result, the animated

hiker will seem more realistic because it comes from personal experience.

Unions and Associations

Membership in The Animation Guild, Local 839, in Burbank, California, and Local 843 in Orlando, Florida, of the International Alliance of Theatrical Stage Employees (IATSE) is highly recommended. Part of the largest entertainment union in the industry, the AFL-CIO's International Alliance of Theatrical Stage Employees and Moving Picture Technicians, Artists and Allied Craft helps secure minimum wages and provides other union support to its members. An association dedicated to helping women animators in the industry is Women in Animation (WIA).

Tips for Entry

1. During high school or college, look into potential internships at film or television animation studios to gain firsthand knowledge and experience of the production process.
2. Network with others in your profession. Making connections with other animators and executives will help your career.
3. Build a diverse portfolio that consists of earlier clips or tapes of animated sequences that display the range of your talent. Include some cartoon or 2-D animation, some short film ideas, and some storyboards to complement your computer animation work.

3-D ANIMATOR

Duties: Create and design computer-animated characters, objects, or effects

Alternate Title(s): CGI Animator; Computer Animator

Salary Range: $33,000 to $130,000

Employment Prospects: Good

Advancement Prospects: Good

Best Geographical Location(s): Los Angeles, New York, San Francisco

Prerequisites:

Education and Training—Degree or certificate from accredited two-year college or trade school in classical animation, film, computer science, or related field, or equivalent production animation experience; bachelor's degree recommended

Experience—Minimum experience working as an animator on film or television productions creating CGI or computer animation

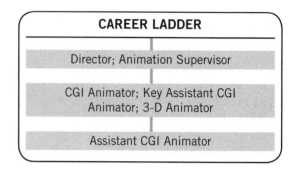

CAREER LADDER

Director; Animation Supervisor

CGI Animator; Key Assistant CGI Animator; 3-D Animator

Assistant CGI Animator

Special Skills and Personality Traits—Creative and artistic; excellent technical skills; observational and acting skills; organizational and communication skills; detail oriented; cooperative; self-motivated

Position Description

Often more realistic than traditional 2-D animation that is used to create classic animated films such as *Snow White and the Seven Dwarfs* and television cartoons that require individual handmade drawings, 3-D computer animation has become the rage in movies such as *Toy Story* and *Wall-E* and computer and video games. The ultimate goal of 3-D Animators, also known as CGI animators, is the same with all animators. The major differences are the tools they use and some of the skills required.

Working under supervision of the director or lead animator, 3-D Animators work alone using highly equipped mainframe computers and 3-D software applications to create realistic and believable designs, layouts, models, static poses, personalities and characteristics, and the illusion of movement of the main characters or objects in computer-animated film and television productions. Most entry-level 3-D Animators animate secondary characters or objects that move as a result of the actions of the main characters in a scene.

3-D Animators have the same background as their 2-D counterparts, including a firm mastery of classical animation techniques, color, drawing, painting, and design, but with more of an emphasis on depth and detail using light, shading, and other techniques. 3-D Animators have expertise in creating animation, visual images, and special effects using high-tech computer tools and software. The 3-D Animator has an eye for detail, from the button of a character's coat to the way hair moves in the wind.

Unlike 2-D animators, whose work is entirely hand drawn, 3-D Animators create animation, visual images, or special effects using computer tools and software. Images can be edited, colored, textured, and animated in programs that use models to simulate the behavior of animated objects or characters in finished sequences. Many start out by making a drawing or sketch before embarking on the process of 3-D computer animation creation. As the Toronto-based 3-D Animator Giovanni Nakpil pointed out in an interview in 2009 with AnimationArena.com, he always makes it a point to sketch out the elements he will be creating in 3-D just so he can familiarize himself with whatever it is he will be doing. Plus, it gives him a visual reference.

Such complex work often involves using independent judgment and can entail creating 2-D or 3-D images that depict lifelike objects, characters, or motion; manipulating light, color, texture, shadow, and transparency; or creating static images to give the illusion of motion.

Most 3-D Animators start by creating character skeletons, or wire-frame models. Possessing excellent creative and artistic qualities and observational skills, they demonstrate a strong sense of physical or environmental movement, timing, and the development of relationship interactions with other characters necessary to produce convincing animation. Once completed, they flesh the characters out into full animated form to set up key frames of animation. In many respects, they employ the special skills and talents of actors—action, comedy, dialogue, and the full range of emotions—using their well-honed technical skills to choreograph, time, act out, and perfect the animation and/or effects assigned to them.

At studios such as Pixar Animation, the producer of some of the most successful and beloved computer-animated films of all time, 3-D Animators receive each assigned shot, including storyboards, story reels, recorded dialogue, and direction, and the director shows each new sequence in layout and describes what is expected for every shot at a "blocking meeting." Afterwards, each animator reads the soundtrack, plans the shots, and blocks in movements in rough animation and shows them to the director for approval in a daily review. Once approved, they finish the sequence in a timely manner, pending the director's final approval.

One area many aspiring 3-D Animators should work on mastering is their execution of "performance" in their animation, a component vital to the success of a character often missing in demo reels. The late Pixar animator Glenn McQueen, who served as a computer animator on *Toy Story* before becoming a supervising animator, recommended in an interview in June 2000 with IGN Entertainment that 3-D Animators work on their action and their motion since "you've got to make a character look like it's thinking—like it's self-motivated." It is also important, McQueen stated, to convey emotion through action, through pantomime. If a character is sad, don't just put a sad face on him, but try and convey that emotion with everything.

Creating such lifelike characterizations also involves knowing how to successfully compose the shot in the frame—in other words, the pose of the characters and how they carry themselves, how they move, and what gestures they make when they talk. Everything about the shot and about the character should say something about the character's state of mind at that moment. "I don't care how well something is rendered, or how well it's modeled, or anything," McQueen added. "The only thing I care about is motion—the performance."

In the demos McQueen used to review from potential new hirers, there was a good sense of motion, and they were entertaining. However, when it came to their acting and performance, they were not great.

McQueen enumerated that it is far easier to teach someone the tools of computer animation than how to act. In his opinion, there was no way he would hire someone as an animator who had only technical skills as opposed to animation skills. To start animating, they needed to have a command of how to make a good performance, how to make it appealing, how to make a character seem alive, how to make a character appear to be thinking, and how to communicate an emotion. These are necessary skills, in his view, that are much more difficult to teach.

Whether the production is big or small, 3-D Animators are expected to deliver the work on time and in tune with the production schedule and budget. In addition to exceptional artistic and technical skills, the key to success for 3-D Animators is the ability to use various 3-D studio software systems and stay current on the ever-changing technological advancements within the industry.

Typically, 3-D Animators work in comfortable office environments and primarily use a computer and mouse as their tools of the trade to create the animation. Sometimes productions require additional field research to better understand and convey characters and environments. For major feature films, many work at a studio location; others freelance as independent animators remotely or from home-based businesses. 3-D Animators employed by studios usually work a standard 40-hour week. However, as is the case with their freelance counterparts, evening and weekend work may be required to meet project deadlines.

Salaries

Salaries for 3-D Animators vary depending on location and whether workers are union or nonunion. Typically, according to Jobs-Salary.com, yearly earnings start at $33,946 and can be as high as $130,000. Animators who work in the film and video industries average around $57,000 a year; those working in the advertising industry earn less, about $48,000. For some jobs, based on collective bargaining agreements negotiated with studios in Hollywood, for example, joining a local guild or union such as The Animation Guild, Local 839, of the IATSE can be beneficial in securing a higher pay scale. Weekly wages for 3-D Animators at Walt Disney Pictures and Television and DreamWorks Animation from July 2011 to July 2012 were $1,552.48, or $38.05 per hour, to start for the first year of employment. For the next year, for journey CGI animators, compensation rose to a maximum of $1,628.56 weekly, or $40.71 an hour. Entry-level 3-D Animators at Pixar Studios in a union state such as California generally start at $45,000 to $50,000 a year, while animators who work at a small studio in a right-to-work state such as Florida make far less, between $20,000 and $30,000. Game-design 3-D Animators, on the other hand, tend to earn more than their industry counterparts in other sectors of the profession. Average annual wages for game animators as reported by AnimationArena.com, are in the $45,000 to $70,000 range.

Employment Prospects

The employment outlook for 3-D Animators is good, as there are frequent openings for this type of position. Most are likely to work for different employers over the course of their career, typically specializing in one particular facet of 3-D animation, such as characters, character effects, or background. Freelancing is also a popular career option. Some work, instead, as character designers, who develop designs for the main characters of a story, or as character effects designers, who draw secondary aspects of a character, such as clothes, fur, or skin. Others become background designers, creating 3-D background images and settings in animated films, television shows, and commercials, or storyboard artists, sketching the framing and shot composition of the scenes in a production. For most, the ultimate goal is to work in Hollywood on major animated features, but less glamorous jobs doing this kind of work are available around the globe.

3-D Animators can also pursue careers outside the traditional movie and video production sphere, in such industries as advertising and computer software development. Certain talented individuals already employed as animators elsewhere, albeit with some training, can quickly progress to the role of 3-D Animators. Studios often fill such positions when they become open.

As the 3-D Animator Liem Nguyen, experienced working in many different fields, including visual effects, video game development, animated children's programs, and television commercials, notes, building good relationships, collaborating, and learning from others is the key to being successful in this industry. "This may sound cliché but it's true—the 3-D animation industry is a tightly knit community where you run into the same people all the time," he said. A majority of the work Nyugen gets is through social networking and receiving recommendations from fellow animators.

Advancement Prospects

Career advancement prospects at studios are mostly good. Some 3-D Animators are promoted from within or move on to become animation supervisors or directors. Others may choose to relocate and apply their knowledge to higher-paid positions at other studios or production facilities, especially if they have been employed in a low-wage nonunion state. Some have used their computer animation skills and knowledge to become instructors at animation art or trade and vocational schools.

Education and Training

A college degree is not necessarily a requirement for success as a 3-D Animator. When making hiring decisions, employers largely consider a candidate's artistic talents and portfolio as part of the equation. However, obtaining a degree from a leading art school or college in animation or computer science can improve an applicant's chances for employment; in other cases, a bachelor's degree in a related field is preferred. Becoming a 3-D Animator requires the ability to draw and an understanding of both traditional hand-drawn and newer methods of animation. Therefore, most undergraduates are required to take courses in life drawing, color theory, composition, and storyboarding as well as computer animation to gain experience using electronic tools such as illustration, scanning, manipulation, and high-end animation software used in creating 3-D animation.

Napkil adds that having good traditional skills in art is very important when doing 3-D animation. Being traditionally trained means having proper knowledge of perspective, anatomy, good composition, and adeptness with whatever art tools are used—the very same elements needed in order to produce a great 3-D image.

Many larger animation studios, such Walt Disney Studios and Sony Pictures Imageworks, offer in-house training and artist-development programs for entry into the industry. Other studios require all new hires to undergo additional training before working on projects. In many cases, animators with traditional 2-D animation experience have crossed over to 3-D after acquiring the necessary computer skills. Some studios will consider training animators in the use of one software program or another if their creative and artistic skills are evident in their demo reels.

The Pixar CGI animator Jason Bosse is one example of an animator who started in hand-drawn traditional animation and successfully made the jump to CGI, or 3-D computer animation. In a published interview promoting his work on the Disney/Pixar movie *Up* (2009), he explained, "With drawing you want something to be a certain way, you draw it that way. In CGI, you have to bend to the will of the computer, because a 3-D model lives in space, it has rules that you can't break."

The best path toward entry into the industry is to learn and spend hours with whatever software is being used in the industry and explore it thoroughly. You can accomplish this either by taking a course in school or by buying the software. Whatever first job in the industry lands in your lap, take it. According to Napkil, "From there, it's just a matter of meeting and knowing people in the industry."

More important, keep yourself "grounded," no matter how good you are or think you are and do not let your talent go to your head, since companies probably will not hire an arrogant animator.

Experience, Skills, and Personality Traits

Most 3-D Animators must have at least two to four years of previous experience as an animator. They should have experience working on well-regarded productions in well-respected studios. It is also helpful in such a relatively small industry to have a good track record and personal reputation, including recommendations from previous employers indicative of high-caliber work and talent.

3-D Animators need to be attentive and sensitive to taking direction in completing assigned tasks. They also should be good listeners and have excellent communication skills, both written and verbal, and strong planning skills and attention to detail, accuracy, and deadlines. Furthermore, they require a clear working knowledge of animation film and television production, budgeting, and scheduling. Last, they must be capable of dealing with various personality types in a professional manner.

As Nguyen, who was influenced to become an animator after growing up watching old Bugs Bunny,

Mickey Mouse, and Tom and Jerry cartoons and visual effects–laden films such as *Jurassic Park* (1993), once explained, it all boils down to the individual's determination, skills, and attitude. The real training begins once an animator gets a job and works with other people in a real-life production environment.

Unions and Associations

Most 3-D Animators are affiliated with The Animation Guild, Local 839, of the IATSE for guaranteed wages and benefits. Others join the CGSociety, one of the most respected global organizations for creative digital artists, which provides a range of services designed to educate and inform and promote the achievements of its members.

Tips for Entry

1. Most 3-D Animators starting out in the field have a bachelor's degree in multimedia animation. Therefore, enroll in a trade or animation art school or a university with a strong animation program to gain a thorough understanding of the tools and programs, including Adobe Flash productions for the Web and Autodesk's Maya and 3-D's Max software.
2. Gain as much experience as possible using various techniques and methods, including stop motion, traditional cel animation, and 3-D animation, as versatility is helpful in developing your skill level.
3. Learn the skills of a programmer, as in many cases programming and animation often go hand-in-hand.
4. In preparing for your career, produce a sample reel of your work demonstrating your ability and skill in everything from storyboarding to character art—talents often required for 3-D animation.

ANIMATION CHECKER

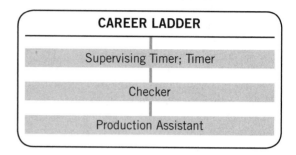

Position Description

After all the artwork is colored with the background art in its place, some productions employ what is known as Animation Checkers or checkers. They are responsible for making sure the animation is consistent throughout each sequence or scene of action. This means identifying any errors or mistakes or elements left out of the process.

As a result, Animation Checkers are detail oriented. They meticulously review every piece of animation, scene by scene, painstakingly checking for errors or omissions. Coordinating their work with other departments, Animation Checkers use extreme vigilance on the job so any errors do not end up in the final production, thereby saving time and costs.

Wendy Jacobsmeyer, now a television continuity checker after working as an Animation Checker on many top television cartoon series, including *Family Guy* and *ChalkZone,* loves the process and helping make it work. It brings a smile to her face every time she finds "a big error" on storyboards or x-sheets because it means "I get to help someone get their stuff 'fixed' before it becomes a retake. That makes them look good and me look good."

One of the hardest parts of her current job is when her input is not heard. There is never enough time to look at everything, and sometimes Animation Checkers end up working with egos that have

no respect for what they do. Jacobsmeyer has a good eye for catching oddities but confesses that a lot of people see her only as "a footage counter and refuse to listen to my input."

If employed by a studio, Animation Checkers typically perform their work in a structured environment on site in assigned work areas that are well illuminated with ample space in which to carry out their specific duties. Like animators, their job involves long periods of sitting and repetitive motion using their hands and wrists to repeat the same tasks. Freelancers, on the other hand, perform such work in the comforts of their own home-based offices. Those employed by studios generally work a standard 40-hour workweek, but like freelance Animation Checkers may work overtime if required to meet project deadlines.

Salaries

According to July 2011 wage scales of the Burbank, California, based The Animation Guild, Local 839, of the IATSE, entry-level Animation Checkers earn $29.18 per hour during the first three months of employment, or $1,167.32 per week; $30.02 an hour, or $1,200.84 per week, during the next nine months; $32.50 an hour, or $1,300.24 per week, for the next six months; and $33.37 an hour, or $1,335.08 per week, thereafter. In the union's 2010 wage survey, Animation Checkers reported minimum earnings of $1,350 and a maximum of $1,800 per week; the median wage was $1,500 per week. Since July 2006, union salaries have steadily increased from beginning wages by as much as $2 an hour, and since 1990 by nearly $11 an hour. For an in-house Animation Checker, the going rate is between $1,200 and $1,500 a week. Journey-level Animation Checkers (those with sufficient on-the-job training and who have completed a formal apprenticeship), on the other hand, are paid $34.84 an hour, or $1,393.72 for a 40-hour workweek. Free-lance Animation Checkers are paid by the foot of film checked—usually $1 per foot. An 11-minute cartoon runs 2,300 feet, so earnings would equal $2,300 for that single job. Freelancers work on a project-by-project basis.

Employment Prospects

Prospects for employment for Animation Checkers are poor, mostly because many studios are phasing out the position. (Exceptions include Walt Disney Television Animation, which still uses Animation Checkers on all of its television cartoon shows regardless of format, and a few studios in other states, due to the increase in CGI-animated shows). "When there is not a position to check timing of the animation, the checker becomes more of an assistant director/production coordinator," Jacobsmeyer noted. "Even Disney has changed my job title to continuity coordinator."

In addition, like many other positions in the industry, work is more seasonal in nature, resulting in periods of unemployment. Most hiring is on a project-by-project basis, but an Animation Checker may occasionally land longer, continuing employment on a weekly animated series. Additional employment may be possible in major markets such as Chicago and New York, which house animation studios that still produce traditional hand-drawn animation productions. Some elect to start out as production assistants or production coordinators and work their way up to becoming Animation Checkers.

Advancement Prospects

The position of Animation Checker is considered entry level. With experience, an Animation Checker can advance to timer and supervising timer and then director. Others cross over to become animators and effects animators, starting as assistants or on the production side of the business as production coordinators, but the career path is not always clear-cut.

According to Jacobsmeyer, the natural progression would be to timer, but only for individuals who have some drawing ability and can convince employers they are worth training. With timing positions being mostly phased out, it's going to become more difficult to move up anywhere from checking. As a result, Jacobsmeyer is currently looking into learning the programs necessary to become a technical director.

Education and Training

A high school diploma or equivalent is the minimum requirement. In addition, two years of animation instruction in school or on-the-job experience, including knowledge of storyboarding, life drawing, and lighting/effects animation, is a necessity.

Experience, Skills, and Personality Traits

Although no set amount of experience is required to become an Animation Checker, a minimum of one to two years of experience and knowledge of production processes would an asset. Some, like Jacobsmeyer, work their way into the position after previously gaining experience in other jobs in the industry. "My background was ink and paint, then animation checking. I'm pretty sure every checker started off as something. Some were storyboard artists, others were timers," she said. "I knew one who was a background designer. There isn't a definite amount of experience needed, just an 'eye' for catching errors."

Patience and a love of details are two additional qualities needed for this position, plus the ability to look at the whole picture as well as dissect it into tiny pieces, making sure each one fits back into the puzzle perfectly. At the same time, as Jacobsmeyer adds, checkers have to cajole artists, directors, and production people into getting them the pieces that are missing or fixing the ones that are "broken."

An Animation Checker should also demonstrate a willingness to learn on the job and work in harmony with the entire crew. Be nice to everyone. As Jacobsmeyer states, "You seriously never know who is going to end up where." As an example: The supply clerk at one of her first jobs ended up becoming the head of development at a major network.

Unions and Associations

Most Animation Checkers are members of The Animation Guild, Local 839, of the IATSE, which acts on behalf of a cross-section of animation professionals in the film and television industry to guarantee wages and provide other job support.

Tips for Entry

1. While in high school, look for internships at local studios or production houses that produce animation or on independent animation productions to gain firsthand experience.
2. Be willing to accept a low-paid position as a production assistant or production coordinator at a studio or company as an entry into the industry to gain necessary knowledge and contacts.
3. Make a good impression and network with others in order to advance.

ASSISTANT ANIMATOR

Duties: Assists in animating specific characters or objects in the sequences of a specific film or television production

Alternate Title(s): Assistant Cel Animator; Animation Assistant

Salary Range: $20,000 to $35,000

Employment Prospects: Good

Advancement Prospects: Good

Best Geographical Location(s): Chicago, Los Angeles, New York, Orlando, San Francisco, Seattle

Prerequisites:

    Education and Training—Certificate from a certified trade school or two-year college degree are basic requirements; bachelor's degree in traditional animation, graphics, illustration, or allied field preferable

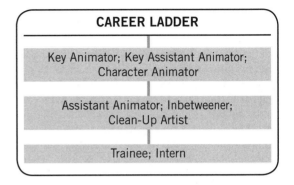

    Experience—Two years in animated film or television industry

    Special Skills and Personality Traits—Animation design; organization skills; flexible and adaptable; reliable; work under supervision and under pressure

Position Description

In this entry-level position, the Assistant Animator serves under the general supervision of the animation supervisor. The primary job responsibility is to assist the animator by polishing and finishing the extremes (a character's pose at the beginning or end of an action) and rough drawings important to the overall continuity and congruency of the animator's shots in the production. At studios and production facilities where animated film and television productions are produced, the Assistant Animator essentially performs the work of a second animator on the production, including preparing scenes for pencil testing during the development stage of the production. Assistant Animators produce at least one drawing between the animator's drawings to smooth out the action from one pose to the next, following the "timing charts" designed by the animator. Their drawings help make the frame-by-frame movement clearer, which makes it easier for inbetweeners to do their job. As with any member of the animation staff, they are expected to produce the best possible work under tight deadlines within a given budget.

"You need to know exactly what the head animator was thinking when he or she drew each drawing," says the freelance animator Sarah Satrun, who has held positions as an animator, Assistant Animator, and preproduction artist. Therefore, Assistant Animators must be aware of the timing charts and how each part of the body is moving. They also must animate it faithfully to what the animator intended.

After the pencil tests (an early stage of animation made from original rough pencil drawings) are approved by the director, the Assistant Animator is responsible for cleaning up the rough drawings, checking the exposure sheets for errors, and determining the pan moves before turning over the scenes to the inbetweener for completion. Afterward, Assistant Animators must check the inbetweener's drawings before a final test is shown to the animator. Furthermore, they are responsible for keeping and delivering accurate log sheets of their work and providing critical feedback to other members of the animation team by attending dailies (unedited footage of animated scenes) on a regular basis.

In time, once Assistant Animators gain the necessary skills and experience, the animator often will give them small assignments of actual animation to do, increasing the amount as they become proficient. Helping with the workflow, sometimes they will be given additional character animation to draw as well.

At smaller studios, the kind of work Assistant Animators perform can vary. At Calabash Studios in Chicago, for example, Satrun essentially performs the duties of both an assistant and inbetweener. When working on a scene with the lead animator, she gets the drawings from him or her along with any notes and thoughts on how to approach it. Then she does the inbetweens accordingly, pencil tests it, and shows him or her the test. As she explained, the lead animator gives her any additional notes of what corrections, if any, are needed. Then she fixes them up, does another test, and turns in the test again until it is approved.

If not working with the lead animator, Satrun is responsible for animating the scene herself and reports to the director. In this case, she will review the animator's timing charts and notes and consult with the director for additional guidance as needed. After finishing the scene, she shows the director a test. She may have to make a few "passes" over the animation if the director requests any changes. "It is also fine to ask coworkers for advice while you're testing your animation before you show it to the director," she adds. "More experienced coworkers often give great advice when you are unable to ask the director." However, the director has the final say and often has different opinions than others. Therefore, as an Assistant Animator, you are often faced with being told to approach a scene in a way you don't agree with. This is where, as Satrun explains, "you need a good attitude and humbleness to do as told even if you don't like it."

At a studio or production company, Assistant Animators work in highly structured environments in cubicle-style work spaces or offices. Like most animation positions, their work involves long periods of sitting and repetitive motion using their hands and wrists to repeat the same tasks. Generally, they work a standard 40-hour workweek; overtime may be required, however, because of project deadlines.

Salaries

Salaries for Assistant Animators in the animation industry tend to be somewhat low because it is an entry-level position. Annual salaries range from $20,000 (entry level) in some urban cities to as much as $35,000, based on surveys by the U.S. Bureau of Labor Statistics. In June 2010, in its annual wage survey of members, The Animation Guild, Local 839, of the IATSE in Burbank, California, reported Assistant Animators made a minimum of $1,072.32 and a maximum of $1799.58 per week based on a 40-hour workweek. As of July 2011, under the union's collective bargaining agreement, Assistant Animators' starting pay was $1,300.24 per week, or $32.50 per hour, for the first six months, and $1,332.48 per week, or $33.31 per hour, for the next six months of employment. Conversely, journeyman Assistant Animators made $1,393.72 a week, or $34.84 an hour.

Small companies tend to pay less than larger studios and tend to hire Assistant Animators on a temporary or subcontracted basis. Rates for freelancers can vary based on the size of the company and the region. Some are paid either by the hour or by the foot (16 frames of film). In the Midwest, for example, freelance Assistant Animators can earn from $20 to $30 an hour. All freelance jobs pay by the hour, but some out of state pay by the foot, which is the norm. Satrun admits that this can be "really bad if you have a complicated scene or a lot of characters, but it can be good if you get an easy scene and are a fast worker." Other factors, such as skill level, speed and accuracy, and negotiation ability, are often involved in determining salary or wages.

Employment Prospects

Opportunities for qualified Assistant Animators are good in major markets, with some exceptions as a result of the current recession. In some parts of the country, far more jobs are available in preproduction in storyboarding and layout than for Assistant Animators; this is also the case as a result of many studios outsourcing animation overseas. To find work, it is better to live in a major city that is home to animation studios and offers opportunities to freelance for different studios. Satrun suggests finding a studio that does animation in-house and learn as much as you can and work as hard as you can. If you're good at your job, then there is a good chance of getting enough freelance work through the studio to make a living, or better yet, get a full-time position there.

The accelerated growth and expansion of the animation industry during the last decade has created additional demand for Assistant Animators. The highest concentration of jobs is mostly in large urban cities on the West Coast, including Los Angeles, San Francisco, and Seattle, and on the East Coast, including New York and Orlando. Satrun suggests candidates research the studios around them to find the best fit for them. Then job seekers should go into a studio with a sampling of their work that reflects the quality and type of work the studio does. When Satrun approached a studio that produces commercials using animation, she submitted an animation reel that showed a lot of hand-drawn animation combined with live action and computer animation. During an interview, she was able to describe the different approaches and how she handled them, and her samples reflected the kind of work studio was doing in its commercials. "Every commercial [they produced] combined hand-drawn animation with either computer animation or live action," she says. "My work was a good fit for that particular studio." However, when Satrun took that same reel to a more Flash- or After Effects–based studio, she did not get the same kind of response. Therefore, she advises finding studios compatible with the work you do to get hired.

In a few cases, studios hire from within, promoting a trainee, intern, or employee from another department to Assistant Animator. Others enter the profession as clean-up artists before moving up the ladder once they gain more practical experience. This is not always the case. Experienced artists with a proven level of accomplishment should have little difficulty in securing work in this position. Relevant to your experience, different grades of this position exist at studios that can lead to being hired for higher-level positions at the studio or department. It is important when contacting studios to "Be nice, respectable, confident, but not cocky." As Satrun, a graduate of Columbia College in Chicago with a bachelor's in traditional animation, explains, "Don't be pushy with your résumé. Don't keep calling them every day. Some people actually do that, and studio heads just find that very irritating." She also advises to never show up uninvited waving your résumé. Just give a call and chat briefly with them to see if you can submit your résumé, portfolio, and animation reel. If they review your work and say no, then ask what skills you need to improve. What are they looking for? Use that as learning experience to improve yourself and try again.

Another important factor to remember in seeking employment is that work of this kind—anything in the arts—is at times cyclical and fluctuates from year to year based on economic conditions. Given the economy right now, Satrun has experienced a huge downturn in her freelance work but hopes that will pick up as the economy recovers. As a result, the work available is mostly freelance. Currently, many studios prefer to hire animators on a project basis as opposed to full time. Satrun adds, "What is the point in paying them when there isn't work in house?"

While freelance animation jobs may last a few months, others, such as full-time studio positions, last much longer, especially when working on a full-length animated feature or television series. These positions can secure regular employment of up to six months or longer at a time.

Advancement Prospects

Prospects for advancement are generally good. Most Assistant Animators work toward becoming an animator, while others choose to remain assistants for the duration of their careers. Career advancement largely depends on natural talent and ability combined with acquiring the necessary knowledge and skills on the job. The stronger and faster an Assistant Animator's drawing and animation skills are, the better. The ability to communicate well is another essential to advancement. Upper-level animators must be able to effectively critique animation, give directions to Assistant Animators, and review and discuss animation with the director. Satrun advises, "Build your reputation as a very good, essential worker and jobs just might present themselves. You should move up in your career either in your current studio or in another."

To start, plying skills at a small studio has advantages over working at a larger studio, as smaller shops offer individuals the chance to do more and work in different areas of animation, thus building their résumé and gaining valuable expertise. Satrun has done character designs, layout, and animation, all within the first year of starting as a freelancer. If she had worked for a large studio, she would not have had those opportunities. Freelancing has provided her with the opportunity to prove herself and move up if positions open up.

Staying at a studio too long, however, means advancing as far as what positions are available in that studio's hierarchy. In regions of the country with fewer opportunities, generally those working in higher positions stay put, diminishing potential for advancement. Going where there is more work will give you a much better chance at getting better positions.

The most successful Assistant Animators are those who do not confine themselves to one style. They can work in whatever style is handed to them and have a good reputation in the industry. Satrun claims the animation community is fairly small, and everyone seems to know each other. Everyone is connected. If someone gets a bad reputation, it will be known and may prevent that person from being hired or advancing. On the other hand, if your peers admire you, then you will find work, and career advancement will become much easier.

Education and Training

A two-year college degree, two years of education and training at vocational or trade school with a strong animation program, or equivalent experience working on animation productions is the bare minimum requirement for this position, although a degree is not always necessary for entry into the industry. According to Satrun, if someone has strong skills, then that speaks more than a degree. Getting a B.A. does help and does "make you more employable."

Most large studios or production houses that produce animation for film or television prefer that candidates have an undergraduate degree, such as a bachelor's in traditional animation or related areas such as graphics or illustration. Coursework in animation design, animation theory, character animation, figure drawing, and film production are among the required courses in such programs. Graduates who studied or have firsthand understanding of traditional 2-D hand-drawn or 3-D computer animation will have a greater advantage. Besides meeting these educational requirements, it is also possible to become an Assistant Animator through internship programs provided by some studios and production houses to train prospective employees. Satrun believes a strong animation program is best, but if that it is not an option, then she suggests going to schools that have strong fine arts departments and developing your drawing skills while doing animation on the side. To do hand-drawn assistant animation, drawing skills are "crucial."

Experience, Skills, and Personality Traits

It is important for Assistant Animators to have a firm understanding of traditional animation principles, acting, film production, and compositional design. Candidates should have a thorough knowledge of the functions and techniques of animation production and moving and timing. They should have superb drawing skills and the ability to work fast under pressure while keeping a positive attitude. They should possess great attention to detail and be able to take criticism and direction. Candidates need to be flexible and adaptable and work long hours as needed to complete work on schedule. Assistant Animators must have sound communication and interpersonal skills to deal with colleagues. They need to be organized, methodical, and capable of working with minimum supervision. For positions in computer animation, Assistant Animators must be experienced and proficient in the use of 3-D animation software, including Maya. Above all else, according to Satrun, be humble. Someone will "always be better than you, and you will always be learning."

Unions and Associations

The Animation Guild, Local 839 (Burbank) and Local 843 (Orlando), of the IATSE are the only unions that represent Assistant Animators and other allied professionals. Members are covered by union contracts and paid union wages for their work at studios and companies sanctioned by studios. While becoming a dues-paying member is not strictly necessary—some animators work for nonunion shops in different parts of the country—it is helpful to guarantee minimum union wages and obtain benefits otherwise not available without membership.

Tips for Entry

1. While attending college or trade school, look for internship programs at a studio or production facility to gain experience in animation production.
2. Take courses to acquire working knowledge in the understanding of movement and timing and observational and acting skills and the techniques of sculpture, graphics, illustration, or traditional drawn animation.
3. Apply for lower-level production positions in animation, such as inbetweener, animation checker, and clean-up artist, at small animation studios or production houses to get the necessary experience.
4. Produce a demo reel demonstrating a strong understanding of animation principles, artistic ability, and a professional approach to animation.

CHARACTER ANIMATOR

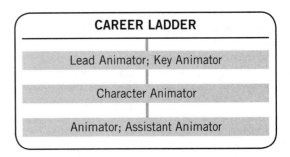

CAREER LADDER

Lead Animator; Key Animator

Character Animator

Animator; Assistant Animator

Position Description

Character Animators are an important cog in the wheel of producing animation for film and television. Considered creative draftsmen, these talented and motivated individuals work closely with directors and supervising animators, taking their directions from them. Like actors, Character Animators have a tremendous amount of creative freedom. Their job is to breathe life into static 2-D or 3-D characters or objects. This is accomplished through implementing exaggerated actions and movements of a human, animal, or object.

Often, the work of traditional 2-D Character Animators entails conceptualizing and creating high-quality animation for one or more characters in a featured sequence. The director tells them what the character has to do, how it will interact with objects and other characters, and where it fits into the story. Character Animators plan their sequences or shots in the context of the story and the character's role in the production. The animation they create is often made to complement voice acting.

To begin, 2-D Character Animators make a sketch of the character or object before implementing changes and completing the shots in accordance with the production schedule. The kind of animation they produce involves the creation of thought and emotion in addition to physical action. They follow the basic rules design animators have been using for generations. Factors such as the character's shape and size, head size in proportion to the body, physical appearance, agility, and relative size to other characters are important in the overall design and character animation.

After completing scenes of animation, Character Animators demonstrate to the director their ideas in a rough cut, combining their drawings and audio dialogue tracks in animation dailies, a test reel of their work in its rawest form.

Unlike their 2-D industry counterparts, 3-D Character Animators, using similar tools of the trade, conceptualize and create the exaggerated actions or motions of character animation using computer animation software. They must meet the standards of quality, originality, and creativity, but their work is delivered in a 3-D environment. Taking directions from the lead animator and project leader, Character Animators perform many of the same essential functions as do traditional 2-D character animators. The greatest difference is they require both artistic and technical skills to perform their job.

A case in point: In realistically animating the penguins in the CGI-animated feature *Happy Feet* (2006), animal logic Character Animator Simon Pickard's tasks involved "an extremely high level of facial performance"—a level of acting shown through characters that went beyond anything ever seen in an animated feature. As he told Softimage XSI's online community, makers of the 3-D animation software of the same name, he still gets goose bumps watching the depth and subtlety of the acting. In terms of the teams he worked with, they had one or more leads per character and then groups of animators assigned to animate the characters. Having an extended period of time with one character, he said, "really helped the quality. Personally, I felt I really knew my character inside out by the end of the project."

The longtime character animator Ethan Hurd, who worked for DreamWorks for four and a half years on such blockbuster movies as *Shrek* (2001) and *Shrek 2* (2004), noted in an interview with *American Chronicle* that creating believable character animation in CGI involves tremendous artistic and technical talent, as animators never meet any of the voice actors, whose lines are recorded months before animation actually starts. He and his fellow DreamWorks character animators received video references of the actors "reading" their lines that sometimes proved useful.

Pixar supervising animator Scott Clark, who started drawing cartoons when he was five and grew up watching reruns of Bugs Bunny on Saturday mornings, believes the greatest challenge for Character Animators is to entertain the audience, while giving them something new or surprising instead of taking the easy out. As a result, Character Animators have to give the characters human flaws to make them "more believable. You want to come up with something real, something truthful. It's believable when you're not doing it perfectly; you're doing it the way a person would do it," he explained in a profile on AllArtSchools.com. The best art, in his opinion, is not predictable. As Clark said, the spine might be a familiar story, but layers on it are the surprises that give the audience more than they expect. The same applies in character animation. Character Animators must be able convey their characters' complexities in their performances, like when "the character is smiling, but they're actually sad."

Character Animators usually work in structured corporate environments, either in assigned work areas or office cubicles. The demands of the job are no different than for any animator. Character Animators spend long periods of time sitting. Their work involves repetitive motion of wrists and hands and eye-to-hand coordination to repeat the same tasks. Most work a standard 40-hour workweek and overtime, if required, to meet project deadlines.

Salaries

Based on experience, years in the industry, and studio and location, Character Animators employed on animated motion pictures and television programs command an annual salary of $54,600 to $90,000. Based on the current collective bargaining agreement of The Animation Guild, Local 839, of the IATSE, weekly earnings for this position are $1,836.14, 15 percent above the minimum journeyman rate. The guild's June 2010 member wage survey reported that Character Animators earned a minimum of $1,018.18 to a maximum of $4,378.95 per week, with a median wage of $2,068.84 a week. Journeyman Character Animators were paid an average of $1,596.64 per week.

Employment Prospects

Employment prospects for Character Animators at film or television studios and video game production houses are generally good. Openings are dictated largely by the need to fill positions as they become available or are based on demand. Due to the intermittency of employment, however, some Character Animators work irregularly throughout the year. The need for Character Animators is mostly evident at medium to large animation studios that produce animated film or television productions or production houses that make commercials and video games.

Advancement Prospects

The next steps up the career ladder for Character Animators are key animator and lead animator. Prospects for such advancement, however, are only fair, as the competition is stiff, and jobs open up infrequently. However, after advancing to the next level, Character Animators can eventually become lead animators, gaining supervisory experience in overseeing a group or unit of animators. Others have also made the jump to assistant director or director after many years of experience.

Education and Training

A bachelor's degree in fine arts, illustration, and computer graphics for the position of Character Animator is preferred. Candidates require a demonstrated understanding of the fundamentals of traditional hand-drawn, computer, or stop-motion animation. They also should be trained in visual storytelling and be capable of demonstrating believable expressions, emotional states, weight, physics, balance, appeal, entertainment, clear timing, and staging. Competence in drawing, storyboarding, concept art creation, rigging, skinning, modeling, texturing, lighting, video editing, and compositing is an asset. Most college and animation school curriculums focus on foundational skills necessary for all aspects of 2-D animation and the process of bringing characters to life, with an emphasis on applying body weight and kinetics to various situations, such as walking, running, and jumping. Courses also instruct students on dialogue, acting, model sheets, time techniques, and more as well as the philosophical tenets of the animation process.

In an interview with *CGexplorer,* Federico Cascinelli, a 3-D Character Animator whose credits include *Charlie and the Chocolate Factory, King Arthur,* and *Harry Potter and the Goblet of Fire,* suggests that beginners choose a good school, preferably three-year courses, so they can build a firm basis in fine arts, acquire solid drawing principles, and "explore animation from A to Z." Cascinelli completed some formal training, the most important of which were a number of master classes with some of the most famous animation artists in the world: Don Bluth and Richard Williams. Bluth, a former Disney animator, went on to form his own studio and produce a series of successful cartoon features, such as *The Secret of NIMH* (1982), *An American Tail* (1986), *The Land Before Time* (1988), and *All Dogs Go to Heaven* (1989) and the popular traditional animation-based laser-disc videogame *Dragon's Lair.* Williams, on the other hand, is best known for his Oscar-winning work on Disney's blockbuster live-action/animated film *Who Framed Roger Rabbit* and is also the author of the animation bible *Animator's Survival Kit.*

The Pixar Character Animator David Tart once explained that ultimately it comes down to "your animation skills, your knowledge of composition, acting, comedy and humor, and all those things."

The Character Animator Jason Taylor, known for his work on many successful films as well as numerous commercials, game cinematics, and film projects, recommends that undergraduates serious about going into character animation acquire a more concentrated education on the fundamentals of animation from the start. He went to a general fine arts college and learned a good amount about experimental filmmaking techniques, such as cut-outs, under lit sand, stop motion, and some very basic 2-D. As he told AnimationMentor.com, "What I didn't learn was how to make characters live and breathe through movement. I spent years slavishly learning character animation on my own."

The most important step to mastering character animation, according to Taylor, is practice. In his case, just learning about the principles of animation was not enough to totally grasp it all. He needed to repeatedly do animation tests in order to figure out how to actually apply those principles and achieve that "sought-after illusion of life."

Experience, Skills, and Personality Traits

Character Animators must have a minimum of two years of production experience. They require expertise in classic animation motion principles and the ability to animate big action and subtle action sequences. They should demonstrate great hand drawing ability and a solid understanding of human anatomy. Natural creativity, a sense of humor, acting ability, and motivation are also important. Understanding how to put themselves into another's shoes is likewise needed. Taking an acting or improv class can be asset in that regard.

Character Animators should be highly organized and knowledgeable of the animation pipeline and procedures of production. They should welcome constructive feedback or suggestions about their work and show a willingness to follow the instructions of the director. Furthermore, they must be able to work and contribute positively in a team environment and complete their work on time. Clark really enjoys his coworkers. Many have the same interests he does and are as talented, if not more talented, than he is. As he notes, "As animators, we have to be collaborative. It's hard for an artist's ego to get in the way when you're collaborating like that."

Unions and Associations

Membership in The Animation Guild, Local 839, of the IATSE helps guarantee union wages even at the lowest scale and can be beneficial in making connections with other professionals in the industry. Other industry associations, such as CG Society, a worldwide organization devoted to digital artists, may be helpful for networking and educational opportunities.

Tips for Entry

1. In school, study how actors prepare to become characters in movies and television shows and apply those methods in creating character animation.
2. Learn from instructions from superiors and from the masters of character development by closely watching examples of the film and television work of successful animators.
3. Read up on the principles and techniques professional animators use to create lifelike physical animation and character movements.
4. Discover how animation is more than good drawing and how emotions play a key role in great animation.

CLEAN-UP ARTIST

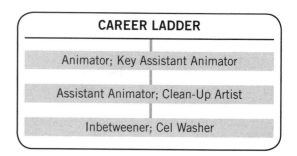

Position Description

After animators draw the rough pencil sketch, followed by the transitional or inbetween drawings they leave for inbetweeners to complete, Clean-Up Artists—appropriately dubbed "unsung heroes"—are next in the chain of animators who produce finished hand-drawn animation.

Clean-Up Artists are excellent draftsmen. They exhibit a high level of consistency in drawing and inking and the ability to interpret the animator's rough drawings and execute them. Their job is to finalize or "clean up" any inconsistencies in the animator's approved pencil animation or rough drawings, keeping with the original character design style. Clean-Up Artists' work is drawn more accurately and consistently than the rough drawings, with impeccable quality throughout. These final drawings are actually used to animate a shot or scene in the finished film. Without consistent drawing and line quality established by the Clean-Up Artist, the drawings, when viewed in sequence on the screen, would "flutter," illustrating their flaws.

It is not the responsibility of Clean-Up Artists to completely overhaul the animation in a scene or to add elements the animator forgot. They are to only modify the penciled drawings, correcting any drawing flaws in character design. Clean-Up Artists give the animation a consistent line look (so the animation follows the exact same style), maintaining the integrity of the animation as originally envisioned by the animator. The consistency of their work creates the illusion that one animator drew every scene before the drawings were finalized. The role of Clean-Up Artists on the production team enables animators to worry more about the action and performance of the characters and less about the finished drawing style.

Ren and Stimpy creator/animator John Kricfalusi says the best way for young artists to break into the industry is as Clean-Up Artists who work under established animators and masters of their craft. "You absorb a lot of information by osmosis . . . ," he notes on his blog. Kricfalusi says this is how the old cartoon animators learned their craft and why the cartoons kept getting "better and better over the years."

The animator Randy M. Santa Ana spent two years working as an artist in the clean-up department at the now-defunct Fil-Cartoons, an animation studio in the Philippines that produced animation for many early Hanna-Barbera cartoons. In 1999, after learning how to be a Clean-Up Artist through the studio's in-house training program, he quickly made a name for himself among his peers due to the "quality of my line work." Paid by the number of drawings he made ("The more drawings you clean up, the more you earn"), Santa Ana realized early on that speed was an important factor in this position. "I was fast, but I also drew with impeccable line quality," he states on his Web site.

Clean-Up Artists are similar to inkers who ink comics in that their work generally falls into three categories: those whose work takes something away from the finished product, those who don't take anything from it but don't really add anything either, and those whose work makes the product even better than what they started with. The long-time character clean-up and character design artist Mark Lewis, whose credits include many direct-to-video animated features for Hanna-Barbera, Mike Young Productions, and Warner Bros. Animation, falls into the third group. "My aspiration has always been to make the work better," he said. He has managed to do that by always giving his best effort.

What Lewis particularly loves about his work is when he is assigned a drawing of an interesting character by a designer whose work he really likes and is able to clean it up and add something to it, hopefully making it "even better than it already was."

Unlike in the past, when traditional, hand-drawn animation reigned, opportunities for Clean-Up Artists have dwindled since the arrival of computer animation. Some 2-D productions still require their animators to produce cleaned-up drawings, but this work now sometimes falls to assistant animators or inbetweeners. However, to achieve greater consistency of design on a multianimator production, Clean-Up Artists provide a valuable service that makes them an important asset to any team.

Clean-Up Artists who work for a studio often do so in a structured corporate environment in individually assigned work areas. Prolonged periods of sitting and repeated use of the eyes, hands, and wrists are among the physical demands of this position. Hours for Clean-Up Artists vary, but they generally work a standard 40-hour week or longer, if necessary.

Salaries

Salaries for Clean-Up Artists are based largely on the place of employment and whether it is union or nonunion. According to the June 2010 member wage survey of The Animation Guild, Local 839, of the IATSE, Clean-Up Artists, grouped into the same classification as assistant animators, make a minimum of $1,160 per week. The middle range for this position is $1,460.00 with a maximum payout of $2,105.26 per week. Journey Clean-Up Artists draw a minimum weekly salary of $1,366.40. However, nonunion studios are not bound by the union's bargaining agreement and often pay considerably less. Freelancers, on the other hand, are paid on a "per piece" basis, so the more work they produce, the better wage they make. Annual salaries for this position are difficult to gauge as the period of employment varies in duration—from two or three months or until landing their next project—and, as a result, fluctuate greatly from year to year.

Employment Prospects

Prospects for bright, talented, artistic individuals seeking this line of work are fair. Much of this is due to waning employment for clean-up work in traditional hand-drawn television and direct-to-video animation as a result of the explosive growth of computer graphics (CG) animation. Despite booming employment in the CG field, little clean-up work exists since full clean-up on most drawings is unnecessary as rough sketches serve as a guide from which modelers build characters and props for CG productions. More people are looking for work than there are jobs. Many venture capital investors who would normally invest in new animated projects have become more cautious with their investments and as a result have cut back in providing a pipeline for funding. Nowadays, Lewis rarely gets the opportunity to do traditional clean-up (pen in hand, on paper, using a light box to see the rough underneath). As he notes, studios are moving toward digital clean-up using Adobe Illustrator. "This is particularly so on Flash-based shows," he adds.

Advancement Prospects

Advancement is possible to some degree to the next level of assistant animator and then key assistant animator and animator. "The top talents will always do well," Lewis said, "but I know some extremely talented people who are having trouble finding work right now. Everyone is hopeful that things will turn around, but right at this moment, they're not great."

Education and Training

Unlike other fields, no real minimum education requirement traditionally exists for this position. According to Lewis, having an art education is "never a bad thing; there's always a value to that." But for a Clean-Up Artist, it is all about what they do on paper or the computer screen. Can they deliver the goods? For clean-up, in Lewis's words, it's about having "sensitivity to other people's work, a good eye, and a controlled hand."

Employers may require some minimum formal education and training. If so, a certificate or degree from an animation or art school in traditional animation, art, or design is usually sufficient to work at smaller studios and production houses that produce film and television animation. Training for a Clean-Up Artist overlaps that of traditional training for an animator. Undergraduate degrees require completion of course work meant to improve drafting skills and understanding of the principles of animation employed in creating a scene. Classes on animal and figure drawing cover the importance of structure, composition, perspective, volume and mass, line density, width, and taper and how to create consistently more realistic and appealing drawings. Other animation courses help students develop a good sense of timing, an essential asset.

Experience, Skills, and Personality Traits

Some experience is required for this position because fewer studios are giving artists the chance to learn on the job. When turning in your portfolio, prospective employers often want to see the exact style of their work 100 percent "nailed already, straight out of the box. So that requires some experience," Lewis explains. On the other hand, too much experience can work against candidates. Lewis knows of people who routinely lop credits off the earlier part of their résumé so as not to appear "too old and be denied work."

Most Clean-Up Artists are skilled in character animation and storyboarding. They are talented and color-savvy draftsmen capable of adapting to any style. They can polish problematic animation with both speed and ease and produce results that usually meet or exceed weekly quotas while maintaining quality in their drawings. "Contrary to what some might think, clean-up is not just simple tracing. It requires the ability to interpret what the designer has drawn, what his or her intent was when putting down a given line (or in some cases, multiple lines, where you have to choose the right one!)," Lewis adds. "It all goes back to what I mentioned before about having sensitivity to others' work, a good eye, and a controlled hand. Being able to execute the work fairly quickly is also a very good thing."

Clean-Up Artists must also be reliable. According to Lewis, some may be the most brilliant artist the industry has ever seen, but if they are "an unreliable flake" when it comes to meeting deadlines and following through on what they have said they will do, "word gets around. You'll find yourself out of work."

A Clean-Up Artist therefore must be an excellent time manager and multitasker able to work on many projects at once and produce high volumes of work under tight budgets and time constraints. As a result, a certain amount of flexibility is required. Working for an employer or a client, a Clean-Up Artist has to do the work to the employer's satisfaction. As Lewis says, "This is why sketchbooks exist; so you can have an outlet to express yourself. If the client wants to see all the models cleaned up in red crayon, the professional attitude is to try to find a way to make that work, not to just "get irate and start an argument," he added.

Clean-up Artists should have strong communication skills, sound judgment, and the ability to take direction. They also boast the ability to function effectively with a wide range of personalities in a team environment and to handle stressful situations on the job.

Unions and Associations

The Animation Guild, Local 839, of the IATSE acts as a bargaining agent for Clean-Up Artists and other animation professionals in the industry. Most belong to the union, which secures minimum wages and other support. The union also serves as a networking outlet for its members.

Tips for Entry

1. While in school, working with live subjects, learn how to do life and head drawings, both quick sketches and long poses.
2. In seeking a position, create a basic portfolio that includes at least two sets of rough keys (key drawings of animation), several pages of life drawings, sketches with gesture-style drawings of people and animals in motion, and cleaned-up drawings of the same reflecting your sense of color, design, and lighting.
3. Produce a demo reel highlighting your eye for realism and attention to detail, cartooning skills, and imagination.

EFFECTS ANIMATOR

Duties: Create animation of noncharacter movements, including lightning, rain, smoke, and water

Alternate Title(s): EFX Artist, Visual Effects Animator

Salary Range: $40,000 to $94,500 or more

Employment Prospects: Poor to Good

Advancement Prospects: Good

Best Geographical Location(s): Los Angeles, San Francisco, New York

Prerequisites:

Education and Training—Undergraduate degree in computer animation or special effects animation, art, or engineering; knowledge and skill with computer animation programs; master's degree optional

Experience—Two to three years experience with simulations of natural phenomena, particle systems,

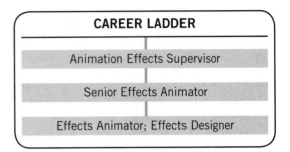

procedural modeling, procedural animation, hard and soft body dynamics, and other similar effects

Special Skills and Personality Traits—Talented; artistic; creative; analytical; strong visual and technical skills; detail-oriented; versatile; patient; problem-solver; collaborative team player; takes direction; works well under deadlines

Position Description

Over the years, groundbreaking work in animation and special effects has forever changed the way audiences experience special effects in motion pictures and on television—from Stan Winston's lifelike computer animation of his menacing "dinosaur animatronics" in the movie blockbuster *Jurassic Park* (1993) to the computer-generated effects in the visionary director James Cameron's monumental futuristic epic *Avatar* (2009). When the size of the production and budgets warrant it, special effects are used to supplement the animator's work and filmmaker's vision in 2-D and 3-D film and television productions. This is where Effects Animators come into play. Working closely with visual effects supervisors, art directors, and designers, Effects Animators create and design believable noncharacter images, elements, and effects using developed effects programs to enhance the action in a given shot or scene.

The effects these specialized animators create vary from simple and traditional hand-drawn effects to highly sophisticated computer-made effects. With 2-D animation, effects include anything from moving waters, flames, and glowing lights that are drawn individually and then superimposed over the character's drawing, to different levels of shadows and highlights layered over the character. Such elements for 3-D animation can mean adding tones, highlights, and shad-

ows to an alien spaceship, adding fire or lightning to a shot, making a superhero fly, creating realistic explosions or massive natural disasters such as a full-scale hurricane or lava-spewing volcano and menacing larger-than-life monsters, intricate physical parts of flesh-and-bone monster with deteriorating skin on top of masses of flesh and muscles, or stars that light up an otherwise blank night sky.

Most Effects Animators determine the best approach to solve effects challenges and develop an approved final look by accurately interpreting the art and design from the art department. In this important role, they creatively solve problems and work to achieve the established goals of art direction. To do this, they employ a strong artistic vision, sense of design and composition, and creativity in how things look, feel, and move.

The animator Harry Moreau, who grew up not far from Walt Disney Studios, is an example of an animator who made his mark as an Effects Animator after starting his career as a traditional ink-and-paint animator. At age 19, after landing a job as a delivery driver with the Haboush Company, founded by former Disney animator Victor Haboush, Moreau became inspired by being around such great artisans, including the animator John Kimball, son of Disney legend Ward Kimball. He rose up the ranks of animation, and after leaving

Haboush, he freelanced on commercials and film shorts before being hired by Doug Trumbull, a former director at Haboush, as an animator to do effects on Stephen Spielberg's classic science-fiction film *Close Encounters of the Third Kind* (1977). As Moreau once explained, "Stars don't show up on film, so we had to actually paint them." As a result, he and the effects team produced them out of an airbrush on black paper and then shot them. The comets and little meteors were all done via animation. They also animated the belly of the mother ship. Most of today's common animation techniques have their origin in that film.

Working conditions vary. For the most part, however, an Effects Animator's job is as physically taxing as most animator jobs. In the confines of a studio or post-production house, their work is highly structured and carried out in cubicles or workspaces equipped with high-powered computers and software. Long periods of sitting and repeated use of the hands, wrists, and eyes are part and parcel of their job in creating animation effects. Independent or freelance Effects Animators face the same physical challenges and usually perform such work in comfortable home-based offices. Regularly employed Effects Animators usually work a standard 40-hour workweek; overtime, however, may apply if deadlines dictate it.

Salaries

Wages and salaries for Effects Animators vary by market, size, budget of the production, and experience level. According to human resources industry professionals in the industry, entry-level animators make a starting salary of $40,000 per year, with more experienced animators making as much as $94,500 or more. Based on the annual member wage survey of The Animation Guild, Local 839, of the IATSE in June 2010, first-year animators who are guild members earn a minimum of $1,309.09 a week. Journeymen animators averaged $1,596.64, and the median weekly wage for the position is $1,818.18. Since 1995, when the average was closer to $1,750 a week, wages have generally decreased because computer animation has become more widespread. Experienced Effects Animators earned a maximum of $2,884.00 weekly for a 40-hour workweek.

Employment Prospects

Current conditions for employment are poor "unless you are a 3-D effects animator or know Flash," explains Rosanna Lyons, a senior effects animator and designer at Film Roman studios in Hollywood. "Hand-drawn special effects jobs are becoming a thing of the past."

The position of Effects Animator is one of the most competitive and intense in the business. In the past, individuals routinely entered the field as effects inbetween artists, but those jobs are nearly obsolete unless working on traditional hand-drawn animated productions. Most Effects Animators start off small, working on independent productions or for small companies before moving up the ladder to larger companies in bigger markets. Demand for Effects Animators remains constant, including at online and video game developers and companies. Furthermore, Effects Animators—called industrial animators—can find employment in government, health care, and private industry for video-related productions; employment prospects in these fields is slightly better. Working as an apprentice or intern at an animation studio or postproduction house is a good way to enter the business.

Advancement Prospects

Opportunities for advancement are good. Advancement possibilities largely depend on talent, reputation, and peer recognition. Most Effects Animators increase their earnings by working as senior effects animators on film and television projects. Others go on to become supervisors of animation effects, taking on greater leadership roles on various productions.

Education and Training

Film and television studios require an undergraduate degree, usually in computer animation or special effects animation, art, engineering, or related fields. Because the industry is so competitive, a master's degree increases the odds of landing top jobs in the field. During their studies, undergraduates usually learn the basics of animation, such as stop-motion and 2-D and 3-D animation, as well as how to plot a story and to bring together different elements—drawings, dialogue, and sound effects—to make animated characters come to life. They also develop knowledge and technical and specialized computer skills in special effects animation, learning how to create jaw-dropping effects like those in the movies. Classes vary depending on the school program, but course work is often of an applied or performing arts nature, including ad design, animation and motion studies, animation storyboarding, 3-D character animation, cartooning, color theory, computer graphics, design, drawing, illustration, film editing, film production, 3-D modeling, painting, photography, special effects animation, television production, and visual theory. This includes instruction in equipment operation and computer programming and the use of computer applications and imaging techniques to manipulate film, video, still photographs, digital copy, and soundtracks.

Lyons found her path into the industry after studying to become a fine artist in college and doing most of her training on the job at Sullivan Bluth Studios in Ireland. She was only 18 years old but succeeded due in large part to the on-the-job training she received and her raw talent.

Experience, Skills, and Personality Traits

In preparing to become an Effects Animator, individuals should possess at least two to three years of experience in television or film production and experience and knowledge of both traditional and digital effects. At larger studios, they work collaboratively in a much larger group of artisans and directors. At smaller studios, Effects Animators may be part of a much smaller group of Effects Animators who communicate with the directors in producing the effects by traditional or computer-aided methods. They must have a thorough practical knowledge of special effects animation and strong visual and technical skills, including an understanding of physical dynamics, natural phenomena, particle systems, procedural modeling and expressions, procedural animation, hard and soft body dynamics, and other similar effects. They should also have a background in all aspects of effects animation, from conception to completion.

Effects Animators need to have excellent design skills and a firm understanding of effects and compositing tools. Experience in writing scripts, programming, and working with established effects programs such as Maya, Renderman, Mantra, Flash, and Photoshop is crucial. They have to keep up with training as well.

Coupled with their knowledge and skill with computer programs, Effects Animators need the ability to take direction and work fast under deadlines. They should be able to work independently and collaborate efficiently with other artists. They also must know how to multitask and solve minor problems on the job as they develop.

Unions and Associations

Membership in The Animation Guild, Local 839, of the IATSE is helpful to secure minimum wages and other union support.

Tips for Entry

1. In high school, take as many art and computer courses as possible and learn everything you can about computer programming. Don't neglect taking more traditional courses in humanities and sciences, as having a broad knowledge base will work in your favor.
2. Take English and writing classes and develop good writing and communication skills, which are vital to any career in the arts.
3. Practice and hone your animation skills on your home computer.
4. Experiment and master new techniques and become versatile in using different software packages used for effects animation.
5. Stay abreast of current technologies and proprietary tools.
6. On your résumé, note any optical or digital training you may have.
7. Develop a strong demo reel and portfolio demonstrating realistic effects animation and drawings that show a variety of work and approaches to design.

FLASH ANIMATOR

CAREER PROFILE

Duties: Create visual images, including characters, or special effects using Flash-type animation and design application software for films, television, videos, computer games, and other electronic media

Alternate Title(s): Flash Artist

Salary Range: $35,542 to $79,090

Employment Prospects: Poor to Good

Advancement Prospects: Good

Best Geographical Location(s): Atlanta, Chicago, Houston, Los Angeles, San Francisco, New York, Washington, D.C.

Prerequisites:

Education and Training—Minimum of an associate's degree in animation, digital design, graphic design, or computer graphics or art school degree in animation media

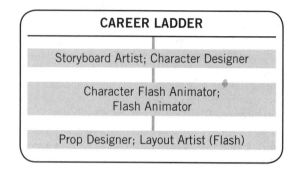

CAREER LADDER

Storyboard Artist; Character Designer

Character Flash Animator; Flash Animator

Prop Designer; Layout Artist (Flash)

Experience—Two years of Flash animation; two to four years of traditional animation experience a plus

Special Skills and Personality Traits—Artistic; creative; understands traditional animation; technical minded; good time management and communication skills; team worker

Position Description

Flash Animators create high-quality Flash-based computer animation and special effects that combine the duties of a Web developer with those of a commercial multimedia artist for a variety of industries, including film and television, gaming, and the Internet. These highly skilled artisans produce remarkably attractive and creative concepts using simple designs at a moderately low cost. They often work for animation studios, entertainment firms, Web hosting companies, and advertising and marketing companies in charge of creating Flash animations that are unique and suitable for the specific needs of the production or company. Most practitioners in this field possess a wide range of artistic and technical knowledge and skills and mastery of techniques, including the use of color and texture, and experience with computer software and computer programming.

Always on the cutting edge of technology, Flash Animators develop and master multiple skills in various genres, including 3-D animation and modeling, drawing, interactive media, sound design and layout, and background design. In doing Flash animation for films and television, their principal day-to-day function is creating and designing overall animation in line with the established vision of the art director. To create images for movies and television productions,

computer games, and special effects, Flash Animators produce a series of images drawn by hand using the studio's desired design application software—the newly popular Harmony, which has replaced the formerly popular Macromedia Flash, and, to a much lesser extent, Adobe Photoshop or Illustrator. Depending on the company, other duties include creating character layouts, making a mock-up for backgrounds if backgrounds have not been created, and drawing additional poses that have not been made yet. Once finished animating a scene, Flash Animators send it on to the director for approval. Afterward, the director and/or lead animator reviews any requested revisions for the Flash Animator to complete, if any. They repeat the process until a scene is finally approved and moved on to editing.

In the day-to-day creation of animation, Flash Animators work closely and communicate with other animators. Unless working independently on a subcontracted basis from home, this collaboration includes helping with each other's scenes. The upside to this position is being able to "bring characters to life and make money doing it," says the veteran animator Gene McGuckin, currently a Flash Animator for Renegade Animation's *The Mr. Men Show* on Cartoon Network. The downside is that sometimes Flash Animators have to work from home as freelancers, without any benefits.

Depending on their place of employment, work environment, or industry, additional duties may be required. When working on video games, Flash Animators may work in concert with art directors, application engineers, and developers. They may draw storyboards for television commercials and animated features and for proposals used to pitch advertising companies and film production facilitators. They may be required to test or improve front-end Flash applications; develop functional prototypes; create interactive sites, banners, and graphics for presentation-based projects; and design specific Web components, Web pages, or advertisements. Their position may also call for them to revise and update programs and keep proper records for software license agreements.

Often, Flash Animators with expertise in a specific area have the most employment options, including animation, commercial or advertising art, digital art, game design, illustration, or Web development. No matter which career path is taken, the animator Anikka Bergstrom, who became serious about Flash animation after working in traditional animation and character design, advises aspiring Flash artists, "Do it for fun!"

Overall, the work of Flash Animators is as demanding as any animation job in the field. Their work is highly structured and is performed in assigned work spaces or cubicles involving long stretches of sitting, repetitive motion of the hands and wrists, and eye-to-hand coordination to use a computer and mouse to draw and create animations. Freelancers perform the same highly demanding work usually out of their home offices or studios. A standard 40-hour workweek applies in most cases, but, as is the case with freelance Flash Animators, overtime may be required if the project demands it.

Salaries

As with other animator positions, Flash Animator jobs are expected to increase at a higher-than-average rate, 26 percent, through 2016, according to America's Career InfoNet. The U.S. Bureau of Labor Statistics projects animation and multimedia jobs, including positions for Flash Animators, to increase to about 109,800 by 2016. Salaries will depend on the position, region of employment, and size of the company. As the industry veteran Shavonne Cherry, who has more than 20 years of experience in both traditional and digital animation as a character layout artist, storyboard artist, and Flash Animator, explains, "Typically, bigger companies pay more and offer more benefits. However, the bigger the company, the more you become just a cog in a wheel, so the balance is up to you to strike." When

it comes to union contracts versus nonunion shops, salaries and working conditions are usually better with union shops, but in the current job market, union contracts are the exception rather than the rule.

According to PayScale.com's National Salary Data, annual earnings for Flash Animators range from $35,542 to $52,179; with bonuses, the range is $36,036 to $56,502. Salary levels were reported much higher in Washington, D.C., at $80,150 and California, at $79,090. Weekly wages range from $1,200 to $1,500 or more. According to the U.S. Bureau of Labor Statistics, in the film and television industry, Flash Animators earn an average yearly income of $71,910 and from $40.00 to $50.00 an hour or more working in temporary or freelance positions, depending on the location, company, and level of experience. On the other hand, members of The Animation Guild, Local 839, of the IATSE make a minimum of $1,078 and a high of $1,600 weekly for a 40-hour workweek.

Contracts for freelance Flash Animators are usually for a shorter duration and are typically paid as a lump sum as opposed to weekly wages. One drawback of freelancing is that, unlike a job that draws a regular weekly paycheck, after the job finishes, sometimes payment for services arrives a month or more later. "If offered weekly wages as an independent contractor for anything lasting over three weeks, be careful," Cherry advises. While the practice is not uncommon, companies are really not supposed to do that, but it does happen.

Supply and demand is driving the market for Flash Animators. As Cherry notes, "It's a free market." Consequently, anyone fresh out of school will be in line with a hundred other people who apply and are considered for one position, so, she advises, don't think "you're Walt Disney's second coming."

Employment Prospects

Since the animation industry's switch from Macromedia Flash to a newer, faster, and more popular Flash software alternative, Harmony, and with this style of animation not being used as much as it once was, opportunities for Flash Animators are a bit harder to find and are therefore classified as only poor to good. Candidates seeking employment must now be Harmony-trained, except perhaps when freelancing for studios where Harmony is not required. "Don't give up after the first try," Cherry says, "or the first 10 tries." It is a competitive field, but opportunities are there if you look for them, and sometimes you must be willing to accept unusual work assignments and conditions. Nothing is ever ideal or "what they explained to you in animation class."

Major urban markets, such as Atlanta, Austin (Texas), Los Angeles, and New York—places that cater to the film business—offer the greatest potential for finding work at a studio. Freelancers, on the other hand, can work from anywhere because they can telecommute. Depending on the budget and scale of the production, studios staff anywhere from 12 to 50 Flash Animators on a single production (a half-hour television series typically has an animation support staff of 50), and they are hired either by contract or on a freelance basis. Flash-animated features and television programs often employ both salaried and freelance Flash Animators. Simple commercials and Internet advertisements, usually done on a freelance basis, may employ only one Flash artist. Duration of employment varies but for a television series can last up to nine months.

Because of the Internet, there are more worldwide opportunities. Whereas it used to be that Flash Animators had to travel either to New York or Los Angeles to find animation employment in the United States, now they can find work in almost every major city across the country. Cherry adds that, generally, to find success as an animator, Flash Animators have to live in a major urban area, at least until "you develop a reputation." Those stories about the artists who live in a cottage on the lake and do all their work from there, generally, Cherry says, happen after "a lifetime of significant experience and work."

Flash Animators new to the business may initially be assigned to perform repetitive work as they establish their careers on the coattails of others. In time, their responsibilities may increase. Many who break into the film and television industries find steady work designing 2-D cartoons and 3-D computer-animated cartoons, special effects, or creating moving images that populate movies, commercials, and other productions, such as network news programs. Some Flash Animators elect to ply their trade in the video game industry, where they use their skills to create characters, animation, and realistic, interactive worlds that delight gamers of all ages. Others end up working for Web-based companies, where they create moving advertisements and other colorful images with sophisticated animation. In some regions of the country, the positions of Flash Animator and Flash Designer are combined; in other cases, employers advertise the position as "Flash Animator/developer," seeking someone experienced in both Flash animation and development.

Advancement Prospects

Advancement prospects for Flash Animators are good. With time and experience, more exposure, and skill advancement, Flash Animators can move up the ladder and become character flash animators, leading to increased creative opportunities, higher salaries, and more advanced positions, such as character designer and storyboard artist. Others who have chosen to switch careers have become 3-D animators. Chances for promotion improve when working in major cities, especially Los Angeles, where most animation studios are located, or New York. The opportunity to enjoy an upwardly mobile career and advance are greater at a larger studio than a smaller one. If one has the ability, people will probably notice.

According to Cherry, in smaller studios, Flash Animators have "a bigger voice" in the overall production. In larger studios, they have less of a say but are attached to more prestigious projects. As she says, it is about "what you like." The secret is to attain a balance—having more duties in a smaller studio may not impress the larger studios, but it may put you ahead of that artist in the big studio in terms of skills.

Developing a distinctive style isn't important for advancement to higher-salaried positions unless, however, that studio likes a particular style and wants to use it in their production. Being a Flash Animator means that you shouldn't have a developed style. In most cases, Flash Animators are hired to emulate the studio style. As Cherry remarks, "The idea is that lots of people collaborate to make one character come to life, not one character coming to life in multiple ways."

In order to advance, it is essential to develop a solid reputation that buttresses the artistic and creative talent displayed on the job. As McGuckin states, having a good reputation and recognition from your peers is "important."

Reputation for being a good worker, for not being "a prima donna," for getting along with coworkers is "invaluable," Cherry advises. A good professional reputation can land you the next job. Without that next job, there is little chance of career advancement. It's a small profession. Bad reputations travel quickly.

The bottom line: There are no shortcuts for advancement and promotion. Hard work, networking, skill development, and a professional demeanor are all important advancement factors. Also, perfecting your skill set and polishing your demo reel helps.

Education and Training

Beginning Flash Animators typically hold either an associate's or bachelor's degree in animation, digital design, graphic design, computer graphics, or a related degree from a certified art or vocational school. Having at least an associate's degree will suffice, and no additional specialized certifications are necessary. Although not all employers strictly require a degree, with the amount of competition for this kind of job increasing each year, employers are more commonly seeking applicants with a solid educational background and some form of training and technical knowledge working with Flash and related programs. According to Cherry, the best experience is "practical experience." There are plenty of trade schools and community colleges that offer Flash training, and if you have the right combination of talent and drive, those will be enough to start you on the path. What really counts is your "knowledge of the program, and the ability to stitch together a good looking demo reel."

Flash Animators are expected to be creative in their thoughts and vision and able to communicate their ideas through 2-D and 3-D images. Therefore, besides understanding both the principles of animation and the particular functionality of the Flash platform, they need to develop strong animation skills and the ability to draw and create characters and objects using the current design application software of choice, Harmony, and others such as After Effects, which is used in the creation of Flash animation and effects. Knowledge of other design programs, including Adobe Illustrator, Adobe Photoshop, Adobe Premiere, and Maya, is likewise useful in doing Flash animation for video game and Web-based productions. Practical knowledge in layering, motion tweening (tweening movement from one position to another), onion skinning (a technique that allows animators to see a faint ghost image of the previous frame of animation and where they want to place artwork for the next frame), morphing, and working with symbols, all basic elements of Flash design, and advanced Flash animation techniques that deal with writing and manipulating images is an asset. Course work varies depending on the school of choice. However, students are usually required to complete classes in drawing, graphic design, sculpture, typography, visual effects, and more.

Along with everything else, Cherry recommends learning about the history of the profession. It is surprising, she says, how many fresh young animators think they are being original when, in fact, what they are doing was done more than 50 years ago. Being aware of styles, trends, and animation history helps to "humble you a bit."

Experience, Skills, and Personality Traits

Most employers want candidates with a strong work ethic, exceptional animation abilities, and applicable technical experience (all are equally important). Two to three years of actual experience in commercial animation, preferably at a studio that produces animation, is the minimum required; more demanding employers require at least four or five years of practical experience. Having as much studio experience as possible is what "puts you on the map" as far as being taken seriously as an animation artist, according to Cherry. In other cases, meeting the appropriate educational requirements may be sufficient without having the necessary work experience. Speed and exceptional drawing and animation skills are highly desired for the job. The most marketable candidates have experience in Flash and traditional animation, character design, layouts, and storyboarding. They can effectively present their ideas both verbally and visually. More important, they are highly proficient in their abilities to employ and manipulate animation using a variety of different kinds of graphics software. They have some experience working with animation scripts. If working in a storytelling medium such as film, television, or advertising, Flash Animators also need a good sense of narrative and storytelling ability in order to storyboard and develop final animation.

The work of Flash Animators is frenetic and fast paced. Thus, they require patience, fortitude, and dedication to see things through to completion. Ideal candidates are passionate about art and layout, have an eye for detail, and are masters at elevating their work to the highest degree. They are comfortable working under pressure and tight deadlines and must be willing to work extended hours when necessary. Typically, Flash Animators work very long hours, so if you are "a regular nine-to-fiver, you may not always get your wish," Cherry notes. Tantamount to all that is the "speed" with which you can complete your assignments. Employers always want it "yesterday."

A Flash Animator has strong problem-solving skills and the ability to accept constructive criticism from peers and withstand challenges and difficulties that may arise. "How well do you handle stress? That's a big one. Being able to handle layoffs is another," Cherry says. "Being able to cope with daily criticism of your work is about the biggest—this is a profession that depends on others telling you what's wrong with your stuff, and if you have a thin skin about things like that, then you might as well not even bother."

To accept constructive criticism and collaborate with peers and superiors, Flash Animators possess excellent verbal and written communication skills. This career path offers few opportunities for Flash Animators to work independently in a corporate environment, unless as freelancers. Those more comfortable working in a more solitary situation most likely should consider a different career choice.

Unions and Associations

Flash Animators generally belong to The Animation Guild, Local 839, of the IATSE. Membership secures better wages and job security. Benefits of membership also include vacation pay and sick leave. Access to continuing education and training programs are also offered. Also of value to Flash Animators is membership in ACM SIGGRAPH (www.siggraph.org), an international computer graphics and interactive technology industry group and sponsor of the annual SIGGRAPH conference. It provides year-round programs and educational exchanges for computer-graphics professionals.

Tips for Entry

1. In this competitive field, developing a strong portfolio to showcase one's work and strengths increases chances for employment.
2. Look for job postings on Internet entertainment industry search engines, such as Animation Network World (www.awn.com), and industry blogs.
3. Submit your résumé, portfolio, and demo reel to as many employers as possible.
4. Network with Flash Animators, or if you have friends in the business, ask for help finding work.
5. Keep learning, studying, and improving to become a better artist.

INBETWEENER (CEL ANIMATION)

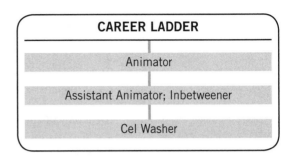

Position Description

Inbetweeners, also known as animator's assistants, are a step up from cel washer and are generally employed at traditional hand-drawn or cel animation studios. Most individuals who fill these positions are new to the business and aspire to become assistant animators and eventually animators. Used for both character and noncharacter animation and visual effects animation, Inbetweeners usually have not yet progressed to the level of a journeyman animator. Inbetweeners have the opportunity to acquire the practical animation skills and experience necessary for long-term career success, and animators who rise through the ranks usually start at this position.

Inbetweeners assist animators and animator assistants in completing the drawings necessary to animate a scene. They perform an essential function in the animation process. Their job is to draw neat and accurate between, or transition, drawings as directed by the director, animator, or assistant animator. These drawings fill in the action between two completed "extreme," drawings (still retaining their essence and never distracting from them) made by the animators. The extremes are key drawings or poses that demonstrate the movement and action in a scene. At most traditional 2-D cartoon studios in the United States, these intermediate drawings are called "tweens," and the process is dubbed as "tweening." In some instances,

since the animators' work may be rough, Inbetweeners also may produce cleaned-up drawings that maintain the same style and continuity of existing animation and model sheets.

After the key drawings arrive on their desks, Inbetweeners are required to thoroughly review them and make sure they understand what is happening in the scene before beginning work. Usually, the main drawings come bundled with an exposure sheet (separate sheets of paper divided into five sections that organize how the animation is to be shot) containing a timing chart. Each exposure sheet is usually labeled at the bottom with a corresponding number written in lead pencil. Numbers representing incomplete drawings are generally written in blue until the Inbetweener completes them. Inbetweeners may also receive special instructions regarding the characters' actions or tertiary actions of clothing, hair, or props involved in the scene to follow.

Once they fully understand the purpose of the scene and have reviewed the work to be done, Inbetweeners proceed with the inbetween process. They start by completing any unfinished breakdown drawings and matching their drawings with the extremes and breakdowns of the animator and the assistant. Although an inbetween animation only appears on screen from 1/24th to 1/12th of a second (if the drawing is "shot on twos"—or one drawing every two frames), every drawing still matters. Any errors that may seem small on paper become visible on screen when magnified many times over. As a result, it is imperative that Inbetweeners learn and imitate the animator's drawings and line quality to reduce "flutter" or "flashing" when they are viewed in sequence on video or projected on film. This helps avoid distractions as well when a "ruff" scene—the first take of a scene that includes the rough or uncleaned line quality, animation, and layout—is cut into the film and viewed.

After the animation by the animators and Inbetweeners is approved, the sketches are then cleaned up so they have clean line drawings before they move on to be traced on an acetate cel and then inked, painted, and filmed afterward.

With less hand-drawn animation being produced today in favor of computer animation, this once vital position in the traditional animation studio hierarchy has virtually fallen by the wayside. However, depending on the individual's skill and talent, the position still offers entry into the industry and a chance to gain valuable experience.

Salaries

Earnings for Inbetweeners are comparatively higher than other entry-level positions in the industry. Based on information provided by various recruiters and human resources professionals in the industry, salaries begin at $39,300 and top out at $61,100. However, with the dwindling amount of traditional hand-drawn animation being produced, annual income for this position is probably far less than actually reported. At film and television animation studios, union wage scales are $26.02 per hour for the first six months; $26.77 for the next six months; and $27.75 after attaining journeyman status. On a 40-hour-a-week basis, this equals $1,041.04 a week to start, increasing to $1,071.12 and $1,110.28, respectively.

Most Inbetweeners work in a studio environment to produce inbetweens for animated films and television shows. They often carry out such tasks in their own individual workspace. Their work can involve long periods of sitting and repeated use of their hands, eyes, and wrists. Although hours may vary, Inbetweeners are known to work a standard 40-hour workweek and overtime as needed.

Employment Prospects

Opportunities for employment as Inbetweeners in commercial film and television animation studios and production facilities that produce traditional 2-D animation for various productions are fair. Despite fewer studios producing this kind of animation, those that do usually hire those with good enough skills as Inbetweeners to work their way up to animator; less experienced artists start at the bottom of the rung as cel washers. Inbetweeners benefit from gaining the experience and follow-through skills they otherwise wouldn't have had. Runners already employed at a studio or production house with appropriate artistic talent sometimes are promoted from within to Inbetweeners. Candidates without qualifications but with tremendous passion and a strong portfolio of drawings, especially life drawings, may also be considered for work at this level.

Advancement Prospects

Many Inbetweeners advance in their careers to become assistant animators or animators. Some advance faster than others. Sometimes they are promoted from within after capably proving themselves in the position. In other situations, competition is so stiff for higher-paying jobs that Inbetweeners move on to other studios and production facilities after outgrowing their current positions.

Education and Training

Most Inbetweeners have an undergraduate degree from an established college or university in traditional animation, illustration, and/or drawing. A diploma from an accredited animation or art school is also acceptable. Good draftsmanship and drawing skills are equally important, along with a working knowledge of animation. Courses that specialize in 2-D hand-drawn animation or art courses such as graphic design and illustration are appropriate for those looking to pursue careers in animation, as employers consider life-drawing ability an asset in judging the talent of applicants. Work experience as an intern on professional productions is helpful, as are apprenticeships with established animators.

Experience, Skills, and Personality Traits

A minimum of experience is usually required for the position of Inbetweener. To become employable, individuals need a thorough knowledge and understanding of the methods and processes of animation. They should be familiar with various styles and techniques of animation. Inbetweeners must possess excellent drawing and illustration skills. Due to the laborious nature of the work, they definitely need patience to excel in the position. They need to perform their work accurately and on time and pay close attention to detail. They should show a willingness to take direction and flexibility in working as part of a team. They also should possess sound communication and presentation skills.

Unions and Associations

Most Inbetweeners in the industry are members of The Animation Guild, Local 839, of the IATSE, one of the oldest animation unions in the country. The guild represents the interests of animation professionals in negotiating better wages and benefits.

Tips for Entry

1. To hone your artistic skills, draw something almost daily and keep a sketchbook of all your work.

2. Take courses in drafting, design, and illustration to further your skills.

3. While in school, accept a job or do freelance work in design and illustration that allows you use your artistic ability on a regular basis.

4. In college, apply for internships and apprenticeships at animation studios and commercial production houses to gain both experience and contacts in the industry.

LEAD ANIMATOR

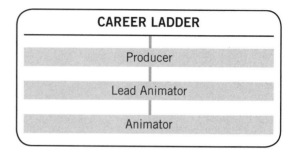

CAREER LADDER

Producer

Lead Animator

Animator

Position Description

As the directing member of an animation team, the Lead Animator successfully completes complex animation sequences in a film or television production as assigned by the supervising animator and/or producer. Acting as team leaders on behalf of their supervisors, they produce animation sequences, including repeated cycles (e.g., walk, run, etc.), meeting specific quotas and exceeding the quality desired whenever possible. Such animation can include facial animation of each character based on the script or agreed-upon guidelines set forth from the beginning of the project and creating model or expression sheets for each character.

During preproduction, the Lead Animator collaborates with the director or supervisor in developing the animation, creating test character models, recommending sequences to be animated, and actively participating in script readings and team meetings. In a supervisory capacity, Lead Animators delegate responsibilities and ensure that other animators productively and efficiently carry out the guidelines and instructions of the supervisor or director. Furthermore, they train and mentor new animators on their team and identify and report problems to the supervising animator or director.

Lead Animators head up units at commercial animation and visual effects studios and production houses that create animation for fully animated as well as live-action productions that use 3-D computer-generated character animation and special effects. The DreamWorks Animation animator Rodolphe Guenoden was a Lead Animator for *Kung Fu Panda* (2008), the tale of a lazy panda who embraces his fate as a great warrior. One of his primary tasks early on was to ensure that his team of animators fully understood how to realistically create animation of the film's martial arts pandas. As he told SI.com, DreamWorks gave martial arts classes to the animators to help them understand the basic mechanics. Every week they had a session of just training and watching movies, and analyzing and drawing from classic movies from the 1970s. Bruce Lee and Jackie Chan movies were also a "big influence."

Faced with the daunting task of developing the signature "Golden Army" sequence in the writer/director Guillermo del Toro's *Hellboy II: The Golden Army* (2008), the Lead Animator Jay Davis led a team of animators in creating thousands of CG-animated robots, which were made out of metal and had mandibles like insects but no facial features and inner workings with glowing bits of nanotechnology. To create the epic cast of characters, he started with roughly 30 hero robots to interact with *Hellboy* actor Ron Perlman. He used cardboard cutouts in their place to see how big the robots were in relation to Perlman, who acted and performed stunts in front of a green screen with the computer animation of the robots integrated into the frames of action in each scene afterward.

Lead Animators typically enjoy creative freedom on the job. Owen Klatte, an experienced character animator and animator director with a background in both CG and stop-motion animation and currently a Lead Animator with Rising Sun Pictures, said two of his favorite parts of being a Lead Animator are getting to design the action in the shows and flow of the sequences, working under the director and brainstorming with the animators to come up with the most effective way of telling the story. Another is working with the animators, teaching the younger ones and learning from the more seasoned animators. And, interestingly, sometimes learning from "the younger ones and teaching the older ones," he added.

Klatte, whose credits include major animated feature films *(Dinosaur, The Nightmare Before Christmas, Charlotte's Web,* and *Spirit: Stallion of the Cimarron),* television series and pilots *(Bump in the Night, Gumby,* and *The Wayneheads),* game cinematics and in-game assets, commercials, and special venue projects, noted that the greatest challenge for Lead Animators can be the technical requirements. As he explained in an interview, he started out in stop motion and got into CG later in his career, so he does not have the technical fluidity of someone raised with computers.

While most Lead Animators work within the entertainment industry, some work in peripheral industries, such as advertising and marketing, and in computer software companies.

Lead Animators employed by a studio or production company typically work within a corporate environment. Freelancers, on the other hand, are sometimes afforded the opportunity to work in their own home or studio. These environments are generally well lit, often with natural light. Lead Animators may work at a drafting table or primarily use a computer. While freelancers set their own hours, those within a corporate environment usually work a standard 40-hour workweek. Overtime may be required if there are specific deadlines.

Salaries

Lead Animators, designated by the producers to be responsible for and supervise the work of other animators, are typically paid 15 percent above the minimum journey rate during an assignment. According to the most recent wage scales of The Animation Guild, Local 839, of the IATSE, this averages out to $1,836.14 per week.

Employment Prospects

In rare cases, it is possible for animators to progress up the ladder to Lead Animator with no prior experience as long as they possess natural talent and passion for the work. Building an impressive portfolio that illustrates your talent and skills is critical to securing a position. People trying to get a start in the animation industry have many more options now than ever before, both because there are more schools and training programs available and because the technology to make animation is so readily available on personal computers. According to Klatte, this also means there are "a lot more people like you trying to break in at the same time, so you need to stand out." What will get you your first job is competency in a demo reel that conveys "a solid understanding of the basics of the craft, ideally with a bit of extra creative spark shining through."

Perseverance, networking skills, and continuing education will also improve your chances. If you have talent, you will eventually get someone to give you an opportunity. Opportunities for more work depend on whether people could "stand working with you" on the first job. Build a career by being a pleasant person to work with.

Advancement Prospects

Advancement opportunities for Lead Animators are fair to good. Progression will depend on individuals' creative talent and skills. Animators typically follow one of two career paths. For those who choose a managerial path, they begin as animators and advance to become senior animators and lead animators before becoming studio managers and producers. For those who choose an entirely artistic path, they start as animators and advance to become senior animators, then character artists, and, with experience, animation directors and art directors.

Education and Training

Many universities and art schools offer both undergraduate and graduate programs in fine arts and animation. A degree or diploma in animation, computer graphics, visual arts, or the equivalent is required to become a Lead Animator. Completed course work in traditional hand-drawn animation, life drawing, acting, and CG animation, including proficiency in the use of CG software such as Maya, is recommended. Klatte believes having a more solid grounding in computers and programming is helpful. Like it or not, he adds, a basic level of technical competence is needed. This is especially true in computer animation with a heavy reliance on evolving technologies.

Experience, Skills, and Personality Traits

Most employers consider both artistic ability and previous industry experience when evaluating potential

Lead Animators. A minimum of three years experience as an animator, a track record of supervising animation teams, or documented success as a project manager in a similar environment is required.

Besides a high level of visual creative skills, artistic flair, and proven leadership abilities, Lead Animators must have senior-level experience in animation, character animation, lip synching, and lighting. A background in classical animation and expert knowledge of high-end 3-D software, particularly Maya, are helpful. Lead Animators must also have a passion for the job.

Being a good animation lead requires a strong understanding of filmmaking in general and animation principles in particular, plus an ability to work well with others. As result, Lead Animators are strong communicators with good observational skills. They are masters at multitasking and prioritizing their workflow and that of their teams. Furthermore, they know how to give and take direction and, more important, manage others in a creative and collaborative working environment. They also need to respond to the direction of the people above them, contribute their own creative and technical expertise, and then lead a varied team of artists and technicians, according to Klatte.

Lead Animators need to effectively and constructively communicate their creative and technical ideas with their peers while training them and providing direction. Humility helps because everyone around them on a production knows more than they do about something, Klatte added. You will succeed if you can effectively channel your talents in support of the director's vision.

Unions and Associations

Most Lead Animators hold memberships in The Animation Guild, Local 839, of the IATSE, which is required to work at major film and television animation studios. The guild secures guaranteed wages and benefits, provides networking opportunities, promotes career growth, and provides general support.

Tips for Entry

1. Get your name known in the industry and build a solid reputation for the quality of your work and leadership
2. Be open to criticism and find the best ways to improve what you may be doing wrong and fix it.
3. Build contacts and network with others in the industry who can help you reach your goals.

STOP-MOTION ANIMATOR

Duties: Creates, uses, and manipulates original and ready-made objects out of clay, latex, or paper for stop-motion animation

Alternate Title(s): Stop-Frame Animator

Salary Range: $20,000 to $60,000

Employment Prospects: Good

Advancement Prospects: Fair

Best Geographical Location(s): Los Angeles, San Francisco, New York, Portland, London

Prerequisites:

Education and Training—A degree from a film or animation school in experimental animation, fine art, sculpture, graphics, illustration, or an allied subject preferred

Experience—Four years or more of stop-motion experience in the entertainment industry

CAREER LADDER

Animation Director; Animation Supervisor

Stop-Motion Animator

Designer; Builder; Lead Animator; Animator

Special Skills and Personality Traits—Artistic; creative; patient and calm; detail-oriented; excellent sculpting and model-making skills; strong character development, acting and timing, and storytelling skills; ability to work without supervision and as part of a team

Position Description

As far back as 1889, stop motion, then commonly known as "object manipulation," involved filming a moveable puppet, lifelike model or creature, or inanimate object, moving it in small increments and filming it one frame of film at a time to bring it to life. Advancements in the field of special effects resulted from the use of this technique in its crudest form in the 1925 silent feature *The Lost World,* considered one of the most influential films ever made for its first-ever use of stop-motion animation on a feature-length scale. Pioneered by the special effects animator Willis O'Brien, who earned his place in movie history through his iconic image of terrifying prehistoric creatures roaming Earth, this technique would gain greater importance in the future, eventually becoming a staple of moviemaking in all forms.

Today, stop-motion animation is still in use, mostly in feature films and short subjects, television series, and commercials. Since the 1990s, despite advancements in computer animation, an increasing number of stop-motion features have enjoyed widespread success. The method of stop-motion—also known as model or puppet animation or table-top animation—though now more advanced, still involves creating realistic, moving miniature-scale models, puppets, and 3-D objects to photograph frame by frame in front of the camera.

In the pecking order of the production staff, Stop-Motion Animators rank below directors and key/senior animators, who establish the characterizations of the people, creatures, and objects they animate from the outset, usually during preproduction. Based on the size of the production, Stop-Motion Animators may also work collaboratively with model makers and riggers to ensure the models, puppets, objects, and other characters are ready for the action required in each scene. On smaller-scale productions, including commercials, Stop-Motion Animators may work solo; on larger projects, as part of a team, they are responsible for supervising and overseeing the work of junior animators.

Stop-Motion Animators apply all the techniques of character animation of either the traditional 2-D or 3-D computer animator. They animate various types of characters or objects originally outlined in storyboard form, bringing them to life and replicating the style of animation set forth by the key/senior animator for each character. They create believable human characteristics, foibles, and pathos in their characters' performances on the screen. People that do stop-motion animation have to be "experts," said the acclaimed director Wes Anderson after his first attempt at animation during an interview promoting his classic-looking stop-motion animated film *Fantastic Mr. Fox* (2009). "They have to be extremely talented."

The biggest difference between Stop-Motion Animators and their traditional and computer animation counterparts is the specialized skills and tools they use. Generally, characters or objects are made from a variety of materials, including clay or pliable material such as Plasticine, and pieces of paper, which are moved one frame at a time. Stop-motion animation is "the slow food of animation," according to Valerie Pirson, considered one of the rising stars of the new generation of French stop-motion animation directors. The work is hands-on, physical, and fun but also "a lot of hard work and very time consuming."

Generally, 1,800 shots, based on the standard film rate of 30 frames per second, are required to film a single minute of animation and create nearly lifelike movement and a range of effects. The main tool in creating believable stop-motion animation is the camera, either mounted in a static position or rigged to control movement and ensure stability in doing time-lapsed photography.

What Carlos Lascano, whose work has earned him international awards, finds most appealing about stop motion is that it provides the "organic look" he considers to be one of the key features of his style. He also likes the way he can control the motion and wiggle of the elements, since he can "completely personalize the movement."

Rigging and puppet making are among two of the biggest challenges Stop-Motion Animators encounter in their work. As the freelance artist and illustrator Kirsten Lepore, whose stop-motion animation has been on television, in international festivals, in print, and on the Web, said in a 2009 interview, "If the puppet isn't well-crafted or has a limited range of motion, then animating becomes a nightmare." Rigging and camera movement is also difficult, and so is keeping track of everything happening in shots, so there are many challenges involved.

Other issues that arise may involve the limitations of the movable figures or puppets used in making the production. "I really love how improvisational stop motion is . . . but a lot of the improvisation comes from limits of the puppet's physical being. Like when a puppet's wire breaks in the middle of a shot or when the puppet physically can't do the pose I want," the Los Angeles Stop-Motion Animator Justin Rasch remarked in a profile of him in Anime8 Stop-Motion. "When they get damaged or break, it's a major slowdown to production."

In recent years, this once computer-free medium has implemented computer technology in new ways to enhance the process. In the director Henry Selick's first all-stop-motion 3-D feature, Coraline, the characters' replacement heads were molded in a computer-controlled 3-D printer that allowed for precise gradations and nuances of expression. As opposed to the lead character in The Nightmare Before Christmas, Jack Skellington, who had around 800 different sculpted expressions, the movie's star, Coraline, had more than 208,000 different possible expressions as a result of advancements in computer technology. As Brian McLean, the facial structure supervisor, charged with the job of introducing the new technology on the film, explained in an interview with Post Magazine.com, they can literally go in and animate scene-specific expressions and use a library with thousands and thousands of faces in digital form. This means that an animator can sit at a computer with a facial animation specialist and go through and help the stop-motion animator pick their faces to create a little movie file of their faces. Throughout this process, the animator was able to focus on the expressions and, when they went out on set, they would have the exact faces that they needed and referred to a little sheet that told them exactly when those faces were needed for a frame of film.

With the face, in effect, already taken care of, Stop-Motion Animators could concentrate on nuances of the body. It is "unprecedented" in stop-motion. As McLean added, "You get this double whammy in Coraline where both [body and facial expression] could be honed and effective."

As is the case with any animated film or television production, Stop-Motion Animators are required to a deliver a prespecified amount of animation within a given period of time, so it is important that they pace themselves accordingly to work under and meet any required production deadlines.

Salaries

Salaries vary according to experience, location, and budget. According to various industry sources, Stop-Motion Animators can earn a minimum of $20,000 and up to $60,000 annually. Based on the July 2011 to July 2012 member wage scales of The Animation Guild, Local 839, of the IATSE, they are paid the same basic hourly rate and weekly wage as standard animators, whether 2-D, 3-D, or stop motion. The starting pay is $38.375 per hour, or $1,535.00 per week during the first six months of employment and increases to $39.25 per hour, or $1,570.04 a week, for the second six months of employment. Journeyman Stop-Motion Animators, on the other hand, make $40.71 per hour, or $1,628.56 a week, during this same period of employment. Stop-Motion Animators are employed on major studio films, television productions, and commercials. Many also freelance or work independently, producing their own short films.

Employment Prospects

Prospects for employment are only fair, as this type of work is highly specialized. It is difficult to break into the industry because larger studios like to promote from within. Occasionally, university or college graduates who demonstrate appropriate talent and skills in a graduation demo reel are hired straight out of school as a trainee and given a chance to work their way up.

Whether creating characters and environments by hand or computer, most Stop-Motion Animators work out of a designated workspace. Inventing the animation involves repeating the same tasks, including intense eye-to-hand coordination and use of the hands and wrists. If employed by a studio, Stop-Motion Animators can work 40 hours a week or more depending on deadlines of the production.

Advancement Prospects

As with most careers in the industry, advancement is largely based on experience, talent, and animation and technical skills displayed on the job. Depending on the size of the studio or production, entry-level Stop-Motion Animators can progress up the chain to junior animators and over time up to higher-level positions, such as key or senior animator and possibly director.

Education and Training

A college degree or diploma from a film or animation school in experimental animation, fine arts, sculpture, graphics, illustration, or an allied subject is a preferred. Programs in experimental animation offer the best framework for undergraduates seeking to become Stop-Motion Animators; in these programs, future animators learn, explore, develop, and refine their skills in a variety of animation techniques and concepts. Courses blend practical knowledge and creative stimulation in 2-D drawn and direct animation (also known as drawn-on-film animation), stop-motion, and 2-D and 3-D computer animation. Accompanying courses in animation history examine all forms of this live art, with special emphasis on experimental art forms. To enter the industry, training in model or puppet animation and completion of core academic courses in life drawing, computer graphics, model building, and performance art is also a necessity. More than these academic qualifications, evidence of your ability, as demonstrated in your show reel, can make you employable on a variety of projects and lead to hiring.

Experience, Skills, and Personality Traits

Four years or more of film or television stop-motion animated production experience is generally required. Stop-Motion Animators must be detail-oriented and exhibit considerable patience on the job, as the work is both lengthy and tedious. Patience is important, Lascano explained, because if "you take a wrong step," you usually have to start over again.

Calling stop-motion "the most unpredictable form of animation," which is endlessly frustrating to "a control freak" like herself, Lepore noted that gravity and the elements are constantly working against Stop-Motion Animators, and inevitably something always goes wrong. However, if you can muster up enough patience to deal with these obstacles, then the payoff is "well worth it."

Among other abilities, Stop-Motion Animators must possess exemplary sculpting (if working in clay) and model-making skills. They need strong and clear character development, acting and timing, and storytelling skills; good knowledge of photographic techniques; and a strong sense of light management. The most important qualities for Stop-Motion Animators, according to Lascano, are good observation skills and a good sense of the different stages of movement.

Furthermore, they must be flexible and able to adapt well to different types of production for a variety of media—including television, films, and commercials—and operate relevant animation and camera equipment. They must remain calm under pressure and coalesce well with other colleagues and members of other departments. Their ability to take direction, accept criticism, and work without supervision and as part of a team with a wide range of personalities is also vital.

Unions and Associations

Membership in The Animation Guild, Local 839, of the IATSE is helpful to secure minimum wages and other union support.

Tips for Entry

1. Stop-motion animation is a "learn by doing" craft. In high school or earlier, learn the basics. Hook up a simple camera to your Mac or PC. Experiment with animating simple objects found around the house, or a plastic action doll, or dominoes—anything—and give them personality.
2. Concentrate on doing short films to learn techniques, such tempo, timing, and movement.
3. Watch and study many different stop-motion animated productions from a filmmaker's perspective. Freeze frame and advance frames one

at a time to study the movement of people, animations, and objects, and replicate the reality of movement in your work.

4. Acquire skills and gain confidence before setting out to create an elaborate short film or tell a story.

5. Create, animate, and produce your own short film and enter it in festivals and competitions around the country.

6. Join animation forums online and attend industry symposiums and conferences to network with other professionals.

STORY ARTIST

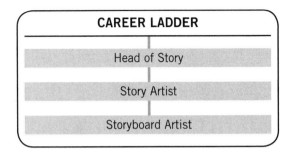

CAREER LADDER

Head of Story

Story Artist

Storyboard Artist

Position Description

The Story Artist position has dramatically changed since Walt Disney created the tedious and intricate concept of storyboarding—a series of sketches visually telling the story before it is actually animated—in the early 1930s, first using the method on his Academy Award–winning Silly Symphony cartoon *Three Little Pigs* (1933). In those days, gag men (those who developed gags used in cartoons) and cartoonists were responsible for building the story with quick sketches; today, these professionals are known as Story Artists. Unlike early storytellers, the current crop must have knowledge of story structure, cinematography, and basic animation in addition to being good gag men and lightning-fast draftsmen.

"A story artist creates the first visual translation of the written script," says the Pixar Animation Story Artist Piet Kroon. "The scenes are broken down in shots. In storyboard, the cinematography is explored. Also, the story artist 'acts' out the scenes in character poses. That way the board artist helps to explore and define the characters' personalities further: not just what they say, but how they say it. In the acting, subtext can be added to the dialogue. In storyboards, bits of business, visual jokes, etc., can be added as well."

While the setup for this position may differ by studio, all Story Artists are a part of the story department and report to the story production manager. Normally, they work with the director and sometimes closely with the editor, who cuts the boards together in animatics, a video reel of the story. In some cases, a head of story (often someone who previously worked as a Story Artist) serves as intermediary between the director and story crew or quasi assistant director, particularly when directors are too busy as the film moves through various departments, with story work often continuing to the very end of production. In every case, their principal role is to develop and create sequential drawings of the story before animation is actually produced.

On animated feature productions, Story Artists contribute to script creation; on television productions, their work begins at script approval, at the same time design starts, sometimes before. Story jobs have changed, however, from artists doing "the basic beats for a story," said the animator, character designer, and story artist Philip Pignotti, "into almost animating, laying out, and the first-pass designing of the entire show or feature."

Television and feature film story work differ in terms of their scheduling. Television production schedules can be short and consistent, whereas in feature work there may be only a few weeks to brainstorm and little time to draw, sometimes leaving only a week to completely draw an entire sequence. Nonetheless, "The Story Artist is one of the most important positions," Pignotti explained. "It's where it all starts to come together. Story Artists are the hands and eyes of the director."

Story Artists support the director's vision for the production. They have to develop a rapport with him or her and be able to interpret exactly what the director wants in "the sequence you draw," said the Pixar Animation Story Artist Christian Roman. One of the challenges of the position is that the director may not always be available to answer questions or provide guidance. Thus, Story Artists find themselves predicting what the director may want in a scene.

For Kroon, one of the main attractions of the job is being a part of the creative process. He loves it when "you start to discover true character and when a script becomes a movie."

What the Blue Sky Studios Story Artist John Hurst, whose films include *Ice Age: Dawn of the Dinosaurs* (2009) and *Rio* (2011), loves is getting the "first crack" at telling the story visually. He is literally the first person to see the movie, even if it's in "my own head," he explained. He gets pages from the writers, but they become his jumping-off point. He interprets their words any way that serves the story best, whether the scene is funny, sentimental, or dramatic. "It's in my hands to put that across to an audience visually," he adds. The absolute best situation for Hurst, though, was when there were no pages, as was the case with Scrat, the squirrel from *Ice Age,* and he was asked to just let "your brain run wild. The wilder, the better."

As a Story Artist, Roman loves telling stories and working on ideas as part of a team, which makes the ideas even better. Like a puzzle, it's satisfying for him to take a simple idea and fit all the parts together to "make a cohesive and engaging whole. And every part of the process serves to improve the idea."

At the start of a production, Story Artists, along with the director and writer if there is one, typically sit in a "story room" to brainstorm on ideas for the movie. They usually start the process working from a script or an outline the director provides. During the course of the meeting, ideas are debated and reworked, and jokes are suggested. The Story Artists produce quick sketches of the story and post them on a wall in sequence. Any time he gets to laugh, whether in the story room during a pitch or in the theater with an audience, Hurst finds his work gratifying. To get that kind of involuntary response from another person in reaction to a gag or a line of dialogue that he came up with, in his words, is "a great feeling."

After the initial brainstorming, Story Artists are given a sequence to draw out. They are responsible for taking their sequence and "fleshing it out" with dialogue; if none is provided, they are encouraged to add it as the scene dictates. Many years ago, much of this work was done by layout artists and animators, but as Roman noted, "The 'story reels' are much more complex and rely on the story artists to produce cinematic drawings and rough animation on the characters to really 'sell' the sequence."

One of the most daunting challenges and greatest thrills of the job, Roman said, is when he begins the first pass on a sequence—it's not just a blank piece of paper, it's hundreds of blank pieces of paper. His mind floods with the possibilities of where the sequence may go, and he has to focus and figure out which is the best way. Fortunately, he does this knowing he works with a team of talented people, and he knows they will catch him if he errs. As he says, Story Artists have to proceed and trust that when they pitch their sequence, the director or fellow Story Artists will point out areas of possible improvement.

Story Artists also strive in their work to keep their ideas and gags fresh and original. They don't try to recycle jokes or gags from other movies that feel tired and unimaginative, Hurst stressed. "Everything that you do must feel surprising and inventive, and [you] shouldn't feel that you've seen it before."

While story problems can seem insurmountable at times, figuring them out as a team can be rewarding. "You all work together to crack it," Roman explained.

After Story Artists complete their first pass on drawing out sequences of the story, they meet and pitch it to either the director or the entire story crew. The director and others in the room review the story in sequence and ideally offer new ideas to improve each sequence. "It's very important that story artists . . . be very humble . . . about their work, because it will almost always be changed or even discarded for better ideas," Roman said.

Often, the storyboard process may involve rewrites by the scriptwriters. As Kroon pointed out, "The script scene gets refined, dialogue may drop out (a picture tells a thousand words). In a sense, a top story artist in features has to be an inventive writer as well as a draftsman."

Afterward, Story Artists take notes from the meeting regarding any changes or revisions and do a second pass, followed by yet another pitch meeting. Depending on time constraints or the importance of the scene, multiple passes might be necessary.

Once approved and the director is satisfied, the sequence then moves on to the editorial department to be made into a story reel—a video of all the sequences in the order of the story with temporary voices and music soundtracks added.

The director watches the completed story reel, and the Story Artists may either advance to drawing another scene or get more notes of changes or improvements or ideas to improve the sequence as dictated by the director. In the end, it is important for Story Artists to accept the reality that they are not in control of the final outcome. "Oftentimes a project will take a turn for what you feel is the worse," Kroon stated, "because time is up, the money is spent, or the people in charge have a different view of what a good story is, or how good is good enough."

Unless hired as independent contractors who work out of their homes, Story Artists employed by a studio work on site in corporatelike environments in assigned work areas. Like animators, their work can involve long stretches of sitting and repetitive motions of the hands and wrists. While work can sometimes be intermittent, if regularly employed by a studio on a production, Story Artists work a standard 40-hour workweek and overtime as needed.

Salaries

This position is one of the most stable and high paying of all production jobs in animation. The Animation Guild, Local 839, of the IATSE has set minimum wages for Story Artists. As of June 2010, according to its annual member wage survey, individuals who worked on feature films earned a minimum of $993.88 a week. With experience, however, the position can be quite lucrative. Story Artists made a maximum of $3,500, with a median of $2,273.68 per week. Journeyman Story Artists, meanwhile, made an average of $1,434.80 a week.

Employment Prospects

Employment opportunities for Story Artists are fair to good. Prospects are tough in animated features but overall better in television animation. "There will always be a need for Story Artists," Kroon remarked, "because it requires a skill set that cannot be easily replaced" through automation.

Most films typically employ eight to 10 Story Artists. Landing work can be difficult, as competition for any opening is intense. Roman observed that there are even more opportunities for Story Artists in the television industry; these artists are concerned with the cinematography and rough animation of a television show but are not involved in writing the story. There are far more animated television shows in production than there

are feature films. Doing television storyboards is, as he says, "a great training ground" for doing features. After moving to Los Angeles, Roman, who has since worked in all facets of animation production, became friends with several artists on *The Simpsons* who ultimately helped him get a job. Once he was in, almost every job since then has come from those connections.

If turned down for a position, it is important to keep trying. Do not give up!

Advancement Prospects

Some Story Artists consider their jobs a stepping-stone in their career to higher positions. Typically, they move up to become heads of story and then directors, which is at the top of the ladder. Advancement comes after years of industry experience, resulting from the abilities they have demonstrated to craft and manage a story and to lead others and their desire to seek greater positions of authority. "A story artist could strive to become a head of story, which in many ways is more an administrative, managerial function and has less to do with drawing/boarding," Kroon said. "Many story artists have also gone on to direct. Obviously, career moves like that are not guaranteed: You have to get extremely lucky."

Many, however, stay put, as they are satisfied with their positions. Mostly, that is because they find it gratifying to be involved in the "gestation of a story and the big picture," Roman explained, which many Story Artists find appealing, whereas the minutia of directing might seem "tedious" in comparison.

Education and Training

A degree from a college or animation school in animation is generally a requirement, as formal education and training in all facets of animation production is invaluable. Story Artists require an innate ability to draw everything—from memory and at any angle. As a result, their course work should include the study of life drawing, cinematography, and story and structure along with drawing every day.

In endeavoring to become a Story Artist, Kroon suggests that undergraduates learn to draw without having to "think about it too much." They need to develop a clear and quick drawing method. Story work is not (or should not be) about beautiful drawings; it's about clearly communicating ideas. Study movies and filmmaking, particularly cinematic staging (how the camera works as a storytelling tool). It would also be beneficial to actually make an entire film to get to know the entire process "inside out."

If they do not attend art or animation school, Story Artists should focus their studies on film and animation as part of their education. Many people are "self-taught," like Kroon, who studied film theory but never went to art school and taught himself to draw.

To gain additional training, most students apply for studio internships, also known as "rookie training grounds," which may lead to job offers. Producing strong student films can also help place students quickly into Story Artist positions.

In Roman's case, he went to school for painting and studied animation on his own before getting an entry-level job doing layouts on *The Simpsons* and worked his way up to become a Story Artist. In order to become a Story Artist, he studied story structure, read many books about story, and watched many movies.

Developing a broad worldview is also essential. Story Artists should live and breathe animation and be able to uniquely tap into the human condition.

The important thing to be successful, as Roman suggests, is, "Keep learning. Get a storyboarding position on an animated television show, where you can hone your cinematographer and character acting."

Besides that, Roman advises people interested in becoming Story Artists to create their own comic books or storyboards to show off their personal storytelling skills. "If you can't come up with original ideas, storyboard a classic fairy tale or joke you heard. Practice the art of telling a story with sequential pictures," he said.

Story Artists need an "encyclopedic knowledge" of movies—any and all kinds of movies, Hearst advises. Their jobs as Story Artists are to find "the most dynamic framing, the clearest way to stage a gag, the strongest pose" to convey what that character is feeling. To achieve this, watch a lot of movies and pick them apart to see what works, what could have been better, and the ways the director developed the story visually. Look at thumbnails from your favorite movies to understand the composition of the frame. Take what you learn and board something to show some samples to prospective employers of what you can do. Being a great draftsman helps, but the studios really want to see that "you know how to tell a story. If your boards are staged well and the ideas are presented clearly in a dynamic way, you're in."

Most of all, Kroon suggests that individuals look beyond the standard requirements of the job and develop their skills appropriately to stand out. As he noted, "Everybody can draw. The most elusive quality a good story artist has to have is a good sense of story and the ability to get ideas." Write your own material and create a portfolio that consists of sketches that demonstrate your creative invention and skills.

Experience, Skills, and Personality Traits

While experience is almost always preferred, that is not necessarily true for Story Artists. Most Story Artists come from other backgrounds and, for the most part, have a few years of experience working on animated feature films or television shows with a portfolio of their body of work that led to them getting hired. "I was a traditional animator for Disney for almost 10 years, so I had a background that taught me draftsmanship and acting, which translated well into storyboards," Hurst recalled.

A Story Artist must be creative and artistic, with great storytelling abilities to match, and have a fine-tuned and flexible creative muscle able to, as Kroon said, "spark their ideas effortlessly in reaction to whatever is before you" without a hitch. They are enthusiastic about their work and able to quickly visualize and conceptualize their ideas to bring them to life through their drawings.

Successful Story Artists possess great improvisational skills they apply in the process of sketching out the story and, like performers, are able to stand in front of the director and other members of the story team to effectively act out and present their ideas. They are similarly fast on their feet when it comes to offering suggestions and improvements to the story at a moment's notice.

Story Artists have a natural gift for brainstorming and bouncing ideas off others. Because creating a story in animation is a team effort, they must work well with others in a team setting and, rather than criticize, support and enhance every idea. They accept criticism and are able to distinguish it as constructive feedback without it becoming personal.

Roman learned when it was truly worth defending his drawings how to explain his reasons without coming across as defensive. "If a director feels like a drawing or sequence I did doesn't work, I try and explain my thought process or what I was trying to achieve. That way we can both get on the same page and work toward making the scene a success."

Another important bit of knowledge that comes with experience is that nothing is random when it comes to creating a story. "Every line you draw, every angle you choose, every expression you create on a character, you have to have a reason for doing it," Roman related. This is especially the case in drawing a storyboard, since they are trying to tell your story as clearly and succinctly as possible.

Unions and Associations

Membership in The Animation Guild, Local 839, of the IATSE will help guarantee wages and can prove beneficial in many other ways, including job protection, networking, and securing other opportunities.

Tips for Entry

1. Draw every day and check your ego at the door, as you will face plenty of criticism as a Story Artist.
2. Immerse yourself in storytelling by watching movies, television, short subjects, and anything that tells a good story.
3. Network with others in the industry.
4. Develop lasting friendships with fellow alumni from school.
5. Once you have your foot in the door, maintain contacts with friends and associates to stay employed and keep progressing in your career.

SUPERVISING ANIMATOR

Duties: Directly supervise the work of a team of animators on an animated film or television production

Alternate Title(s): Animation Supervisor; Supervising Director of Animation

Salary Range: $1,889.68 to $3,062.50 per week

Employment Prospects: Fair

Advancement Prospects: Fair

Best Geographical Location(s): Los Angeles, San Francisco, New York, London

Prerequisites:

Education and Training—A degree from a university or film and animation school in computer animation or traditional animation and fine arts with an emphasis on classically drawn and computer-rendered animation

Experience—A minimum of five years of experience is required along with a minimum of three years in a leadership or supervisory role

CAREER LADDER

Director; Senior Supervising Animator

Supervising Animator;
Animation Supervisor;
Supervising Director of Animation

Lead Animator; Animator

Special Skills and Personality Traits—Artistic; highly organized; knowledge of acting and traditional animation principles; good communication and interpersonal skills; management and problem-solving skills; able to work well with personalities for long hours

Position Description

Since the role was created in the 1930s, Supervising Animators have assumed the position of leadership through their execution of memorable scenes and character performances in countless animated motion pictures and television programs. Functioning as the director's "right hand" in animation, Supervising Animators, also known as animation supervisors on CG-animated films and supervising directors of animation on television cartoon programs, supervise a unit, or team, of animators in the execution of animation sequences to represent and articulate the director's vision while upholding animation quality. As the Pixar animator Glenn McQueen told the FilmForce correspondent Kenneth Plume, "The directors can say, 'We want Woody to look sad in this shot.' So we will help the animators make Woody look sad. Also, depending on the show . . . sometimes we only have the director's time for an hour or two in the morning, and then we're pretty much on our own for the rest of the day. So Supervising Animators, or directing animators, are here to act as almost surrogate directors when the directors aren't around. You look at someone's shot, and you try as best you can to nudge them in directions that you think that the actual directors will want the shot to go."

To that end, Supervising Animators are in charge of overseeing the shot continuity and workflow of each individual sequence and the work of each animator in their group in meeting the artistic and technical requirements established for the production. In many ways, McQueen equated the work of supervising animators to that of being an assistant coach. Part of their job entails running each scene through several filters. The first is what they think the shot should be. The second is the justification for each shot. Everything must be clearly defined and tailored to the purpose of the shot. They must also consider how visually appealing the shot is and what the director will want or like in framing every shot.

In most cases, Supervising Animators represent the animation department in meetings with other team leaders and interact with other departments to artistically and technically guide each shot through the animation production pipeline, all while maintaining a "long-term" view and overall perspective and understanding of the story and its execution. In a 3-D computer animation environment, they are additionally responsible for model development and designing, testing, and approving the functionality of character rigs for animation in an individual sequence or shot while meeting the director's artistic interpretation of the production.

Supervising Animators also work with the other departments: story, layout, set direction, lighting. The Pixar Supervising Animator Scott Clark is responsible for many pieces of the production pipeline and is "constantly in contact with people who are before us and the people down the line."

Supervising Animators may handle animating certain character scenes or sequences along with their team. In an average week, out of 24 frames for every second of film, they may produce a 100-frame shot in three or four days, which translates into only four seconds of film, depending on how complex or difficult the scene is. Some scenes take longer, some shorter. Supervising Animators also develop schedules and identify delivery dates of animation. In this leadership position, they also coach and motivate animators under their supervision to meet the needs of the production schedule.

On any given production, Supervising Animators, along with the directing animators, can be responsible for guiding an animation team of 28 to 50 animators. Characters differ in size and behavior, and the challenge is to make them believable on screen. As Dylan Brown, the Supervising Animator on Pixar's *Finding Nemo* (2003), explained in an interview on CGSociety's features page, "Each film has its own unique set of challenges and we always begin by trying to figure out what they are and how to solve them." Aiding Brown and his animation team were visits to aquariums, diving stints in Monterey and Hawaii, study sessions in front of Pixar's well-stocked 25-gallon fish tank, and a series of in-house lectures from a noted ichthyologist to help produce "caricatured reality" of the movie's fish characters in their animation.

The Disney animator Mark Henn, a Supervising Animator on many classic traditional 2-D Disney full-length features, routinely uses certain elements to guide him in supervising character animation in a scene. As he told AnimatedViews.com, he looks at the challenges of the role and approaches it like an actor would upon receiving a big offer for a particular role in a film.

Most Supervising Animators use other tricks of the trade to capture the exact expression, movement, or action of the characters they are animating in a scene. Dick Zondag, the Supervising Animator for the evil character Bowler Hat Guy on Disney's *Meet the Robinsons* (2007), uses both traditional and modern devices. As he once confided, "I watch myself acting into it and try to copy what I see into the animation. I also have a little Web cam so I shoot myself—especially my facial features—and replay it as inspiration for the animation."

The most challenging shots for Supervising Animators to oversee and animate can be those involving no dialogue. In these cases, it can be helpful to write down an internal dialogue of what the character is thinking and to let that guide the decision-making process.

Overall, at the end of the day and the production, the Supervising Animator's performance on the job is part of a much bigger picture. "While supervising, you learn that it's not about you. It's about your team and about making them successful by giving them the tools, the help and the creative environment," Brown explained. "Sometimes you have to support or criticize other people's work. But retaining the respect of my peers is very important to me. They are so talented and much smarter than me."

Like most of their animation counterparts who work for major or independent studios, Supervising Animators work within the confines of a corporatelike environment in a separate work area or in a dedicated workspace that allows them to interact with various units of animators and other departments. Their work involves a moderate amount of sitting and use of their physical extremities, including eyes, hands, and wrists, to perform required tasks. Full-time Supervising Animators usually work a standard 40-hour workweek and overtime as needed on a project-by-project basis.

Salaries

Salaries vary widely depending on many variables, including experience and location. Annual salaries, according to SalaryList.com, for a Supervising Animator on animated feature films at major studios range from roughly $100,000 to $145,000 a year; on television productions, salaries are much less. According to the June 2010 member wage survey of The Animation Guild, Local 839, of the IATSE, wages start at $1,889.68 to a high of $3,062.50 per week. The median salary for Supervising Animators is $2,265.00 a week, an increase of $83.18 over the previous year. Journeyman-status Supervising Animators, however, draw a minimum of $1,836.13 per week. Major feature films often employ as many as four Supervising Animators along with a pair of Senior Supervising Animators.

Employment Prospects

Most major commercial animation studios usually employ two Supervising Animators on a CG- or computer-animated feature and one on a weekly animated television series. The job requires considerable experience, and competition is usually intense whenever positions open up. Most Supervising Animators are promoted after working several years as animators or as lead animators in a supervisory role. As a result, overall chances of becoming a Supervising Animator are fair.

Advancement Prospects

Advancement opportunities are fair. A small number of well-established Supervising Animators may become directors for animated feature films or television series. Others may accept more responsibility by becoming both producers and directors, while some take a much different course by dropping down a peg and finding steady work as animators and character designers. There is not always a clearly defined career path.

Education and Training

An undergraduate degree in computer animation from a university or film and animation school or traditional animation and fine arts with an emphasis on classically drawn and computer-rendered animation is essential. Individuals who seek this career path need to develop a strong understanding of entertainment, acting, and traditional animation principles. As part of any arts education and training to work in 3-D computer animation, candidates need to gain knowledge of other departments in the production pipeline, including character modeling, effects, layout, and lighting.

Experience, Special Skills, and Personality Traits

A minimum of five years of professional animation experience is required along with a minimum of three years in a leadership or supervisory role. Individuals who seek this position require a strong understanding of acting and traditional animation principles. They should have a "good animation eye" and the ability to uphold animation quality and lead by example. They must have excellent communication and interpersonal skills coupled with the ability to motivate and support the creative work of others. Supervising Animators must proactively anticipate the needs of their animation team to produce work on schedule and within the director's vision, while advocating their animators' artistic interpretations, all within a fast-paced production environment.

Supervising Animators must also be skilled managers, able to identify and isolate problems as they occur with models, layouts, software, and hardware. They need working knowledge of other departments (e.g., character modeling, effects, layout, lighting, etc.) in the production pipeline to facilitate the creative process.

Unions and Associations

Supervising Animators who work for major-market studios and independents are usually members of and are represented by The Animation Guild (TAG), Local 839, of the IATSE. Other than TAG, there is no other union or professional organization that represents Supervising Animators.

Tips for Entry

1. During your early years of schooling, get involved in any aspect of animated filmmaking available to you, including creating, producing, and directing student films.
2. Accept college internships at studios and production houses to learn the specifics of animation production.
3. After becoming established in the industry, take on more supervisory positions, such as key animator and lead animator, to gain valuable experience to work your way up the ladder.

ART

ART DIRECTOR

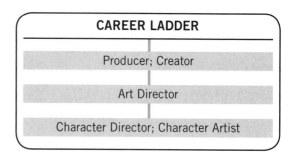

Position Description

Whether it be a full-length animated film or animated television series, Art Directors are responsible for developing the overall style and look, creative direction, and visual consistency of the animated production, including final designs for both characters and environments, in conjunction with the producer and production designer on a feature film or the show runner/supervising producer or creator on a television program. Often starting their work before the production commences, they carry the visual standards they establish from the outset throughout the production, usually performing their jobs within the confines of a studio or production facility.

For 2-D animation, Art Directors produce model sheets and turnarounds of characters with corresponding key backgrounds. Conversely, for 3-D animation, they play a larger role designing characters, backgrounds or environments, and special effects. In most cases, regardless of the animation technique, their initial designs will be hand-drawn.

On animated television series, Art Directors work directly with the show runner/supervising producer and/or creator to create the right synergy and clear vision for the show so they can properly explain it to the art department and to the series directors. In this case, the show runner sets the parameters of the world in which the art director is free to create his or her design.

As the Cartoon Network Art Director Nollan Obena explained, "Art directors are responsible for creating the overall look, mood, and tone of the show through color

and design, from the design aesthetic of the characters, to vehicles and backgrounds, to the color theories of the environments."

Kevin Gallegly, who served as the Art Director on Cartoon Network's popular *Adult Swim* series *Tom Goes to the Mayor,* added that the Art Director's job sometimes goes beyond creating entire original worlds in which the characters reside. "Sometimes the art director's job is to faithfully recreate or flesh out an existing style as well," he said.

For Obena, developing an appropriate look and design for *Generation Rex,* a series involving monsters and a military agency, required unique rules of design. "The monsters [could not] look too alien and too animal-like," Obena explained. "They [were] abominations, so there [was] no rhyme or reason for their anatomies or proportions." Thus, as part of his job, he had to establish rules when designing these creatures. Obena applied the same approach in designing the military agency. As an agency whose purpose was to "cleanse the world" of the monsters, he gave the personnel a sterile look and made their headquarters clean and orderly. In being charged with the responsibility of creating a diverse range of characters and environments, while the task can be challenging, most Art Directors know instinctively what elements they need to pull it together; they have a natural sense of what fits and does not fit in a given reality.

The work of Art Directors in animation typically involves many different tasks. In conjunction with the producer and production designer, they develop and communicate their artistic vision with members of the design team and across different departments involved in the implementation of designs—animation, lighting, modeling, visual effects, and special effects. They supervise, lead, and mentor their team of designers throughout the creation of designs while monitoring the look, mood, and quality and making final decisions regarding these different assets with the producer and production designer.

As an Art Director, finding time to do the artwork can sometimes be a challenge. "It's very easy to let the managerial aspects of the job eat up all the time. It's a constant struggle to carve out creative time," explained Dan Krall, an Art Director for such top-rated Cartoon Network shows as *My Gym Partner's a Monkey* and *Samurai Jack*.

Having finished creating their unique world and characters and established design rules, the second phase of art direction begins. This includes complementing the story in art direction using different colors in both indoor and outdoor environments. Drawing inspiration and ideas from a talented group of writers, Obena usually incorporates reds for emergencies, blues for dimly lit scenes, and greens and oranges for subterranean locales. "Working with them has always been a pleasure," he said. He finds inspiration from them while guiding them to create what he called "a common visual language."

In addition to overseeing the preparation of model sheets, characters, backgrounds, environments, and special effects, Art Directors analyze the script to identify any additional props or effects that are needed and determine the required lead times to produce them. As a result, they work closely with these departments. They also help maintain continuity of characters and environments during the production, along with monitoring any changes to the scripts where required.

Because they have so many responsibilities, Art Directors often work long and irregular hours that may include evenings and weekends, and scheduling can be among their greatest challenges. As Obena remarked, "In this modern animation industry, where shows are shipped overseas, it's always hard to produce an episode in a week or two."

Art Directors employed by a studio or on a production perform their jobs in designated work areas with ample space to create hand-drawn or computer-generated designs and renderings for the production. The mental and physical demands of this position involve long periods of sitting, repeated use of the hands and wrists, and intense eye-to-hand coordination. Hours range from 40 hours per week or more depending on the needs and deadlines of the production.

Salaries

Earnings for Art Directors vary widely depending on the medium in which they are employed. According to various industry professionals in the field, the entry-level salary for Art Directors is $30,000, and the position can pay up to $100,000 or more. Television animation Art Directors can make around $2,000 or more per week, depending on the studio. Otherwise, average weekly earnings are between $2,200 and $2,500. Art Directors working on full-length animated features can draw significantly more. In a member wage survey conducted by The Animation Guild, Local 839, of the IATSE in June 2010, earnings ranged from a low of $1,625.00 to a high of $4,750.00 with a median of $2,340.00 per week. The minimum weekly wage listed in many cases was for persons who worked at non-union shops or those who were less than journey level. Journey level Art Directors, on the other hand, made a minimum of $1,836.13 a week.

Employment Prospects

Prospects for employment are poor to fair. Limited employment opportunities for this position exist across the board in film and television animation.

Television animation studios are forgoing hiring full-fledged Art Directors; instead, they are using show runners, character design supervisors, and background supervisors to absorb the work Art Directors would usually perform. According to Obena, "Sometimes it's just the show runner and the design crew, including one character designer, one prop designer, and one background designer. If the show runner is too busy with the art direction, the series director takes the lead."

Openings are more likely with local studios or production facilities of prominence in smaller markets or in other industries, such as advertising and marketing and gaming.

One recommended career path is working your way from a design or painter position to a supervisory position. "This way, you are familiar with the ins and outs of animation production," Obena said, "namely creating a show which is 'produce-able' with the schedule."

Advancement Prospects

The possibilities for advancement for Art Directors are fair. Most Art Directors consider their job the ultimate step up in their career and, with competition so high in their field, stay the course. There are no other positions to shoot for above art directing outside of being a show creator. Some, however, go on to become producers and creators.

Still others eye other elevated positions in the industry to advance their careers, such as heading a development department for an animation studio—what Gallegly calls "the holy grail of animation" and ultimate goal in the business for an Art Director.

Being especially talented and skilled make the possibilities for advancement more likely. "Work your way up the ladder and have patience. If you have the skills and just as importantly, the drive and work ethic, you will get noticed and you will get your shot," Gallegly explained. "I worked from being a color stylist, to crew supervisor, to department supervisor and was able to translate those skills and experiences into opportunities."

Diversifying your portfolio and not staying in one place of employment for too long can also speed up the process of advancement.

Education and Training

A bachelor's degree in graphic design or fine arts is acceptable; a degree in art, preferably illustration, is also useful. Most Art Directors have backgrounds and training in fine arts or 3-D design, including special effects. Before advancing to college, high school students can get a taste of college-level offerings and an idea of the skills necessary for this position by taking courses in art, drawing, art history, graphic design, illustration, advertising, and desktop publishing.

Many universities and professional art schools offer degreed art programs. Course requirements usually include classes in figure drawing, painting, graphic design, and other art courses as well as classes in art history, writing, business administration, communications, and foreign languages. Taking specialized courses in typography, animation, storyboarding, Web site design, and portfolio development may be required.

Given the growing use of computer design in animation, a thorough understanding of how computer animation and layout programs work, particularly the technical skills needed for the job, is also essential. As Gallegly said, "Knowing what resolution you could get away with is a time saver. I sent many files to the editor that were way too big. I could've worked a lot smaller and saved some time, but our show was more 'shot from the hip' so I always played it safe and worked larger to have the option of close-ups if needed."

Most universities and animation and art schools offer additional programs to undergraduates in their final year, including training opportunities and internships, to further develop their animation design styles and skills as well as their portfolios. Obena, who spent parts of his career as a background artist as well, suggests learning and becoming comfortable working with color for backgrounds, characters, props, and special effects in school in preparation for becoming an Art Director. It is imperative, he adds, that Art Directors know how to find "harmony" with so many colors overlapping in their designs.

Since art directing is not only about the look of the show, developing time management skills and the ability to turn around work quickly with the expedited schedules of the modern animation industry are also essential. "There's a learning curve in the industry that illustrators have to be accustomed to if they are thrust into the art directing position from the start," Obena related. "So a working knowledge of the industry is very helpful."

Experience, Skills, and Personality Traits

Three years or more of production-related and industry experience is required to become an Art Director. Certain core skills are needed to advance and become successful in the position. These include creativity, imagination, excellent free-hand drawing and technical and visual skills, and strong aesthetic and artistic abilities for sketching and illustrating ideas. "You have to have an intuition for story. Art direction's only role should be to support and tell the story and should try not to be a distraction from it," Krall explained. "Also, you need to be very creative from one project to the next. No one wants their show to look like anything else that's been done so you have to constantly figure out ways to be inventive."

Art Directors are competent in the design and creation of characters, sets, props, vehicles, lighting set-ups, and the use of 2-D and 3-D application programs, especially Maya, Photoshop, and others to develop a wide range of visual concepts in all forms of animation. Accuracy and attention to detail and an understanding of the workflow of animation production and related departments are also important. They are also well rounded in character design, background design, color, and storyboarding, especially those who art direct television shows.

Successful Art Directors have superb leadership, supervisory, and management and office skills. They are well organized and very good at multitasking, scheduling, and prioritizing their work; they know how and when to delegate, and quickly zero in on what's important. With deadlines a constant factor in their work, Art Directors possess good time-management skills to handle the daily stress and pressure of their positions. They establish clear directions and objectives, create support for their artistic visions and make it sharable with everyone. They work well with different people; assign and distribute the workload appropriately; monitor process, progress, and results; and provide constructive feedback. They create a positive, productive, and exciting work environment that inspires and motivates others.

Art Directors must be able to communicate and manage the needs of the production and various artists under their leadership throughout the duration of the production. Not all artists are the same—some are slower or not as technically inclined as others. Therefore, it is important that Art Directors keep them on schedule. This is especially the case when they do a "hand-out"—when they present their vision of the show—to the artists before they start the design or color process. "There may be a handful of artists designing or painting a show and all need to be headed the same direction," Obena explained. "It's important to communicate the ideas beforehand to avoid revisions after everything is finished."

Art Directors also need good presentation and pitching skills; they must be able to stand up before a room full of professionals and make a strong case for their ideas. Not all ideas will be approved. Many pieces will not end up in the production or even make it past the pitch stage, so Art Directors must be patient and be able tolerate criticism and rejection.

Furthermore, Art Directors are excellent problem solvers and troubleshooters. They know how to evaluate and adjust for problems and roadblocks during the various stages of production and come up with solutions to difficult problems as they arise. Seeing the broader picture, they effectively coordinate work with other departments and artists, such as modelers, prop designers, and riggers. At the same time, successful Art Directors learn from those they supervise.

Unions and Associations

The Animation Guild, Local 839, of the IATSE represents many Art Directors. All artists who work at a union studio must be members. Some are members of the Art Directors Guild, Local 800, of the IATSE, which represents Art Directors in both film and television. Both labor organizations negotiate wage minimums and working conditions, provide health and pension plans, and act as advocates in disputes between employees and employers. There are also some who join the Academy of Television Arts and Sciences, the only major organization devoted entirely to television, which is made up of more than 15,000 members who represent 28 professional peer groups, including performers, directors, producers, art directors, and various other artisans, technicians, and executives. Membership enables artists to nominate themselves for an Emmy in Art Direction along with their fellow members.

Tips for Entry

1. Draw and paint on a daily basis.
2. Develop an understanding of color and texture and where to apply them.
3. Be patient and learn your craft, honing both your artistic and technical skills.
4. Network and learn from experienced professionals, many of whom are approachable and willing to help.

COLOR STYLIST

CAREER PROFILE

Duties: Create and design animation backgrounds, characters, and props used for film and television productions

Alternate Title(s): Color Designer; Color Key Stylist; Colorist

Salary Range: $35,000 to $45,000 or more

Employment Prospects: Fair to Good

Advancement Prospects: Good to Excellent

Best Geographical Location(s): Los Angeles, San Francisco, New York

Prerequisites:

　Education and Training—Undergraduate degree in art and design helpful

　Experience—One year working as an inker and painter on film or television productions

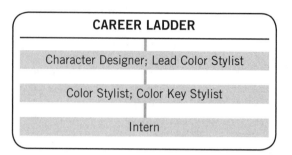

CAREER LADDER

Character Designer; Lead Color Stylist

Color Stylist; Color Key Stylist

Intern

Special Skills and Personality Traits—Strong artistic and technical skills; excellent color sense; design talent; attention to detail; good communication, time management and follow-up skills; ability to adapt to the style of the production; understanding of animation production; able to take direction and criticism; team player

Position Description

During the preproduction stages of an animation production, Color Stylists play a vital role by creating the look of the entire animation using their unique artistic style and visionary talents. As part of the animation design team, they work closely with the art director while reporting to their immediate supervisor to create all the elements of an animated scene that come together for the first time in color. They create animation drawings, such as backgrounds, characters, and props using traditional and digital rendering methods in collaboration with the art director. The goal is to establish the overall direction of the animation and continuity of the project. Part of the job is also giving directions on how effects and color will be handled.

For traditional 2-D renderings, Color Stylists use such common tools of the trade as color pencils, pastels, and acrylics; for 3-D digital renderings, the design software is the choice of the studio producing the production.

Working with the Color Stylists' color keys (different groups of colors), black and white renderings are turned into full-color master production backgrounds, adding depth and achieving the effect through paint or digital renderings to the background art. The day-to-day duties of the position can be challenging. For example, some scenes can be highly complex, and many companies, in an effort to simulate "the theater experi-

ence," will have Color Stylists work in dim lighting, sometimes for long hours, which can result in eyestrain. As a result, the demands of the position, as the Color Stylist Celine O'Sullivan pointed out, can be rigorous, with long and unpredictable hours, but can be "tremendously satisfying, including generous salary and benefits." While the atmosphere on most productions is generally lively and creative and each crew is unique, dealing with deadline pressure can be stressful. "I love working with the most talented and creative group of people," said the longtime Walt Disney television animation Color Stylist Nancy Ulene. "Sometimes the workload is so great for the time allotted. It is tough to be creative when one is faced with such pressure, but when it is done, it is quite an accomplishment." Physically, the job can be taxing, especially in a studio environment where Color Stylists often work in a cramped workspace with other artists seemingly right on top of them.

Color Stylists work even when they are off the clock, something Ulene has learned from experience. To this day, when she is driving or taking hikes, she observes the world around her, such as various shades of green in nature, how water flows in a creek, and the color of the clouds at different times of day to use in her work. As a Color Stylist, you are constantly being challenged to duplicate "real life in fantasy," she explained. "Truly this is a hard thing to do if you do not observe it in real life first. Never stop looking at things and taking in what the surfaces and textures are made of."

Color Stylists who freelance work out of home-based offices or studios. Similar to working in a studio environment, they spend long hours behind a drafting table or computer to create their colors and renderings. As a result, prolonged sitting and repetitive motion of the hands and wrists are among the demands of the job. Full-time Color Stylists generally work 40 hours a week and overtime if project deadlines require it.

Salaries

Color Stylists on the West Coast are members of The Animation Guild, Local 839, of the IATSE in Burbank, California. Hourly wage scales for this position as of July 30, 2011, start at $29.18 during the first three months of employment and top out at $31.45 an hour. For journey Color Stylists, hourly wages begin at $33.37. Union member Color Stylists make a minimum of $1,167.32 per week for a five-day, 40-hour workweek. With experience, their weekly salary can be $2,500.00, while average weekly salary is $1,446.00, down from $1,550.00 a week in 2009. On the other hand, journeymen Color Stylists earn an average of $1,366.40 a week to start. Entry-level freelance stylists are paid roughly $1,000 per episode, which varies if it is for a nonunion shop. Overall income also varies, as most Color Stylists do not work steadily throughout the year, so their weekly, monthly, and annual incomes will depend on the number of days they are employed on film or television projects. As is the case with most positions, as they become more established and their reputation grows, Color Stylists are often able to negotiate a higher rate of pay.

Employment Prospects

Opportunities for Color Stylists in the field of animation are only fair due to two factors: the animation industry's transition from doing less 2-D traditional hand-drawn animation to more 3-D computer-animated productions and the economic recession in the United States that has resulted in many animation studios cutting budgets and eliminating positions. However, with some studios still producing 2-D animation for television and motion pictures, such as Nickelodeon and Walt Disney, the services of Color Stylists are still needed in certain cases.

With an abundance of trained Color Stylists currently seeking employment, the number of qualified candidates outweighs the number of openings. With so few opportunities available, many who are currently employed hold on to their jobs and stay with the same studio or company for as long as possible. If laid off, they are also usually the first to be called back when a position reopens.

As Ulene added, "Most [Color Stylists] have been replaced by the character designers who do their own color as they create characters on the computer. This is not to say there are not exceptions, but there are far fewer opportunities than there used to be."

The veteran animation professional Carol Wyatt, who has worked as a stylist on numerous hit Cartoon Network shows, concurred that for individuals who have "good connections and a great portfolio," the market, on the other hand, is "good." For someone with no experience, the noted Warner Bros. Animation Color Stylist Brian Smith suggested that perhaps an internship would help new artists gain entry into their field of interest.

Opportunities are greater in major urban areas, such as Los Angeles, San Francisco, and New York, where many major animation studios are located and the majority of animated film and television productions are produced; others work as freelancers on a project-by-project basis in major cities or at home. The specific number of Color Stylists hired for a production largely depends on its size and budget. For lower-budget productions, usually one Color Stylist is employed.

Before the advent of 3-D animation, demand was high for trained Color Stylists. Many studios recruited and retained artists for these positions on a long-term basis, thus resulting in great job security. Today, Color Stylists' tenures usually last the duration of the production and end upon its completion. Production of a television show lasts nine months, but continued employment is possible if, as O'Sullivan noted, "you are very lucky" and the show is picked up for another season.

Finding work in a bad or highly competitive market, however, is possible and up to the individual. Be persistent, show confidence, and try to show that you want the chance to prove yourself.

Jennifer Nelson, currently a freelance storybook Color Stylist for Nick Jr., offered that the best opportunities right now are for entry-level Color Stylists, designers, and illustrators. "You can obtain this position with the right education and a strong portfolio," she said. "It is not necessary to have prior professional experience, and a great opportunity to gain experience in design and storytelling areas." Another direction candidates can take is to start as storybook Color Stylists. This position offers upward mobility to become a color stylist, then background painter, and eventually color supervisor. Far more freelancing opportunities exist than full-time jobs, providing another alternative for employment.

Advancement Prospects

Prospects for advancement are poor to fair for Color Stylists depending on the talent level and goals of each individual artist. As Ulene explained, if the Color Stylist has training in other fields, then this position could be the entry level job. Once connections are made, advancement is a possibility. Ulene has seen this happen many times. Opportunities for advancement can also arise because of pure talent.

In some cases, prospects are good based upon the quality and quantity of the work the artist has produced. There are more opportunities to advance in larger cities and at larger studios. A good reputation and respect within the industry are also important for obtaining a better position.

Gaining the support of upper management and being afforded some latitude in the position, including the ability to take initiative and make decisions independently, can hasten advancement. The key is to strike a balance between working on one's own and taking direction from superiors.

Most Color Stylists advance to become color model supervisors and to positions in other departments, such as character designer, if they show potential. Demonstrating certain attributes can help. These include excellent color sense, technical knowledge, attention to detail, a professional attitude, being consistent in your work and approachable by your peers, and following directions and working well with colleagues and coworkers.

Education and Training

No special certification is required to become a Color Stylist. However, due to the competitive nature of the industry, obtaining as much relevant formal education as possible is helpful in landing a job. A bachelor's degree in art, design, graphics, and computers from a college or art school would be beneficial.

When applying for this position, some studios require that applicants pass a "color blindness test," a written exam in color theory, along with a test demonstrating aptitude and ability. Therefore, taking courses in composition, drawing, design, painting, and illustration is recommended. Color Stylists also need training in color theory. Color is "a science in itself," Ulene offered. She took many courses throughout college and learned about how color is used in various environments and media.

In addition, film and animation classes are a must, as it is important to know the medium, including all genres and styles of animation. This includes watching cartoons and studying how color and certain values and lighting are used to create the mood in a scene or in a production, how animation works, and how a production is put together. "It is important to know your craft," Ulene said, "as each show has it own set of issues. By making your skills more well-rounded for all scenarios, your options and chances at success in the future are greater."

Becoming a Color Stylist also requires knowledge of computers and proficiency in various application design software, including Photoshop, Illustrator, Flash, and Maya for 3-D animation. Any computer skills should be matched with strong painting and illustration skills, a necessity for the job. Any additional course work and specialized training should be relevant to animation as much as possible.

Experience, Skills, and Personality Traits

A minimum of one year of experience working in the ink and paint department serves as a qualification for becoming a Color Stylist. Since one of the primary duties of Color Stylists is to establish color designs that cel painters follow, working as an inker and painter provides a concrete understanding of how to simplify colors and inks and how to create character and prop color palettes, essentials of the trade.

Ultimately, Color Stylists need to demonstrate a good balance of artistic and technical skills and a foundation in color theory. Therefore, they must be absolute color whizzes. They need to be versatile in both color key and background painting. They should display excellent design and color sense and produce work that is attractive, consistent, and well thought out with colors that are fresh, vibrant, and eye-catching. They also need a deep understanding of animation production and the theories of color schemes. "Having a distinct style is great, but you must be able to adapt to the style of any show," Nelson explained.

Conscientious and dedicated, Color Stylists take their work very seriously. They care about the success of each project they complete and the people they work with. They are self-motivated and highly organized, creative and energetic, and work with considerable speed to complete every assignment they are given, no matter how challenging or difficult. Most people think being a Color Stylist is a "fun art job," which is partly true, but it is also a lot more paperwork and organization than you would think, Smith pointed out. Thus, you should have a good memory for details and be very well organized.

Color Stylists require patience, a positive attitude, an outstanding work ethic, and the ability to think quickly on their feet. They must be able to anticipate problems in advance, devise and communicate solutions, and work collaboratively with fellow artists as well as producers to stay on track while producing high-quality work under tight deadlines and stressful conditions.

As Wyatt added, "The final decisions rest with the art director and director when all is said and done. By using your trained skills in color theory and knowing the mood of the show, you should be able to take direction and implement the information into the color work. If there are changes needed, do them with a smile on your face and be happy you are working. Never feel you know it all."

Because they receive criticism from superiors, Color Stylists must be "tough enough to handle daily critiques of your work," Wyatt remarked, "and listen to art directors and directors and implement their ideas or translate their suggestions into the style you are working on. Also, make on-the-spot decisions with directors and producers looking over your shoulder, talk up your creative decisions, and be able to see your mistakes and know how to correct them yourself." Above all else, don't be a "whiner, complainer, depressed and angry person," she said. "No matter how good you are, producers will get tired of your attitude."

Unions and Associations

Most Color Stylists are members of The Animation Guild, Local 839, of the IATSE, which handles collective bargaining with studios to secure better wages while protecting the rights of its members. Members also qualify for many benefits, including medical, dental, and a 401K pension. The guild also offers animation-related classes at The American Animation Institute and keeps members informed by publishing a monthly newsletter, *The Pegboard*.

Tips for Entry

1. Take classes at the The Animation Guild Union or enroll in industry-related classes at art schools. Most are taught by people in the industry, so try to network.

2. Create an art portfolio and store it in a nice case. Show various styles of color uses, and show monochromatic setups with backgrounds included, if possible. Be creative and try to make your portfolio memorable. Give copies to people you meet who may have industry connections so they can pass your work along.

3. Be confident. When on job interviews, be sure of yourself. If you believe in your ability and training, it will be obvious to the interviewer. Make follow-up calls to show how interested you are.

4. Watch cartoons and as much animation as you can.

5. Maintain a positive and professional attitude at all times when working with others, as developing a good reputation is important to staying employed.

STORYBOARD ARTIST

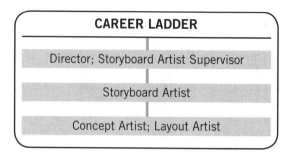

Position Description

Flourishing as a craft after its introduction by Walt Disney Studios in the early 1930s, storyboarding has been around for decades. It has played a vital role in the development of film and television animation as well many other parts of the entertainment industry, helping both animators and live-action film directors envision how a story or scene will unfold. Storyboard Artists are the individuals responsible for this task. Their primary role is to conceptualize the story or screenplay in visual form by producing a series of sketches called storyboards that, besides articulating the exact vision of what the director wants to achieve, graphically present the story for members of the production team.

Today, storyboards are widely used on animated film and television productions, including CGI, or computer-animated productions, and on live-action big-budget films, many of which are storyboarded before shooting begins. The requirement of storyboarding in live-action films, which emerged in the 1930s after film directors took notice of the practice among animation studios, has become a sensible way of avoiding over-shooting, especially in light of spiraling budgets.

Storyboard Artists generally create two kinds of storyboards, a presentation storyboard and a production storyboard. When called upon to help sell the con-cept of a project to a potential backer or network, they produce a slick, finished visual presentation in color known as a presentation board. During planning and development of a production, before it commences filming, they create a series of sequential drawings that serves as a visual roadmap—a production storyboard. Depending on the requirements of the production, Storyboard Artists may be asked to produce rough or cleaned-up drawings. Clean and tightly drawn panels of the characters are less relevant for computer-animated film productions. However, for television animation, it is often necessary that characters be drawn precisely with great attention to detail and clear written directions, especially if the animation is outsourced and produced overseas.

During what is known as preproduction, most Storyboard Artists work in the story department within a studio and start working before filming commences. They report to the story supervisor (when there is one), the director, or the producer when he or she is involved in the process. For feature-length animation, Storyboard Artists commonly work with no script, only from an outline or a concept. From there they develop sequences, actions, and dialogues, and the storyboard will demonstrate if a sequence visually works or not. When it fails, the director will instruct the writer to rewrite that sequence. "It is a back and forth process," explained the Storyboard Artist Christian Lignan, who has more than 25 years of experience in film and television animation. Overall, storyboarding allows the director to explore various means of depicting a story before going into production.

In television animation, the Storyboard Artist usually works from the script only. Because these productions have smaller budgets than feature animation, the work involved is more of a one-way process. As Lignan noted, "Unlike in feature animation, there is no exploration process of the characters or it is rather limited."

During the conceptual part of the process, Storyboard Artists attend relevant meetings and contribute ideas as needed. Later, they pitch the storyboard itself to the director and members of the production team. On most animated productions, the script and storyboard are created simultaneously; in this scenario, Storyboard Artists, working with writers, storyboard gags and visualize story ideas with quick sketches as the story develops. When reading the final script, as in the case of television cartoon productions, Storyboard Artists create thumbnail sketches and write notations and questions in the margins before meeting with the director and beginning to storyboard the project. Afterward, they sit down with the director to get feedback regarding whether they are have the right sense of the overall mood and atmosphere of the production and are heading in the right direction, making notes of any verbal descriptions the director offers. They likewise meet with their creative supervisors to discuss objectives and what is desired before sketching out the story into storyboard form.

Once sketches are approved, Storyboard Artists begin the creation of storyboard art that implements the storytelling objectives of the story supervisor or director and producer. They create rough, full-sized sketches that carefully detail and break down what happens in each scene. In most cases, their "roughs" block the action, dialogue, and characters in a scene, establishing the continuity and technical aspects to best convey the character interaction, psychological impact, and dramatic elements of the story. During this phase, Storyboard Artists consider various factors in storyboarding each sequence, scene, or shot. The most basic of these is the camera shot, or how they will frame the characters from different viewpoints in each scene; examples include extreme long shots, long shots, medium shots, close-up shots, extreme close-up shots, single shots, two shots, and insert shots—each of which serves a different artistic purpose. Another important element they take into account in storyboarding is the camera

angle, such as high-angle, low-angle, eye-level, bird's eye, canted, tilt, three-quarter, frontal, profile, and over-the-shoulder. Camera movement must also be considered, including crane, pan, dolly, and tracking shots and zoom. Likewise, when planning a project, Storyboard Artists add further definition to each scene according to three different camera perspectives—objective, point of view, and subject shots—whereby the characters will be placed in the different shots or scenes.

Some Storyboard Artists prefer to produce their drawings using a range of manual tools, from simple graphite pencils to more elaborate tools such as charcoal and paints, for presentation storyboards and concept illustrations, since they have more control over the movement and flow of their drawings than when using computer software. However, they frequently use popular 2-D/3-D visualization software, such as 3-D Studio MAX, StoryBoard Artist, Storyboard Lite, Storyboard Quick!, and other animation software packages, including Flash, Maya, and Adobe Illustrator or Photoshop. Working with computers allows Storyboard Artists to easily collate and change their work.

The drawings they produce tell the story in a series of framed panels linked sequentially, like comic book art. There is definitely room for creativity, as Storyboard Artists often take certain liberties when interpreting the preliminary drafts of a screenplay or sequences. Their work involves careful analysis and planning, especially when developing drawings of complex sequences that can't be left to improvisation. The initial storyboard illustrates the narrative and planned shots as well as the action and continuity between scenes. Each simple sketch and panel in sequence provides a visual interpretation of the script and story, including dialogue, character performance, and camera moves.

The cleaned-up and inked storyboards consist of as many as four individual panels per page. Each panel is numbered according to the corresponding scene in the screenplay and shot number. Camera angles and action are described at the bottom of each panel, including a brief description of the shot and any special effects, if required. When significant movement happens in a scene, directional arrows are used for clarity.

In such a deadline-oriented position, most Storyboard Artists tend to work long hours that frequently run into the weekends. Most big-budget feature films employ two or three full-time Storyboard Artists; on other productions, including both animated and live-action television programs, commercials, and music videos, only one Storyboard Artist is used, with employment lasting for the term of the production. Given the high turnover rate of the job, it is not uncommon for many to work as freelance illustrators and Storyboard Artists on many different productions at once.

Storyboard Artists work either on a full-time basis or on a freelance basis in work areas that are comfortable and well lit. The job involves inordinate amounts of sitting at drafting tables and similar workspaces to create storyboards by hand and by computer. The work entails the repeated use of their physical extremities, including their wrists and hands. Most usually work a standard 40-hour week. Many, however, work overtime in order to meet deadlines.

Salaries

Based on various industry sources, the entry-level salary range for this position is from $30,500 to $45,000 a year, depending on experience and location. Individuals working in the epicenters of the film and television animation industry, including Los Angeles and New York, can expect to earn even more. According to SimplyHired.com, as of June 8, 2010, the average salary for Storyboard Artists in Los Angeles was $44,000, with a high of $73,000 per annum. As reported on Salary List.com, an experienced Storyboard Artist working on computer-animated feature films for major studios such as Sony Pictures Animation and DreamWorks Animation SKG earns between $100,000 and $109,200 a year.

Employment Prospects

The employment outlook for Storyboard Artists is fair to good. Most new college graduates do not find work immediately because often others already in the industry work their way through the studio system to attain such positions. Those who have been animators or those who alternate between careers as Storyboard Artists and animators fill most positions. Others are promoted from the layout department. In addition, it is not uncommon for live-action film Storyboard Artists to move into animation. Therefore, most newcomers have to move up the ranks of the animation studio for which they work to become a Storyboard Artist. In Lignan's opinion, "a good first step" for those who want to begin their career in storyboarding is to do revisions of existing storyboards. "Working under the authority of an experienced storyboard artist or a director is a good way to build up experience."

While most candidates come from within the film and television industry, individuals with experience as graphic artists and illustrators or employed in animation and design studios have successfully transitioned to working as Storyboard Artists as well as production designers. Furthermore, graduates from art schools interested in film technique and storytelling who have taken courses in graphics and illustration also have made similar switches in their careers.

Advancement Prospects

Opportunities for advancement are generally good. Experience especially counts when it comes to moving up in your career. Most people become Storyboard Artists after having worked their way up from various jobs in the industry, such as animator, layout artist, or background painter. On the career ladder, Storyboard Artists can take the next step up to become storyboard supervisors or directors. Lignan recommends knowing the job from the "bottom up," including becoming skilled in animation, layout, or background painting so people will want to work with you again. This will also give you the necessary managerial skills to advance.

Education and Training

A college degree or diploma in animation, graphics, or illustration is a minimum requirement. Attending an art school to develop skills in drawing is helpful, but going to animation film school is even better, as developing artistic skills is part of the program and parallel to learning filmmaking.

As part of any required curriculum, graduates complete course work mostly specializing in animation. This includes courses teaching the process that most interests them, storyboarding during the preproduction phase of a production, and a basic understanding of film theory. Undergraduates usually are required to produce a storyboard for a film and attain as much drawing experience as possible by serving in internships before graduating.

Experience, Skills, and Personality Traits

Excellent drawers with the natural ability to adapt to various styles, Storyboard Artists must also be good storytellers. Skilled in visually interpreting other people's ideas in 3-D form, they need to quickly draw and produce storyboards that combine their well-honed layout, composition, sequential drawing, and editing abilities. Storyboards must be consistent with design standards established for the production.

Highly competent draftsmen and artists, Storyboard Artists possess great design sense and an all-around understanding of what is necessary to make cartoons. They are film literate and work independently and as part of a team ("Teamwork is the key in the film industry," Lignan said). A pleasant manner and professional attitude toward their work and their peers, along with a capacity to take direction or make necessary changes to their work, as needed, are vital. "Skills in human relationships and communication are very important, too, as working with various people most of the time under pressure is common," Lignan stated. "Being adaptable, eclectic, open minded, positive, always ready to cooperate, and being reliable are part of what will make the difference in the long run."

Because of the constant challenges of learning varied styles and working with different people and different teams, in addition to the necessity of consistently performing tasks well under pressure, the job requires good listening and quick comprehension skills. The most effective Storyboard Artists not only listen carefully to the intentions of the director to be sure they understand what they are asked to do, they also perform their tasks efficiently. They can accept criticism and have the ability to start over from scratch and redo something they had finished.

Basic technical knowledge of the filmmaking process, particularly the operation of film cameras and lenses, and the ability to think cinematically like a director are invaluable. In some cases, computer literacy and a thorough working knowledge of storyboard software and image manipulation applications, such as Adobe Photoshop, may be required. Excellent presentation skills are also essential, as Storyboard Artists often have to present their ideas to groups of people.

Unions and Associations

Many Storyboard Artists belong to and are represented by The Animation Guild, Local 839, of the IATSE for employment in the industry. Membership is beneficial in guaranteeing wage levels and bargaining and providing opportunities for networking.

Tips for Entry

1. Develop excellent drawing skills and the ability to draw quickly.
2. Read a film or television script and storyboard a few scenes; draw them by hand in black and white and color.
3. Build a portfolio that reflects your abilities. Make sure it displays your drawing skills and that it tells a story through a sequence of images. Enclose a variety of your work, including many concept drawings that show you are creative and can come up with interesting ideas. Show that you can work in different media and use different styles.
4. Move to a major urban area, such as Los Angeles or New York, where the majority of animated film and television productions are made.

VISUAL DEVELOPMENT ARTIST

CAREER PROFILE

Duties: Visually explore, develop, and design all aspects of an animated feature film, including sets, props, characters, background environments, visual effects, color, and style

Alternate Title(s): None

Salary Range: $25,000 to $40,000 or more (entry-level); $50,000 to $97,000 or more (with experience)

Employment Prospects: Good

Advancement Prospects: Fair

Best Geographical Location(s): Los Angeles, San Francisco, New York

Prerequisites:

    Education and Training—A bachelor's degree or equivalent in fine arts, computer arts, industrial design, illustration, or related field plus one year of visual development, graphic design, 2-D illustration, or related experience in the above areas

    Experience—One to three years of visual development, graphic design, 2-D illustration, or related experience in the film, animation, or digital gam-

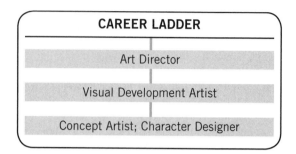

CAREER LADDER

Art Director

Visual Development Artist

Concept Artist; Character Designer

ing industry, conceptualizing and developing storyboard artwork, including environmental and character designs; and creating illustrations and presentation artwork, using Adobe Photoshop or similar software

Special Skills and Personality Traits—Artistic; creative; motivated; excellent color, design illustration, and painting skills; good visualization and conceptualization skills; good technical and computer skills; well organized; flexible; team and goal oriented

Position Description

While the art department is largely responsible for conceptualizing and executing the unique look and feel of animated films, from the earliest stages, Visual Development Artists have a profound influence on a film as their "free-form exploration" inspires fresh thinking about everything from the personalities of the characters to the story itself. Unlike the days when they did thousands of paintings for traditional animated feature films, today, much more of Visual Development Artists' work is done digitally and is more focused. This phase, known as "visual development," sets the "optical stylist elements," including concept art and 3-D previsualization, which visually translate the script and function as a style guide for the many artists involved in creating their designs and for all eventual visual possibilities from pre- to postproduction. It is an entirely chaotic process—as these artists consider visual ideas coming from all departments, including from the director and the art director—that defines the look and vision of an upcoming film.

    Working closely with directors, art directors, producers, and production designers, Visual Development

Artists are responsible for creating and developing artwork for the early story process. This includes storyboards, action plans, graphic work, and designs and themes for all aspects of animated feature film productions, including sets, props, characters, visual effects, color, and the overall style. In collaboration with the director, after analyzing the script, they develop unique visual ideas to illustrate key story moments. Visual Development Artists realize their ideas from concept to finished presentation by preparing hand-made rough sketches; clean-up renderings and tonals; paintings; sculpture; 3-D environment illustrations; technical drawings and digital imagery using high-end software that display a sense of caricature, imagination, background color, and texture; and characters in different modes and environments. Sometimes a Visual Development Artist will design entire sequences as well, emphasizing color, mood, and time of day. When the director or studio executive has a difficult time visualizing a CGI set being used in a production, Visual Development Artists may also have to build a whole 3-D set, even though only a small fraction of it will be visible in the final film.

Afterward, they determine the technical feasibility of their work with the director. They then work with story and layout artists to convert and execute their designs in 2-D or 3-D before passing them on to other artists, including modelers and technical directors, in the production pipeline for further development. In a job that is both complex and simple, their work must serve the movie in terms of storytelling and "fit with visual style" established by the art director and the production designer, noted the DreamWorks Animation Visual Development artist Nicolas Weis.

Explaining the process of visual development of characters and environments in computer animation, James Wood Wilson, a DreamWorks Animation Visual Development Artist, told the BBC in an interview, "Basically, we create the forum and mood for the characters' performance. It used to be that the visual developer would develop the look of the movie, but now it's been modified so that we take the story after it's been written, storyboard it, and develop all the visual ideas and design. . . . All the props, the characters, the environment, the surfaces, we have to do all of that within the art department."

Shelly Wan, a Visual Development Artist, once stated that her process of visual development starts with her visualizing "a mood" she wants to capture. She listens to a song again and again that catches the mood somehow and starts composing her ideas from there. Sometimes she does not start drawing until after thinking constantly about the idea for two weeks. She can work "on the fly" when needed but prefers working slowly. Otherwise, her work suffers.

Visual Development Artists may come up with one or more design styles or themes for the characters. In the animated feature *The Prince of Egypt* (1998), artists used two design styles for two contrasting groups in the film: a straight, formal, grand look for the Egyptians and a twisted and organic design for the Hebrews.

In creating the right "feel" for the film, Visual Development Artists find inspiration in all places. *Madagascar* directors Eric Darnell and Tom McGrath were originally keen on giving the movie "the feel of classic Tex Avery and Chuck Jones cartoons," but Wilson instead patterned his visual look after the work of the former Disney conceptual artist Mary Blair, known for her work on the 1948 cartoon short *Johnny Appleseed*. As he stated, "People looked at Blair's work and thought that either she was a genius or a naive artist. She was very advanced in doing stylized work that appealed to both children and people who had once been children. We took a lot from her—keeping things simple even though it was a complicated world." Deter-

mining the best arrangement and effectively bringing together all the visual components often presents the greatest challenge.

Visual Development Artists often find inspiration for their work by examining the work of other artists. Mike Kurinsky, who served as a Visual Development Artist on Sony Pictures Animation's computer-animated comedy feature *Open Season* (2006), once told a group of animation professionals how he and his fellow artists looked to the work of a legendary Disney color stylist and background artist on the classic film *Sleeping Beauty* for inspiration.

Visual Development Artists play an equally important role in the final visual presentation and success of live-action films that require realistic 3-D computer-animated effects. The German-born matte painter and visual development artist Sven Sauer, who has worked mostly on live-action films doing visual effects, claims the role of visual development is akin to "crash test dummies." In discussing his work on the made-for-television drama *Vulkan* (2009), about the after-effects of a volcanic eruption in the middle of Germany, he said he tried to walk in "every imaginable trap" which might appear during the production in order to reduce mistakes. He tested which colorings adapted to the single scenes, which light changes happened, and which elements reflected in the landscape. Proceeding this way, the look of the film became more cohesive and controllable. He planned in advance in order to prevent protracted phases of adjustments during the proper production.

Four persons were employed during the first stages of development: a 3-D artist who made camera tests of the single shots, a 2-D artist who defined the look, a composer who constructed a technical pipeline for production, and an individual to coordinate it all. They laid out the tasks of creating a huge water vortex, a disastrous volcanic eruption, an explosion, and entire full digital landscapes totaling as many as 65 shots. This work amounted to two months of intensive visual development.

According to the visual effects supervisor Sven Martin, the optical stylistic elements are set in preproduction; it is the visual translation of the script in the form of a style guide. The artists get the style guide as soon as it is created and implement it. Thus, everything about the design seems like it came from a single source.

Visual Development Artists work either as regularly employed artists for studios or on a contract basis for as long as the animation production lasts. Generally, they perform the duties of their job in designated work areas that are comfortable and well illuminated. Freelance Visual Development Artists carry out the same tasks in home-based offices or studios using identical tools of the trade. As a result, they spend a considerable amount of time using their wrists and hands and sit for prolonged periods of time when it comes to creating their artistic works. Visual Development Artists generally work a standard 40-hour workweek but on occasion work overtime hours as needed to meet important deadlines and keep the production on schedule.

Salaries

Salaries for Visual Development Artists vary from one studio to another and depend on the size of the studio, the salary policy, and the artist's negotiation skills. Entry-level salaries range from $25,000 to $40,000 a year, while more experienced artists at studios such as DreamWorks Animation earn between $89,000 and $97,000 annually.

As of June 2010, weekly wages for members of The Animation Guild, Local 839, of the IATSE ranged from $1,013.48, including persons working at nonunion shops, to a high of $3,300 per week. The median rate for the same position was $2,115.38 per week, up from $1,818.18 the previous year. Based on union wage scales from July 31, 2011, to July 31, 2012, Visual Development Artists at Warner Bros. Animation were paid $38.375 per hour, or $1,535.00 per week, during their first six months and $39.25 an hour, or $1,570.04 a week, for the next six months of employment. Journey-level artists, on the other hand, made $40.71 an hour, or $1,628.56 per week, during the same period.

Employment Prospects

Visual Development Artists are an essential part of the production process on most major animated feature films and other large productions. As a result, prospects for employment are fairly good. In addition, they are protected against most modern threats other fields might suffer from, such as technological advances that make human labor irrelevant. The education and creativity the position requires assure that talented individuals will be in demand.

Advancement Prospects

The chance of advancement for a Visual Development Artist is only fair, as opportunities for moving up to another position are limited. There are only two positions artists can aim for: art director and production designer, both of which usually take years to attain. This does not mean you cannot negotiate a better salary and stay a Visual Development Artist for a long time, especially since being an art director or a pro-

duction designer requires other skills in the management field.

Education and Training

A minimum of a bachelor's degree or equivalent in fine arts, computer arts, industrial design, illustration, or a related field is required. At least one year of additional visual development, graphic design, 2-D illustration, or related experience may be required in the above areas to work as an entry-level Visual Development Artist; three years or more of experience is required to land more advanced positions.

Experience, Skills, and Personality Traits

Experience for this position varies. Some Visual Development Artists are hired straight out of school at the entry level after completing internships in partnership with certain leading animation schools; others who land jobs have previous studio experience. Although the production pipelines vary from one studio to the next, most prefer candidates who have three years of visual development, graphic design, 2-D illustration, or related experience in conceptualizing and developing storyboard artwork, including environmental and character designs and creating illustrations and presentation artwork using Adobe Photoshop or similar software, in the film, animation, or digital gaming industry.

Visual Development Artists must exhibit a mastery of drawing, including human and animal anatomy, design, painting, or digital media as it pertains to feature film or television design and a strong art technique that feeds their imagination and creativity. They must be comfortable working in a variety of styles, from "cartoony" to highly realistic. They should have expertise in one or more areas, such as set, location, and props design; character or costume design; special effects design; and/or color styling. They must also have a solid understanding of 2-D and 3-D translations and hands-on use of 2-D or 3-D tools in the design process, with a demonstrable ability to think and design from concept to finished product independently. Working knowledge of Photoshop and Maya is a plus.

In working in a growing and complex pipeline on a production that can last for months, Visual Development Artists must have excellent communication and interpersonal skills so they can successfully work with colleagues and superiors. This means forgetting "your ego" as much as possible, constantly adapting to the frequent changes of the production, and being able to work as part of a team. Overall, as Weiss said, the job is "a pretty delicate balance" between individual talent and the ability to work as part of a team.

Unions and Associations

Membership in The Animation Guild, Local 839, of the IATSE is required to work on union-sanctioned productions in the industry. The union represents its members in bargaining agreements with studios besides providing other support, including health care benefits and a pension plan.

Tips for Entry

1. Tap into your imagination and art skills at an early age and draw every day.
2. Take classes in life drawing, figurative drawing, cartooning, and color and design.
3. Create your own personal universe of original characters and works, including drawings from live subjects, gesture-style drawings of people and animals in motion, head drawings (both quick sketch and long poses), comic strips, comic book and fantasy illustrations, and samples reflecting your color and design sense.
4. Assemble a portfolio of samples of your work in which everything is crystal clear and well organized. Your portfolio should be built for the specific studio you are targeting, fitting as perfectly as possible with their needs or a particular project to stand out among other artists who have applied.
5. Develop your own professional network by meeting other artists at conventions or through mutual friends to get advice and make important contacts.

BACKGROUNDS
AND LAYOUTS

BACKGROUND ARTIST

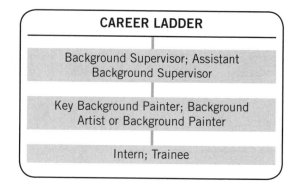

CAREER LADDER

Background Supervisor; Assistant Background Supervisor

Key Background Painter; Background Artist or Background Painter

Intern; Trainee

Position Description

Background Artists, also known as background painters and background stylists, are considered one of the most important members of the animation team. Backgrounds make up nearly 90 percent of the animation an audience sees and are fundamentally important to the story. Background Artists are responsible for creating lifelike and visually compelling 2-D or 3-D backgrounds or environments vital to the interactions of characters or objects and for completion of each scene in the overall story. Such backgrounds are commonly the bottom layer that rests beneath the hand-inked and hand-painted drawings or computer-rendered drawings of the characters or objects that are animated and photographed in sequence for film or television.

Enhancing the quality of the animation, Background Artists play a key role in establishing the color, style, and mood in each sequence through their work. They emphasize attention to detail, lighting and shading, and atmosphere in their work and employ many styles and techniques to produce the desired results. Backgrounds are usually created using background layout drawings to create one single, painted piece of work that goes behind all the animation action while the main animation is being inked and colored. The two layers—the foreground and background elements—are composited afterward. Sometimes, backgrounds are

stand-alone pieces of art; other times, several matching backgrounds are needed for successive scenes that make up an entire sequence of action. In each case, backgrounds are consistent with the films preestablished line and color styling throughout.

In the case of 2-D traditional animation, Background Artists create backgrounds using a rich palette of tools—brushes and paints, including watercolors, acrylics, oils, and pastels—and cutout paper. For 3-D computer animation, they rely heavily on popular authoring software, such as Adobe Illustrator and Adobe Photoshop, and animation programs such as Maya. Background Artists use these programs to produce multilayered realistic or simulated colorful backdrops. First, they make sketches of the backgrounds according to the design team's specifications and, when satisfied, shape and adjust the brightness, shadowing, color, and intensity of the environment to evoke a particular mood or time of day in the finished virtual version.

The attractive backdrops Background Artists create are meant to showcase the animation, with values, colors, and elements that stand out but don't detract from the characters or action in the scene. Among their many duties, they are responsible for spotting problems the directors have missed, such as an overlay that is needed or a background that is not hooking up right to the scene. In most instances, Background Artists are given a copy of the script or storyboard and character lineup or model sheet so they know how things are supposed to progress and to make sure the characters will work in the different backgrounds and environments they create. The veteran background painter Carolyn Guske noted that she always knows when there is a problem if she focuses on how beautiful the backgrounds are and forgets what the movie is about.

Different grades of Background Artists exist, usually at much bigger studios and pre- and postproduction facilities with larger production crews.

When employed on a production, Background Artists generally work in structured corporatelike studio environments; freelance artists work out of home offices or studios. They create hand-drawn and computer-made backgrounds and environments for animation in amply lit and mostly comfortable clustered or cubicle-style work areas. As work is generally done on a project-by-project basis and part time, hours vary. Some work a standard 40-hour workweek with occasional overtime; others work far less and must seek additional jobs to supplement their income.

Salaries

Background Artists tend to have decent salaries to start. According to various industry sources, the national average is $48,900 a year and with experience can go as high as $169,000. According to the June 2010 Member Wage Survey by The Animation Guild, Local 839, of the IATSE, they earned salaries ranging from $62,400 to a high of $149,500. The minimum salary for a 40-hour week is $1,347.37, increasing to a maximum of $2,200.00, based on experience. The average weekly wage is $1,850. Salaries differ depending on the size of the studio or production facility, market, and geographical location. The larger the market, generally the higher the pay. Therefore, the best-paid positions are often found in larger markets. Freelance Background Artists who work from home for animation studios make considerably less, from $250 to $450 a week, with no benefits.

Employment Prospects

Prospects for employment are fair. Most Background Artists start at small-market studios and production facilities in art departments that employ small production staffs on a project-by-project basis or part time. Some artists start their careers as freelancers doing graphic design and other work-for-hire design jobs until they can find long-term work at established studios or production facilities. Work as a traditional paint-and-brush Background Artist is virtually nonexistent. Fewer opportunities are available for 2-D artists than 3-D artists, who work in computer animation and in the gaming industry. Jobs as environment artists, who paint backgrounds and other elements and also lay out images, are more plentiful.

Today, many fewer Background Artists are needed on film and television productions compared to earlier years. Much of this is due to the conversion from traditional hand-drawn animation to computer animation. Guske notes that when she worked on the DreamWorks Animation film *The Road to El Dorado,* which blended traditional 2-D and computer animation, they had 24 painters on staff. On her next DreamWorks film, *Spirit: Stallion of the Cimarron,* only 19 painters were hired; for its next production, *Sinbad: Legend of the Seven Seas,* only nine. In 2010, DreamWorks Animation planned to hire only one to four new Background Artists that year. As of this date, there are no background painters at DreamWorks, according to Guske. Only texture artists or lighters/shaders—five per movie—are needed. At other studios, art directors now handle painting background keys (concept art sketches used to establish the color scheme and mood of an animated scene), with backgrounds being produced by animation studios in other countries as well. Studios used to hire Background Artists to perform this function or in postproduction to correct backgrounds produced overseas, but, thanks to budget cuts, that type of work is hard to find. Presently, Nickelodeon employs 10 freelance background painters to create all of its backgrounds for its animated programs in a month as opposed to hiring one artist to produce the same work in three months and at a much higher rate of pay. "I'm doing keys for Nickelodeon freelance at $250 each," Guske said. She gets only about three [background] keys done each week, so she is not earning much for her efforts.

Background Artists who are members of The Animation Guild, Local 839, of the IATSE, the oldest animation union in the country, must work 30 years and accrue 60,000 hours of employment to retire through the union with full benefits. With work being so seasonal, however, reaching that milestone is often difficult. In Guske's case, she has 31 years in the business and has worked nearly 50,000 hours in that span. "To get 60,000 hours, you basically have to work at least four days a week for 30 years," she explained. She is not even close to that number. In the past, when Background Artists were laid off, studios would lay them off for three months—from November to February—and hire them back. Now they are lucky if they are given more than a few months on a project. Many of Guske's colleagues have traveled overseas on work visas to seek employment at animation studios in such far-flung countries as Australia, England, Ireland, Japan, Poland, and neighboring Canada, only to be laid off and stuck in a country where they cannot get work.

Guske recommends that artists who want to do "color" work in the animation industry put themselves on a different career path from background painters, color stylists, texture artists, or matte painters, thus increasing the likelihood of employment. Secondary career choices for those with excellent layout and design skills would be to seek work as layout artists, character designers, and storyboard artists.

Advancement Prospects

Opportunities for advancement for Background Artists into creative and better-paying upper-level positions at commercial animation studios or production houses are only fair. Part of this is due to the relative scarcity of higher-level positions that open up and intense competition that results when they do. Depending on experience, they can advance to higher-level positions, such as key background artist, assistant background supervisor, and background supervisor and earn a higher grade of pay as a result.

Background Artists' talent and level of experience, however, can put them in an excellent position to work in other promising production and technical positions in film, television, and related entertainment industries. They can find work as texture artists, creating different textures and environmental elements, such as grass, ground, and leaves, for others to light and composite and for matte painters, who paint basic backdrops. Some become visual development artists, which, Guske adds, "is much fun because you help design the look of the show."

With years of experience, including a clear understanding of camera movements and how animation works in a scene, Background Artists can advance to become art directors. In this demanding position, they are responsible for establishing the color and style of a production that animators and other artists match in the animation they develop from beginning to end.

Education and Training

Most major studios require a bachelor's degree in painting, illustration, or animation for this position, whereas smaller studios and production companies generally accept a two-year degree or certificate from a credible animation or art school in the same fields. Most industry insiders recommend that students obtain extensive art training and take classes in life drawing

and painting to master the art of figure drawing and adding colors and depth to subjects. Traditional and computer animation classes teach everything about animation production, including the importance of direction, staging, and camera moves. As Guske explained, Background Artists must be able to draw the figure accurately from start to finish. They should be able to paint any type of lighting or subject. Many artists have problems matching the style of the show, which can be a serious problem if they are unable to adjust.

After obtaining education and training, the most successful artists are those who never stop learning and stay current on new developments, trends, and changes in software and technology. Every really good artist draws all the time to "stay fresh and keep learning," Guske said.

Experience, Skills, and Personality Traits

As an entry-level position, Background Artists must be proficient in concept illustration, texturing, and production of backgrounds in traditional 2-D animation or 3-D animation. Candidates should know how to use programs such as Adobe Photoshop, Adobe Flash, or equivalent 2-D paint programs. They must exhibit a strong knowledge of figurative drawing, color and design, and lighting. They should be skilled in the production of detailed illustrated renderings in a wide range of media (pencil, pen, marker, paint, and digital). Background Artists likewise require a strong understanding of form, shape, structure, silhouette, illustration, and design. They must be self-motivated and well organized, with strong analytical and problem-solving skills to deal with unexpected situations. Furthermore, a cooperative attitude and strong interpersonal communication skills are required to work with diverse personalities and deal with the day-to-day pressures and deadlines.

"Because background painting is one of the higher-paid positions, the competition is fierce. It's important to be well liked and do what the directors ask with a positive professional attitude," Guske stated. "Sometimes you have to work on projects that fight your aesthetic style, are ugly, and disrupt every artistic bone in your body. You do it how they want with a smile on your face. You really can't have an ego."

Unions and Associations

Many Background Artists join The Animation Guild, Local 839, of the IATSE, whose members include animation artists, writers, and technicians in the industry. The guild negotiates and enforces collective bargaining agreements with studios and companies that employ members under its jurisdiction. It sets minimum wages, hours, and working conditions and provides other benefits, including sick pay and vacation time.

Tips for Entry

1. In school, improve your skills by painting or drawing on your own. Develop a quality portfolio that represents your best work, and search for people who can help you become a Background Artist.
2. Volunteer or seek paid positions in local theater productions doing set design or any artistic endeavor involving painting and drawing while networking with others in your creative sphere.
3. Contact local casting agents who know about local film and television shoots. They might need the services of a Background Artist.
4. Use the Internet to network with other professionals, and join online forums in your area, posting examples of your background art and your résumé, to make progress in the field and connect with the right people who can show you the ropes.

LAYOUT ARTIST/SCENE PLANNER

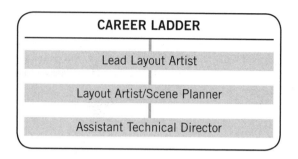

CAREER LADDER

Lead Layout Artist

Layout Artist/Scene Planner

Assistant Technical Director

Position Description

Layouts for characters and backgrounds are important components of animated productions. They are required to demonstrate the exact size, position, design, and location of the different pieces in each scene. This is where Layout Artists/Scene Planners come into play. They determine how lighting affects the animation and how the camera moves through space and create the very foundation upon which the production stands. The Layout Artist has much to do with the lighting of the film and the way the camera moves through the sets, explains Frank Gladstone, manager of Animation Training at the Disney-MGM Studios at Walt Disney World. In many ways, the Layout Artist is the cinematographer of the animated film.

Like set designers in live-action films, through their rough drawings, Layout Artists/Scene Planners set up the scene and establish the basic size relationships between the characters and their environment—backgrounds or props—in every frame or scene on a film or television production. The character layouts show all the key positions or poses of the characters as they appear over the background; the background layout defines the setting in which the characters perform. Each characters layout they produce communicates the essential emotion, storyline, and major action poses in relation to the size and location in those scenes as well.

The two-time Emmy Award–winning director, producer, and designer Mike Milo, who started his career in Los Angeles doing character layout for $600 a week on Warner Bros'. Taz-Mania animated cartoon series, was required to do six scenes per day and a total of 30 scenes per week. As he once wrote, "Doing character layout was essentially animating without doing lip synching because you were required to flesh out the storyboard, add all necessary poses to make the gag work, the acting believable, and the staging work to maximize the jokes." Character layout artists were also required to put the characters "on model" and make sure the size relationships stayed consistent from scene to scene. "Finally, they had to work out the pans and make sure that the characters took enough steps to get them from point A to point B and act while they were doing it. It was a tricky job, but I loved it."

Character layouts serve another important purpose: They give the director the chance to work or rework poses as needed.

At studios that produce 3-D computer-animated films such as Pixar Animation, Layout Artists/Scene Planners, known as camera and staging artists or 3-D Layout Artists/Scene Planners at other studios, create the sequences of shots that convey the story in a 3-D computer graphics environment using such propriety software as Maya. They stage and plot the action and are responsible for establishing the lengths of shots within a scene. They also ensure continuity and flow within and between each shot and sequence, block the positions of characters, select camera angles and movements, and prepare major shots that take place within each assigned scene, using storyboards as reference. They rework and change rough timing of shots as necessary and provide technical setups to other production departments in the production pipeline.

Before the scenes are passed on to the animators, Layout Artists/Scene Planners resolve screen direction for cut-to-cut continuity and timing for the shot. They do this by creating a low-resolution animatic, video layout, or story reel of all the shots of the environment, even temporary ones, and specific poses of the characters for the shots. "We then string them all together to see how the sequence of shots work in continuity," explained Thomas Baker, a 3-D Layout Artist/Scene Planner at Walt Disney Animation Studios. Once this has been worked out, the sequence goes to the animation department.

The stage that comes after the animation is completed is called final layout, when set dressing is added, background models are built in high resolution, and last-minute adjustments are made to camera moves and shot lengths. Depending on the size of the production, lighters/compositors are responsible for carrying out these tasks.

In coloring their layouts, Layout Artists/Scene Planners use various media and tools. For traditional 2-D animation, they may use pastels, watercolors, and ink markers; for 3-D animation, digital software is used for rendering, painting, and texturing. The process, says the character layout artist André Medina, of designing the art in general is time consuming and "pretty difficult, but rewarding." He warms up by drawing for four hours straight to get "into the groove" and finds doing layout and design work much easier.

The storyboards and approved designs Layout Artists/Scene Planners create are subsequently used as starting points by animators to create and draw the original drawings for every scene, which are inked and painted for a traditional 2-D animated production or scanned and digitally colored for a 3-D computer animated production. In this role, Layout Artists/Scene Planners calculate the field or area captured by the camera and changes that may occur within the scene. On most larger-scale productions, Layout Artists/Scene Planners work directly with the director, designers, editors, and animators; on traditional cel-animated productions, designers and animators may perform this work. At postproduction facilities, if the job exists, Layout Artists/Scene Planners are known as layout technical directors or setup technical directors, and they perform a more technical role.

Like most animation professionals, Layout Artists/Scene Planners work in structured work environments and in workspaces that are ordinarily comfortable and well lit. They spend long periods of time sitting and using their eyes, hands, and wrists to create background and character layouts that define the animation in each scene of the production. Layout Artists/Scene Planners generally work a standard 40-hour workweek; if contracted, they work until the production is completed. Additional hours may be required on an as-needed basis.

Salaries

Wages for Layout Artists/Scene Planners vary based on experience, location, and the going rate for each area. Major urban areas such as Los Angeles, San Francisco, and New York pay much higher wages than Orlando, Toronto, London, and Paris. According to PayScale. com, median annual earnings of salaried positions at major studios and production houses in markets such as Boise, Idaho, and Los Angeles range from $60,000 to $135,363. Overall, the salaries range from $1,000 to $3,000 per week for a 40- to 50-hour work week. As of July 2011, according to The Animation Guild, Local 839, of the IATSE in Burbank, California, earnings of Layout Artists (called Scene Planners) ranged from $34.75 per hour, or $1,390.12 per week, for first-year hires to $36.19 per hour, or $1,447.96 per week, for those with journeyman status. Nationally, Payscale.com reports that Layout Artists working in 3-D animation made $12.87 to $20.30 an hour for a 40-hour work week. Each studio has different requirements in terms of the hours they expect employees to work. For example, in Los Angeles, Layout Artists/Scene Planners generally put in 45 to 50 hours a week; in Paris, 35 to 40 hours a week.

Employment Prospects

Currently, the climate for employment is fair. Animators sometimes land more regular jobs at big studios, such as Walt Disney, DreamWorks, and Pixar, but, as in the entertainment business as a whole, much of the work is on a job-by-job basis and "it's extremely tough to land a job and keep it year-round for several years," Baker explained.

One of the best entry-level jobs central to becoming a Layout Artist/Scene Planner is working as an assistant technical director, or ATD; ATDs perform many tasks that assist directors to get their thoughts onto either paper or images and do little movements in a 2-D compositing package such as After Effects. Working with animators, they assist them in creating their shots and prepping the environments before they start. Layout Artists/Scene Planners watch a lot of film to learn about camera composition and different staging techniques.

Some have been fortunate enough to enter the position after completing training programs offered by animation studios. In the case of Medina, after graduating from Laguna College of Art and Design and taking additional classes, he was hired at Omation in suburban Orange County, California, to help redesign a character for the computer-animated film *Barnyard* (2006). Two years after originally testing and applying, he was then accepted into a two-week training program for character layout to work on *The Simpsons* and was immediately hired after completing his training.

Besides working for film and television animation studios and production houses, some opt for careers in advertising and marketing, where earnings can be higher.

Advancement Prospect

Opportunities for advancement are fair, as competition for the position is strong. Some studios tend to pick favorites and advance them over others, but "those people are few and far between or extremely talented," Baker said. He advises that the best way to advance is to never refuse to do a task or turn down a job because of a poor pay structure. Individuals who follow such advice can build connections and ultimately get the job they want, but they should also prepare for the day that job may not be there.

While Layout Artists/Scene Planners are employed on many medium- to large-scale film and television productions, smaller productions use their special talents as well. Thus, the best course of action is to start working on small-scale, low-budget productions to gain skills and experience before advancing. Depending on the type of production—2-D traditional hand-drawn or 3-D computer animated—different studios look for different experience, so appropriate artistic and technical skills and experience are a must.

Layout Artists/Scene Planners who advance generally move into positions in the area of lighting/compositing, and some become layout supervisors or layout technical directors. With experience, Layout Artists/Scene Planners can attain other high-level positions in design, animation, production, or possibly editing. Many others move into the special effects world of live-action movies, while others stay in animation. In the animation industry, Layout Artists/Scene Planners can become lead layout artists, a rewarding and demanding job, as Baker did, working six different feature films at one time over six years.

Education and Training

A college degree from a two-year college or qualified art or trade school in design is beneficial, though a bachelor's degree from a four-year university is recommended. While some people with natural talent have been mentored without completing any additional education, obtaining a formal design education is becoming an absolute necessity to become a Layout Artist/Scene Planner and can be useful in both learning the rigors of the position and landing a job. Degree holders also stand to earn significantly more than those without degrees. "Anyone that wants to get into the higher-end computer-driven areas will probably need exposure to a college or university," Baker said. Most of the software-support professionals he knows have master's degrees or Ph.D's. Even working in other areas, such as hair simulations, rigging, rendering, lighting, and compositing, is getting so complex that without a solid education "you can't break into the industry."

To become a Layout Artist/Scene Planner, a background in art or film and a strong understanding of traditional art skills, including a strong sense of composition and perspective, are critical. Education in classical or 3-D animation, art fundamentals, or other relevant areas of study, such as cinematography, composition, film structure, and screen direction, is also a must. A working knowledge of cinematography, composition, film structure, and screen direction is an asset.

Experience, Skills, and Personality Traits

Since this is not an entry-level position, Layout Artists/Scene Planners must have a strong aesthetic sense of traditional drawing and design. They must understand the principles of composition, continuity, timing, and mechanics to create visually appealing layouts. As Baker noted, "You have to have a good awareness of staging a camera for the best emotion for the particular shot and an understanding of timing and continuity based on the emotion of the sequence you are working on."

Besides creative intelligence, Layout Artists/Scene Planners require a keen eye for detail, visual flow, and accuracy in their work. According to Medina, "Being a good artist takes years." Most of the people he knows who are "really awesome" have been working for seven years or more. Growth happens sooner if you start when you are young. Try not to get discouraged. Be patient. In Medina's words, "Lots of bad drawings, years of bad drawings" have to come out before great ones follow. Being an artist is a very time-consuming job. An understanding of weight and physics and how gravity and environments affect your characters will improve your work.

A good working knowledge of animation, compositing, and different stages of production is essential. With most camera work now digital or computer animated, Layout Artists/Scene Planners must have compositing experience as well as 3-D graphics experience using various high-end design software, such as Maya. "There are plenty of low-budget projects or even student projects that one can gain a wealth of experience on if one is willing to work really hard for little or no pay," Baker recommended. "I don't know of anyone breaking into the industry without what most refer to as 'paying your dues.'"

As is the nature of this job, Layout Artists/Scene Planners work collaboratively as an essential part of the production for extended periods and, given the intense demands of the position, require dedication, passion, professionalism, and, most of all, patience.

Successful candidates exude a high intellect, sense of humor, engaging personality, easygoing manner, and flexibility. They are highly reliable, well organized, and efficient. Layout Artists/Scene Planners have good time-management skills and are capable of managing workflow under the constraints of tight production deadlines. Furthermore, they are strong problem solvers who anticipate, communicate, and troubleshoot creative or technical issues and suggest solutions as they arise. They also handle feedback and constructive criticism well and react rapidly to comments and changes from directors during production.

Unions and Associations

Membership in The Animation Guild, Local 839, of the IATSE is advantageous, particularly in securing minimum wages, benefits, and other union support as well as for networking with others and attaining a solid professional standing in the industry.

Tips for Entry

1. In school, fine-tune your ability to create character drawings for layouts and clean-ups of roughs from another artist's work.
2. Gain work experience by doing freelance work or internships during college, and establish industry contacts for future employment.
3. Create a diverse work portfolio demonstrating your versatility and innovation, as well as a strong sense of staging, design, lighting, and perspective.
4. Read up and stay abreast on design trends and theories, and become acquainted with the work of contemporaries in the industry.

DESIGN

CHARACTER DESIGNER

Duties: Create the visual representation of a character to be animated

Alternate Title(s): None

Salary Range: $35,000 to $60,000

Employment Prospects: Fair

Advancement Prospects: Poor

Best Geographical Location(s): Chicago, Los Angeles, New York, Orlando, San Francisco, Seattle

Prerequisites:

Education and Training—College degree in fine arts or commercial arts field beneficial though not required

Experience—Depending on skill level, one to two years doing character design at a studio

CAREER LADDER

Director; Assistant Director; Art Director

Illustrator; Prop Designer; Character Designer

Layout Artist; Inker; Production Assistant

Special Skills and Personality Traits—Creative flair; design and style sense; computer- and software-design savvy; patience; able to multitask; good written and verbal communication

Position Description

Many graphic elements go into determining how characters act and move, how big or tall they are, how many fingers they have, and even what color they are. As a member of the production team, Character Designers are responsible for creating the character designs and determining how those physical and behavioral characteristics all come together in an animated film or television production. At most studios, character design is undertaken by a variety of individuals, while at larger studios, such as Pixar and DreamWorks Animation, for example, Character Designers perform their job separately, with a design team that includes concept artists, illustrators, storyboard artists, layout artists, and animators. Either way, Character Designers play a very important role in helping shape both the direction and outcome of the final production.

Using their experience, they work with the creator, director, and lead character director to design the fictional main and secondary characters to be portrayed in the production. They determine what the characters will look like physically and generate concepts for their design after reading the finished script, and, in some cases, they create characters that were roughly designed by the storyboard artist. Character Designers then create their visual depiction of the characters—drawing the characters in different poses doing different things and showing various expressions (e.g., smiling, laughing, yelling, etc.)—taking into account the designs,

styles, directions, and guidance set down by the producer and art director.

Designing characters is difficult. "You really do have to find the right personality and shape design to communicate who this person or animal is," Mark McDonnell, a Walt Disney Company digital painter/designer told CGAdvertising.com. He usually starts with shape design and determines the overall design and personality of the character through the acting that comes out of his design and comes to life on paper or on screen. Character designing is, as he noted, all about acting and interesting shapes that can be moved around in "interesting ways."

Before designing anything, most Character Designers like to do a little research on the subjects they need to design to get the characters into their heads. As the Character Designer Shannon Tindle, who has created character designs for many popular cartoon series, explained in an interview, before designing a character, she likes to know more about the character, such as where it lives and comes from before she starts developing "a specific picture" in her mind of who the character is before drawing and designing it.

After completing their research, Character Designers start drawing rough visual designs of the characters and environments in order, blocking in shapes and adding color. The initial visual designs they produce based on their research may be the first of dozens of roughs they draw; they end up picking the ones they like best, refining the shapes and adding the necessary details to each drawing or design. Once she has the rough detail blocked in and likes the overall silhouette, Tindle starts toning the piece and wrapping it up.

For many, the most fun part of the job is sketching the characters and the creative process of coming up with the definitive drawings that set the tone for the production. Many initially draw their sketches in pencil, and, after doing any clean-up work required, they color the final designs using either traditional hand-drawing tools, such as Pantone markers, or digital computer paint software. The hope afterward is that what they designed and drew on paper and translates to the finished product, such as 3-D models, in computer animation.

The work is very difficult, but the best part of the job, according to Ricky Nierva, a Pixar Animation Character Designer, is creating 3-D models that capture the "essence" of the characters to make them widely appealing.

Successful Character Designers possess the talent to create compelling characters and character scene sketches that can be modeled in traditional 2-D or computer-animated 3-D productions. From their designs, their characters are then used to create the production storyboard that serves to tell the production's story as well as demonstrate the characters' interactions throughout. In doing so, Character Designers rely on their own artistic sense for design, keeping in mind lighting, spacing, color, texture, and size of the characters in the context of the production. Likewise, they interact with other designers and artists as well as programmers (on 3-D projects) in the completion of their tasks.

Studio Character Designers work in a structured environment in clustered workspaces with other members of the production's design team. Their work demands long periods of sitting, eye-to-hand coordination, and repetitive motion of the hands and wrists. On an animation production, Character Designers generally work a standard 40-hour week but may work additional hours if deadlines and the production require it.

Salaries

Salaries for Character Designers are low to mid-range and, based on multiple industry sources, range from $35,000 to $60,000. Salaried union positions start at $1,187.50 weekly, with experienced Character Designers earning a maximum of $2,100 weekly. Reportedly, the average union salary is $1,737 a week; for journey Character Designers the salary is slightly slower, $1,534.64 a week. Salaries at nonunion shops can be considerably lower, around $800 a week. At major studios, the average weekly pay is a minimum of $1,300 a week and can go as high as $3,500 a week or more, depending on the job level and whether the project is a television cartoon series or animated feature.

Employment Prospects

Current prospects for Character Designers are fair to poor, mostly the result the nation's troubled economy. Most college students start their careers right out of school as production assistants and generally scan the designs of the Character Designer or work as an assistant to the art coordinator or line producer. Others, based on their artistic ability, start as inkers and work their up to layout artist, where they learn the ins and outs of layout and design before becoming Character Designers. Often, when the production loses an artist, instead of finding a replacement due to lack of time or budget, they will give that opportunity to the production assistant, which can lead to becoming an artist on the production, possibly as a digital inker.

Most studios generally hire only one to two Character Designers on an animated series, compared to five to six storyboard artists on the same show or movie, but many new opportunities are popping up daily. Based on the number of jobs available and the current state of the industry, the Character Designer Jason Jones says, job seekers might have a better chance getting a storyboard position.

While opportunities for work are few, dedication and hard work can lead to success. Carrying a sketchbook and drawing from everyday life and attending art conventions as much as possible can help aspiring Character Designers get their foot in the door.

Advancement Prospects

Advancement for Character Designers is difficult, and prospects are generally poor. Seldom do opportunities for promotion within studios or production companies arise. When they do, they are usually for the next posts up the ladder—prop designer and illustrator. "The best way to advance your career as a character designer is to really put yourself out there," Jones stated. A good friend of his is successful as a Character Designer because he really "sells himself" as an artist. He has many different business cards that he creates that really represent him as an artist.

Earning a good reputation as a hard worker and a fun person can be huge. People want to work with others who are reliable and pleasant to be around.

Some aspire for much loftier positions as art directors, which requires many years of experience and, in some cases, have made the jump to assistant director and ultimately director. The best way to advance to art director is to be reliable and have storyboarding talent.

Education and Training

A bachelor's degree in fine arts, commercial arts, or animation is the usual educational background for most in the field, though it is not necessarily required. A certificate or diploma from a leading animation or art school is often enough for entry. Many vocational schools offer curricula that cater to this field. Skill and an understanding of the fundamentals of design and construction can sometimes substitute for a degree.

Some background in digital character design is recommended, as are courses in related subjects. In most cases, undergraduates also study puppetry and maquette building (a technique used to create a preliminary model) to gain a thorough understanding of the principles and practices used in character design in the film, television, and gaming industry. Future Character Designers also usually master the art of model sheet creation and devising character profiles, important assets they will use later in their careers. Likewise, they develop their creative and conceptual proficiency in creating characters in 2-D and 3-D environments. Most start in graphic design positions within the art department of a television studio or production house to gain experience before moving to larger commercial studios. Some pursue careers as animators before switching to character design.

Experience, Skills, and Personality Traits

Generally, one year of experience in film and television work is necessary to obtain the position of Character Designer. In addition, a strong understanding of 2-D or 3-D character design and modeling is required. Proven abilities in managing projects from concept to completion are also important.

To succeed in this line of work, candidates must be talented, hard working, and passionate about their work. They should produce character designs that exceed expectations. The most successful are dependable, dedicated, and highly innovative artists with expressive styling and highly developed drawing ability.

To that end, an important part of being a Character Designer is having the ability to caricature people, draw strong shapes, and convey personality in drawings. Another is absorbing or matching various styles, an ability that takes a couple of years of honing observational skills to develop.

In overcoming challenges to find the right look for characters and environments, Character Designers require a positive attitude, patience, and an easygoing temperament. They need strong artistic sensibilities and an understanding of various techniques to zero in on the right design style and produce final designs. Most studios want designers who take direction well and don't "fall in love" with their own drawings. Because of this, Character Designers must be willing to rework their designs to the fit a director's vision.

Jones's advancement to Character Designer was due to his experience working in an entry-level job doing digital inking and clean-up. He worked under some "incredible" Character Designers. His first job was to digitally clean up their rough drawings. In the process of cleaning up many of their drawings, he picked up many of their strengths. In some cases, he cleaned up an artist's designs. If they were not totally happy with the results, they would put a Post-It note over the clean up and have him clean up the design again. He never took it as a slight against him or his work. Instead, it all came down to what the Character Designer preferred. Overall, he learned from his experiences that a big part of designing characters is to always revise and rework ideas until they are as close to perfect as possible.

Unions and Associations

Membership in The Animation Guild, Local 839, of the IATSE is helpful to secure minimum wages and other union support. As Jones said, "The union sends out e-mails letting you know of new career opportunities in animation."

Several associations for animation and cartoon professionals are also worth joining. One of them is the National Cartoonists Society, with 16 regional chapters throughout the United States and one in Canada. Founded in 1946, the organization promotes a social, cultural, and intellectual interchange among professional cartoonists of all types.

Another is the International Society of Caricaturist Artists (ISCA), an international nonprofit trade association with 550 members worldwide whose purpose is to promote "the art of caricature, educate the public and the media about the art of caricature and to provide its members with helpful information about caricature as an art form as well as a profession." Members receive a quarterly magazine, *Exaggerated Features,* featuring in-depth articles about caricaturing, well-known artists, tips, and other useful information. The ISCA also holds an annual convention featuring notable figures in the industry, lectures, seminars, and more.

Although more geographically limited to artists living in the Los Angeles area, a third recommendation is the Comic Art Professional Society (CAPS) in Burbank, California. Formed in 1977 by the cartoonists Sergio Aragonès and Don Rico and the writer Mark Evanier, members of this organization meet monthly to discuss happenings in the comic art business, exchange market news, give state-of-the-industry reports, and feature guest speakers who are at the top of their professions.

Belonging to these groups has untold benefits, one of which is getting to "talk to the pros," learn new techniques and tricks of the trade, and get inspired by others more knowledgeable and experienced.

Tips for Entry

1. To start out, copy other drawings to learn why an artist drew something a certain way.
2. Take a character and copy it. Draw the character doing different things and making different expressions, such as smiling, yelling, and laughing, and keep drawing the same character until you become comfortable with it. Then find another character and do the same thing. When you feel ready, design a character of your own and follow the same process.
3. Contact studios and reach out to professionals in the industry.
4. Don't be afraid to show those in the industry your work to get feedback on how to improve.
5. Realistically assess your strengths and weaknesses as an artist, and work on becoming the best artist, you can be.
6. Build a Web site with your portfolio showing your talent.
7. Above all else, be persistent in pursuing your goals.

GRAPHIC ARTIST AND GRAPHIC DESIGNER

CAREER PROFILE

Duties: Plan, design, and create graphics and other graphic elements used in computer-animated and live-action movies and television shows

Alternate Title(s): None

Salary Range: $36,000 to $45,000 or more

Employment Prospects: Good

Advancement Prospects: Fair

Best Geographical Location(s): Chicago, Los Angeles, New York, San Francisco

Prerequisites:

Education and Training—Minimum of an associate's degree in commercial art or graphic design; a bachelor's degree in art or graphic design is preferable

Experience—At least one to two years experience as a commercial artist or designer

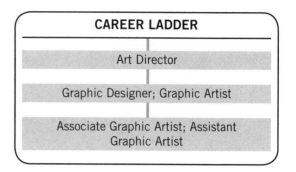

CAREER LADDER

Art Director

Graphic Designer; Graphic Artist

Associate Graphic Artist; Assistant Graphic Artist

Special Skills and Personality Traits—Creativity; drawing ability; sense of design; technical skills; detail-oriented; self-disciplined; versatile

Position Description

Production of computer-animated films is a collaborative process that involves many different artists and technicians in the creation of each image. One vital element used to create a clear and consistent representation of the director's goals for the story and the production designer's vision in supporting it is graphic design.

Every 3-D animated feature, and every animated feature in general, is made up entirely of human-made creations—from characters, to cities, to the weather—and Graphic Artists play a part in thinking up every billboard, poster, interface, and important graphic element embodied in the story and film. The role of graphics is significant, as many productions rely heavily on graphic design when it comes to illustrating the story right down to the smallest detail. Graphics are integral in three key areas: textural, which entails adding visual complexity or authenticity to a scene; informational, which involves communicating special plot information; and subtextual, which helps convey emotion, symbolism, or character information to audiences. Graphics also help set the tone through clever and original designs of opening and ending titles in animated movies and television shows.

The development of graphic design follows the normal design process of any other art being developed in the art department, with the majority of responsibility usually falling on the shoulders of Graphic Artists and Graphic Designers. Usually under the direction of the production designer, they are assigned specific design tasks and develop various graphic elements that are important to the story and production. In the earliest stages of development, they prepare sketches or layouts, drawing by hand or with the aid of a computer using specialized design software to help them create their vision for the design. During the process, they may incorporate various supporting design elements to flesh out their ideas, selecting colors, artwork, photography, style, and other visual elements. Next, they decide on the size and arrangement of the various elements and how they want them to appear on the page or screen. At most studios, designs are reviewed for approval by the production designer and director on a weekly or biweekly basis.

Afterward, turning these artists' designs into reality is dependent on many other departments in the animation production pipeline. The modeling department creates an exact model or set on which the graphic can be applied and appropriately formatted. The layout and lighting artists determine the best design for the graphic in the context of a shot—whether it is full frame, in the background, in the dark, or out of focus. Set dressing artists review how each graphic relates to other graphics or design elements in the shot. Upon final approval of the director, graphics are effectively applied to the models for use in the intended shots.

Mark Holmes, Pixar Animation's so-called graphics guru, has worked as a Graphics Artist on some of the studio's biggest releases. On a given day, he spends his time attending department check-ins, scheduling time with his production designer or manager to discuss the week's goals and progress, reviewing art with the director, and assessing graphic designs in shots. Depending on his role on a film and how deeply involved he is in the process, he usually splits his time between design work at his desk and checking in with other artists and technical directors, he stated in an interview with Thunder Chunky, a design and illustration hub in operation since 2003. Early on, he devotes his time to planning and design, but as production progresses, he spends increasing time fixing problems and tries to end each day by setting an agenda for the next workday.

Assisted by a talented crew of designers and motion Graphic Artists, Holmes was given the task of planning and designing the film graphics for a significant portion of *Wall-E* within a short window of time. Sequestering himself for the first weeks with his colleague Philip Metschan, he developed a plan for every character, set, shot, and sequence that required graphic or motion-graphic treatment, a list that only grew as the film evolved. They created a style guide and stuck to it as much as possible throughout the production.

While overseeing the work of other artists, Holmes focused on the high-level designs in the film and developed the immense Times Square and other major set pieces of planet Earth and every design element of the Axiom, including architectural signage, robot graphics, holograms, computer screens, control panels, and so on. Over the course of the production, he also supervised the design and execution of the film's static graphics and many motion graphic components.

Susan Bradley, who served as the manager of Walt Disney Studios' title graphics department for six years before moving on to design titles for many live-action films, was involved in graphically developing a number of scenes in *Ratatouille* (2007). Working with the production designer, one of the first steps in developing their graphic designs was to conduct vast research on the landscapes in and about Paris and create designs consistent with the style of the film's director. Bradley also designed and created a custom hand-made typeface for the movie's opening and ending credits.

Other Graphic Artists and Graphic Designers produce the credits that appear before and after live-action television programs and movies; design prominent scripted items used in such productions, such as authentic-looking logos, signs, props, set decorations, and period or historical pieces; and design many nonscripted items that come up suddenly during filming, usually under the direction of the production designer, who approves their designs. Occasionally, they also do previsualization work (creating hand-drawn sketches or using digital technology to plan and conceptualize elements in a scene) using Adobe Photoshop. Many more work behind the scenes in studio marketing departments and advertising agencies, creating visual solutions and the most effective designs to promote movie and television productions in print and electronic media. Their duties include developing the overall layout and production design of corporate publications, promotional displays, packaging for products, distinctive corporate and product logos, and material for Web pages, interactive media, and multimedia projects.

Working conditions for Graphic Artists and Graphic Designers vary. Generally, they work regular hours in bright and comfortable settings. Freelance artists and designers adjust their workday to suit their clients' schedules and deadlines and tend to work longer hours in smaller, more congested environments. In any case, the work of Graphic Artists and Graphic Designers involves prolonged sitting and repeated movement of the hands and wrists. On occasion, they may work additional hours, including evenings and weekends, to meet production deadlines.

Salaries

No exact salary or wage information is available for this position from representative unions, such as The Animation Guild (for whom the position is overly broad and therefore currently has no information from its member wage surveys fitting this category) and the Art Director Guild, which was unresponsive to such requests, as it applies to the animation film and television industry. According to the American Institute of Graphic Arts, the median salary for entry-level Graphic Artists and Graphic Designers was $36,000 in 2010. Nationwide, experienced Graphic Artists and Graphic Designers earned around $45,000 a year.

Employment Prospects

Employment prospects for Graphic Artists and Graphic Designers are good. The U.S. Bureau of Labor Statistics predicts employment of Graphic Designers to grow by 13 percent through 2018 as demand for professionals in this field increases. Graphic Artists and Graphic Designers with animation and design experience will be especially needed, as demand will probably increase for designers of interactive media, such as Web sites and mobile phones, and Web marketing and promotional materials for a growing number of products and services. Most typically hone their skills working in entry-level positions for small design studios, graphic arts companies, advertising agencies, and marketing departments of companies both outside of and related to the entertainment industry. *The Princeton Review* reports that 40 percent of all Graphic Artists and Graphic Designers leave the profession entirely in the first two years. After proving themselves and building their reputations, most have an easier time getting a foot in the door at a studio and production company working as designers on various productions or for different departments or divisions under the corporate umbrella of major animation and entertainment companies or cable and television networks. Most employers seek candidates who can "think outside of the box" and whose design and illustrative work shows talent and personality.

Advancement Prospects

Opportunities for advancement for Graphic Artists and Graphic Designers in the animation industry are only fair. Most are generally satisfied with their work despite the long hours and average salaries. Only individuals with proven records, solid connections, and excellent professional references move up in the industry. About two-thirds who started their careers as Graphic Artists and Graphic Designers stay in the profession; about 10 percent elect to work independently as freelancers or as designers-for-hire, producing work for various film and television productions, which can be fairly lucrative in some cases. Those who start their own businesses may reap significant profits if their ventures turn out successful. Others go on to become production designers, art directors, and producers, and many more with established reputations and whose designs remain fresh work in supervisory roles in design departments. A significant number leave the industry to take in-house positions as design consultants and as magazine layout editors.

Education and Training

Most employers in the industry, including studios, production houses, and companies that design, develop, and produce animated film and television productions, require a bachelor's degree in art and/or graphic design.

Bachelor's degree programs in fine arts or graphic design are offered at many colleges, universities, and private design schools. The National Association of Schools of Art and Design accredits around 300 post-secondary schools in the United States with programs in art and design; most award degrees in graphic design. Most allow formal entry into a bachelor's program only after the student successfully completes a year of basic art and design courses in high school. Applicants also may be required to submit a portfolio of sample sketches and other examples of their artistic ability.

Curricula usually require the study of studio art, principles of design, computerized design, commercial graphics production, printing techniques, and Web site design. Basic undergraduate course work may also include art history, color theory, figure drawing, illustration, painting, sculpture, typography, and specific courses related to the chosen area of specialization. Creative individuals who wish to pursue a career in graphic design require technical skills and a familiarity with and understanding of computer design software, such as InDesign, Fireworks, Quark Xpress, Adobe Photoshop, Adobe Illustrator, PowerPoint, and other painting and graphic design tools to work competitively in the industry.

Experience, Skills, and Personality Traits

Backgrounds in film, television, animation, and comic design are helpful for job candidates, with many employers requiring a minimum of three years of experience for this position. Versatility and a facility in a wide variety of techniques and styles are often a prerequisite for employment. Most employers are attracted to candidates whose portfolios demonstrate a diverse array of attractive work and come highly recommended by their peers. Successful candidates are able to communicate their ideas well visually and verbally. They are well read, open to new ideas and influences, and quick to react to changing trends. As exhibited in their work, they have a strong sense of design and a keen eye for details. They are, of course, proficient in the use of computer-generated graphic systems and software. The ability to work independently while under pressure is equally important. Most people in this field are self-disciplined and take the initiative to start projects on their own, to budget their time, and to meet deadlines and production schedules. They are also able to work long hours and withstand criticism and rejection in a professional manner.

Unions and Associations

Some Graphic Artists and Graphic Designers in film and television belong to The Art Directors Guild,

Local 800, of the IATSE, which provides guaranteed wages and health and pension plans and offers various resources and opportunities for sharing and enhancing their skills in and knowledge of different areas of the industry. Others join the American Institute of Graphic Arts (AIGA) and the Society of Illustrators, both of New York. Founded in 1914, AIGA is a not-for-profit association whose mission is to advance design as "a professional craft, strategic tool and vital cultural force," offering professional resources and educational opportunities for its members. Established in 1901, the society promotes the art of illustration through exhibitions, lectures and education, and awards and competitions that serve the welfare of its members.

Tips for Entry

1. In high school, take as many art classes as possible, and take advantage of the different resources offered by your school's art department.
2. Join and get involved in extracurricular art clubs in school.
3. Brush up on your drawing skills daily.
4. Create a portfolio that consists of drawings from life for admissions to an art school.
5. Have your art instructor review and provide constructive feedback.
6. Choose a university or college that offers a strong fine arts curriculum as a foundation.

ILLUSTRATOR

Duties: Design and illustrate characters, objects, and environments in vividly realistic or cartoonish form for movies, television shows, and games

Alternate Title(s): Concept Artist; Conceptual Illustrator; Production Illustrator

Salary Range: $18,650 to $80,000

Employment Prospects: Fair to Good

Advancement Prospects: Good

Best Geographical Location(s): Los Angeles, San Francisco, New York, Orlando

Prerequisites:

Education and Training—Bachelor's degree in animation, illustration, or related field preferred

Experience—Up to two years of experience and training in animation, film, television, or game production

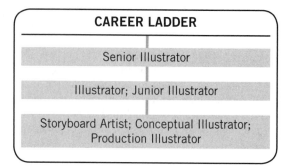

CAREER LADDER

Senior Illustrator

Illustrator; Junior Illustrator

Storyboard Artist; Conceptual Illustrator; Production Illustrator

Special Skills and Personality Traits—Artistic; imaginative; excellent drawing, illustration, and painting skills; visualization, interpretation, and conceptualization abilities; proficient in 2-D and 3-D computer design and paint; work well under pressure

Position Description

Exploding buildings, emotionally charged action, and colorful characters are just part of Illustrators' handiwork. It is their job to bring thrills and excitement to big and small screens everywhere, from animated film and television productions to video games. Illustrators are skillful artists who apply the same processes and techniques in these fields that directors, producers, and game developers rely upon to make their visions for a project come to life.

Illustrators ply their artistry and visualization talents in a number of ways. Most films employ only one or two Illustrators. However, major productions may require five or more Illustrators; they are usually grouped in three classifications, none of which are mutually exclusive: production Illustrator, conceptual Illustrator, and storyboard artist.

Production Illustrator is the overall term for so-called film Illustrators. These Illustrators create detailed black-and-white or color renderings in a wide range of media, including pencil, pen, marker, paint, and digital. They illustrate specific sets, locations, and major dramatic moments in the production, usually drawn on large-format paper. The director uses these renderings to establish the overall look and mood of a film. However, on 3-D computer-animated films, contracted production Illustrators at PDI/DreamWorks, for example,

use their unique illustrative abilities in other areas of the design process, such as prop design, environment color keys, and texture painting.

Conversely, conceptual Illustrators—also known as concept artists—do what their title suggests: They produce detailed drawings done very early in the preproduction process that illustrate and define the concept and visual look of a proposed film. Specialization often occurs among conceptual Illustrators. For example, Illustrators whose specialty is hardware design may specifically deal in making conceptual drawings of weapons, spaceships, and other objects. In other cases, producers call them in to produce conceptual illustrations as a "sales device" to help raise funding for a film, a specific sequence, or production. In the gaming world, conceptual Illustrators, or concept artists, perform many of the same services, putting conceptual ideas of a game in a visual form for the game development team.

As a storyboard artist, Illustrators create the first look of the film, laying out a visual map of the story in a series of comic book–style drawings reminiscent of something found in vintage action superhero comics. Originated in the early 1930s by Walt Disney, storyboarding has been a vital component of the preproduction process ever since. "In large productions, especially those with complex physical or effects sequences, storyboarding is an absolute necessity," stated David Russell, a noted concept Illustrator and storyboard artist in an interview with storyboardart.org. "But any film can benefit from storyboarding."

When working as storyboard artists, Illustrators cooperate in a kind of storytelling partnership with the director that can be creative and satisfying. The primary role of the storyboard artist is to lay out a sequence of well-designed shots that "serve the needs and ideas of the screenplay, as well as support the mood, style, and intentions of the director," Russell added. The boards the storyboard artist renders for the director serve as a visual representation of the script that subsequently becomes the basis for the animation (or live-action production) and how the film will be shot and directed. Storyboards are also useful as budgeting tools and to sell a concept of a production to producers or studio heads so it can be made.

Some Illustrators in the animation industry double as animators. They work as animators or character animators, creating a wide array of entertaining and appealing characters for animated films, television series, and Web-based cartoons. They might do illustrative work on the side for leading publications, including magazines and journals, as well as comic books, children's books, and in other media.

Illustrators face working conditions similar to other industry professionals. They routinely perform their work in areas that provide sufficient comfort, lighting, and space. Their work can be mentally and physically demanding and require long periods of sitting and extensive use of the eyes, hands, and wrists. Illustrators are known to work a standard 40-hour work week, but hours vary.

Salary

Salaries for Illustrators vary greatly depending on industry and career path and whether they work in-house at a major studio, production company, or video game company or as independent or contracted freelancers. Nationally, as reported by *The Princeton Review,* the minimum salary is estimated at as low as $18,650 to as high as $48,110 a year. Top Illustrators who build solid reputations after years of experience often make much higher wages of around $80,000 a year. Illustrators in the motion picture industry have the highest mean pay compared to artists in other industries of around $36.47 an hour.

Employment Prospects

With opportunities in animation—in film, television, and gaming—often going to individuals with solid track records and experience, it is difficult to find employ-

ment right out of school. Thus, prospects for employment are only fair. However, Illustrators often enter the industry via a circuitous route. As a gateway to using their illustration skills in film and television animation, many Illustrators choose to become storyboard artists at studios; this can also provide valuable industry experience. Storyboarding is one of the most stable aspects of the industry, and currently more opportunities are available in this area. Others have taken the path of becoming digital painters as a means to become production Illustrators on 3-D animated movies. Illustrators who seek to become conceptual Illustrators, or concept artists, have a tougher road ahead, as usually the most qualified and experienced land such positions. This does not mean it is virtually impossible to attain work in this field, but it is more likely only after carving out your career as a storyboard artist doing boards for either live-action or animated films and building a strong reputation and contacts within the industry.

Advancement Prospects

Technical skills combined with the ability to draw or paint to create pictures that communicate ideas, sensations, feelings, and emotions are the qualities and skills necessary to advance. Most Illustrators stay on an artistic career path, either specializing in a specific area or diversifying their talent to increase prospects for advancement. Some Illustrators are satisfied working strictly as storyboard artists on live-action or animated film and television productions. Others take the next step up to become senior Illustrators at a studio or company. Other Illustrators use their abilities to become character designers or character artists who draw, paint, or create 2-D and 3-D characters and imagery in online and video games, work that can be both challenging and rewarding at the same time. In other cases, individuals find it more stimulating and lucrative to assume a wide range of roles—pitching concepts and designs as preview or previsualization artists and working in character and prop design.

Education and Training

A bachelor's degree in animation, illustration, or a related field is sufficient. Under most school curricula, students acquire skills in traditional animation and general illustrative skills focused on their specific areas of specialization. They may be required to take courses to become proficient in 3-D animation and design, character design, color theory, computer illustration, digital imaging, life drawing, storyboarding, and typography as well as producing illustrations in a variety of media. In addition, students may be required to apply and serve as interns or apprentices in the industry through school programs. Likewise, in their senior year, most programs require students to complete a portfolio, a culmination of their body of work, that meets professional standards and demonstrates their artistic and creative development.

Experience, Skills, and Personality Traits

Most employers require one or two years of on-the-job production experience and training or a combination thereof. The primary skills Illustrators require, regardless of the positions they seek, are creativity and imagination. They must have solid drawing, illustration, and painting skills and visualization, interpretation, and conceptualization abilities. They must have a good sense of color, size, composition, and other techniques. They also must be able to create their work using common tools, such pens and ink, watercolors, charcoal, and oil or computer design and paint software, including Photoshop and Painter.

Illustrators must be skilled in drawing, illustrating, and sketching a variety of subjects—characters, buildings, models, vehicles, and other objects and environments—in either realistic or cartoonish style. They must be skilled in developing visual elements that convey desired effects, emotions, and moods. They also need to quickly and efficiently produce high-quality art that satisfies the needs of the production, often under tight deadlines.

Unions and Associations

Many Illustrators in the motion picture and television industries, whether employed on live-action or animated productions, belong to the Art Directors Guild, Local 800, of Los Angeles, which, in January 2003, merged with the former Illustrators and Matte Artists, Local 790, of the IATSE. Union membership is required to work on a studio or union film or television production and to receive union wages and other benefits, including health and pension plans. Other associations, such as the Graphic Artists' Guild and Society of Illustrators, each featuring a diverse membership of artists and regional chapters, may also be beneficial for networking purposes.

Tips for Entry

1. At an early age, take drawing and art classes in school and develop a unique, consistent style—one of the most important keys to having a successful career as an Illustrator.

2. Become proficient in creating art using different media—pen, pencil, watercolors, paint, etc.—and acquire the necessary technical skills to draw and paint using computer programs, including Adobe Illustrator and Adobe Photoshop.

3. Market yourself and your skills. Create your own Web site. Post samples of your work on your site, and browse others that showcase portfolios of artists in your particular field of interest.

4. Confer with other artists and professionals on online forums. Obtain feedback regarding your work, and link up with individuals in the industry with experience and contacts to find job opportunities.

MOTION GRAPHICS ARTIST AND MOTION GRAPHICS DESIGNER

Duties: Conceptualize, design, and produce motion graphics productions in various forms and formats, combining 2-D or 3-D animation, live footage, typography, graphics, and other visual effects or elements

Alternate Title(s): Mixed Media Animator

Salary Range: $38,000 to $65,000 (Motion Graphics Artist); $31,637 to $90,000 or more (Motion Graphics Designer)

Employment Prospects: Good

Advancement Prospects: Fair to Good

Best Geographical Location(s): Major urban centers

Prerequisites:

    Education and Training—A bachelor's degree in digital design, graphic design, computer animation, or a related field preferred

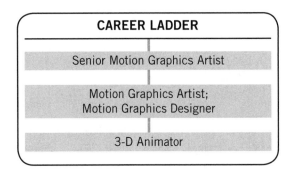

    Experience—At least five years of experience working in motion graphics

    Special Skills and Personality Traits—Creativity; drawing ability; keen sense of design; technical skills; detail oriented; self-disciplined; versatility

Position Description

Whether in animated movies, titles for live-action films and television shows, commercials, 3-D logos for television channels, videos for distance education courses, or Web-based animated advertisements, Motion Graphics Artists, also known as mixed media animators, and Motion Graphics Designers are the so-called magicians of the technology world. Masters in graphics design, special effects, and 2-D and 3-D animation, they produce captivating imagery needed in many industries. Part artist and part technician, Motion Graphics Artists and Motion Graphics Designers have been around for decades in some form or another.

The principles of motion graphics, combining graphic design, typography, and illustrations that move and that they apply in their work, technically date back to the origin of the first flip book published by the British lithograph printer John Barnes Linnett in September 1868. The term *motion graphics* actually originated in 1960 with the animator and computer graphics pioneer John Whitney's founding of his company, Motion Graphics, Inc. He used his invention of a mechanical analog computer to create memorable animated title sequences for motion pictures (for directors including Alfred Hitchcock, Stanley Kubrick, and others), television shows, and commercials after creating sequences for television programs and commercials during the 1950s using his renowned mechanical animation techniques.

Ever since 1955, when the Academy Award–winning filmmaker and well-known American graphic designer Saul Bass designed the first modern movie title sequence, opening credits have grown into a cinematic art form of their own. Bass set the bar high for other Motion Graphics Designers through his innovative title sequences in numerous films, including the text racing up and down what eventually becomes a high-angle shot of the United Nations building in Alfred Hitchcock's *North by Northwest* (1959) and the disjointed text that raced together and pulled apart for *Psycho* (1960). Since the 1980s, three forms of media that rose to prominence resulted in huge demand for this art form: cable television, videocassettes, and video games. The cable giant MTV broke the mold with its use of dynamic motion graphics logos designed to attract young viewers. Since 2000, demand for Motion Graphics Artists has exploded due to the affordability of technology. The medium has become much more elaborate and sophisticated, using design graphics, typography, animation, and other visual elements that made it widely popular in films and television, in video games, and on the Internet.

In most cases, Motion Graphics Artists and Motion Graphics Designers work closely with the art director to match appropriate design results and animation solutions that meet or exceed the intended objectives of the project. Preliminary tasks they undertake include developing concepts and designs for storyboards and animation; motion for audio and tempo, including music and voiceovers; motion graphics in eye-catching title sequences in major motion pictures; tags and bumpers for cable television networks; and movie trailers for theatrical film releases.

On the job, Motion Graphics Artists and Motion Graphics Designers display a strong artistic aptitude with an exceptional sense of design and design-related technology. They must deliver high-quality results and pay attention to all the details. They are masters in the use of traditional media, digital media, and new technology to make their conceptual designs a reality. These artists use cutting-edge industry-standard software on high-end computer platforms, both Mac and PC, to render their designs and bring together the many different audio and visual elements into one cohesive and visually striking presentation.

At times, professional Motion Graphics Artists and Motion Graphics Designers also act as animators/designers and art directors, although this role is usually within much smaller studios and production houses where such jobs overlap. In smaller markets, besides creating motion graphics–based productions in many different forms, they may also perform video editing for television commercials and corporate videos.

Jeff Bannister, a 2007 graduate of the Art Institute of Dallas, works as a lead Motion Graphics Artist/art director for CRM Studios, interacting with other 3-D artists, compositors, editors, directors, producers, and clients besides managing his staff in producing 2-D and 3-D animations, developing concepts, and art directing finished pieces. In discussing the process of bringing different projects to life, he explained in an online interview: "The project starts with compositing host wraps, prep artwork for sections, and creating motion graphics packages—which [constitutes] up to 60 per cent of a two-hour show."

Motion Graphics Artists and Motion Graphics Designers provide a high level of creativity and innovation in both large and small markets and other industries, including biotech, medical equipment, and pharmaceutical companies; computer and online video gaming; and professional sports franchises (baseball, basketball, football, and hockey) throughout the country.

In the case of online and video games, Motion Graphics Artists and Motion Graphics Designers help create visually compelling in-game movies, high-quality animated graphics, and functional art. Working with concept art teams, they use their strong visual aesthetic and creative and technical knowledge to tell the game's story within the requirements and constraints of the game's design and platform.

Motion Graphics Artists and Motion Graphics Designers also play an important role in the creation of motion graphics for live broadcasts and broadcasts of videos during sporting events and musical concerts. The Dallas Cowboys, for example, like many major sports teams, employ Motion Graphics Artists (called Motion Graphics Artists/broadcast designers) to create original motion graphics for their television broadcasts and for display on large electronic and video screens during games at Cowboys Stadium. Similarly, they create high-energy, fast-paced, 60- to 90-second mini music videos from storyboards to key frames to be shown during rock and country music concert, as well as Web demos and in-store demos for the latest PCs and high-definition televisions.

Working conditions for Motion Graphics Artists and Motion Graphics Designers are highly structured and intense at times. Generally, they carry out their tasks in comfortable and well-lighted work areas, but the work itself can be both mentally and physically demanding. It involves lengthy periods of sitting, hand-eye coordination, and repetitive use of the hands and wrists. Freelance Motion Graphics Artists and Motion Graphics Designers face the same challenges but generally in smaller, more congested work areas in home-based offices or studios. Studio- and company-employed Motion Graphics Artists and Motion Graphics Designers work a standard 40-hour work week, but they may work more if project deadlines dictate. Freelance artists and designers generally work longer hours, including evenings and weekends, to meet scheduled deadlines.

Salary

Salaries for Motion Graphics Artists and Motion Graphics Designers vary greatly due to company, location, experience, and ability. Nationally, according to Job-Salary.com, salaries range from $31,637 to $90,000 or more. According to the 2010 Motion Graphics Design Census, an unofficial Web-based survey of professional Motion Graphics Designers, artists made from $30,000 to $80,000 or more, with a median salary of $50,000. As of July 2010, Indeed.com reported salaries for this position in San Francisco at $83,000, 14 percent higher than average salaries nationwide, while Simply.

Hired.com listed the average salary for Motion Graphics Artists in Los Angeles during this same period at $38,000 a year. Conversely, in a wage survey posting on Mograph.com, experienced freelance Motion Graphics Designers made between $500 and $600 a day, while others with decent skills and less experience earned as much as $400 a day.

Employment Prospects

According to the U.S. Bureau of Labor Statistics, employment of Motion Graphics Artists and Motion Graphics Designers is expected to grow about as fast as the national average for all occupations over the next decade. Leading the demand for professionals in the industry is the proliferation of motion graphics in live-action and animated motion pictures and television shows and commercials and huge growth in other fields, including cell phones, PDAs, and handheld computers. Many freelance in addition to working as 3-D animators, while others elect to use their skills to teach computer animation and video production at animation and trade schools.

Advancement Prospects

The prospects for advancement for highly talented and resourceful people—those with especially solid technical and drafting skills—are good. Many Motion Graphic Artists and Motion Graphics Designers become senior Motion Graphics Designers or senior Motion Graphics Artists for television and video production companies. Others advance to become motion graphics directors, managing and overseeing a team of artists/designers. Some may use their experience to attain more senior positions as art directors within production companies, major-market television stations, networks, and other corporations and organizations.

Education and Training

An undergraduate degree in digital design, graphic design, or an equivalent is required, as is applicable training in design and 3-D computer animation. Students considering a career in this field should prepare with courses in computer operations and basic programming languages. Prospective college applicants should have some experience with graphic design at the high school level along with creative and technical ability.

Most bachelor's degree programs explore the fundamentals of graphic design. Students are usually instructed in such areas as digital video production, digital video editing, graphic design, illustration, digital media and design, fundamentals of digital imaging, drawing, 3-D motion graphics, and principles of interactive design.

Courses taught may include traditional fine arts and design basics, 2-D and 3-D animation, 3-D modeling, composition, compositing, color theory, interactivity/screen design and mobile device design, layout, motion theory, typography, and concept creation and instruction in common graphic design and editing using such software programs as After Effects, Dreamweaver, and Final Cut Studio. Classes at most schools are project-based and incorporate all aspects of visual design and production. Projects may include creating and developing network I.D. packages, Web sites, podcasts, commercials, public service announcements, music videos, corporate logos, and cross-platform marketing campaigns.

Students become equipped to work in the movie and television industries, creating special effects and animation. They learn related skills in 2-D and 3-D animation, audio and video editing, camera and lighting, design and composition, drawing and color, storyboard and layout, motion graphics, visual effects rendering, camera and lighting, and audio and video editing.

With extensive lab time, students become adept in a variety of computer hardware and industry-standard software applications, including After Effects, Dreamweaver, and Final Cut Studio, and acquire video editing and pre- and postproduction skills by shooting and editing projects. Students may also be given the opportunity to work with real-world clients on out-of-class projects on a volunteer or internship basis. Students also complete a mandatory senior-year project, which may include a portfolio and motion graphics demo reel that demonstrates their overall expertise, before graduating. In addition to a career in motion graphics, graduates are able to pursue other options, including supervisory roles, as art directors and digital video editors.

Experience, Skills, and Personal Traits

Five years or more of experience is the minimum preferred for this position. Most employers seek individuals with an exceptional contemporary design style and mastery of the tools involved in developing motion graphics. The right candidate must be a self-starter who is well organized, has a sharp eye for motion, thinks creatively, and articulates well-designed visuals that are cohesive and stylish. Motion Graphics Artists and Motion Graphics Designers should be experienced in all facets of motion graphics production, including designing, editing, and executing and integrating mixed media. They must generate ideas on time and within budget parameters, and they must have the ability to multitask in a fast-paced environment.

Motion Graphics Artists and Motion Graphics Designers should have superb technical abilities and well-honed art direction skills. They should be proficient in using 2-D and 3-D animation and design and video editing software—Adobe Photoshop, Adobe Illustrator, After Effects, Avid, Cinema 4D, Final Cut Pro, Flash, and Maya—on both Mac and PC platforms. They also should be solid technical troubleshooters and problem solvers who always put the needs of the project first. In addition, they must have excellent communication skills and be willing to take direction to fulfill the requirements of a project. They must have a proven track record of adapting easily to team-based project workflow, but they should also be comfortable working independently. Finally, they must cooperate with both technical and nontechnical staff, including animators, producers, editors, and other artists, in a creative environment.

Unions and Associations

Many Motion Graphics Artists and Motion Graphics Designers are members of ACM SIGGRAPH, a leading volunteer organization that offers year-round programs, resources, and support for computer graphics professionals. Others belong to the Visual Effects Society, the entertainment industry's only organization dedicated to visual effects professionals in film, television, commercials, music videos, and games. Motion Graphics Designers may belong to the American Institute of Graphic Artists, the oldest and largest professional membership organization for design, whose mission is to "empower the success of designers at each stage of their careers."

Tips for Entry

1. Develop a strong sense of depth, space, geometry, and visualization techniques.
2. In high school, take art, photography, computer science, and television production or video classes to learn different methods of creating fine art and using and combining various media using animation, design, and video editing software.
3. Shoot, produce, and edit your own mini digital or hi-def video motion graphics production using an inexpensive video camera and application software and hardware.
4. Motions graphics consists of different disciplines wrapped up into one complex package. Learn as much as possible. Read and surf forums and blogs on the Web. Download tutorials and technical training videos. Share and learn from others.
5. Become completely dedicated to your motion graphics career, technically and artistically. Network online and in person at special events with industry professionals and package yourself and your talent to suit what is needed.

PRODUCTION ARTIST

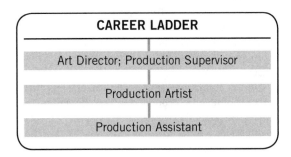
Position Description

Production Artists perform a critical function in the creation of animated films and television shows. They work closely with the production designer and art director in the execution of the production's overall design. Depending on the structure of the job, they handle both design and production roles at once and make sure all technical aspects are in order in a typically fast-paced and frenzied environment.

In many respects, a Production Artist is equivalent to a film or television production assistant in that the job is sort of a "jack-of-all-trades." However, unlike the latter, the position is often higher paid than a graphic designer, as it requires more technical knowledge.

Job descriptions for Production Artists are often tailored to a company's specific needs. Ben Jammin Chow, a production artist for Chicago-based Calabash Animation, serves as an assistant to the production manager and directors. He mainly manages the art production team at all stages of production and fulfills needs of the entire project, from creative to the final production. He determines what needs to be done and when. Consequently, he delegates and assigns specific tasks to members of the team and those he deems are best suited to handle certain parts of the production efficiently.

In other cases, Production Artists perform a variety of design tasks in producing 2-D traditional and 3-D computer animation. They may work as color key artists, background designers, character designers, background painters, and layout artists. Essentially working as supporting artists, they use their knowledge of color, line, and form to create visually appealing elements needed in a single frame of animation. ASIFA-Hollywood, a branch member of the Association Internationale du Film d'Animation (ASIFA), specifically honors film and television production artists at its annual Annie Awards for best individual achievement in the category of "Animation Production Artist."

Peter Sohn joined Pixar Animation Studios in September 2000 as a production artist to work on Brad Bird's blockbuster CG-animated feature *The Incredibles* (2004). However, since that film was still in development at the time, he started instead on *Finding Nemo* (2003), working in the art department. As he told CG Society, "I was asked to draw designs for people in the dentist's office. But, I didn't just want to draw default people, so I put them into a little scenario with kids looking into the fish tank and reacting to the dental equipment."

Sohn is an example of a production artist who didn't stay in the position for long; in nine years, he soared to the position of director to direct his first Pixar animated short, *Partly Cloudy,* which simultaneously opened with Pixar's *Up* (2009).

Unlike animation artists who spend inordinate amounts of time in a confined workspace, Production Artists are generally more mobile. Their job involves both periodic sitting in comfortable and well-lighted workspaces and standing to oversee phases of the production. At times the work is intense and pressure-packed. Production Artists generally work 40 hours per week, but, like most jobs in the industry, additional hours may be required to meet deadlines and keep the production on schedule.

Salaries

Earnings for Production Artists vary as determined by the studio and the size of the studio. According to multiple industry sources, salaries range from $25,000 to $45,000 based on experience, the amount of responsibilities, and the type of studio. At larger studios with larger staffs and bigger projects, the pay may be higher than at smaller studios with a core staff that relies on freelancers and outsourcing.

Production Artists who carry out the tasks of supporting artists—color key, background design, character design, and others—are paid according to wages set by The Animation Guild, Local 839, of the IATSE, and by their respective classification: color key, from $1,125 to $2,500; background layout/design, from $1,309.09 to $2,400; character design, from $1,093.75 to $2,335; background painter, from $1,347.37 to $2,200 per week.

Employment Prospects

Employment prospects for Production Artists are only fair. Demand is generally low since most productions are now being done overseas to lower costs. However, industry jobs occasionally pop up on a need-to-fill basis. When applying, play up your strengths in line with the requirements of the job, but always be truthful about your abilities.

Advancement Prospects

Overall, chances for advancement for Production Artists are fair. Individuals with managerial aspirations can work their way up to become production supervisors, who supervise all processes and delivery of animation in a production either at a studio or production company. Others more artistically driven strive to become art directors. Still others move up within their respective job rank (i.e. color key, background design, character design, etc.) to key artist or supervisory positions with an eye toward becoming art directors, assistant directors, and directors.

Education and Training

Most film and television animation studios prefer that individuals seeking to become Production Artists have a four-year degree or certificate in animation, art, illustration, or a related field from an accredited college or school that specializes in animation arts. Most programs require undergraduates to complete classes in traditional and computer animation, color and design, life drawing, painting, and becoming proficient in developing characters and physical environments in both 2-D and 3-D animation.

Experience, Skills, and Personality Traits

At least two to three years of production experience is required to become a Production Artist. Individuals must be extremely patient, disciplined, and driven. They require creativity, a sense of color and design, and competency in traditional and computer animation. They require excellent organizational, time-management skills, and problem-solving skills and must be focused on meeting deadlines. They need to prioritize and handle the most important to the least important tasks in a fast-paced environment. Production Artists must have the ability to work in groups and also independently. Long hours are sometimes required, so Production Artists should be dedicated to their work.

Unions and Associations

Like most supporting animation artists, Production Artists may belong to The Animation Guild, Local 839, of the IATSE to work on union and nonunion productions. The guild provides oversight on wages, benefits, and working conditions in the industry.

Tips for Entry

1. In high school, take art, art history, and computer graphics and develop an understanding of the techniques and approaches in creating animation in traditional and 3-D form.
2. In high school, talk to a career counselor and investigate colleges and degree programs that

will help round out your knowledge of all aspects of the production process.

3. Apply for apprenticeships or internships at local studios or production companies to learn from professionals and possibly work your way into a regular position after completing your education.

4. Post your résumé and cover letter on animation industry employment boards, such as AWN (Animation World News), Career Connections (http://jobs.awn.com), FilmStaff.com, and ProductionHUB.com. Contact anyone you know, including fellow graduates, to find and apply for work in your field.

PRODUCTION DESIGNER

Duties: Plan, conceive, and create the visual style and appearance of an animated film or television production

Alternate Title(s): None

Salary Range: $35,000 to $40,000 (entry-level); $1,625 to $4,750 per week

Employment Prospects: Fair

Advancement Prospects: Poor

Best Geographical Location(s): Los Angeles, New York, San Francisco

Prerequisites:

    Education and Training—Undergraduate degree in commercial art, fine arts, or design

    Experience—Two to three years as an art director and/or five years as a graphic artist

CAREER LADDER

Production Manager

Production Designer

Art Director

Special Skills and Personality Traits—Creative; innate design skills; keen visual sense; good communication skills; supervisory and administrative abilities

Position Description

Every animated film or television program starts with the production design, which sets the tone and overall look of the production. Everything that exists in the final production must be conceived, designed, and created from scratch, including characters, locations, sets, props, lighting, and more. The responsibility for developing the visual appearance of those items falls on the shoulders of Production Designers. Their principal role is to visualize and conceptualize the stylistic theme of the characters and environments. In this way, Production Designers illustrate the narrative and vision of the film and are crucial to its success.

In the early stages of the project, they work in partnership with the director and sometimes the producer and take into consideration technical resources of the production and any budget and scheduling restrictions. On smaller-scale productions, the Production Designer position may be combined with that of art director, character designer, and/or background designer.

Most Production Designers develop their designs as drawings or paintings, even for 3-D CG or computer animation. Whether working alone or as part of a team, they establish designs for characters, props, color schemes, and other elements as needed; in other instances, they may be contracted only to produce key designs that define the style of the production and are implemented by art directors. How much work

is required depends on the style of the project, the requirements of the production, and the size of the studio's art department. In some cases, they may also serve as the creative head of the department, supervising the work of a team of art directors, concept artists, character designers, layout artists, sculptors, prop designers, background artists, model makers, set builders, set dressers, storyboard artists, and previsualization artists.

In most cases, Production Designers determine what the director and producer are hoping for in regard to the look of the film or television show. Much like architects or theatrical set designers who come up with a basic framework, they usually draw colorful sketches on oversized drafting paper or build conceptual models from which to start drawing upon ideas from conversations with the director and producer and from reviewing an early draft of the script or treatment of the story.

When embarking on the design of an animated film, one of the first things Production Designers consider is the look of the film. They consider a host of different options and styles—"cartoony, realistic, stylized, primitive, retro, graphic, cutesy, high tech, wacky, dimensional, flat, etc." before developing the design, according to Paul Lasaine, who served as producer designer on Sony Pictures Animation's computer-animated film *Surf's Up* (2007), after previously working as an art director on all three of Peter Jackson's Lord of the Rings films. The tone of the story generally dictates the visual look of the film.

The original designs Production Designers create not only set the direction of the storyline, but also many different elements that are animated throughout. For Walt Disney's animated film *Hercules* (1997), to push the movie beyond the traditional Disney design and give it something unique, the studio hired the services of an outside artist, the well-known British caricaturist Gerald Scarfe. A self-proclaimed Greek mythology buff who did much of his work from his London studio, he first started developing production designs for *Hercules* two years before its release. Working from an early draft of the script, he came up with designs for the full range of characters, drawing some of them a dozen different ways. Standing at his desk and using large pieces of drafting paper, he used his whole shoulder to create the long sweeping lines in his designs that combined "the grotesque and cute, the hideous and comic—all executed with the simple flowing lines and angular shapes" that were his trademark.

Execution of the Production Designer's vision within the context of the actual production involves various stages of creation. After designs are approved by the director and producer, they are circulated to various departments throughout the studio. Artists use the designs to create storyboards, layouts, backgrounds, animation, and visual elements.

After Lasaine came up with the design for *Surf's Up*, it was the job of 10 highly talented artists in the studio's visual development department, working for three solid years in tandem with other departments—story, look develop, visual effects, modeling, animation, texturing, matte painting, and lighting—to produce the huge amount of visual designs and animation necessary for the production. Similarly, when the Production Designer Dan St. Pierre dreamed up the stylish look and design of the luminescent underwater world for DreamWorks Animation's *Shark Tale* (2004), it took approximately 150 artists pushing the limits of commercial animation software to create the look of simulated soft shadows with ambient light, among other designs.

Even after developing the design and the teamwork involved, it is difficult to know how well it will all translate on screen. According to the DreamWorks Animation production designer Kathy Altieri, in the beginning of working on the 2006 film *Over the Edge,* she and the team of artists had no idea they would be able to come up with a film that they had envisioned and pull it off. As it turned out, three years later, everybody came together and exceeded their original vision.

Ordinarily, Production Designers carry out their work in structured studio environments in workspaces that are generally bright and comfortable. At times, their work is intense and done under pressure. Creating various animation designs demands protracted periods of sitting, good hand-eye coordination, and repetitive use of the hands and wrists. Production Designers generally work a standard 40-hour work week, but they are known to work longer hours to meet deadlines and keep the production on schedule.

Salaries

Salaries for Production Designers vary according to union wage scales, whether the designer is union or nonunion, and the individual's standing in the industry. As reported by various industry sources, the entry-level salary for this position ranges from $35,000 to $40,000; highly experienced designers have higher earnings. According to The Animation Guild, Local 839, of the IATSE, Production Designers earn roughly the same weekly wages as art directors who are members: a minimum of $1,625 to a maximum of $4,750 per week. The median salary is $2,340 a week, down from an average of $2,763.64 per week in 2009.

Employment Prospects

Overall, employment prospects for Production Designers who have previous experience as art directors or graphic designers in the film or television industries are fair. Most have worked their way through the art department, starting as production assistants; the position provides a bird's eye view of what the job entails as well as top-notch training to help prepare for career advancement. Others gain valuable experience as character or set designers. Since Production Designers supervise various art and design functions in the preproduction phase of an animated motion picture or television show, some management experience is necessary and usually gained working as an art or assistant art director.

Advancement Prospects

Career advancement for Production Designers can be difficult. Thorough knowledge of film or television production and the animation pipeline and supervisory and management skills can lead to promotions to production manager, but such opportunities at most major studios and production houses are rare. Most Production Designers who have reached the top of their craft earn top salary levels after years of toiling in the industry and thus rarely leave their posts in pursuit of other jobs.

Education and Training

Most companies and studios require that Production Designers have degrees in architecture or environmental or theatrical set design. Most studios prefer individuals who have an established track record. Candidates are often selected on the basis of their style, reputation, and suitability for a particular project. While experience in animation is not always necessary, an understanding of the techniques and pipeline for animation is extremely helpful.

Experience, Skills, and Personality Traits

Most employers expect their Production Designers to have at least two to three years of experience, preferably as an art director, in film or television production design.

Production Designers must possess basic design skills, a strong imagination, and artistic flair. They need to be able to visually conceive ideas and then accurately explain them to those who must animate or physically build them. They must be well organized and have good management and leadership skills. They must be experienced in prioritizing their own work and that of others and managing a diverse team of creative subordinates, including production and technical professionals. They must have the discipline to work on a schedule and within a budget without supervision. Good communication and presentation skills are also assets.

Unions and Associations

Membership in The Animation Guild, Local 839, of the IATSE is required on major film and television productions, except for nonunion productions and nonunion shops. Such membership is also beneficial for networking within the animation industry and securing wages and hours. Production Designers are also represented by United Scenic Artists for bargaining purposes for work on major and independently produced theatrical features, hour-long television shows, pilots, and commercials.

Tips for Entry

1. Develop an artistic style and sense of design early on by taking art and design classes in high school.
2. Gain practical experience by working on theater productions in school developing designs for sets and props.
3. Volunteer your time to design student films or low-budget productions in your community to build a résumé.
4. Enroll in animation or art school to obtain a formal education in design.
5. Land an internship or apprenticeship at an animation studio or production facility that produces film or television animation.
6. Work as a production assistant or in the art department to gain hands-on experience in the industry.

PROP DESIGNER

CAREER PROFILE

Duties: Create and design various objects for use in an animated motion picture or television show

Alternate Title(s): None

Salary Range: $25,000 to $35,000

Employment Prospects: Good

Advancement Prospects: Poor

Best Geographical Location(s): Los Angeles, New York, San Francisco

Prerequisites:

Education and Training—No minimum educational requirement, though a bachelor's degree in fine arts or equivalent work experience is desired in some cases

Experience—Some prior industry work experience necessary, though requirements vary

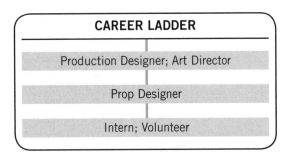

CAREER LADDER

Production Designer; Art Director

Prop Designer

Intern; Volunteer

Special Skills and Personality Traits—Creative; drafting and design skills; mechanical and technical skills; flexible; reliable; organized; problem solver; time-management skills; meets deadlines

Position Description

Whether they are futuristic forms of rapid transportation, such as cars, planes, or helicopters, out-of-this world spaceships and spacecraft, or never-before-seen high-tech gizmos and gadgets, props play an integral part of any animated production. Prop Designers, whose artistic contributions are just as important to a production as the animation, design, and direction, have grown in importance in recent years, with their artistic and creative work front and center in countless full-length cartoon features and weekly cartoon series that call for their specialized talents.

Depending on the studio and how the production is structured, Prop Designers work closely with the art director (if the show has one), the episodic director on series where there is a lead producer/director with directors working under him on specific episodes, or with the series' overall producer/director. In other instances, character designers also are part of the hierarchy in the creative process. As Mark Lewis, an experienced character and Prop Designer who created prop designs for Warner Bros. Animation, noted, "I've never worked on a show or series where things were quite so formal as to have actual 'departments.' I know that things tended to be structured more that way years ago, but that hasn't been so much my experience during my animation career."

While other specialized positions in the industry are dwindling in number, the need for Prop Designers continues to flourish. They are an asset, particularly on animated action/adventure shows that require their expertise in building, designing, and creating various dynamic props and custom objects for each episode. As with clean-up artists, freelance Prop Designers work on a "per-piece basis." "Some days you get to draw a pencil, other days you have to draw a complex and detailed spaceship," Lewis related. Although different items do not take the same amount of time to draw, freelance Prop Designers are often paid the same amount for each item.

It is the responsibility of the Prop Designer to meet with the art director and/or other creative decision makers to identify props needed for the show, review storyboards to ensure continuity, and complete all prop designs, special effects, lettering, schematics, and any other prop-related art that may be required. Initially, they produce interpretive designs of props based on the needs of the production in rough and then revised and final draft form, resolving any design problems with the art director, episodic director, or lead producer/director during the process. Rarely do Prop Designers have official meetings with an art director beforehand, according to Lewis. Mostly, he is handed "a prop list" generated by someone on the production side. On rare occasions, he is handed a script and asked to go through it and break down what he thinks is needed.

Prop Designers review the script as well. "Often there are design cues that you wouldn't have picked up if you were only working from the list," Lewis offered. Sometimes the production staff will miss some items, or possibly list things that are not absolutely necessary, and the only way to catch these oversights is by reading the script.

In developing various prop designs, Prop Designers usually refer to certain actions called for in the script, which must be taken into account. Their designs are also influenced by whether the art director (if there is one on the project) or the director have specific ideas in mind about what they want to see for certain props.

The number or variations of designs Prop Designers typically draw—usually three (a rough or first draft and then revised and final drafts)—varies depending on the type of production. As Lewis explained in an interview, "In a CG show, clean-up is basically irrelevant." All that is really needed is a relatively clean rough drawing that the CG modelers can use as a reference guide from which to build. Sometimes, Prop Designers can create a guide without having to make revisions. Usually, Prop Designers create a rough draft and, if that is approved, they might go straight to clean-up. If there are minor notes, they would revise it first and then hopefully be able to take it to the clean-up stage. If their design is not liked, they will scrap it and start over with a new rough design.

Lewis added that the above is true only for a show or production where "the look" is already established. If working on a project for which the design is still in the process of being developed, Prop Designers can end up doing multiple versions of the same thing, "experimenting" and trying to "figure out the right overall look for the project."

On 2-D hand-drawn animated productions, Prop Designers generate their props the old-fashioned way, using pencil and paper, possibly with the assistance of ellipse templates, French curves, and/or a ruler after roughing out what the prop is supposed to look like. On occasion, some use 3-D software such as Lightwave to help work out particularly complicated props that need to be shown from multiple angles. For 3-D CG or Flash-animated productions, for which Prop Designers are required to create signage or other kinds of graphics that are used directly on the surface of the final build of the prop design, they use software such as Adobe Illustrator.

Some high points of the job are those occasions when Prop Designers come up with designs that the director and the client like. It is satisfying when they are able to design something that not only meets the needs of the story and the actions called for in the script, according to Lewis, but is also "an interesting object in its own right."

What also makes the work rewarding is seeing the final product on the screen. For Lewis, there is a bit of a "kick" when he recognizes things he designed on the screen. He has a certain pride knowing that his designs are part of the finished product.

Prop Designers who work on film and television productions do so in mostly structured conditions in comfortable and bright workspaces. Their work requires hand-eye coordination and lots of movement of the hands and wrists. It can be both physically and mentally draining. Studio Prop Designers generally work a standard 40-hour workweek but may work more hours as needed.

Salary

Annual earnings for beginning Prop Designers range from $25,000 to $35,000. In its June 2010 member wage survey, The Animation Guild, Local 839, of the IATSE reported starting salaries for Prop Designer at $1,568.18 to a maximum of $1,960.33 for more experienced artists. The median average based on the lowest and highest rate response of members was $1,700 a week, with journey level Prop Designers making slightly less, $1,596.64 a week.

Employment Prospects

Employment opportunities are good, as the demand for Prop Designers is steady. Generally viewed as a position that requires previous experience, many have made a name for themselves by being exceptionally capable. If prop design is your career goal and you are talented, you may be able to negotiate a much better rate for yourself than someone just starting out as a Prop Designer. Plus, the better you are at meeting the needs of the show, the directors, and the production staff, the better your chances of longevity in your career.

Lewis suggests that aspiring Prop Designers cultivate a good eye for mechanics and work on their perspective. They may be able to come up with a "really cool" three-quarter front view of a spaceship, but can they then turn it and draw it from a different angle? That is where perspective is important.

Prop Designers should also have good instincts for how to put shapes together in interesting and appealing ways. According to Lewis, the more styles Prop Designers are comfortable working in, the more shows they will be able to get work on.

Some artists could also do well working outside of animation in areas such as production or automotive design.

Advancement Prospects

Prop Designers who want to advance their careers will encounter difficulty. Currently, there are more people available than there are jobs for them. Many artists have to settle for positions far below their capacities. Prop Designers with well-honed drawing skills are more likely to advance. Many options are available to them. They can move over to character design to become background layout artists or into storyboards. From character design or background layouts, depending on artistic skill level, the next step up is art director, followed by director and then producer. From storyboarding, individuals can move into a storyboard supervisor position and then to director and possibly producer.

Education and Training

There is no standard educational path or minimum education requirement for becoming a Prop Designer, but some major studios desire a bachelor's degree in fine arts or equivalent work experience. The only set-in-stone requirement is, as Lewis said, the ability to "deliver the goods on a piece of paper or on the computer screen." For most Prop Designers who are hired and working on both animated film and television productions, additional education or training in association with work experience in 3-D design, sculpture, architecture, or theater design, including methods and techniques in creating and making visually appealing props that work with the specific vision or standards of the production, is beneficial.

Experience, Skills, and Personality Traits

Prior experience is desirable but not always required. Different studios and shows and/or productions may require different qualifications. However, more often than not, a studio will desire candidates with real-world industry experience.

First and foremost, Prop Designers must have exceptional drawing and mechanical skills and comparable time-management skills to quickly render and construct high-quality props within assigned deadlines. Knowledge of or willingness to learn applicable design software and hardware is an asset. Furthermore, Prop Designers should have a keen perspective on how to draw complex items from different angles. They also should have the ability to read and break down a storyboard and to adapt to working in different styles to suit the look of the show or production. For example, a bicycle on one show would probably look out of place on another. Prop Designers must ask questions when necessary and be able to come up with creative ways to cooperatively solve design dilemmas that arise, so communication skills are important.

Prop Designers must be reliable, flexible, and able to change direction and make revisions as necessary. In addition, they should be conscientious at all times—in putting in long hours, in meeting deadlines, and in working with their colleagues. Remember that you are doing the work for a client, not to express yourself. You may not like it, but the client is paying for it and should get what he or she wants.

Unions and Associations

Membership in The Animation Guild, Local 839, of the IATSE is required to work on major film and television cartoon productions and is beneficial in guaranteeing at least minimum wage levels for various Prop Designer positions, in addition to benefits such as medical and dental coverage and pension plans, and access to networking opportunities with other industry professionals.

Tips for Entry

1. Enroll in animation, film, and television production courses that cover such subject areas as set and prop design in high school and college.
2. Volunteer to work for local theaters, nonprofit film companies, or community cable television stations to gain experience in designing and constructing various sets and props.
3. Pursue internships and on-the-job training in the art department of an animation studio or production company to learn about production and prop design as well as to make valuable contacts.
4. Be willing to do any task you are asked to perform, learn from others, and meet with as many other professionals in the industry as you can. Remain friendly at all times, and stay in touch with people.

ENGINEERING

PRODUCTION ENGINEER

Duties: Realize the collective vision of a scene by establishing the technology and technique required for necessary optical and/or digital aspects

Alternate Title(s): (Digital) Research & Development Engineer; Research & Development Technical Director; Pipeline Engineer; Character Technical Director; Look Technical Director; Lighting Render Technical Director; Photogrametric Technical Director; Matchmove Technical Director; Camera Technical Director; POV Technical Director; (Visual) FX Super; Pyro Tech; Character/ Animatronic; Motion Control or Motion Capture Engineer

Salary Range: $40.00 to $120.00 per hour; for management roles, an extra $100 or more per hour

Employment Prospects: Excellent

Advancement Prospects: Good

Best Geographical Location(s): Los Angeles, New York, San Francisco

Prerequisites:

    Education and Training—Minimum of a bachelor's of science degree in engineering or programming with a minor or additional training in art and/ or film or visual media; master's or Ph.D. optional

CAREER LADDER

Supervisor; Advisory Engineer; Senior Engineer

Production Engineer

Junior Technical Director; Junior Engineer; Assistant Supervisor; Camera Assist; Production Assistant

Experience—At least two to five years of experience in engineering and computer systems management, preferably in computer animation

Special Skills and Personality Traits—System administration skills; mathematical and analytical skills; large software system and script abilities; knowledge of relational database concepts; understanding of industry workflow standards; problem-solver; verbal and written communication skills; ability to handle a variety of tasks and personality types

Position Description

Behind the creation of every 3-D computer-animated film, a highly creative and technically skilled team is responsible for designing, implementing, and maintaining the software that "glues" together the software and data in the production of the animation. Managing and overseeing the software development of the entire computer animation process and animation pipeline is the Production Engineer.

Job titles and duties are generally broken into "digital" and "visual" production assignments. Digital assignments fall under research and development and technical production; professionals in these positions serve as engineers or technical directors and have titles such as research and development engineer; research and development technical director; pipeline engineer; character technical director; look technical director; lighting/render technical director; and photogrametric,

matchmove, camera, or POV technical director. Visual assignments cast engineers in either design or consulting roles for other supervisors; titles include FX super, pryo tech, character/animatronic, high speed/special camera engineer, and motion control or motion capture engineer.

Motivated and experienced Production Engineers maintain existing software systems; enhance, modify, and redesign systems to accommodate the ever-changing requirements of productions; interact with animators and technical directors; and use their understanding of computer animation to come up with creative solutions to difficult technical issues. They usually report directly to production supervisors and to a director or department manager. Other times, Production Engineers report to department heads, the director, or the company owner during the research and development phase of a production.

Production Engineers build plans and teams, establishing criteria and goals and applying tools, practices, processes, and procedures of computer engineering to support and carry out the director's vision of the production. To this end, they collect data, evaluate input, listen and invite ideas, and establish more than one perspective in applying protocols and standards of math, programming, and physics in documenting, tracking, adapting, and implementing their plans. Demonstrable art skills are also required. As the longtime production engineer Rich Wolf explained, "Production engineers are responsible for breaking down a script and scene into shots and determining the equipment, optical or virtual approach, safety, cost, and other requirements to provide continuity and imagery that supports the shared vision of that part of the animated production."

Production Engineers hired for animated productions usually work in offices in structured studio environments and on the sites of productions. Many work a standard 40-hour workweek; at times, deadlines bring added pressure and require longer hours.

Salaries

Salaries for Production Engineers vary. A mix of knowledge and on-the-job experience with accomplishments and proven capability can drastically impact wages. Starting salaries as culled from various industry sources are about $40.00 per hour. Depending on the specialty, the rate can be higher. A senior Production Engineer or specialist can demand hundreds of dollars an hour. Typically, major companies or studios cap salaries at $120 per hour; in a management role, the cap can increase another $100 or more an hour. "I will not work for less than $65 per hour, ever," Wolf explained. "I have charged as high as $250 an hour."

Salaries are often based on a Production Engineer's knowledge and training ("The more disciplines you are a familiar with, the more valuable you are," Wolf said), their set and production experience in such areas as set design, film technique, pyro certifications, safety and prop management protocols, stunt assessment, special materials, controlled dynamics, and machinery, robotics and capture control, and their digital production experience, including pipeline workflows, program structure and integration, scripting and programming, data management and workflow, ingest and scene prep, cross platform and networking, asset management, and much more.

Production Engineers may charge overtime during an assignment but usually are salaried otherwise. "A production salary can go as much as 30 percent higher as a crew member," Wolf stated. This happens when an engineer is called on to stay on-site during production with the crew at all times. Most countries deny work visas that would take away a skilled job from a citizen, but Production Engineers can get union waivers and freely work in any country with a "skill exception" (establishing their work as a unique skill needed by the production). The United States, Canada, New Zealand, and India often require that "waivers" be approved so that visas can be granted, accompanied by a statement and testimonial to allow workers to work overseas. Workdays of 10 hours are standard, as are frequent seven-day "forced calls" (to report to work outside the normal or agreed-upon commitment). "If I travel out of the 30-mile radius of a Los Angeles production zone, it will cost more," Wolfe stated. "I need to have accommodations and per diem. If I travel to another country, I need to have all my applications, waivers, etc., done for me. I also usually have a higher salary when I work out of the country."

Employment Prospects

Prospects for employment for Production Engineers are excellent. Much of this is due to the "conservative grip" loosening (allowing the substitution of nontraditional methods that use new and custom technologies and techniques) in filmmaking and a huge jump in demand for newer technologies that may take up to 15 years to be fully met. "Games, 3-D, special effects, nearly seamless motion capture–based filming techniques, and higher demand for realism all bear great weight on company recognition and placement in the industry," Wolf noted. "The engineer will always be [important] in assessing and providing new technologies and workflows for integration into the production method, many times for even a single production, and often for many productions."

However, one requires "an absolute passion for the biz," Wolf added. "If there is *any* other alternative you might be interested in, it's probably going to be less demanding, more lucrative, and better security given the same amount of commitment."

Production engineering opportunities are more plentiful in major urban areas such as Los Angeles, San Francisco, and New York, home to many film and television animation studios and effects houses. The number of engineers employed on a production varies from one to as a many as a dozen. Multidisciplined engineers attract the most opportunities; technical directors and research and development or specialist engineers are given assignments much broader in scope.

Accepting an entry-level job is essential to becoming a Production Engineer. Candidates should work as on-set production assistants for at least 100 hours to gain practical experience as the first step toward becoming engineers. As his colleague Edward Diguilio suggested to him earlier in his career, "You can't do filmmaking without learning filmmaking first hand . . . go do your boot camp [on-set training] . . . watch everyone, know 'the line' and find your place in it."

Thereafter, additional stepping-stones can include working as a camera assistant, assistant supervisor, or other team management and building position. This can lead to becoming a junior tools engineer, providing a learning path on software and math every engineer requires, and then a junior technical director, offering production exposure and a good mentoring approach to becoming a Production Engineer.

It is imperative that Production Engineers begin their careers under seasoned, structured engineers. In addition, established corporate standards teach documentation, planning, tracking, teamwork, and chain of command much better than the more loosely structured environments at smaller companies, according to Wolf.

Advancement Prospects

Advancement prospects for Production Engineers are mostly good. Becoming a Production Engineer requires a lot of studying and keeping up with technology and the business. As Wolf explained, it also takes a well-built and trusted network of coworkers and company relationships.

Some negatives, however, can stall advancement. Production Engineers solve problems, and at production time, nobody wants their work associated with problems. "Engineers are often resented and scapegoated if anything is less than ideal in the production workflow," Wolf remarked. "Many people will simply refuse to work with engineers, and some will actually actively try to block progress in favor of 'how it was always done.'"

Good Production Engineers may also unintentionally work themselves out of a job if the techniques, workflows, and technologies are established and documented well enough that technicians or supporting staff can run the processes and responsibilities without the engineer.

Many climb the ladder to become senior and advisory engineers and ultimately supervisors who oversee a group of engineers. Others work up the scale to become directors, production managers, and producers. However, it is not unusual for Production Engineers to advance into many disciplines, often jumping into management, effects supervisors, or other production roles outside the engineering sphere.

To improve their prospects of advancement, Production Engineers need to meet their commitments, build a network of professional contacts, earn the respect of their colleagues, not criticize others without offering support and training (and lots of assurance and feedback), work as a team, know the art and know how to be an artist, and listen and learn. Essentially, "The more you learn how to read a director's 'vision' and assess what it takes to meet that vision, in any technical-art assignment, the [quicker] you progress and move up," according to Wolf.

From Wolf's experience, networking is important, and companies are more inclined to "keep you if there is another company down the street that wants you and can use you to compete." As he added, "If you don't do all of the above, you won't work very long" in your career.

Education and Training

Most Production Engineers have a bachelor's of science degree in engineering or programming from a four-year university with a minor or supplemental training in art and/or film or visual media from a private film school. A master's degree and Ph.D. are also a plus. Some entry-level positions can have thousands of applicants, and few beginners possess the skills necessary to do the job well. It can take six or seven years to be fully qualified, and a master's degree and/or Ph.D. is not overkill in terms of education.

Courses in math, programming, art, and creative media along with some film history and script analysis are helpful. Knowledge of muscle systems and anatomy, bipedal and quadrapedal locomotion, fluid dynamics, and physics as well as common industry computer and network methods and principles, including render theory, Renderman standards, mental ray standards, CPU theory, graphics stands, and SAS and NAS networking, is also necessary. Additional training and certification in C++, scripting and networking, special effects, and state safety programs and OSHA laws is an asset.

Experience, Skills, and Personality Traits

Most employers expect Production Engineers to have at least two to five years of experience, depending on the responsibilities and skills required for the position.

Production Engineers must possess keen mathematical and analytical skills, including an understanding of 3-D linear algebra, render and color theory, optical and camera theory, and Euclidian math. They should have some basic knowledge of human anatomy and bipedal locomotion and experience in pre- and postproduction planning and breakdown, plus scriptwriting, scene design, and shared vision techniques. They must have a solid understanding of industry workflow and visual media standards and limitations on the job. They should have extensive scripting and object-oriented C++ and UNIX/Linux development experience working on large software systems, including knowledge of relational database concepts.

In addition, Production Engineers must be highly skilled in systems administration and establishing and managing resources, materials and dynamics, and "product development" talent. With the line between special effects and visual effects becoming more blurred, Production Engineers need to have more "level of detail knowledge" on how to assess and integrate teams that provide exactly what is needed in production pipeline support. They need good documentation, presentation, and writing skills. They must be superb problem solvers and able to handle high-pressure situations. Production Engineers must fully define all aspects of an assignment's problems, roadblocks, timeline, and budget before deciding what the team will or will not do.

Using strong verbal and written communication skills, Production Engineers must know how to handle different personality types as part of a team or group. They must have the ability to rapidly break down "unsolvable" problems into manageable elements and solve them intelligently. They must know how to work with sometimes difficult high-profile celebrities, directors, and producers.

Unions and Associations

Most Production Engineers hold memberships in ACM SIGGRAPH, the New York–based Special Interest Group on Graphics and Interactive Techniques, which has more than 8,000 members and more than 90 chapters worldwide. Membership offers countless benefits, which include keeping pace with industry standards and rapid technological changes and schmoozing with other professionals in the industry at special symposia and summits throughout the year.

Others also join such long-standing organizations as the American Society of Mechanical Engineers (ASME), a professional association specifically focused on mechanical engineering, and the American Society for Engineering Education (ASEE), a nonprofit member group dedicated to promoting and improving engineering and engineering technology education. Another organization is the Visual Effects Society (VES), the entertainment industry's only organization that represents the full breadth of visual effects professionals in all areas of entertainment, from film, television, and commercials to music videos and games.

Tips for Entry

1. Develop an absolute passion for the business.
2. In school, learn the arts of animation and filmmaking and their techniques and histories.
3. Study a script. Break it down. Look at a scene and how it contributes to a dramatic element.
4. Master the tools and technologies of the trade, and learn how to solve and define programming and engineering problems.
5. Strive to become the best in your field. Only top performers get opportunities.
6. Become part of the industry by joining collaborative groups and societies. Network and socialize with other professionals at meetings and special events.

SOFTWARE ENGINEER

Duties: Responsible for the design, development, and support of the proprietary and application software used in the production of a computer-animated production

Alternate Title(s): CG Software Engineer; Software Technical Director; Research and Development Engineer

Salary Range: $60,000 to $140,000

Employment Prospects: Very good

Advancement Prospects: Excellent

Best Geographical Location(s): Los Angeles, New York, San Francisco

Prerequisites:

  Education and Training—Bachelor's of science in computer science or related field and/or equivalent experience

Experience—Prior studio experience is a plus, though not a prerequisite for entry-level positions

Special Skills and Personality Traits—Computer and technical skills; design and programming knowledge, including scripting; problem-solver and troubleshooter

Position Description

When the idea that feature-length animated films could be created using computers first emerged, a common reaction was, as Dr. Evan Smyth of DreamWorks Animation once wrote, "nothing could replace the richness of images produced by dedicated artists toiling over their drawing boards, that the days of animated epics would be over." Instead, computer animation has been responsible for creating a resurgence in animated features, not to mention some of the most successful animated films of all time.

A key area in the innovation and delivery of CG, or computer-generated, 3-D animation is the deployment of large-scale computer clusters—systems built around a dual-processor, multicore architecture, used to render some 100,000 frames in a computer-animated feature film. Typically, such films can take more than 10 million CPU hours (the time it takes for the computer to process something) of rendering to complete, requiring enormous computational abilities requirements and solutions.

Behind the scenes, Software Engineers, serving as members of the studio's systems group, are responsible for developing, designing, writing, and debugging code for the studio's proprietary application software, tools, and libraries. This technology is used for high-performance computing to create the animation on advanced supercomputers and computer clusters used during each production. Working closely with lead programmers and development teams, these pragmatic programmer-analysts lend a hand to others artists and technicians when needed, harnessing their technical know-how, innovation, and user experience to latch on to "the best, most practical and sometimes most obscure but smart solution," noted Erick Miller, the technology manager of Walt Disney Animation Studios. Since most systems groups are typically small, even though each engineer usually has a specialty, they all must possess general and interdisciplinary knowledge as well.

Live-action visual effects and fully computer-generated filmmaking both rely on an infinite number of machines and capable infrastructure and resources to render each frame of animation as quickly as possible. Although many variables go into producing computer animation, high-performance computing allows the animators to set a parameter and see results without having to wonder how long it will take. Software Engineers are there, to a great extent, to explore all possible solutions to improve turnaround time and performance. This is especially critical when a studio has more than two films in production and demand for high performance computing becomes large, especially in the second half of production, when the manpower and computer demands increase dramatically. As Dr. Smyth once told *Primeur Weekly,* "One of our recent films required 12 million CPU-hours, which is a pretty big demand, especially when you consider we have more than two films in production at the same time. . . . It's clearly critical to artistic effectiveness to get the results back as quickly as possible. If they change the lighting in a scene and they can see the results immediately, they can either make further changes or move on to the next one."

Vast amounts of computer time are needed to iterate the best lighting settings that go into creating the final images that appear on the screen. One part of the Software Engineer's job is to see how they can make the rendering software be "faster and more efficient."

Software Engineers are also called upon to apply principles of computer science to solve practical problems that include UNIX system-level programming, data translation, interprocess communication, and scripting, including writing scripts to automate or assist operating systems or network systems. Their duties can include developing specific capabilities for requested features in system software for the creation of certain effects or animation. For example, Software Engineers make it possible for an artist to drag a slider to change the intensity of light in a frame and instantly see the final quality of the rendered image; animators may also effect incremental changes that enable and speed up different work flows and phases and the level of performance to make them much more efficient. Software Engineers are involved in the investigation of new technologies for integration into new software as well.

Mike King, a CG supervisor at Pixar Animation Studios, entered the business as a Software Engineer with Walt Disney Feature Animation in 1995, after the much-heralded boom of computer animation in the industry. He found the most challenging part of the job was figuring out to make many different third-party software packages talk to one another—still one of the challenges of the job today—by writing a code to help get data from one package to another. About a month or two after he started, he was asked to add a critical new feature to one of Disney's data translation programs for a show that was currently in the midst of production. The learning curve was steep and the deadline was tight, but by asking many questions and reading lots of documentation, as he told GraduatingEngineering.com, he "managed to implement the feature, and in the process became the data translator specialist."

Software engineers receive gratification from learning something new on each project and knowing that each frame of a finished project passed through something they designed.

Studio-based Software Engineers ordinarily work in highly structured work environments. The job requires frequent sitting and standing and use of the hands and wrists to troubleshoot and run computer systems and create or improve the performance and functionality of animation software. During the crunch time of a production, Software Engineers are affected the most and often must work more than a standard 40-hour workweek.

Salaries

Salaries vary greatly by studio and experience. As reported by multiple industry sources, at much larger studios, a low-end junior engineer may make $60,000 a year and an experienced principal engineer could earn as much as $140,000 or more. Information on salaries at smaller studios was unavailable as of this writing.

Employment Prospects

Opportunities for Software Engineers are very good. Jobs are plentiful in nearly all areas, including animation, lighting, rendering, rigging, database, user interface design, mathematics and physics, and pure research. "Not all studios have a large software department, but most of the major ones do, and even the smaller studios have a strong need for software engineers," explained Brendan Duncan, a research and development Software Engineer at PDI/DreamWorks. "Typically, the larger the studio, the more room they have for junior-level engineers, and smaller studios tend to need more experienced people since they have fewer people to work with."

There is really no defined career path or ladder to becoming a Software Engineer. Most are hired as Software Engineers (also known as junior Software Engineers) directly out of college. Individuals' skill levels and experience can influence the position for which they are hired. As Duncan noted, those without professional experience usually are hired as junior-level engineers. Some have joined the software department from other groups, such as hardware, but that is not typical.

King thinks the key to landing work is to become a good Software Engineer and programmer first and worry about 3-D graphics knowledge later. As he once iterated, "While both are important, [studios] look for good engineers familiar with computer-generated imaging, and have turned away 3-D experts who lacked design experience or sound programming skills."

King recommends becoming familiar with the industry and deciding on a niche. He also suggests that those serious about the field read popular cinematography magazines, such as *Cinefex* or *American Cinematographer,* to understand how visual effects are produced, as well as graphics and design publications, including *Computer Graphics World* or *3-D Design,* to learn about the latest computer graphics industry news and techniques. "And unless you happen to be an accomplished artist with a killer demo reel as well as a software engineer," he remarked, "don't expect to work directly on a scene in your first job."

Furthermore, in pursuit of employment, do not apply for a position under any circumstances for which you are neither qualified nor experienced. Take your time to acquire the requisite skills and experience.

Advancement Prospects

Prospects for advancement in software engineering in the animation industry are excellent. Different studios use different titles for Software Engineers—some may have only junior and principal positions. Some also may add an additional title to denote a career step. Many climb up the ranks to become senior Software Engineers and then principal engineers. "Senior engineers typically work on larger projects, with influence on the design and implementation of the project," Duncan stated. "Principal engineers also work on larger projects and have significant influence on the project itself, as well as a larger vision of how the software fits in with the other software in the studio as a whole."

Others rise to supervisory roles as managers, overseeing Software Engineers instead of writing and developing software.

Education and Training

The minimum educational requirement for this position is a bachelor's of science degree in computer science or a related field and/or equivalent experience. A master's and doctoral degree in computer science will make you more appealing to a studio but are not necessary for most entry-level positions.

Many young people, unfortunately, think that they can skip a degree because they have spent so much time on a computer. "Sometimes it works out that way, but typically not," Duncan said. "Completing a degree is important because it shows dedication and discipline, and typically improves the breadth of knowledge a person has."

Required core subjects usually include computer science as well as math and art. Higher-level math such as calculus and linear algebra are useful, especially for writing animation software, a key element of the job. Art courses are also important since engineers will be

working in animation, an artistic field. A strong appreciation of art also helps engineers understand artists and create tools for them.

Attending a prestigious school is not as important as any personal experience and independent study work you gain, which is often equally, if not more, valuable than the courses you have taken. Experience rounds people out and gives them exposure to working in group environments and to subjects they would not necessarily study on their own outside of school. During job interviews, studios often pay more attention to the experience candidates have had outside a school environment.

Independent study work, such as working on a game, an animation system, a dynamic simulator, or any number of related subjects that go beyond what you learned in school can be a huge bonus, making you more visible to studio recruiters and interviewers.

Overall, your education and experience need to demonstrate a level of dedication, personal interest, and knowledge that makes you stand out.

Experience, Skills, and Personality Traits

Prior studio experience is a plus but is not a requisite for entry-level positions. As mentioned earlier, work done outside school that demonstrates personal interest and investment in software engineering is particularly valuable.

Most Software Engineers are solid designers and programmers who work quickly. They have superior knowledge of computer science and programming languages (such as C++—the most widely used language for compiled software—and occasionally Java and Perl, and Python for scripted software) necessary for writing applications software, tools, plug-ins, and scripts (including a grasp of 3-D and shading software combined with the ability to design and implement solutions that make things run better or faster). A Software Engineer's job is to write software, so knowing how to write software is an obvious but important requirement. There are hundreds of different programming languages, and it does not matter what your favorite is or if you like following the latest trends, as you will need to be able to write for the languages and systems used by the studio. If you do not have experience with a particular programming language, then a strong background in computer science and languages in general will help you learn quickly.

Along with the ability to write software, Software Engineers are accomplished debuggers able to quickly sleuth out complex conflicts and issues between Maya and other applications and implement fixes and new features that save time and get productions back up and running. Since most studios work with Linux computers, experience with Linux and programming in that environment is a bonus.

In addition to their technical prowess and strong work ethic, good communication skills to effectively relay ideas clearly and concisely in working within groups, with other developers, and for coordinating tasks with others in the production pipeline are vitally important. Communicating with managers and the like often requires distilling detailed tasks into a more concise, less technical form. The ability to get along with coworkers is an asset because Software Engineers often work on tight deadlines under a certain amount of pressure, so maintaining friendly relationships with others in the group greatly reduces the stress involved and leads to better results. In addition, the industry is very small, and Software Engineers often move between studios, so it is important to maintain a strong network of friendships for the sake of your career.

Unions and Associations

Presently, no unions exist for Software Engineers. However, many join ACM SIGGRAPH, an international computer graphics association involved in current research in the field. The association holds an annual conference for its members featuring keynote speakers and forums on the latest research and an opportunity to meet others in the industry. "Often recruiters are there for the various studios," Duncan related, "so it's a great place to talk directly with [potential employers]."

Tips for Entry

1. Keep close tabs on the graphics industry and technology. Read industry publications and graphics-related postings in industry newsgroups and online forums.
2. Send polite e-mails to newsgroups or forum members asking about different positions and seeking advice for someone breaking into the industry, including how to focus your cover letter and résumé.
3. Immediately send or post your résumé in response to jobs openings and postings on company Web sites and newsgroups, and keep your résumé on file for future opportunities.
4. Register and attend major computer graphics conferences, such as ACM SIGGRAPH, to make contacts and network with other industry professionals, and continue dialogue and keep in touch with them afterward.

DIRECTING

ASSISTANT DIRECTOR

CAREER PROFILE

Duties: Assist the director on film or television animation production

Alternate Title(s): Assistant Animation Director; First Assistant Director; Second Assistant Director; Third Assistant Director

Salary Range: $1,312.50 to $3,412 per week

Employment Prospects: Fair

Advancement Prospects: Fair

Best Geographical Location(s): Los Angeles, New York, San Francisco

Prerequisites:

    Education and Training—Undergraduate degree in art, film, or related field

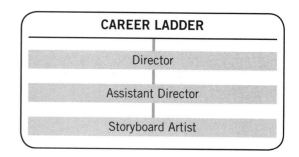

CAREER LADDER

Director

Assistant Director

Storyboard Artist

Experience—Minimum of two years of animation production and storyboarding

Special Skills and Personality Traits—Hard worker; diligent; detail-oriented; drafting and animation skills; organizational skills

Position Description

Whether it is an animated movie or television show, Assistant Directors (or ADs) essentially serve as "the right-hand man" to the director. They are responsible for coordinating various aspects before, during, and after the production.

On major stop-motion animated and live-action/ animated feature film productions, usually there are two Assistant Directors, a first Assistant Director and a second Assistant Director. First Assistant Directors handle a number of important responsibilities to free up the director to concentrate on the creative process. During preproduction, they break down the script into a shot-by-shot storyboard and determine, in collaboration with the director, the shooting order and how long each scene will take to film. Next, they draw up the overall shooting schedule (a timetable for the filming period). Once the film enters production, they ensure that every aspect of the shoot or filming keeps to this schedule.

Second Assistant Directors, on the other hand, support the first Assistant Director in managing the daily operations of the shooting floor, acting as points of contact for questions and issues to relieve the first Assistant Director of more routine inquiries and tasks. They are responsible for creating the daily call sheet (a document that contains useful information including that day's schedule and what scenes and script pages are to be shot) and production report, calling crew to daily rushes, wrangling animators and cameramen to

editorial sessions, and managing the shooting units. They likewise inform the camera crew and animators of upcoming shooting schedules, start dates, and estimated completion dates. The second Assistant Director also monitors the stage to ensure that props, puppets, sets, and rigging are ready; this includes troubleshooting animation and camera department issues that may need to be rerouted to other units to prevent wasted time. The second Assistant Director also provides guidance to the third Assistant Director, if the production has one.

In television animation, only one Assistant Director is employed. These professionals assist the director but work in a much more creative capacity than their motion picture counterparts. They help out with storyboarding during the preproduction phase, when storyboard artists create the first visual representations of the story before the actual animation can commence. "You are first off a storyboard artist, but you generally get less pages than the board artists assigned to a show," explained the Assistant Director Jon Hooper. "The idea being that you will be able to help at the end of the board if the director or board artists aren't able to get their pages done."

In assisting with the storyboards, Assistant Directors play a role in the direction of the story and program. Storyboarding in animation is "basically directing in the sense that you are the first person to visualize the script," Hooper added. With today's layout style boards, Assistant Directors essentially animate the project.

Hooper finds the creative puzzle solving of the boarding to be one of the most rewarding aspects of the job.

After the storyboards are completed, an animatic, or story reel, comprised of countless individual sequential drawings is produced and screened for the director, who provides critical feedback and makes any changes and/or revisions to the structure and flow of the story deemed necessary. "The assistant director is like a second set of eyes for the director, helping him get through the revisions. . . . Any difficult changes [are] done by the assistant director," Hooper said.

Afterward, the television animation Assistant Director is responsible for managing all revisions made to the storyboard, doling out tasks to revisionists and making sure they meet the director's specifications. In delegating work to the revisionists, Assistant Directors must make sure to elicit the best drawings for the director in the allotted time.

Assistant Directors who work in television also help the director with timing the animation, although animation timers usually handle most of this. In this case, Assistant Directors help to take the storyboard panels and detail what is happening on certain frames for each character or effect in the scenes. They write out all the small actions that are needed, frame by frame, on exposure sheets, like a big spreadsheet broken into frames and columns for each character. If any action is not drawn on the boards, Assistant Directors produce thumbnail drawings and written instructions to flesh out what needs to be provided on the exposure sheets. The exposure sheets also map out the lip assignments (mouth poses for each part of a word) for lip sync of the character voices. "Along with the storyboards, they serve as a blueprint for the animators of how the animation will look and be timed," Hooper said. "So, in essence, how long all drawings will be on the screen is timed on the exposure sheets."

Working conditions for Assistant Directors vary by studio but are generally pleasant, including a suitable workspace stationed near other animators. The work involves frequent sitting and standing and repeated movement of the hands and wrists. Assistant Directors generally work a standard 40-hour week, except for times when overtime may be required to meet production schedules and deadlines.

Salaries

According to The Animation Guild, Local 839, of the IATSE, the minimum weekly salary as of June 2010 for Assistant Directors was $1,312.50. The median salary range for the position was $1,468.75, up $15.63 from the previous year, with more experienced directors making as much as $1,672.73 per week. Journeyman Assistant Directors draw a weekly salary of $1,500.60, slightly below the median salary for this position. Conversely, Assistant Directors who fall under the contract union guidelines of the Directors Guild of America (DGA), which represents film and television directors and motion picture first Assistant Directors and second Assistant Directors, earn higher guaranteed wages and salaries. For their minimum rates, effective November 1, 2010, to November 30, 2011, first Assistant Directors are paid $853 a day and $3,412 a week; second Assistant Directors are paid $466 daily and $1,864 weekly over the same time period.

Employment Prospects

Assistant Directors have one of the most coveted and highly desired positions in animation. As a result, it is difficult to attain, and candidates may be better served gaining experience in storyboarding or as revisionists. Television animation directors often hire storyboard artists who are talented and quick workers and have acquired sufficient experience and expertise to serve as Assistant Directors.

Advancement Prospects

Most Assistant Directors use the position as a pathway to becoming a director or associate producer at major-market film and television animation studios and some smaller-market and independent production companies. Due to strong competition, only the most skilled and talented—in storyboarding, animation timing, and coordinating the various elements of an animated production—are promoted. Consequently, prospects for advancement for Assistant Directors are only fair.

Education and Training

To become an Assistant Director, one must have an undergraduate degree in film, art, or a related field or an equivalent combination of education and experience. Most studios that produce motion picture and television animation favor applicants with a bachelor's degree with prior experience in animation and production scheduling. Any course work in storyboarding, composition, and drawing can be assets on the job.

Experience, Skills, and Personality Traits

Most animation studios and independent production companies require a minimum of two to three years of prior experience, preferably in animation and storyboarding, for advancement to Assistant Director. Sometimes, experienced and successful storyboard artists are elevated to this position.

Besides having a well-rounded background in all aspects of animation production, Assistant Directors must be highly motivated and diligent. They must be good draftsmen with some animation skills. In addition, they must be highly organized and detail minded, with the ability to handle many complex duties involved in working on an animation production. Likewise, they must be capable of dealing with various creative and technical issues and diverse personalities within a demanding and stressful environment.

Unions and Associations

Most Assistant Directors working in the film and television animation industry are members of The Animation Guild, Local 839, of the IATSE, which negotiates bargaining agreements and guaranteed wages and other benefits for its members. Others also belong to the Directors Guild of America, which represents film and television directors as well as Assistant Directors in the motion picture industry.

Tips for Entry

1. Candidates for Assistant Director are usually promoted through the ranks from storyboarding. If you want to take this career track, become a great storyboard artist first.
2. Learn and execute the tasks of storyboarding. Show that you are reliable, organized, and thorough. Have a good work ethic and eye for quality in your work.
3. Talk to various directors you work with. Express an interest in learning to become an Assistant Director.
4. Find a director who will mentor you and can give you some training in timing and some of the more arcane tasks. Directors who like your storyboarding work are likely to make the decision to promote you to Assistant Director.

DIRECTOR

CAREER PROFILE

Duties: Bring together all the creative and technical elements of an animated production into a single film or television program

Alternate Title(s): None

Salary Range: $48,005 to $132,257

Employment Prospects: Fair

Advancement Prospects: Good

Best Geographical Location(s): Los Angeles, New York, San Francisco

Prerequisites:

Education and Training—Undergraduate degree in animation, art, computer science, or related field; some film and/or art training

Experience—Varies from studio to studio; some require as much as five years or more experience in film or television animation

CAREER LADDER

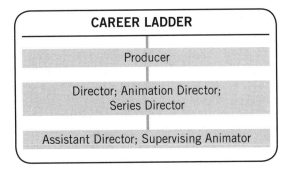

Producer

Director; Animation Director; Series Director

Assistant Director; Supervising Animator

Special Skills and Personality Traits—Creativity; organizational and leadership skills; motivational abilities; technical knowledge of animation production; understanding of animation timing and posing; effective communicator

Position Description

Much like their live-action counterparts, Directors of animation oversee the creative planning, design, and direction of a production as a whole. They are ultimately responsible for the on-screen interpretation of the story and for the quality of the final product.

In the motion picture field, Directors helm everything from 2-D traditional to 3-D computer animated short-subjects and feature films. In each case, they have a creative responsibility for the entire production, providing both vision and leadership. In principle, they supervise all the work that ends up in the final released film, working with animators, background artists, layout artists, modelers, riggers, technical directors, engineers, visual effects technicians, editors, and many others involved in its creation and success.

During preproduction, Directors work closely with producers, art directors, production designers, and scriptwriters to determine and approve the final narrative content and visual style of the production. They are particularly involved with the design, storyboard, layout, and animation and whatever creative decisions and choices must be made with respect to the project's overall direction, tone, pace, and performance from beginning to end. In directing 2-D traditional or cel animation, some of which is produced today with the assistance of computer ink-and-paint software, the Director traditionally oversees eight overlapping stages: scripting and storyboarding of the story, recording the soundtrack dialogue, creating exposure sheets (giant spreadsheets to log sound and direction for the animation), painting backgrounds, drawing the animation, pencil testing (producing a test reel of the actual film in its rawest and crudest form), inking and coloring characters, and compositing the images to be photographed in sequential order. During postproduction, the Director and editor shape the final product before it debuts on television or in movie theaters.

Even with the rapid expansion from 2-D animation to 3-D computer animation, Directors essentially supervise the same basic stages that have been the basis for how all animation has been produced for more than a century. First, they oversee designing the story and then the characters to "the point where they are sometimes even built [created] in the computer at the time we cast [the film]," stated the Pixar Animation director Pete Docter in an interview following the release of the animated film *Up* (2009).

In preproduction, before a single frame of animation is produced or a single line of dialogue is spoken, the Director meets with story artists or storyboard artists to create storyboards, a sequence of crude drawings on paper that visualize each shot of animation and the direction of the story. During this stage, unlike live-action films, for which they produce the final cut of the film at the end, the film's editor, who ultimately melds everything together—the images and sound—up until final rendering, provides input for the Director and the story team in shaping the plot, characters, and look and style of the film.

Casting of the voice actors actually precedes the animation. The Director listens to demos or voice samples of different actors until finding something fitting. Then the Director guides the actors in separate recording sessions of them reading and performing the character dialogue as written in the script, along with any improvised lines they happen to create on the spot. Usually, this is only the first of many recording sessions to follow. According to Docter, this first session is "almost like a learning session, and we hardly use any of it because we're starting to figure out the cadence and type of words they use, finding and discovering and they end up—the actors—in that way really influencing the characters."

After the storyboard is completed, the Director sits down with the story artists or storyboard artists, animators, and writers to review, discuss, and approve every shot and the direction of the story as a whole. This often results in multiple drafts before the Director fully signs off on it. Once approved, the Director produces a story reel featuring thousands of individual drawn scenes from the various boards that the editor culls together with temporary voice tracks of the actors' character dialogue for review and approval.

Afterward, the Director assigns specific characters and scenes to animators, under the direction of supervising and lead animators, who oversee them. Their job includes matching the movements and lip movement of the characters with the dialogue—including the subtle nuances of the way the actors deliver their lines—in their animation. As the Pixar Animation lead animator Bobby Podesta explained in an exclusive online interview, "You—the animator—will get a shot and the director will tell you, this is what's going on in the sequence, who the characters are, and what they need to achieve. You'll also have the voice recorder of the actor acting out the scene. However, the director will not tell you how to act. You get to bring that to the shot."

As part of the trial-and-error process that characterizes much of the animation, the Director produces a test shot of a usually high-quality rendering of a detailed model to see how a single frame of animation and the final product will look. The Director also usually performs a pencil test of the animation using either simplified models or low-quality and/or low-resolution renderings of the characters synced with the dialogue.

The test provides the Director with real-time calculation and playback of the animation used to analyze and address any creative and technical issues requiring further modifications and revisions. Potential issues include any that affect the timing, posing, movement control (the movement of an object from one spot to another), and kinematics (the human characteristics) of the character in each sequence.

After the character models are painted and textured, the Director advances the production to the camera and layout stage of the animation and 3-D environments, including decisions about the final editing by the editor of all the elements, before final rendering is done on networked supercomputers to bring the production to life.

In television animation, Directors, also sometimes known as animation Directors and series Directors, are responsible for actualizing the vision of the project or show. They participate in the scripting process and development of compelling stories. In collaboration with a storyboard artist or editor, they determine the artistic interpretation of the story/script in keeping with the vision of the series and design shots. They direct the storyboarding team throughout the boarding of each episode and communicate and recommend solutions that better interpret the script visually.

"In my current position, I oversee the storyboarding of individual episodes," commented the Nickelodeon Animation Studios animation Director Gary Conrad. That includes the creation of animatics that guide the animators. However, the duties of animation directors vary from show to show. As he explained, titles are "tricky in this business."

Television animation Directors are also responsible for approving the final storyboard panels, recommending revisions as needed and cutting together the final boards into an animatic, or story reel. They direct and work with other department directors throughout the production to maintain continuity and quality. They oversee with the voice director recording sessions of the cast and sound mix sessions, making creative suggestions as they deem fit. They comment on and approve the final cut of the show to ensure that the editing serves the story and action of the production.

"Probably the biggest challenge in television animation is working within the constraints of budgets and schedules," Conrad added. "Both tend to be tight . . . it's simply the nature of the medium."

For Conrad, who entered the business in 1984 and has directed countless episodes of numerous Nickelodeon hit cartoon shows, the main attraction to his work is "Simple: getting to make cartoons . . . doing the thing I love to do for a living. Also, working in a creative environment and collaborating with many talented, supportive, and fun people."

For the most part, Directors work in animation studios. Ordinarily, these environments are highly structured and equipped with comfortable and functional workspaces. Tasks involve repeated sitting and standing, talking, drawing, and viewing of demo reels and finished animation. Hours for Directors are often longer than the standard 40-hour workweek, especially during critical stages of production.

Salaries

Wages vary widely for this position. According to Payscale.com, as of June 2010, salaries for animation Directors ranged from $48,005 to $132,257. The minimum for a television animation Director, based on the 2010 member wage survey of The Animation Guild, Local 839, of the IATSE was $1,375 per week. Actual wages tend to be around $1,800 per week, above union minimums. However, the median rate for television animation Directors was $2,500, with a maximum of $4,000, per week. Feature film animation Directors earned significantly higher salaries, from $2,000 to as much as $6,009.38 per week. The average salary, meanwhile, was $3,054.55 a week.

Employment Prospects

The current chances of becoming a Director are fair. The job requires considerable experience. Competition is usually strong, and hiring has slowed in the animation industry due to the economic slowdown. However, "business appears to be on an upswing," Conrad remarked, "and employment opportunities are likely to increase."

Most Directors achieve their positions after five years or more of moving up the ranks through various departments as storyboard artists, animators, lead animators, supervising animators, and assistant directors within a single studio or for multiple employers. Most are hired or promoted on the basis of talent and track record.

Advancement Prospects

Many successful film and television animation Directors consider the position to be the crowning achievement of their careers and stay the course. However, the value of their experience and skill in the business often leads them to additional opportunities or directions. After a number of years directing, some become producers or produce and direct. Most attain these positions at major-market animation studios as well as comparable positions at independent and smaller-market production companies. With experience, some Directors advance to higher-paying directing jobs or producing positions, while others specialize in directing either film or television animation.

Education and Training

An undergraduate degree in animation, art, computer science, or a related field is required. Some film and/or art training is also beneficial—"anything that gives hands-on experience," Conrad said. "I graduated from the California Institute of the Arts with a B.F.A. in character animation, and the training I received there was valuable for me. But hiring is based on ability, and skills are more important than degrees."

As a Director who oversees all creative and technical aspects of the animation process, you need to complete course work covering animation practices and principles, including traditional and 3-D computer animation, character design, character animation, story structure, storyboarding, and sound and video editing. Completion of required courses will provide a hands-on learning experience and understanding of the importance of mechanics, movement, style, and continuity relevant to creating an entire animated production. Similarly, apprenticeship opportunities, available through most undergraduate programs, provide useful knowledge of all aspects of the production process and entry into the industry after graduation as well.

Experience, Skills, and Personality Traits

Experience is certainly beneficial, but no set number of years or a particular background is needed to become an animation Director, even though some studios require five years or more of experience. Directors require a mix of creativity, imagination and artistic flair, a sense of story and structure, and technical knowledge of animation principles and techniques, including timing and posing. Likewise, they need to have strong leadership, management, and organizational skills necessary to direct and manage the story, design, layout, animation, and technical teams. "An ability to keep an eye on the 'big picture' while also keeping a grasp on details is important," Conrad said. "Also, [Directors should have] a passion for [the] work combined with the ability to work with people, communicate, and . . . balance the creative and administrative sides of production."

Directors must be self-confident, decisive, and deadline-motivated. They need to effectively evaluate and communicate their ideas, specific viewpoints, processes, plans, and concepts. They must have the vision to identify and manage various needs of individuals and production teams. They must arbitrate sensitively between creative desires and production requirements. In addition to being deadline oriented, Directors must also work well under pressure and budgetary constraints.

Unions and Associations

Directors who work for most major-market film and television animation studios and independent production companies are usually members of, and represented by, the Directors Guild of American (DGA) and/or The Animation Guild, Local 839, of the IATSE, the only professional organization that represents Directors and animation professionals.

Tips for Entry

1. Study the many different animation styles and techniques used by contemporary and legendary cartoon Directors of the past.
2. In high school, learn how to create animation. With simple editing and animation software, teach yourself and start making short movies—maybe one a week.
3. Practice your planning, timing, and posing of shots and the pacing of your stories, and don't be too ambitious to start. For your first film, start small. Take stick figures and animate them to look realistic doing anything you want, from changing a bicycle tire to chasing a butterfly, and add clever dialogue to demonstrate your staging and timing of such simple characters. You can even do the same with available objects, such as Legos, to produce a stop-motion animated film using an inexpensive video camera and your editing and animation software.
4. Gradually work your way up to do more advanced films using various angles, color, lighting, shadows, and other elements as you become more proficient in your technique as a Director.
5. In college, pursue internships to gain professional experience.
6. Network with professionals in the industry.

GAME ANIMATION AND DESIGN

3-D ARTIST

CAREER PROFILE

Duties: Creates animation for multimedia interactive projects, including games

Alternate Title(s): 3-D Game Artist

Salary Range: $30,000 to $100,000

Employment Prospects: Good

Advancement Prospects: Good

Best Geographical Location(s): Austin, Dallas, Los Angeles, New York, Redmond, San Francisco

Prerequisites:

Education and Training—A two-year associate's or four-year bachelor's degree from a college or university in animation, computer design, computer science, technical design, or a related field; background in graphic design, 3-D lighting, rendering, and particle systems, and knowledge of application design software

Experience—At least two years of game animation experience; more than three years experience in game development; and/or four years in computer-

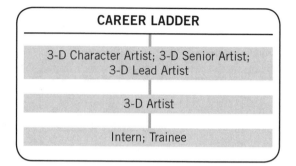

CAREER LADDER

3-D Character Artist; 3-D Senior Artist; 3-D Lead Artist

3-D Artist

Intern; Trainee

generated 2-D and 3-D animation in a game environment and platforms

Special Skills and Personality Traits—Artistic; enthusiastic and outgoing; technical minded; well-organized and detail-oriented; analytical skills; strong team player; creative problem solver; good communicator with strong written and oral communication skills

Position Description

3-D Artists create game art or game animation using design and editing software as their primary tools. As animation and technology has advanced in recent years, 3-D Artists have become a necessity for various firms that design not only video games but also computer-animated movies.

3-D Artists thrive on the innovation and creativity the job offers. Most of their day is spent drawing pictures and developing art for projects. When working on deadline, they easily can put in a 12-hour day, and 10-hour days are the average. They are expected to create specific elements within a game environment, including low- and high-resolution characters and texture maps for multiple game formats. One of the important aspects of their job is to create and prepare 3-D high-poly models rendered from 3-D drawings, modified from 3-D CAD drawings, or with 3-D scanners.

As the Black Isle 3-D game artist Dennis Presnell, perhaps best known for his work on the computer game Icewing Dale, once explained, "3-D Artists are responsible for creating different characters, backgrounds, and environmental props that make up these virtual playgrounds."

3-D Artists employ conventional modeling techniques and common toolsets in the course of creating video or online game animation. They mostly use popular design programs such as 3-D Studio MAX or Maya as well as Photoshop. One of the most important skills demonstrated in their work is a strong sense of creative expression. As the 3-D artist Raphael Lacoste noted in an interview at raph.com, 3-D CG allows him to give life to his imagination in ways that are extremely realistic. He works faster with CG than if he had to do models and light them with torches, filters, and other effects. Also, 3-D allows him to "fake" immersive and plausible environments and increase their size with depth fading and volume effects. As a result, he can create a huge setting and make it "almost real," with great depth and a large range of details. This kind of animation also allows him to mix his "passion for photo, lighting, and scenery."

Most 3-D Artists start by making rough concept sketches or drawings of the characters, environments, or props on paper. This preliminary process gives them a vivid mental picture of what they will create. It outlines various aspects of the image, including the lighting, textures, and colors, before they are fully developed on the computer screen. Nothing is set in stone, however. Changes can be made as the process moves along.

Afterward, 3-D Artists scan their rough sketches into a design and illustration program, such as Photoshop. Then they drag it to an empty canvas to polish it, add texture, and modify anything they desire before creating the final 3-D image and environment through which a game player will travel. 3-D Artists usually use Maya to accomplish this.

In addition to creating characters and environments for 3-D video or online games, 3-D Artists also develop animation for what are known as motion-capture games. To do this, they use the same techniques used in producing animated movies such as *The Polar Express* (2004), *Monster House* (2006), and *A Christmas Carol* (2009). The process is known as performance capture. In it, actions of human actors are recorded and turned into realistic, digitally animated characters in 2-D or 3-D computer animation. When performing this function, 3-D Artists usually work under the direction of an art lead.

3-D Artists are likewise entrusted with the job of creating animation in various other fields. They work in the medical field to create realistic 3-D images of human anatomy and internal body structure. These images are helpful in the diagnosis of diseases. In the field of architecture and construction engineering, many 3-D Artists are responsible for creating graphs and digital drawings of buildings that help engineers visualize their tasks in an efficient manner. In addition, they are often responsible for producing still images, posters, presentations, and brochures for various companies.

3-D Artists have the flexibility to work on a full-time basis or on a freelance/per-project basis. Most prefer to freelance, select the projects they like, and work with several companies at the same time. Some artists prefer to work from a home-based office or studio. They work a standard 40-hour workweek or more in mostly comfortable and casual work settings.

Salaries

Starting salaries depend on an individual's experience and knowledge, the size of the company, and location. While competition is the toughest for animators and illustrators, 3-D Artists are much more sought after. According to multiple industry sources, individuals with one year of experience can expect to make from $30,000 to $40,000 a year. Artists with one to four years of experience can earn from $38,000 to $52,000. After sharpening their skills and gaining more work experience, earnings for 3-D Artists can increase exponen-

tially. After 10 to 19 years of experience in the industry, they can draw from $60,000 to $100,000. According to *The Princeton Review,* artists with 10 to 15 years of experience can see their earnings climb to $78,000 a year. On average, professionals in the field work 50 hours a week.

Employment Prospects

As reported by AnimationArena.com, career prospects for those wishing to enjoy a lucrative career as a 3-D Artist are good. Josh Harvey, a 3-D Artist and art manager for Liquid Development, an outsourcing company, says individuals starting out in the industry need to demonstrate a broad range of skills to be hired. The best way to attract attention is create a portfolio that breaks down different examples of their work. "Most [employers] when looking at a portfolio want to see you have solid skills in your area of expertise, that you can clearly demonstrate your abilities," he said.

Harvey suggests that beginners avoid specializing in a certain area of the industry until they gain more experience. Only then are companies more willing to hire artists as specialists.

Advancement Prospects

Overall, the prospects for advancement as a 3-D Artist are good. Artists who enjoy creating character animation often become 3-D character artists. Experienced artists with proven track records and the ability to both create art and manage art creation often move into leadership and upper-level positions. Individuals with three to five years of experience and the ability to direct others are often promoted to 3-D lead artists; others with at least six years of professional experience can move up the scale to become 3-D senior artists.

Education and Training

With competition increasing considerably in this field in recent years, many employers now require either a two-year associate's degree or a four-year bachelor's degree in animation, computer design or computer science, technical design, or a related field and/or certification of completion of advanced 3-D animation in some cases. An education should include courses in the fundamentals of art, including design and color theory, and specialized classes, such as 3-D modeling. Some curricula also require classes in drawing, painting, and sculpting.

On the importance of having traditional art skills in order to be a good 3-D Artist, Lacoste stated, "In my opinion, 3-D is just a tool; it is like a pencil, and if you have a good basis in traditional art, you'll be a better 3-D artist." Strong traditional art skills will help 3-D Artists develop a good sense of perspective and lighting.

Besides an art education, developing good technical skills is equally important. Presnell confirms that employers really look for these skills in a 3-D Artist. They can learn a lot along the way in terms of art training, but it really depends on what the employer is looking for. Some artists are more technically skilled, while others are more classically trained.

3-D Artists must constantly try to improve and keep up with the emerging trends and changes in hardware and technology. As Presnell said in an interview with deviantART.com, "A school won't make you a good artist. That is something that you do on your own." In his opinion, schools help up-and-coming 3-D Artists learn the basics, but to really become a good artist, they need to study and learn things on their own. Artists must take the knowledge they have gained from school, apply it, and use it every day. Presnell has met many students who, for example, take a Photoshop class, but then they do not apply those skills after the class is finished, and by graduation they become rusty. To succeed, he says, 3-D Artists need to constantly push and challenge themselves. If they do not use the skills learned and improve upon them, they will fall behind. The industry is constantly changing, too, as newer hardware and technologies come out, so it is essential to stay up-to-date and current to be successful.

Experience, Skills, and Personality Traits

Generally, companies require at least two years of game animation experience, and three or more years of shipped (completed) games experience for motion-capture animated games. Most employers seek 3-D Artists who are self-sufficient self-starters. They should have proven experience and abilities in producing top-notch work on at least one or two published games. Industry experience is important but not essential in all cases. Some companies will consider artists so long as they have examples of high-quality work.

Successful 3-D Artists are creative and enthusiastic, with excellent animation skills and a positive attitude. They possess a passion for animation and a strong interest in gaming. They are experienced in creating detailed and realistic characters and environments with convincing motion and complex, fluid simulations for a wide variety of subjects for various gaming platforms. Most 3-D Artists have excellent traditional art skills and are proficient in modeling, texturing, and rendering. They must have a strong grasp of color, scale, propor-

tion, and lighting. They have a strong technical background and mastery of 2-D and 3-D software and tools, 3-D Studio MAX, Character Studio, Maya, Motion Mixer, and Motion Flow for motion capture animation, as well as Adobe Photoshop and After Effects. They must understand composition, mapping, and gameplay flow.

In addition to game personality animation requirements, 3-D Artists doing motion-capture games must be able to create realistic hand-keyed human motion (painstakingly capturing the movement of characters) as well as edit motion-capture assets. They should be capable in the creation of conceptual 3-D mockups and simple effects animation to be synced with motion capture.

3-D Artists must be well organized, detail-oriented, and meticulous in their approach. While creativity and imagination are important attributes, they should have a good work ethic and be good troubleshooters and task managers. 3-D Artists must be able to follow directions while also taking the initiative in meeting any challenges and completing tasks. Knowledge of 3-D art production processes, pipelines, proper building techniques, and platform performance restrictions is also helpful, as is the ability to use various animation styles. Because every project involves teamwork, excellent communication and team collaboration skills are important.

Unions and Associations

Currently, no union exists for 3-D game artists. However, many become members of the CGSociety, a respected global organization for creative digital artists that offers support at every level and a range of services, including online workshops and showcasing of your portfolio. Those involved in developing computer games join the Computer Game Artists Association, a community of computer game artists who network with each other.

Tips for Entry

1. Learn everything you can about the art of game making, including the required skills of the profession. This includes interface design, character creation, conceptual design, and special effects. Take relevant courses on the subject to brush up on your technical and creative abilities.
2. Familiarize yourself with the basic theories and operations of 3-D art.
3. Master your skills in the use of high-end 3-D industry software, such as Maya and others.

4. There is no better pathway into the game industry than an internship. Many game companies do significant recruiting through their intern programs, providing the perfect opportunity for newcomers to work hands-on in the industry.

5. Join an online creative gaming community, such as CGTalk (www.cgtalk.com), Gamasutra (www.gamasutra.com), GamingArtist (www.gamingartist.com), and others that showcase top art talent, share tips and tutorials, conduct contests for cash and prizes, and advertise job openings. Many also offer forums that are frequented by industry professionals who share their personal insights.

ANIMATOR

Duties: Animate characters and objects in scenes for multiplayer online or console video games

Alternate Title(s): 3-D Animator; Game Animator

Salary Range: $35,000 to $75,000

Employment Prospects: Good

Advancement Prospects: Good

Best Geographical Location(s): Austin, Dallas, Los Angeles, New York, Redmond, San Francisco, Salt Lake City

Prerequisites:

Education and Training—Minimum of a two-year art degree in 2-D and 3-D animation with an emphasis on character animation or equivalent work experience; bachelor's degree in related field preferred

Experience—At least three years or more experience with one published game in the appropriate format

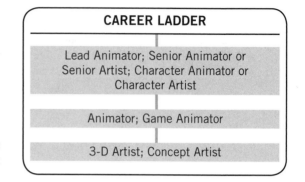

CAREER LADDER

Lead Animator; Senior Animator or Senior Artist; Character Animator or Character Artist

Animator; Game Animator

3-D Artist; Concept Artist

Special Skills and Personality Traits—Creative; imaginative; self-disciplined; artistic and technical skills; knowledge of traditional animation and computer 2-D and 3-D animation; communication and presentation skills; ability to work independently and as part of a team

Position Description

One of the fastest growing segments of the animation industry is video and Internet games. As in developing and producing animated film and television productions, games rely on realistically rendered animated characters to create a sense of involvement and interaction for game players.

The role of game Animators is no different than traditional and 3-D computer film and television animators. They are responsible for breathing life into characters and creatures using realistic behavior, movements, objects, and scenery. The realities they create must enthrall and entertain players in the game's target audience. Unlike film and television, for which animators are hired on a project-by-project basis, game Animators work as permanent employees for either development studios or independent and publisher-owned game companies.

On the job, game Animators work as part of the art department team in game production. Their work is both complex and collaborative. They require patience and attention to detail as they combine artistic and technical skills to work as efficiently as possible under the constraints of a game environment. Using characters, objects, and models created by 3-D artists, they

employ popular 3-D animation software and tools and techniques of the trade, painstakingly creating an underlying sense of believability through behaviors and movements. At the same time, Animators make the best use of the game's engine technology while maximizing game play and interactivity of its users. Since game animation can involve a complex combination of different types of movements, game Animators often rely on an extensive library of reusable animation for each character that makes the process more efficient. They are also responsible for other technical processes in game production, including rigging and skinning of characters. This entails creating what is known as an underlying structure, such as the bones of the skeleton, and attaching skin to it using 3-D computer animation software.

Game Animators have to keep in mind how their animation and movements will work within the context of the game and often have to limit the number of key frames used or number of characters that appear on the screen at one time. As a result, they work closely with programmers and artists to create the right balance to produce a smooth, seamless movement and optimize the performance of the characters and scenes.

Game Animators typically work indoors in offices or rooms equipped with high-powered computers and specialized software. The environment is usually hectic and fast paced. Most work 40 hours or more a week to meet project deadlines.

Salaries

According to Jobs-Salary.com, the beginning salary for game Animators is around $35,000. Experienced Animators with three years or less in the industry make an average of $46,700 a year. With three years of experience, most animators make $67,000 annually; for game animators with six years of experience, more than $75,000 a year.

Employment Prospects

Based on the assessment of industry leaders, employment opportunities are mostly good. There are many openings for people who have the "talent and drive but no track record—certainly much more so than in older industries—and the constant bubbling up of new startups and boutique companies mean there should always be a 'backdoor route' for outsiders," explained Steve Theodore, a games industry animator/character designer for Valve Software.

Unlike the early days of the gaming industry when companies were usually smaller and "amateurish" in some cases, eager to hire people, and there were more opportunities for bright and talented individuals who didn't have formal training and were largely self-taught, today companies prefer those who are paper qualified, meaning they meet educational qualifications and required training and experience.

Most Animators who break into the industry have achieved some proficiency in computer animation either during their undergraduate work or after. Some have come from other sectors of the animation industry, such as film and television. Either way, it is important to know before getting into the field that although playing video games can be fun, working as a game Animator can be demanding. As the Ubisoft lead video game animator Patrick Beaulieu noted in an interview on AnimationArena.com, "Animator is a job that a lot of people think working for a video game company is a synonym of playing video games all day. Unfortunately, it's not the case. . . . Being an animator on video games is hard work and not a game."

Beaulieu added that most video game companies look for animators with "unpolished talent." "It doesn't matter what software he or she uses. What's important is can that person animate," he remarked. When interviewing potential candidates, he looks for certain things in their portfolios and demo reels—mostly original animation that avoids clichés or movements that

have been used or seen before. "Only put your best stuff in a demo," he said. "It's better to have three good animations than 15 bad ones." He suggests assembling a variety of the most interesting examples that demonstrate the range of talent and what a potential employer wants to see. Above all else, be original and make a good impression.

Advancement Prospects

Opportunities for advancement for Animators with exceptional drawing and technical skills are generally good, depending on location, size of the company, and motivation. The next step up is to become a character animator or character artist responsible for creating character animation for games. Others choose to move up and become a senior animator or senior artist and take on more supervisory roles within the industry, such as lead animator in charge of directing the work of a group of game Animators.

Education and Training

A two-year degree in 2-D and 3-D animation with an emphasis on character animation or equivalent work experience is the minimum requirement. However, most employers prefer candidates with four-year degrees since they generally have "a broader set of experiences to bring to their work than people who've spent two or four years isolated in a studio," Theodore remarked. Degrees and courses are available at a wide range of colleges and universities and vocational and trade schools across the United States. Any education should include courses in general art, life drawing, and computer animation. Background in practical arts, such as keyboarding and computer technology, is useful.

Anyone considering a career as a game Animator needs to have a thorough grasp of the technical aspects of game animation. This includes understanding the interactive nature of games and various aspects involved in their creation, including character modeling, rigging, skinning, cinematics, and basic cinematography, and the constraints associated with real-time rendering. Furthermore, they must have a good command of one or more of the most commonly used software packages, including 3-D Studio MAX and Maya, to carry out the duties of the position.

Besides the inherent creative and technical skills needed, the single most important tool a game Animator can have is an outstanding demo reel. "Companies will be glad to know if you have a portfolio of figure drawings, a scrapbook of performance art pieces, or a straight-A transcript in your studio classes, but the thing that will make or break your job search is the demo," Theodore stated. "A good reel is concise, under five minutes. It showcases only your best work. The choice of material will say a lot about you as an artist and as a person, so consider carefully what kind of impression you want to make." Most recruiters look for candidates who demonstrate mastery of a variety of genres and styles, walk and run cycles, and more fully developed sequences with the ability to portray a character's personality through behavior and movement.

Experience, Skills, and Personality Traits

Most game companies require at least three years or more experience and one published game, preferably in the type of format they produce. Along with a strong sense of creativity and imagination, game Animators require knowledge of traditional and computer 2-D and 3-D animation techniques. Since game animation requires a combination of artistic and technical skills and is simple and expressive, Animators should be equally skilled in human and animal movement, timing, and appearance and know how to create memorable characters that convey real attitudes, emotions, and moods that will appeal to players. The ability to lip sync is also an asset.

In this fast-paced and deadline-oriented business, successful game Animators are self-disciplined, well organized, and able to work independently and as part of a creative team. They have the ability to manage and produce their work under the constraints of production deadlines. They communicate effectively and have good presentation skills. Some understanding of the production pipeline for games is also helpful.

Unions and Associations

Membership in the CGSociety (www.cgsociety.org) is beneficial; it provides forums, workshops, and job support to its members. Other industry associations, such as the International Game Developers Association (www.igda.org) and Computer Game Artists Association (www.vectorg.com/cga/CGA.htm), are useful for career advice, educational opportunities, events, and networking.

Tips for Entry

1. Having a passion for video games is a good starting point. Develop good drawing and technical skills and take courses to master the art and methods in both areas.
2. Be ambitious and original in your work, and fine-tune and develop your craft.
3. Stay up to date on the latest trends and software in the industry.
4. Join online game industry communities and forums and post examples of your work on Web sites seen by other gaming professionals.

CHARACTER ARTIST

CAREER PROFILE

Duties: Create animation-friendly character models and textures under given art direction

Alternate Title(s): 3-D Modeler/Artist; Character Modeler; Creature Modeler/Artist

Salary Range: $30,000 to $100,000 or more

Employment Prospects: Poor

Advancement Prospects: Fair

Best Geographical Location(s): Austin, Chicago, Los Angeles, Portland, Orlando, San Diego, San Francisco

Prerequisites:

Education and Training—A bachelor's degree in fine art or visual art/design from an accredited art or design school or equivalent level of experience

Experience—Two to five years of experience developing characters for many types and genres of games or styles and platforms with at least one shipped game preferred

Special Skills and Personality Traits—Eye for art; understanding of work flow/pipeline; team player

CAREER LADDER

```
Art Director or Character Art Director;
Lead Artist or Character Lead Artist
            |
Senior Character Artist; Character Artist
            |
Junior Character Artist, Character Artist
Intern, or 3-D Artist/Modeler
```

Position Description

Characters that fill the modern game world come in all shapes, styles, and levels of abstraction, from cartoonish to hyperrealistic. Making such characterizations and variations in virtually any style possible are Character Artists, who use their creativity in countless ways to dream up appealing and unique characters that encompass an array of body types, costumes, personalities, and facial features.

Character Artists create assigned characters, or "assets," as they are called, under the direction of the art director and lead/senior character artist. Usually, they are given at least one piece of 2-D concept art for a character or come up with some ideas for a character and show them to the art director. "When starting a new character, I receive a package containing instructions," stated the Cinematico freelance Character Artist Matt Corcoran, "including poly count, texture size, color charts, reference images, and hopefully (but not always) orthographic drawings of the character. From the beginning to end, I report directly to the character art director, and occasionally I'll get further instructions for quality assurance."

Afterward, Character Artists begin creating the character in 3-D, applying their understanding of geometric functions, rigging, and weighting in their design. First, they create a high-resolution source computer model using ZBrush, Mudbox, or other digital sculpting tools and then a lower-resolution version of the same model with UV (to map out the character or object) within Maya or 3D Studio Max for actual in-game usage. In addition, Character Artists may use Photoshop to produce high-quality textures of the character. Next, they "map" the character by producing specific maps—a normal map, ambient occlusion map, spec maps, and others—from the source model for the in-game model; these maps contain normal or color information for the game engine to use in animating the character. Sometimes, they will be provided with a proprietary game engine into which they import assets of the character.

Throughout the process, Character Artists work closely with the art director, animators, tech artists, and other animation professionals on the game development team. The art director meets weekly or biweekly with Character Artists to review their character models to ensure they follow the art direction and fit the game needs. They also provide critical feedback and suggestions on how to make the character even better. Upon further review, the quality assurance department provides a "draw-over" list of revisions for Character Artists to make until the character is fully approved for production.

As a Character Artist, knowing a bit about conceptualization and character rigging, animation, and even design really helps. This way, when something goes wrong during developing the character, you can figure out what went wrong and fix it faster and easier.

Character creation from inception to completion takes about four to six weeks or longer for a single character. "Usually we create a model that is 60 percent done and send it off to tech artists, who will then create and set up the rigging for the character," explained the Monolith Productions senior Character Artist Luis Lu. "Then an animator will take the file and do a rough first-pass animation. If anything goes wrong on the model, the tech artist or animator will kick back the file to the modeler to fix the problem and then start the process again until the character is done."

Character Artists, however, do not always have the creative freedom they once did. Because developing game characters takes so much time, some studios now prefer that Character Artists follow the concept they are given without input or making any modifications.

Being a Character Artist means keeping up with changes in the industry. Technological improvements are frequent, so artists should be prepared to learn new tools throughout their careers.

Character Artists are either employed full-time by game studios or on a freelance or contracted basis. In either case, they spend an inordinate amount of time using their wrists and hands and sit for long periods of time in generally comfortable and bright workspaces. While the hours can be long and vary from six to 14 hours a day, the upside is creating "fun" characters, sometimes being able to work from home, and having a "more flexible schedule," Corcoran says.

Salaries

Salaries for Character Artists vary and are based not so much on the size of the company, but rather what the client is "willing to pay" for a job, Corcoran related. "The company will then give you an offer based on the client's needs. Paychecks vary with each client. The bigger named clients aren't always the highest paying."

Beginning salaries, according to multiple industry sources, are in the $30,000 to $40,000 range. In high cost-of-living areas, artists can negotiate for a higher salary as opposed to an area where living costs—and consequently salaries—are much less. Highly experienced artists have been known to earn as much as $100,000 or more per year.

Freelance/contracted Character Artists are paid several ways: hourly, daily, and by the model. Others charge on a case-by-case basis; for "rush" or "special request" work, normally the rate they charge is higher. Such rates are usually negotiable. Experienced freelancer/contractors with more skill earn more, and contracted artists are guaranteed a certain amount, whereas freelancers have no such guarantees. While there is no average price range, based on Corcoran's experience, daily rates are from $275 to $300 and anywhere from $800 to $1,500 on a per character basis. Year-round employment for freelancers is not guaranteed.

Employment Prospects

Employment conditions for Character Artists are poor to fair. There was a wave of layoffs in 2009 and 2010, resulting in limited opportunities and fewer jobs across the board. A career as a Character Artist is very desirable, but it is a very hard position to secure. Many companies are not hiring, but things are slowly getting better; companies may start to expand as the U.S. economy recovers.

Before the recession, studios actually brought people from overseas and took care of their visas if they were the kind of talent they needed.

Major urban areas offer the most job opportunities because most game studios are located in bigger cities. Game companies employ anywhere from three to 15 Character Artists; the greater the scale of the game, the more artists they have on a team. New hires, such as college graduates, start out as 3-D artists creating assets not limited to just characters, including props, weapons, and other game pieces. More experienced and knowledgeable Character Artists have an easier time finding work, especially with game companies that focus more on storytelling and character development.

Given usually tight budgets these days, most companies are hiring more freelance artists than contractors. Basing yourself in areas where game studios are located may improve your odds of employment. The length of employment varies per game—anywhere from two weeks to eight months or longer. Recent college graduates have a greater chance of being hired in this instance since companies then can see if they are a good match with little invested in them and, depending on their skills, either boost them to full-time status after a few months or let them go after their contract and the project ends. There are usually full-time Character Artist positions in every studio. Most of the games studios still want to keep major characters' work in house because art direction and tech problems are easier to deal with in house.

While some jobs are posted on game Web sites and job boards, it is important before seeking work to study the market and network with others currently working in the industry. Gaming professionals usually seek talent from people they know first. One way to gain visibility is by posting samples of your work on online 3-D game communities and forums.

Those who are new to the industry and seeking employment should work hard on improving their skills. Classes in sculpting and anatomy are helpful, as are tutorials on various subjects. Whatever you do, never stop learning, and never give up. Keep updating and refining your demo reel, and find people to give you honest feedback on your work.

Advancement Prospects

Advancement prospects are fair to good. Advancement is based on experience, skill level, and interests. After two to three years, artists may move up to a specific type of job, including Character Artist, while those already in the position go on to become senior character artists, lead character artists, and eventually lead artists or art directors. Others change their area of focus and become concept artists or technical artists.

Major cities have more studios and more job opportunities in general, increasing the likelihood of advancement. However, advancement opportunities at smaller studios located outside major cities are stronger because it is easier to be noticed. In addition, smaller companies allow Character Artists to work in different specialties, thus diversifying their skill set and increasing chances for advancement. Rapidly improving your skills and knowledge and learning from your fellow colleagues can also hasten your advancement. Learn from those who have more experience and knowledge than you. In addition to making you a better artist, this will help you get an idea of where you want to go in your career. Moving up requires a solid reputation and recognition from your peers, who must be willing to recommend you for positions not only within the studio where you are working but outside as well.

Education and Training

A bachelor's degree from an accredited art or design school, college, or university in art and design, with an emphasis in 3-D, is usually required. A degree shows employers that you have undergone formal training. Before graduation, most undergraduate programs offer internships in the gaming industry, which can provide valuable on-the-job experience.

Course work in traditional and 3-D animation, life drawing, human anatomy, color and form design, sculpting, and rigging are important. Proficiency in all aspects will enhance your chances of employment.

Experience, Skills, and Personality Traits

Character Artists are expected to have had at least two to five years of experience developing characters for many types and genres of games or styles and platforms with at least one shipped game to their credit. Qualified artists must be exceptionally creative and gifted character animators. They should have a solid understanding of human and animal anatomy, facial animation, cloth and clothing dynamics, character rigging, and application of classic animation principles (e.g., staging, timing, cameras, etc.) with the ability to creatively translate concepts and ideas into 3-D.

As Character Artists usually handle modeling and texturing their own characters, they require good 3-D modeling, including high-resolution and low-resolution modeling, UV (to map out characters or objects), and texturing skills. They must consistently demonstrate an excellent sense of form and shape, proportion, color, and design. Fluency in the application and use of one or more major 3-D software programs, including 3-D Studio MAX, Character Studio, and Softimage XSI as well as Adobe Photoshop is preferred.

Ideal candidates are open-minded and flexible. They are multitaskers with time-management skills and an eye for detail. Character Artists are natural team players able to work long hours and collaborate and communicate effectively with a range of team members. They have the ability to see things from a different point of view and accept constructive criticism without taking it personally.

Most Character Artist positions tend to be about 20 percent art and 80 percent problem solving. Therefore, patience is needed to dig into complex problems and find quick solutions along with the ability to adapt to new or changing technologies on the job.

Unions and Associations

Many Character Artists belong to an array of guilds and associations, each a good source for learning and networking. Some belong to the Graphic Artists Guild (www.graphicartistsguild.org), which represents the "social, economic and professional interests" of its members, including graphic artists, animators, cartoonists, designers, illustrators, and digital artists and offers an extremely useful handbook that describes contracts, prices, and common business ethics especially helpful to artists working as freelancers. Others also hold memberships in ACM SIGGRAPH (www.siggraph.org), the leading professional organization for computer graphics, which convenes an annual conference attended by thousands of computer professionals; the International Game Developers

Association (www.idga.org), the largest independent, nonprofit organization serving individuals who create video games; the CGSociety (www.cgsociety.org), considered the most respected global organization for creative digital artists; and Game Artisans (www.gameartisans.org), an online community that features art competition galleries to motivate and inspire artists of all levels for purposes of professional growth and making new contacts with other professionals. Joining Game Artisans is entirely free.

Tips for Entry

1. Create an online portfolio on your own Web site so people can see it. Put your finished work and in-progress work on it, as well as your résumé and contact info. Do not use a lot of Flash animation unless you are looking for that type of work.

2. Post your work frequently on 3-D/CG forums to network and get feedback. Find a professional willing to look at your work and honestly critique it.

3. Talk to your teachers. Some teachers are from the industry or know people in the industry, so treat them well. Also, contact fellow college alumni in your desired field.

4. Visit game company Web sites or online job boards such as Gamasutra and CreativeHeads to find jobs. To find game studios by geographical location, visit http://gamedevmap.com/.

5. Go to game shows or conferences such as the annual Game Developers Conference, the largest annual gathering of professional video game developers, where some studios have booths and will accept resumes.

6. Be patient. Good things come to those who wait.

CONCEPT ARTIST

CAREER PROFILE

Duties: Create and design original characters, objects, environments, and worlds used within video games

Alternate Title(s): Conceptual Artist

Salary Range: $20,000 to $100,000

Employment Prospects: Fair

Advancement Prospects: Fair

Best Geographical Location(s): Atlanta, Dallas, Chicago, Los Angeles, Seattle, San Diego, San Francisco

Prerequisites:

Education and Training—A fine arts or visual design degree or equivalent work experience and background in design and illustration

Experience—Two to five years of experience in video game production preferred

Special Skills and Personality Traits—Artistic; creative; illustration, painting, and technical abilities; proficiency in 3-D design and painting systems; organizational and analytical skills; problem-solver; ability to work with minimal supervision and within a team setting

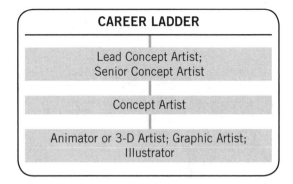

CAREER LADDER

Lead Concept Artist; Senior Concept Artist

Concept Artist

Animator or 3-D Artist; Graphic Artist; Illustrator

Position Description

Concept Artists work with like-minded professionals to create fun and innovative themes for video games. Reporting to the art director and lead concept artist, with whom they work closely, they are principally in charge of creating all conceptual artwork and assets, including sketches, color comps, storyboards, and more. They assist in the production of artwork that illustrates concepts and ideas that drive all visuals within a game in a specific style. Their creative renderings define the overall artistic design, aesthetics, look, style, and function for various elements in a game environment.

Most Concept Artists produce their art traditionally and/or digitally in order to effectively convey the artistic direction and environments pertaining to the game. From the outset, they regularly participate in concept art and project development meetings. These meetings provide a number of design principles, or "kernels," that Concept Artists use through the course of developing their art. Their creations and designs must be captivating and believable. Concept Artists apply the rules of construction and pose as applied in doing life drawings to develop the necessary conceptual artwork, including character and creature sketches; detailed drawings of environments, including real buildings and lush landscapes; other elements, such as moving automobiles, props, or weapons; and drawings and paintings suggesting atmosphere, lighting, and form of the environment in which characters interact.

During initial meetings with the development team, Concept Artists are assigned to produce art from initial idea to final concept. Everything they design they first create on paper as a rough concept that must fit with the general look and feel of the game. For example, if they are assigned to design a futuristic spaceship with personality, first they gather source material before commencing with their actual design. Working from existing art and photographs or a basic notion of what they have in mind, they may next create preliminary drawings on paper to work out the object's appearance and shape.

In discussing his process of creating concept art, the Concept Artist Wayne Barlowe explained in an interview with PasteMagazine.com, "I can come to the drawing table either with a complete notion of what I want to do or with none at all. It varies quite a lot depending upon the subject. I frequently let my pencil do the thinking. Technically speaking, I use the side of my Wolff's carbon pencil to rough in forms, and in that process many abstract shapes emerge, which I exploit in a design sense. Interesting solutions that otherwise might not have presented themselves come through, and I find that it keeps the drawings fresh and alive."

The Avalanche Software Concept Artist Ryan Wood, who set out originally to pursue a career in illustration until finding his calling as a Concept Artist in the video game industry, tackles developing conceptual art of characters once he has "a good idea" of specific character traits. An understanding of backstory and other character relationships also helps. After that, he likes to have a few actors' voices in mind to help him visualize the characters' behavior. Wood uses an illustrative approach that makes it challenging to visualize how he is going to animate sometimes. He usually tries to make the characters interesting looking in some way.

The approach to creating concept art for a video game is basically the same as for a film. It all starts with a good design, and "the reality of a character having to move is pretty much the same in both cases," Barlowe added, "which means, of course, that the character has to look good from all angles."

The process of completing a concept varies. Concept Artists may start a new concept and finish it within hours or a few days. Once their artwork is approved, Concept Artists clean up the artwork. This step involves scanning the designs onto a computer and using art painting software, such as Painter or Photoshop, to modify and perfect the line work and add needed details. At this stage, they also derive what colors will be used to create the right color balance, from which texture artists create the correct textures for the character, object, or environment. Wood, whose work has been featured in video games for Nickelodeon and Disney, uses Painter almost exclusively for his drawings. He creates a full black and white value study after he scans in his line drawing. After he gets to a point where he is happy with it, he does a selection using image luminance and pastes it onto a separate layer. After that, he paints some rough color washes underneath the sketch on the base.

After the concept artwork is completed, it is passed on to the 3-D modeler and animator to create a final animated version. At some studios, Concept Artists also participate in game play test sessions of the completed game to assess whether additional adjustments are needed before it is mass-produced and distributed.

The business of concept art extends beyond games. Concept Artists are also employed in the film and animation industry and are responsible for creating concept art for blockbuster movies and big-screen adaptations.

Work conditions for Concept Artists are similar to those for other positions in the industry. They work either in a studio or home-based setting (for freelancers) that offers sufficient comfort and work space. The work itself requires long periods of sitting and extensive and repeated use of the eyes, hands, and wrists. Concept Artists work 40 hours or more a week.

Salaries

Salaries for Concept Artists depend on experience, skill, training, and location. Full-time employees usually receive fringe benefits, including 401(k) plans and health insurance. Entry-level salaries for this position, based on multiple industry sources, range from $20,000 to $40,000, and the more skilled and experienced you are, the better you are paid—an average of $61,925 and up to $100,000 per year, according to Job-Salary.com.

Employment Prospects

Employment opportunities for Concept Artists are mostly fair, as hiring is limited to the most qualified individuals. Finding work is therefore difficult and is as much about experience and networking as it is about innate artistic talent. Many Concept Artists begin their careers as graphic artists, illustrators, and graphic novelists. Others working in the animation or special effects industry move into concept art, jumping to this area of production via storyboarding. According to the U.S. Bureau of Labor Statistics, Concept Artists being hired are those with the best training and portfolios. Your best course of action is to take what you can get at first. Focus on working for a single game company or working in a single style, and pursue other artistic opportunities to broaden your talents and bolster your résumé. Continue to network with others in the industry as you continue to gain experience.

Advancement Prospects

Some artists with leadership or supervisory aspirations become lead Concept Artists who collaborate with art and design leads to shape the vision and lead a concept team in creating art for games. Previous lead-level or equivalent experience is usually required. Others with five years or more experience working as an artist, Concept Artist, or illustrator become senior Concept Artists, who creates sketches and digital paintings and mentor junior Concept Artists in fulfilling the product's vision.

Education and Training

Becoming a Concept Artist requires a heavier focus on experience and networking compared to other jobs. Many have attended or graduated with degrees from art schools or universities, but this is not always required. A fine arts or visual design degree or equivalent work experience is usually sufficient, including training and course work encompassing all aspects of art and design. One of the most important aspects of becoming a good Concept Artist is to develop strong skills in drawing, painting, illustration, graphic design, and 3-D art. Part of any curriculum should also include classes in life drawing to learn as much as you can about anatomy, proportion, and skeletal structures, and design, which teaches how to compose and produce realistic and captivating landscapes and environments that will help you know how to make unreal creations seem real. Additional study of animation, graphic design, illustration, and technical drawing are vital in further developing your illustration and rendering skills, both essentials on the job.

Concept Artists come from many different professional and educational backgrounds, but as the conceptual designer and illustrator Francis Tai told ImagineFX.com, "There are many different paths you can take to achieve this, but they all involve certain elements . . . probably the main thing to remember is that the job is principally about design—yes, illustration and rendering skills are very important. Getting a concept design job in the games industry means being able to define and solve problems given varying amounts of information and being able to communicate ideas clearly and effectively."

Experience, Skills, and Personality Traits

Employers require anywhere from two to five years of video game production experience for this position. To achieve great success in the game art industry, Concept Artists must possess a creative passion for games and outstanding character and animal illustration skills. They require a critical eye and a solid grasp of anatomy proportion, perspective, and motion. They should have superior painting skills and the ability to illustrate concepts in a variety of forms based on verbal and written directions or ideas. Concept Artists require expert knowledge of industry-standard 3-D software packages, including 3-D Studio MAX or Maya, Adobe Illustrator, and Photoshop. A strong traditional art background, including color theory, lighting, and shading, is a plus.

Concept Artists must also be able to adapt to the visual intent of the project and work with a high degree of self-direction and self-motivation. They require proven organizational and analytical skills to meet designated production schedules and deadlines and to think critically and resolve complex issues on the job. They need to work well under and respond well to pressure. Concept Artists also should be receptive to constructive criticism.

Unions and Associations

Concept Artists in the gaming industry are currently without union representation. However, individuals find membership in one or more leading organizations beneficial in terms of providing a host of resources and networking opportunities. They include the International Game Developers Association, devoted to industry professionals who create games, and the Graphic Artists Guild (www.graphicartistsguild.org), which represents graphic artists, animators, cartoonists, designers, illustrators, and digital artists. Others join ACM SIGGRAPH (www.siggraph.org) for computer graphics professionals and the CGSociety (www.cgsociety.org) for digital artists.

Tips for Entry

1. Develop your love of designing and never put your pencil down. Always keep imagining, and focus on being creative. Pick an aspect of drawing you really enjoy, and practice everyday in order to produce your best work.

2. Learn the principles involved in the creation of traditional animation and background art—character attitude, emotion, and motivation—all of which are important in creating believable characters and environments for games.

3. Watch industry-related DVDs, such as the Gnomon Workshop series, which provides professional training for artists in the entertainment and design industries, and video tutorials showing how artists create their works and discuss the process.

4. Team up with other artists interested in gaming, and make a game or "mod" (modification of a popular game). You can include this work in your portfolio.

5. Sign up and become part of online communities such as ConceptArt.org to see how professionals work and to get valuable feedback.

ENVIRONMENT ARTIST

Duties: Build, model, texture, and light different environmental assets from 3-D inception to a finished game

Alternate Title(s): None

Salary Range: $38,000 to $65,000.

Employment Prospects: Good

Advancement Prospects: Good

Best Geographical Location(s): Atlanta, Austin, Dallas, Chicago, Los Angeles, Seattle, San Diego, San Francisco

Prerequisites:

Education and Training—Undergraduate degree in game and art design

Experience—Up to two years experience in 2-D and 3-D animation in a game environment with at least one shipped title for a major game platform

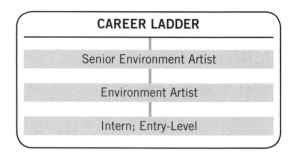

CAREER LADDER

Senior Environment Artist

Environment Artist

Intern; Entry-Level

Special Skills and Personality Traits—Creative, expressive, and imaginative; artistic and technical skills; strong color, design, and composition skills; well organized; team player

Position Description

As part of the game art and design team, Environment Artists create all aspects of environmental artwork. They produce all level models, textures, and surfaces for a compelling scene within specifications and allocated time.

Environment Artists usually work for an art director, an environment lead, and a game producer, who makes the ultimate decisions regarding what goes in the game and how it will look. Once such decisions are made, during preproduction, Environment Artists are assigned different pieces, or "assets," to create for specific regions in the game. They employ various tools and common industry toolsets, including such 3-D applications as Maya, 3-D Studio MAX, and ZBrush, to create models and apply textures and surfaces used in scenes. The environment lead then reviews them to make sure they meet the desired vision. Tasks of Environment Artists usually involve the construction of a diverse visual range of environments, terrains, hard-surface objects, props, characters, models, and hand-painted textures. In the process, Environment Artists demonstrate a strong grasp of color, scale, proportion, and lighting. In collaborating on and building required assets, they may find or use reference images and other sources of inspiration before creating any game assets. As Megan Sawyer, an Environment Artist for Bethesda

Softworks, stated in profile of her career on Gaming Angels.com, "I find inspiration in everything, from board games to movies to random photos I come across on Flickr. I've learned a lot from my coworkers, and people are always sharing new tips and techniques with each other."

Working closely with senior artists, Environment Artists create and maintain an art style and cohesive look and feel throughout the game by a consistent quality of work. Throughout the process, they also communicate with designers, programmers, and fellow artists, in addition to troubleshooting or fixing "bugs" in the process and providing constructive feedback on outsourced assets, if applicable.

During the course of a day, Environment Artists spend most of their time in front of a computer. On a typical morning, they load up all the files on the computer they are using and work for several hours before breaking for lunch and then picking up where they left off while checking in with their respective environment leads. Once a week, they meet as a group to review every artist's work and progress.

One of the most challenging aspects of the job is the technical limitations. Even though technological advances are being made at a breakneck pace, Environment Artists must always work within a given set of parameters, which may be frustrating at times. Furthermore, the job itself can be both physically and mentally demanding. It requires prolonged sitting in front of a computer and repetitive movement of the wrists. Environment Artists are known to work a standard 40-hour workweek; additional hours may be required to meet project deadlines.

Salaries

Earnings for Environment Artist, as reported by Payscale.com, range from $38,000 to $65,000. As with all positions in the gaming industry, wages vary by location, size of company, and experience level.

Employment Prospects

With ramped-up production of games in all formats and continued explosion of the gaming arts, employment opportunities, based on various industry reports, are good. Getting a foot in the door as an Environment Artist is relatively easier than for a character artist or concept artist. However, given the competition for such positions, beginning artists have a better chance of finding employment with smaller game studios to start; with experience, they can gradually work their way up in their careers. Larger studios draw a mix of more experienced and up-and-coming artists.

Aaron Canaday, an Environment Artist at Bioware Austin, decided to pursue the field while attending the Art Institute of California, San Diego, where he received a bachelor's degree in game and art design. He learned from his instructors, many of whom worked at local game studios, which jobs were less competitive within the industry. As he explained in an in-depth online interview, "It became clear to me very early on that environment art would be a much easier way to get my foot in the door as opposed to character art or concept art. Although I do have friends who landed positions in character or concept art, I'm really glad that I made the decision I did. Not only are environment jobs more widely available, it's a type of work I enjoy doing a lot. I tend to be a 'people person,' and environment art interfaces with many different jobs such as concept, design, visual effects, and animation. It's a really cool experience to see the ins and outs of other people's job, as well being able to meet and become friends with such a wide range of people."

Canaday broke into the industry after getting an internship at a local game company, High Moon Studios, working on a game version of the movie *The Bourne Conspiracy*. When the internship became available, he was one of the "lucky" people to be accepted. After his internship ended, he applied for environment art jobs at many places before landing a full-time gig

at Bioware Austin, which thought his art style was well suited for them, within a few months of graduating. As he candidly stated, "I can honestly say that between my internship, finishing up school, and working on my portfolio, that was by far the hardest I have ever worked and the least I have slept! If I hadn't have spent that extra effort, I'm convinced I would have needed an extra six months or more after graduation to polish my portfolio and land a job."

A visually dynamic and well-assembled portfolio can often make the difference. Applicants should include in their portfolio, however, only artwork that is unique and that makes you the most marketable for the job.

Advancement Prospects

Based on recent reports by various industry sources, advancement prospects for Environment Artists are particularly good. After establishing themselves, with only three to four years of experience, they can become senior environment artists leading a small team of Environment Artists in creating assets for a variety of games.

Education and Training

An undergraduate degree, usually in game and art design, is preferred. Many Environment Artists obtain their education at art schools that offer accredited programs in game arts. Instructors who actually work in the industry usually teach these programs. Programs are often a combination of fine art and technical art classes. Typically, courses cover drawing, human anatomy, color, design, composition, modeling, texturing, and lighting—all valuable skills an artist needs to work in the trade. Film or theater classes are extremely beneficial, as students learn how to set up a physical stage with props, which is good practice for arranging game scenes.

Experience, Skills, and Personality Traits

At least one to two years of 2-D, 3-D, and/or animation or game experience developing games for next-generation (future) game consoles and computers with at least one shipped title is usually preferred. Top-level Environment Artists must be talented and self-motivated. They must have strong traditional art skills with a great eye for detail and a natural flair for color, composition, design, and architecture. Exceptional drawing abilities to accurately create models from concept through to final output are essential. Environment Artists must have a complete understanding of modeling, texturing, and painting practices and proper building techniques to produce realistic 3-D models. They also require up-to-date knowledge of current art and lighting techniques, development processes, and methods of optimizing art assets for game engines of different types.

Apart from their creative abilities, Environment Artists must possess good time-management and follow-through abilities and a thorough knowledge of one or more high-end 3-D modeling packages, such as Maya, 3-D Studio MAX, and ZBrush, and other third-party software, including Photoshop or Painter, to bring their creative vision to life. Furthermore, they must have a strong grasp of game development, 3-D art pipelines, and platform performance restrictions. In addition, they must have the ability to take artistic and technical direction. They must have good written and verbal communication skills so they can successfully work in a team environment.

Unions and Associations

Membership in the International Game Developers Association (http://www.igda.org/), the largest nonprofit membership organization serving individuals who create video games, is beneficial to Environment Artists, as it brings together game professionals and developers at conferences, in local chapters, and in special interest groups to network and improve their craft. Other industry associations, such as the National Video Game Association (www.nvgaonline.com), which features four regional chapters across the country and member forums, and online organizations, such as Gamasutra, a division of United Business Media and publisher of the print magazine *Game Developer,* which features resources for game professionals, including a job posting board, may be helpful for networking as well.

Tips for Entry

1. Take an hour each day to draw and learn about anatomy, color, design, and composition. Keep up the practice. Know that it may take at least a year before you produce something worth looking at, but do not give up.
2. Spend a large part of your time playing games and getting to understand what makes a game entertaining.
3. Show professionals your work to get feedback on how to improve and make your environments better.

GAME DESIGNER

CAREER PROFILE

Duties: Use graphic design, animation, and coding techniques to invent and build interactive games

Alternate Title(s): None

Salary Range: $10,000 to $150,000

Employment Prospects: Good

Advancement Prospects: Fair to Good

Best Geographical Location(s): Atlanta, Austin, Dallas, Chicago, Los Angeles, Seattle, San Diego, San Francisco

Prerequisites:

Education and Training—Bachelor's degree in game art and design, video game design, or a related field

Experience—Three years or more of professional game design experience

Special Skills and Personality Traits—Creative; artistic; innovative; good planner; organized; under-

standing of game theory and design, game play, scenarios, activities, and game development and production; interface design and technical skills; knowledge of gaming trends; communication skills; creative problem-solver and troubleshooter

CAREER LADDER

Executive Producer; Creative Director

Game Designer; Lead Game Designer

Intern; Entry-Level

Position Description

Ever since the introduction of Atari and the first Nintendo game, video games have come a long way—very close to reality in their 3-D graphics, interplay, and visual presentation. Games have moved from arcades and consoles to personal computers and the Internet. The professionals responsible for creating them and making the gaming industry so successful are Game Designers. They create the compelling games that become popular with users and profitable for game companies. Ideally, each one is more exciting than the last and entertains, challenges, and even teaches gamers something in the process.

Game Designers create interactive digital environments for all types of gaming platforms, from cell phones to the latest Xbox. The field has broadened from traditional video games meant only to entertain to games that sell products and teach specific skills in strategy, design, and business that can be applied to a variety of professions. Some games raise awareness about important social issues.

As part of a game development team that often includes artists, animators, designers, technical directors, and programmers, Game Designers conceptualize the game from beginning to end. They design and define various aspects, including background story and plot, structure and story flow, rules and core game play,

difficulty levels and modes of play, interface design and community features, and props and avatars. It is a creative job that requires originality and visualization of game play experience. The challenge is designing an interesting game within the constraints of budgets and schedules. Successful designers have a broad range of intellectual interests that inspire them in their work, including books, movies, games, and more. When initiating a project, they usually determine what their objective is and explore ways to reach their goal until they come up with a satisfactory strategy to implement their design. Some designers first develop a scenario for the game, follow a game-genre heritage, or start from a technological premise and then build on their idea; others believe establishing a clear set of goals at the outset is the important factor in being successful.

Chris Crawford, considered the "dean of American game design," who made his game design debut at Atari in 1979, stated in a 2008 interview that the first step is deciding "what you want to accomplish, then do it. It's so simple, so obvious, yet so rarely done." He added, "For example, my last game, *Patton Strikes Back,* was designed with the goal of creating 'a war game for the rest of us.' Before that, I did *Balance of the Planet* with the goal of 'showing people how environmental problems interact with economic and cultural issues.' My most creative design, *Trust and Betrayal,* was built with the goal 'talk to the animals.' . . . If you don't know where you're going, you'll never get there."

The work that goes into design and development depends on the type of game—multimember online role playing game (MMORPG), role playing, story, battle, puzzle, arcade, learning/education, racing—and whether it is a single game or episodic. The creation of each game follows a similar pattern and has three basic phases: idea, prototyping, and conceptualization. Just like a book or movie, the design process begins with the idea. The Game Designer takes the creative lead in devising the plot that the game will revolve around. Most designers routinely review or evaluate competitive games, films, music, television shows, and other art forms as well as industry trends and audience interests, from which they generate their new game ideas. For example, if the designer wants a game in which the main character is supposed to restore order, he or she will develop a plot to fit that purpose; the game's levels and play will be based on the plot idea, and the characters will be created to the fit the designer's vision. During this stage, Game Designers, using 2-D and 3-D graphic design software, develop a design document of their vision and structure of the game they want to develop. Using 2-D concept layouts and 3-D mock-up screenshots, the document covers all aspects of formal game design, including sample menu layouts, game play flowcharts, and other graphic devices defining the core game features, role-play mechanics, missions, challenges, functionalities, audio direction, and required art to create it. They also write or supervise the writing of the game text and dialogue. After presenting the game design concepts to management and technical personnel, including artists, animators, and programmers, they collaborate with fellow designers, developers, artists, and others in developing the various elements of the game, including characters and environments, and achieving the appropriate visual style based on their approved concept.

Next, a prototype—or basic and early version of the game—is produced from the Game Designer's design. During prototyping, the designer works with the program lead to determine the feasibility of the design. They conduct regular design discussions among development teams in addition to managing its production to create a game-play prototype and solicit feedback from the creative design and technical staff. Afterward, they make adjustments as needed to the workings of the game, such as the rules, the plot, or player dynamics to make them more effective and improve the game play experience and to ensure the critical and commercial success of the product. Such refinements to their original conceptual framework may be in response to technical constraints, as not all concepts are possible. The early prototype may change several times before the actual game is rendered and produced.

After the designer's game design, narrative, plot, and level designs have been worked out during prototyping, the game is programmed and designed with 3-D artists, animators, character artists, and environment artists creating the actual animation and backdrops. Programmers and technical directors, including audio technicians, take what they have created and integrate it into a 3-D world for production, after which the game is tested and fixed under the Game Designer's oversight to ensure it meets the original vision and intended gaming experience before it is packaged, sold, and marketed.

The former Microsoft PC and Xbox game designer-turned-executive producer Paolo Malabuyo feels the most enjoyable part of designing games is "being able to create stuff—to come up with a cool idea and actually see it happen."

One growing trend has been toward producing more episodic adventure games, as they typically have a faster turnaround than the "more soul-crunching . . . 18-plus-month slog on a game that you're never entirely sure is going to work," said the game designer Mike Stemmle, formerly a lead designer with Lucas Arts. The development process is different for these games in that each game has a small cadre of designers in charge of the overall story and design for an entire season. After the core design for the season is approved, then specific designers are assigned and responsible for the design details of individual episodes and usually the script. It can take a few months to work out the overall story before any models are built or animation commences. As Stemmle enumerated in an interview with GamePro.com, "Once that's in place, designing the first episode begins in earnest. This usually takes a month. Then, while the script is being written, sets and character models are starting to get built, and rudimentary code writing begins. By the time the script is recorded (which takes another week), the animators have begun their work and are starting to hand things off to our 'choreographers.' Now the fun begins, as everyone piles on to cram everything into the game, all at once. This usually takes another four to six weeks, including time for a pick-up recording session and an external play test. All in all, it takes about three to four months to bring an individual episode from a vague idea to a finished product."

Computer Game Designers focus largely on making game-play decisions, such as how a specific monster should act and what the overall concept of a game should be. They do not worry as much about low-level game programming, fixes, or testing the game to make sure everything functions as intended before the game is released.

Aside from the artistic and creative challenges, there are many social and managerial dimensions to the job. Depending on the size of the company, Game Designers collaborate and interface with dozens of people, including the executive producer, creative director, animation artists, and sound and technical team to ensure the intent of the game design is upheld. Game Designers need creativity and vision coupled with communication skills to articulate their ideas to a team of people to get them to do what needs to done. "You need dedication to see your vision through—to work your way through the disappointments and failures," Malabuyo said. "When you're three months from shipping, working until 2 A.M.," you need to be dedicated.

Game Designers must make games that are difficult enough for success to be rewarding; at the same time, they must make sure games are not so challenging that players become frustrated and stop playing them. According to Malabuyo, a "game should quickly become an extension of [the player's] own ego, so [he or she is] no longer fighting the controls, but just doing it: flying the plane, doing cool moves, trying to shoot down the guy in front of them, and feeling" a sense of accomplishment.

Much of the game's success rides not only on its look, functionality, playability, appeal, and numerous other factors. In addition to these factors, game concepts must be innovative and original, which is a major challenge.

Game Designers often work hectic and long hours, including evenings and weekends, to meet project deadlines. Working conditions are mostly informal and provide opportunities to work with interesting people in games development. It is worth noting that game development is largely a male-dominated field. This is not to say, however, that talented female designers with a passion for gaming cannot find success.

Salaries

Salaries for Game Designers are difficult to pinpoint due to persistent changes in the market and the fact that game design is a fairly new field. According to Game Develop Research's ninth annual Game Developer Salary Survey in 2009, the salary for the position was up 3 percent to $69,266; the average design salary, including design leads and creative directors, is listed at $61,859. The range may vary depending on a variety of factors, including experience, talent, location, and the size of the projects worked on. Because of these fac-

tors, salaries range from $10,000 to around $150,000 a year for highly experienced and high-level designers. Most Game Designers with a modicum of talent usually start at $35,000 to $40,000 a year. Extraordinarily talented senior designers are more likely to make $80,000 to $90,000 a year. Typically, Game Designer with four to five years of experience—classified as junior Game Designers—can make from $42,000 to $60,000 per year. Experienced Game Designers, on the other hand, usually draw from $72,000 to $96,000.

Employment Prospects

With sales of games generating billions of dollars annually with no letup in sight, prospects for Game Designers are good. The U.S. Bureau of Labor Statistics projects average growth of 7 to 13 percent for this and other computer specialists' jobs through 2018. The tremendous growth of many established and renowned international game companies and the rise of new independent and individually owned game design and outsourcing companies producing higher-quality and large- and small-scale games should translate into a strong demand for Game Designers in the immediate future as well. A hotbed in the games industry remains major urban areas throughout the United States, where games companies have sprouted up. Outside the United States, places such as Vancouver, Canada, and Singapore provide solid opportunities for employment.

The field, however, is hard to break into, and only qualified people generally land jobs in this field. Professionals with design expertise and original ideas to back up that skill usually have a leg up on landing opportunities in this field. Most work for small, privately owned studios and sell the rights to their creations to game publishers who then market and sell the games to the public. With so many different career paths to take in this field, some opt to use their design and technical skills to work as concept artists and 3-D artists, animators and level designers, or programmers and quality assurance testers. Others apply their talent and skills to marketing and game distribution.

Advancement Prospects

Overall, advancement opportunities for Game Designers are good. For professional Game Designers, the most likely career progression is into more administrative and managerial positions. Game Designers with at least five years of experience often make the leap to lead Game Designer, leading a team of designers in producing a game design for the creative director. In some markets, the most highly talented and experienced individuals move up to become senior Game Designers and then senior designers, overseeing design from conception to completion. Others choose to take on more executive management roles as creative directors—employed mostly by development studios and publisher-owned and independent game companies—who oversee multiple projects at once, make high-level decisions that affect how the game plays, and oversee the entire game development process. Successful designers with senior-level game development experience usually fill these positions. Some climb the ladder to the highest position possible, executive producer. Executive producers manage all phases of project development.

Education and Training

While the best preparation for a career in game design is having a love of games and playing them, a Game Designer must meet certain educational criteria. In the past, an associate's degree from a two-year college or vocational and trade school was accepted, but many companies now require a bachelor's degree in game art and design, video game design, or a related field from a four-year university. Based on a survey of employees in the computer science field (including games) age 25 to 44 by the U.S. Bureau of Labor Statistics, 68 percent of respondents have a bachelor's degree or higher, and only 25 percent have some college background. Individuals need a base of knowledge in game programming and 3-D design skills in addition to strong creative abilities and conceptual thinking skills. To excel in this position, candidates should become well-versed in game design, particularly computer and video games, by developing strong math and computer skills in high school in preparation for taking college-level programming courses. English and creative writing classes will help students hone scriptwriting and story development abilities. Art classes in drawing and design are also necessary.

Undergraduates in game design typically gain artistic and technical knowledge through course work that focuses mostly on game design. Most curricula give students hands-on experience as well as a broad knowledge of the field. Classes usually fall into three categories: art and design, technology, and business. Art and design classes include 2-D and 3-D animation principles, drawing, effects animation, level and character design, modeling, painting, sculpture, visual storytelling, story and character development, storyboarding, and creative writing. Technology classes generally cover computer programming, game development and supporting technologies, game theory and game production, history of games, sound production, motion capture, and artificial intelligence. Business classes focus on project management and marketing.

The key to landing a good job is to create a portfolio of original work to show prospective employers that effectively illustrates your talent and game design skills.

Experience, Personality Traits, and Skills

Most game companies prefer to hire Game Designers with three years or more of professional experience in game design. A career as a Game Designer requires artistic and technical skill and a passion for games. Game Designers have the ability to create innovative concepts, mechanics, and ideas for compelling game play, scenarios, activities, and encounters for the advanced and casual game audience. Therefore, they have a thorough understanding of major elements of game theory and design for many different game platforms, including story, dialogue, character interaction, mission and environment design, AI (artificial intelligence), combat, strategy, flow, balance, difficulty, and what makes a game appealing to different audiences. Consequently, they are great creative thinkers with meticulous analysis and planning skills. They are able to conceptualize, communicate, and implement their game ideas using their interface design skills and various tools, technology, and knowledge of gaming trends.

Game Designers are highly organized and efficient in terms of allocating work within a team environment. They possess the ability to productively discuss their ideas with both the creative and noncreative stakeholders and make decisions and communicate their ideas to effectively influence members of the design, art, and programming teams to produce the desired outcome.

Unions and Associations

Most Game Designers are members of the International Game Developers Association (www.igda.org), a leading not-for-profit organization that gives designers a chance to network via conferences, events, and online forums to advance their careers. Another option is the Academy of Interactive Arts & Sciences (http://www.interactive.org/), which serves the needs of professionals in art and graphics, animation, interactive design, production, software engineering, sound design, testing and quality assurance, and other aspects of the interactive software industry.

Tips for Entry

1. Play a lot of games, and develop a passion for them. Keep a list of the games you play, including their strengths and weaknesses, and share your views with other gamers on online bulletin boards and newsgroups.

2. Read about gaming and design at your local library and on the Internet. Write and draw whatever interests or inspires you. Create your own graphics, and polish your art skills. Develop good habits of working on projects and completing them.

3. Get actively involved in the industry while building your career. Host multiplayer game parties. Act out or perform the roles of your favorite characters. Volunteer for beta testing of games as they become available (for announcements of public betas, visit http://www.bluesnews.com).

Get involved in building levels or modifications for games; use them as demos of your work, and add the best ones to your résumé.

4. Create and design your own pencil puzzles, brainteasers, crosswords, card games, board games, and others. All make great additions to include in your cover letter and portfolio.

5. Build a portfolio illustrating your talent and game design skills. Post your work on online game community forums to get feedback and improve your work while getting your name known and building important contacts in the industry.

LEAD ANIMATOR

Duties: Direct the animation team to ensure quality and consistency of style for all motion throughout a game; realize the director and art director's overall vision while collaborating with the programming and design departments

Alternate Title(s): Animation Director; Directing Animator

Salary Range: $65,000 to $90,000

Employment Prospects: Excellent

Advancement Prospects: Good

Best Geographical Location(s): Atlanta, Dallas, Chicago, Los Angeles, Seattle, San Diego, San Francisco

Prerequisites:

Education and Training—Bachelor's degree in animation, computer science, or a related field from an art or technical college recommended

Experience—Equivalent years of experience (however long it takes) producing two shipped games

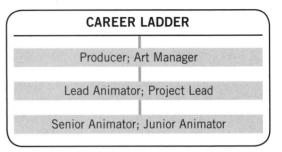

with a background in animation, character rigging, character weighting, and tool development

Special Skills and Personality Traits—Supervisory and leadership abilities; eye for animation quality assurance; technical knowledge of animation software; time management skills; understanding of other departments and disciplines related to the animation department; communication and mentoring skills

Position Description

In the development of every video game, Lead Animators are the driving force in the creation of high-quality animation that defines the game-play experience and contributes to the success of the project as a whole. Talented animators themselves, Lead Animators have an undying enthusiasm and passion for animating games and characters. Relying on their leadership and mentoring abilities and creative skills and knowledge of their craft, they manage a team of in-house animators and storyboard artists. Their responsibilities include showing their staff how a character should look, move, and interact within a game environment and checking the content and technical integrity of their work so it meets the creative vision of the director and art director. Furthermore, they may oversee the work of other artists, designers, level builders, and scripters in the game pipeline to make sure the animation meets production standards.

From the outset, Lead Animators establish, with the art director, the desired level and quality of animation assets (characters and objects) and style of the major animation, including character and creature animation and design of the project. At least once a week, Lead Animators hold animation team meetings to talk about

their progress and any relevant issues or priorities. They work in collaboration with both lead or system designers and game play programmers throughout a game's creation.

Lead Animators guide their teams through the various stages of creation. In the early stages of development, supervision of their team's creation of fleshy and flexible human characters and creatures, allowing for precise humanlike behavior and a full range of motion required, is an involved and iterative process. First, they produce the initial character animation to perform key poses and actions required of them in a game-play setting. Working with programmers, Lead Animators manipulate the animation using a controller to check its overall fluidity and how well it plays in the game's engine system. Following this game-play review, they direct their animators to make any required fixes. Once the necessary changes are made and the Lead Animator approves it, the animators make the final animation.

If motion capture—importing and animating subjects filmed in live action—is used, Lead Animators also plan and execute all motion capture sessions. Likewise, they may also serve as the primary actor/director for character and creation motion capture, in addition to directing both game and cinematic animation if required.

Lead Animators employed by game companies typically work in a corporate environment. Freelancers, on the other hand, are sometimes afforded the opportunity to work in their own home or studio. Lead Animators may work at a drafting table or primarily use a computer. While freelancers set their own hours, those in a corporate environment usually work a standard 40-hour workweek. Overtime may be required if there are pressing deadlines.

Salaries

Level of experience, quality of work, and supply and demand are among several factors game companies used in determining the salary or wages paid for this position. The salaries of Lead Animators, based on multiple industry sources, typically range from $1,800 to $2,200 per month. In the Seattle and West Coast region, where many game companies are located, salaries average around $1,600 per week. The size of the company can mean about a 10 percent difference in wages from smaller to bigger studios. Lead Animators with three to five years of experience can earn from $4,000 to $5,000 and, with six years or more, up to $7,000 or more a month. Wages for freelancers include added pay to cover insurance costs

Employment Prospects

Based on industry reports, prospects for employment are excellent. Even with the trend going more toward outsourcing, Lead Animators are needed to direct the work being done out of house by such companies. "More junior animation jobs are getting outsourced overseas, but the casual games industry has opened up a floodgate of opportunities [for those] who know Flash [animation] and can animate in 2-D," explained the Seattle-based games industry senior animator and Lead Animator Ted Warnock. "Junior and senior positions are also going more toward a Hollywood model of contracting to prevent traditional development studios from laying people off."

Game companies often employ only one Lead Animator per project, and positions are usually full time and considered part of the permanent upper-management staff. Most start out in the industry as junior animators and advance to become senior animators. Those who choose a managerial path tend to become a project lead and then Lead Animator. Those set on an exclusively artistic path start as animators and instead work to become senior animator, then character artist and, after considerable experi-

ence, animation director and art director. Opportunities for Lead Animators are limited according to area and region and by how much game development is presently going on in each area.

Major game development hotbeds like the San Francisco and Seattle areas have huge pools of talent, with some areas also having game development schools to add to their already existing pools and therefore are more competitive. DigiPen Institute of Technology, a games school based in Kirkland, Washington, that offers associate's degree programs in 3-D computer animation and associate and bachelor's degrees in computer science is a good example.

To land work as a Lead Animator, an individual must first and foremost be a good animator with a high-quality demo reel. Warnock recommends individuals seeking this position research other film and gaming industry animators through sites such as mobygames.com and honestly compare their reels. "The closer you get to their quality, the better chance you have of getting the job," he added. It is also imperative that you stay ahead of the curve in other areas, including technology, management skills, and present game quality standards to be considered for positions.

Advancement Prospects

Overall, chances for upward mobility from this position are good. Lead Animators typically advance to upper-level positions such as studio manager and producer. Advancement is generally easier at smaller studios than larger ones. Progression will largely depend on your creative talent and skills, your distinctive style, your reputation, and your recognition among your peers. "This is 50 percent of your advancement," according to Warnock. "The other 50 percent is the quality of your work and the titles you have shipped."

Education and Training

Most game companies require a bachelor's degree in animation, computer science, or an equivalent. Sometimes some education combined with game experience will suffice, however. "A BA doesn't hurt, but is unnecessary," Warnock offered. "A BA with a low-quality demo reel, however, means nothing."

Warnock recommends that candidates attend a specialized animation school to learn the basics, including extensive course work in computer science to cover the technical aspects of the job and how to produce a good-looking show reel that will get you your first junior level animator job. Among technical schools, Animation Mentor.com graduates and students have solid job opportunities.

Both art and technical schools and universities offer undergraduate programs to prepare individuals to work in the field. Complete course work in traditional hand-drawn animation, life drawing, acting, and CG animation, including proficiency in CG software, such as Maya, is recommended.

Experience, Skills, and Personality Traits

Experience equivalent to producing shipped games is the minimum requirement. Successful Lead Animators must thrive in a team environment. They are self-motivated, organized, and effective managers and teachers. Ideally, they have experience working closely with directors and clients doing lead animation on games or on prototypes. In addition, Lead Animators require a strong understanding of the computer graphics production process in the game production pipeline.

Lead Animators must have working knowledge of 3-D animation tools, preferably Maya, and tool development, plus an understanding of animation principles and work methods. They should be skilled in developing characters, character rigging, character weighting, and creating animation in a variety of styles and formats. Animation, drawing, and sculpting skills are a plus. Lead Animators should bring passion and enthusiasm to the job.

Unions and Associations

Some Lead Animators are members of the CGSociety (http://www.cgsociety.org), which provides forums, workshops, and job support to its members. Other industry associations, such as the International Game Developers Association (http://www.igda.org) and Computer Game Artists Association (http://www.vectorg.com/cga/CGA.htm), are useful as well for career advice, educational opportunities, events, and networking.

Tips for Entry

1. Produce a high-quality demo reel of comparable quality to leading game animators in the industry and whose work you admire.

2. Contact game animators you admire through their Web sites to seek their advice and feedback.

3. Join online game communities, such as Gamasutra (http://gamasutra.com/), and professional recruitment sites, including Creative Heads (www.creativeheads.net), to post your profile, résumé, and a portfolio of your work to be viewed by others. Do not be afraid to apply for opportunities in the industry.

4. Become involved in your school's alumni association, and participate in activities and events to share and network with others.

TECHNICAL ARTIST

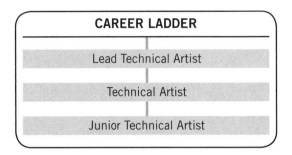

CAREER LADDER

Lead Technical Artist

Technical Artist

Junior Technical Artist

Position Description

Generally speaking, the job of Technical Artists is to balance the aesthetics and technical performance of the creative elements in producing computer and video games. As a member of the art team, they are also known as technical directors and sometimes are differentiated in their title by their designated specialty, such as character rigging, shading, or tools.

Technical Artists mostly act as a liaison between art and code to ensure the smooth running of asset creation, artist workflow, and production pipelines. They help bridge the gap between art and programming that spans multiple platforms, including multiplayer and next-generation games. They identify potential workflow and production pipeline improvements and develop various content creation tools and solutions, supporting 3-D artists and animators in their creation of game assets.

Part of Technical Artists' job is pipeline cohesion and getting art packages—on computer systems and software—to "talk to each other," which is a real challenge. "I've always enjoyed learning the new software and trying to figure out how to get complex data like skeletons and animation from [one] package to another," stated Jason Parks, a senior Technical Artist at Sony Online Entertainment in an online interview.

"All the new technologies will at a minimum need some sort of scripts and infrastructure set in place to facilitate data transfer. This takes an intimate knowledge of the data you're trying to transfer."

Technical Artists and technical directors have one thing in common: They solve technical problems in the creation and implementation of the varied aspects of game animation. Most Technical Artists have advanced knowledge of programming, text editing, scripting, and computer toolsets such as MEL, Python, Eclipse, and Visual Studio. They use this knowledge to create real-time scripts, debugging features, commands, interacting controls, and nonbuild type scripts that do everything from making 3-D software, such as Maya or MotionBuilder, run faster to improving building/rigging of animation models, DDS creation and light mapping, and export content in the production pipeline.

Technical Artists solve a variety of problems that arise in the production process. In some cases, they come up with the solution and instruct other people to fix it, but most video game houses are not staffed that way, so any solutions Technical Artists propose are usually drafted, documented, coded, and implemented by them. In their "free time," they may step in to make everything work better for the artists they interface with on a daily basis. For example, if they see an artist doing a repetitive task multiple times a day and there's a better solution, they may put down what they're doing, ask the artist why they do that task a specific way ("So how many times do you click those same 3 buttons in a day?"), and then write a script that circumvents the problem.

One of Technical Artists' greatest challenges is getting rigging (the setting up of) characters to be animated in 3-D form to work properly; they therefore need to know everything about animating skeletal models.

It is of paramount importance that Technical Artists stay current with developing technology and upgrades and be willing to adapt. According to Parks, "It seems like a TA is reinventing his or her skills all the time, so I don't think any technologies will change our roles much. Except for the fact that we need to be there to figure out, understand, and support the technology." Technical Artists have evolved into full-fledged tools programmers, database administrators, software architects, and more.

Ordinarily, the work environment for Technical Artists is highly structured. The job demands periodic sitting and standing and repetitive motions of the hands and wrists to work on computer systems. Deadlines and project scheduling may require working more than a standard 40-hour workweek.

Salaries

As video game technical directors, Technical Artists are among the highest paid in their profession. According to a Game Makers Salary Survey, Technical Artists with less than three years of experience make an average of $60,700 a year. With three to six years of experience, Technical Artists can earn as much as $73,000 and, after six years or more, about $110,000 annually.

Employment Prospects

Based on reports by leading industry sources, employment opportunities for Technical Artists are good. They occupy an extremely important niche in game production and preparation that will likely expand with continued industry growth. There will always be a need for professionals with technical know-how to figure out and solve technological issues and problems.

Advancement Prospects

Advancement opportunities are mostly good for those with exceptional technical and management skills. Some position themselves to become lead technical artists, who are responsible for establishing the art style and game technology of forthcoming titles for a studio or company. Positions open up less frequently higher up on the career ladder, with experienced artists taking most top spots as senior technical artists.

Education and Training

A degree in applied science, computer science, mathematics, physics, engineering, or technical arts is desirable. This includes formal training in 3-D computer animation (including human and creature anatomy, character and environment setup for animation, and animation principles), computer graphics, computer science, engineering, programming, and scripting. In some programs, additional courses in psychology, sociology, or interpersonal speech communications may be required. A well-rounded art background acquired through education and/or work experience, showing thorough understanding of color, form, light, texture, and visual balance and of commercial graphics packages, such as Maya, 3-D Studio Max, or others is an additional asset.

Experience, Skills, and Personality Traits

Individuals must have two years or more of professional game development experience, including at least one shipped title, and experience designing and troubleshooting art pipelines on three or more game consoles or systems to become Technical Artists. To be successful leaders, they must be self-motivated, reliable, friendly, and approachable. They must have strong visual and technical skills and be comfortable explaining technical concepts to artists. Technical Artists require a working knowledge of 3-D computer graphics, including lighting, rendering, and modeling. They must have strong programming, coding, and scripting skills and basic or advanced knowledge of scripting and coding languages, such C++, C#, MEL, Python, MAXscript, HLSL, and Cg. Basic knowledge of 2-D image manipulation tools for programs, such as Photoshop, is desirable. They must be skilled in developing content creation tools and pipelines, including scene exporting and in light mapping techniques. Furthermore, they need to have good communication skills and interpersonal skills to work alongside others in providing technical support as needed.

Unions and Associations

Technical Artists generally belong to ACM SIGGRAPH (http://www.siggraph.org/), the largest organization for computer graphics professionals. The organization offers events, forums, and educational and career portals for its members. The International Game Developers Association (http://www.igda.org/), a professional society for video and computer game developers and artists worldwide, is another option.

Tips for Entry

1. Learn problem-solving skills and how to simplify and abstract problems to their simplest components. Develop a strong understanding of modular techniques to know how to create scripts to automate repetitive work or "helper files" to load or bridge things in a scene.
2. Study the underlying principles, guidelines, and methods of artistic anatomy and basic mathematics used in creating 3-D game animation.
3. Develop and hone your art skills and your use of traditional and industry-standard software tools. Design, develop, create, and integrate your own assets to improve your skills. Include your best work in your portfolio.
4. Go to industry conferences to network with industry professionals. Participate in online forums to obtain critical feedback and guidance to further your career.

PAINTING AND TEXTURING

DIGITAL PAINTER

Duties: Scan and add color and details to animators' drawings using digital ink-and-paint systems

Alternate Title(s): 2-D Digital Painter; 3-D Digital Painter

Salary Range: $18,000+

Employment Prospects: Poor

Advancement Prospects: Good

Best Geographical Location(s): Los Angeles, San Francisco, New York

Prerequisites:

    Education and Training—A degree from an accredited art or animation school or two-year college

    Experience—Two years or more of production experience with 2-D or 3-D animation systems; for CG-animation, experience on a feature film or game preferred

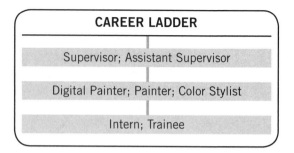

Special Skills and Personality Traits—Creativity; color, design, and drawing skills; knowledge of traditional and 3-D animation methods and systems; communication skills; ability to take direction; able to work collaboratively in a team setting

Position Description

For decades, until the manifestation of 3-D computer animation, animated motion pictures and television shows were produced in traditional hand-drawn animation, whereby animated drawings were usually inked (traced) and then painted onto transparent acetate by artists known as inkers and painters. Steady-handed professional inkers used fine brush strokes to painstakingly copy the perfectly cleaned-up work done by the clean-up artist onto clear acetate cels; a single complex drawing takes hours to ink by hand. They would draw animation on different levels with colors, purposely varying them based on their position and to compensate for table lighting of the animation before dispatching it to the paint department. There painters individually and meticulously hand-colored and painted the cels to be photographed. Many years later, to expedite the process, inkers and painters used a faster and cheaper process known as Xerography. This process consisted of using Xerox machines to produce exact copies of the animator's pencil drawings by photocopying them onto cels; it handled most of the coloring and inking of them as well.

The advent of computers advanced traditional hand-drawn animation by leaps and bounds. In the late 1980s, Walt Disney Studios introduced the now-defunct digital ink-and-paint system known as CAPS. The process, at its best, combined the precision of Xerography with the clean look of hand-engineered inking, doing what normally would take hours of painstaking work and largely eliminating the need for individual inkers and painters, though traditional background painters are still used on some 2-D animated productions.

Today, background paintings in 2-D animation are created using computers rather than traditional tools. Digital Painters perform much the same tasks as traditional background painters, only they set the scene, lighting, and mood and emphasize the joke or feeling in a scene using popular digital paint programs, such as Adobe Photoshop, Illustrator, and Painter. Some cartoons combine hand-painted and digital backgrounds.

In this entry-level role, Digital Painters work closely with production designers, production supervisors, and matte painting supervisors. As members of the production team made up of color stylists, scanners, painters, and compositors under the supervision of the head of color and compositing, Digital Painters are principally responsible for adding color to each frame of animation created by the animators. In this job, it is important that they exhibit a keen sense of detail, color, and continuity in their work as they apply to the standards of animation approved for the production.

First, they methodically scan the animators' original series of drawings onto a computer for processing using one of several kinds of digital ink-and-paint systems such as Photoshop, Illustrator, Painter, and others, including Animo, Toon Boom, Opus, and Toonz, to make necessary adjustments to colors, shapes, and details of the animation. In 2-D animation, this process is much cleaner and more economic. Drawings are combined in layers to layer each color with washes of transparent colors applied to each, respectively. The systems are far better than the old-fashioned ways of hand-painting because the artist has only to paint the area once, and the paint never strays from the lines, nor are they ever limited by what colors of paint or how much of that color they have in inventory. In 2009, the entire character animation (rough and clean-up) for Walt Disney's return to traditional hand-drawn features, *The Princess and the Frog*, was produced with pencil on paper and then scanned into Toon Boom for digital ink and painting.

On 3-D computer-animated productions, Digital Painters take direction from the director, production designer, and art director. They handle digital painting of models for shades, textures, patterns, and surface details needed to create depth, richness, and complexity. They demonstrate artistic versatility in their ability to match and adapt their painting style to suit a range of production designs and are generally resourceful in their approach to gathering needed references using a variety of media. In many instances, Digital Painters also supervise and train other 3-D painters while contributing to the painting process and production of the animation as a whole.

Digital Painters work in mostly comfortable and bright work areas. The job requires long stretches of sitting and repeated use of the eyes, hands, and wrists and can be mentally and physically taxing. Digital Painters usually work a standard 40-hour workweek, but additional hours may be required due to project deadlines and scheduling.

Salaries

The Animation Guild, Local 839, of the IATSE sets wages for this position. 2-D Digital Painters working in television make from $1,500 to $1,900 a week. 2-D painters working on full-length features are paid higher than those on television animation, as are digital painting supervisors. Hourly wages for 3-D Digital Painters in computer-animated features employed by a signatory studio such as DreamWorks Animation are $24.50 for the first three-months; $28.28 for the next nine months; $30.63 for the following six months; and $31.45 per hour thereafter.

Employment Prospects

Despite more cartoons using CG animation these days, according to industry sources, some popular cartoons and features still need painters, whether digital or traditional. However, given the state of the national economy and its sweeping impact on the arts, current prospects for employment are poor.

Advancement Prospects

Prospects for advancement for Digital Painters are good. Factors that affect advancement include experience, knowledge, and attitude. Talented and savvy individuals with working knowledge of multiple programs have the best chance to progress in the field. Generally, those who fit this description advance up the ladder to positions of greater responsibility, including color supervisor, art director, and director.

Education and Training

To work for a major-market film or television animation studio, a bachelor's degree in fine art, design, painting, or a related field is required. In some situations, a degree from an accredited art or animation school will suffice. To become a Digital Painter, undergraduates must hone their artistic and technical skills, as a strong background in composition, color, design, and painting and a working knowledge of computer programs, such as Adobe Photoshop and Illustrator, is required.

Experience, Skills, and Personality Traits

More than two years of related experience is usually required; for CG productions, experience working on a feature film and/or game is ideal. Most Digital Painters require strong knowledge of the animation process, 3-D animation systems, and compositing. They must have solid design and drawing skills, an eye for color, a sense of sculptural detail, and strong organizational and follow-through skills. Digital Painters need to be able to paint projects in a fast-paced, dynamic, and deadline-driven environment, in accordance with expectations and budgets. In addition, they must have exceptional knowledge of traditional art skills—color, lighting, and composition—and be proficient in an array of programs, including Adobe Photoshop, Illustrator, and Painter, with an understanding of commonly used 3-D systems, such as Maya, and proprietary software used by studios. Furthermore, they must have excellent communication skills to clearly and effectively present their ideas, be able to take direction and meet objectives under direct supervision, and work collaboratively with a diverse team of professionals.

Unions and Associations

Membership in The Animation Guild, Local 839, of the IATSE is necessary to obtain union-guaranteed wages and other benefits, including health and pension plans. Likewise, being a member offers opportunities to interact and network with other industry professionals and learn of job opportunities in the field.

Tips for Entry

1. In high school, take art classes, and learn how to draw and paint traditionally. Master your drawing ability to render finished details.

2. Develop a good sense of color, lighting, and perspective in your work. Become familiar with digital paint programs, such as Adobe Photoshop and Painter, to produce solid digital art.

3. Find online sites that will help you in the production of your craft, and become actively engaged in forums.

4. Never stop learning, and never stop growing as an artist.

MATTE PAINTER

Duties: Paint backgrounds and landscapes to interact with characters or objects in an animated scene

Alternate Title(s): Digital Matte Painter, Matte Artist

Salary Range: $30,000 to $120,000

Employment Prospects: Good

Advancement Prospects: Good

Best Geographical Location(s): Los Angeles, San Francisco, New York

Prerequisites:

Education and Training—A bachelor's degree in fine art, painting, or illustration preferred

Experience—Two years or more of related experience in 2-D painting and 3-D matte painting on animated productions

Special Skills and Personality Traits—Artistic; composition, color, and layout skills; knowledge of matte painting techniques; visual skills; proficiency in 3-D compositing software and 3-D animation system software; understanding of architectural design, landscape photography, and camera positioning; communication skills

CAREER LADDER

Art Director; Lead Matte Painter
Matte Painter; Compositor
Storyboard Artist; Layout Artist

Position Description

Working with the art director and under the paint or visual effect supervisor, Matte Painters, appropriately dubbed "scene makers" in the industry, are responsible for designing various environments in an animated film or television production. In this all-important role, they conceptualize and visualize ideas, including creating complex digital backgrounds and landscapes in which characters interact and that are vital to each scene.

Visual environments they produce for 2-D or 3-D computer-animated productions include realistic foregrounds, mid-grounds, and background paintings and landscapes that may include entire cities. Working with layout and models, they take such ideas from visual development to production-ready elements and provide troubleshooting of background components created when necessary. All of Matte Painters' work must adhere to the director's and production designer's overall vision of the project.

Most Matte Painters start their day by checking their shot list, a series of scenes they have been assigned to create and paint, as well as any notes regarding revisions and enhancements they have been asked to make to any shots in progress previously completed for approval. The work is physically demanding and laborious. Typically, Matte Painters work 40 to 60 hours per week, depending on their workload. They work on computers for long periods of time, requiring patience and hand-eye coordination as they create and paint a myriad of landscapes and environments with the click of a mouse using the paint software of choice.

Their renderings and paintings of imaginary worlds and landscapes not only establish shots and visually help the scene, but also convey mood, atmosphere, and depth. As Ronn Brown, the head of DreamWorks Animation's matte-painting department at its Glendale, California, facility, once attested, "Matte artists have, and always will be, a great alternative both financially and artistically for shots where it's not feasible to film in live action or build entire 3-D environments. The matte painters always bring a quality aesthetic to vista and set extension shots."

On CG animated features, Matte Painters are usually required to follow a specific style that they have to match that represents some semblance to reality without coming across like full-blown live-action, whether creating shots of landscapes or cities. On most productions, they work hand in hand with the art and light departments. Creating matte paintings for CG or computer animation requires a much different approach than for live-action films that use digital effects. For DreamWorks Animation's 2006 summer movie *Over the Hedge,* for example, Matte Painters were responsible for rendering two sets of extensive digitally painted images—both interior and exterior shots—throughout the film. This included creating compelling CG backgrounds, one indoor, the other outdoor. These series of images were then composited with shots of the characters into one image for each individual scene in the film.

Salaries

Wages for this position vary. According to its June 2010 Member Wage Survey, card-carrying member Matte Painters of The Animation Guild, Local 839, of the IATSE earned a minimum of $1,464 and maximum of $2,152.32 per week for a 40-hour workweek. The median weekly salary was $1,818.18. By comparison, journeymen Matte Painter made a minimum of $1,596.64 per week. Inexperienced nonunion Matte Painters can make around $20 an hour, and the rate can be higher depending on hours and experience. Freelancers with experience charge slightly more, while some charge the same hourly rate for freelance or contracted work. Most work on a project-by-project basis or are subcontracted to work for a certain amount of time at a negotiable hourly wage. Depending on the project, gigs can last from two weeks to six months or longer.

Employment Prospects

Prospects for this position are mostly good. According to the Los Angeles–based Matte Painter Holli Alvarado, demand for this position is solid, as the industry is "always going to need things painted, fixed, and created." Painting is also a cheaper option than, say, filming on location. Also, matte paintings are starting to be used in new, unique ways, which can create new positions for painters.

Most who work in the industry recommend that candidates research what kind of studio they want to work for and what type of employment they want—full-time staff at a studio versus freelancing for many studios—before applying. Apply even when there are no current openings because when a job suddenly opens up, having your résumé on file ahead of time can be a big advantage.

The best opportunities are in major urban areas where studios and postproduction houses are located. Depending on the size and nature of the production, employers may have as little as one to three Matte Painters. Freelancers can live anywhere and find work via the Internet. Alvarado, who freelances, has had many clients all over the world, but working in-house in a studio has its benefits.

Advancement Prospects

The chances of advancement from this position are mostly good. Some Matte Painters use their experience and skills to become senior Matte Painters. Other seasoned and talented Matte Painters seek to advance to more supervisory positions, such as matte painting supervisor, visual effects supervisor, and art director. The best way to increase chances of advancement is to start at the bottom, learn as much as you can, and work your way up.

Major cities offer more opportunities to move up and move around. As Alvarado explained, "I think it doesn't matter where you start—just that you learn, grow, and challenge yourself."

Education and Training

Most employers require a bachelor's degree in fine art, painting, or illustration. In some cases, a high school education and some postsecondary technical or vocational training will suffice. A strong background in art and knowledge of computers are essential. Most Matte Painters take courses in color theory, compositing, digital painting, and visual effects. They learn necessary computer skills and proficiency in painting and compositing techniques for matte painting in both animated and live-action productions. Specialized training may cover color theory, perspective, light-shadow concepts, camera mapping, modeling, texture (painting), photo manipulation, layering, and 2-D and 3-D projection and composition techniques on computers. Students can expect to use digital and 3-D application software, such as Photoshop, After Effects, Nuke, Maya, and 3-D Studio MAX.

Experience, Skills, and Personality Traits

Matte Painters typically have years of artistic training—a minimum of two years or more—and some animation and background experience as well as live-action visual effects experience. Many are able to do concept designs for visual development as well.

Matte Painters require a sophisticated eye and a strong skill set. They must have a good fundamental understanding of frame composition and components of painting. A solid résumé of postproduction work should attest to that, including experience in painting mattes and set extensions on traditional or computer-animated productions. Most studios want Matte Painters who are deadline oriented and exceptional team players with a high skill level in painting, composition, perspective, color, and traditional skills, such as painting in acrylic, oil, and pastel. Besides an understanding of basic compositing, Matte Painters must be able to use software for 3-D animation systems, such as Maya and Renderman, for painting, compositing, modeling, and more.

Alvarado had six years of Photoshop experience, but that was not enough to land her a job because she was switching industries. A studio internship proved invaluable to securing employment. Putting that experience on her résumé helped her secure full-time employment. She had a great mentor who not only talked with her about technique and process but also shared stories about the industry.

Employers generally prefer candidates who are patient, flexible, and dedicated to their work. Possessing good communication skills and a collaborative nature in working with others and solving problems is also important.

Unions and Associations

Many Matte Painters belong to The Animation Guild, Local 839, of the IATSE, and some are also members of what was formerly known as Illustrators and Matte Artists, Local 790, of the IATSE, which, in January 2003, merged with the Art Directors Guild, Local 800, in Los Angeles. Union membership is required to work on a studio or union film or television production and is beneficial for networking purposes and set wages and benefits, including health and pension plans.

Tips for Entry

1. Apply for internships to gain practical knowledge and experience.
2. Create an eye-catching portfolio featuring sample images of matte paintings and animation background paintings, along with traditional paintings. Include a shot breakdown to identify sections of the images or shots that you painted.
3. Get involved in online animation forums where others in the industry congregate to talk shop and connect with other professionals.
4. Practice your craft doing speed painting every day.
5. Post your speeding paintings, sketches, doodles, and masterpieces online—anything to get your name out there.
6. Know your assets, and sell yourself.
7. Be professional, organized, and creative in selling your skills.
8. Be humble. No one likes a know-it-all.

TEXTURE ARTIST

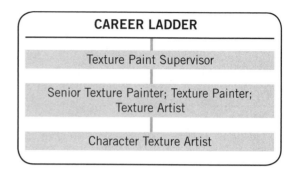

Position Description

In the chain of production, Texture Artists handle the complex and technically demanding job of painting the surfaces that define the look and feel of 2-D and 3-D animation in computer-animated movies, television shows, and video games.

In the film and television world, under the direction of the art director and director, Texture Artists' work entails creating a wide variety of textures and types of surfaces using computer paint tools and systems. Early on in the process, as part of the design team, they work with the look development technical directors (on a CG-animated film) to create materials that define the look of 3-D characters and objects used in the production. They also help determine painterly and realistic texture styles and various design solutions for material creation and appearance as well as unification and variation of such methods. In painting a variety of digital textures, Texture Artists perform their visual magic using a proprietary and expression-driven computer toolset that may include a variety of other popular paint programs, from Maya to Photoshop, to efficiently create procedural textures and manipulate shades of colors to define the organic surface qualities of 3-D animation.

Working with the animation supervisor, Texture Artists create optimal UV layouts (mapping of the characters or objects) and collaborate with the modeling department and the lighting department regarding scheduling and the complexity of the setups and to ensure that surfaced and textured items meet specific standards and are complete and ready for lighting. In their specialized role, Texture Artists are held accountable for producing their work in an efficient and timely manner, meeting specific quotas and production deadlines as well as troubleshooting any creative and technical issues that may arise in the production of their work.

The Texture Artist Aharon Charnov starts by laying out UVs and building up texture networks to make the character or object look and feel as it should. "There's something magical about taking a bland [model] and building it into a robust, good-looking prop for a CG television show or movie," he noted. "When you take a model and bring it to life with detailed and interesting textures, it moves beyond the level of graphics up to visual art, and there's something very wonderful in that often-challenging process."

For Texture Artists, one of the greatest challenges of the job is being able to consistently produce exceptional work all day for 10 to 11 hours per day at least five days a week. Deadlines can be tight, especially on television production schedules. Successful Texture

Artists find ways to save time by automating repetitive computer tasks.

Remaining successful as a Texture Artist involves continuous learning and improvement and constantly striving to get ahead of the artistic, creative, and technological curve in a field in which technology and trends change every year. As a result, Texture Artists spend time looking at other artists' work, attending industry talks, reading industry magazines and Web sites, and learning new software.

Salaries

Salaries for Texture Artists, based on multiple industry sources, are between $52,000 and $67,000, depending on experience. Hourly and weekly wages vary by location and range from about $20 to $26 per hour and from $1,000 to $1,300 a week. On the other hand, members of The Animation Guild, Local 839, of the IATSE (listed as Texture Painters) make a minimum of $1,110.28 (including working at nonunion shops) and a maximum of $2,181.82 per week. The middle rate as of the guild's most recent wage survey for the position was $1,852.63 weekly. Journey-level Texture Artists, meanwhile, draw approximately $1,534.64 a week.

Employment Prospects

Current job opportunities, in Charnov's opinion, are only fair. Outsourcing of lower-end television texture work overseas has resulted in huge losses in domestic jobs while driving down salaries in the United States as studios try to compete with the cheaper foreign labor force. In addition, positions in the United States are usually on a contract basis, and there are limited periods of employment. This means that Texture Artists might work fewer days in a year, but hours are long when they do work. In addition, securing a job that has medical benefits and sick days is very difficult.

When it comes to finding work, it is important to come across as highly motivated. You must have good credits on your résumé—equally important later in trying to advance to do more high-level work and work at the most successful studios. Artists must constantly improve their demo reels when applying for jobs.

The application process can seem like a job in and of itself. Candidates often spend more time applying for artistic positions than actually making art, which can become a serious drawback to attaining stable, full-time employment. It is important to avoid being overly critical in assembling your portfolio and demo reel to the point that it seriously wastes your time and cripples your career. If you keep putting your work out there and applying for jobs, you will eventually get hired.

It is very rare for college or university graduates to immediately secure work at a major studio. Aspiring Texture Artists should be prepared to pay their dues and put in time at smaller employers.

Advancement Prospects

Individuals seeking to advance will find prospects only fair. In the last few years, there have been many studio layoffs, resulting in a large amount of talented artists competing for a dwindling number of jobs. As a result, most Texture Artists move from company to company on a per-job basis, and there is not much chance of making a good impression on a manager and secure a permanent staff position, let alone being promoted.

Education and Training

An associate's degree in film and animation or video and game design is the minimum requirement. A bachelor's degree in art, fine arts, illustration, computer graphics, computer science, cinema studies, mathematics, engineering, or an equivalent is usually preferred, although some are hired with no formal training. Course work required includes drawing, painting, 3-D modeling, texturing, animation, and rigging.

As Charnov noted, the type of degree is not nearly as important as the quality of the work. He tells people that to be successful in CG animation, you have to be very good with computers and art. How you acquire these skills is not especially relevant.

Experience, Skills, and Personality Traits

Most studios require at least three years of production experience and a background in visual arts. Individuals who want to become Texture Artists need to have a good artistic eye. They must have exceptional artistic skills and an understanding of concepts as they relate to the creation of CGI, traditional artwork, construction, and painting of complex 3-D characters, props, and environments. As a result, Texture Artists require well-developed technical knowledge and proficiency in using 2-D or 3-D paint programs, including Maya, Painter, Photoshop, StudioPaint, and other paint tools. The ability to navigate UNIX/Linux operating systems is also a requirement.

Texture Artists must have a strong desire to create art every day. Jobs come and go, and the odds are that someone starting out today is not going to be a millionaire immediately, so a strong artistic drive is essential to success and happiness in this career.

In a highly demanding and structured work environment, Texture Artists must possess a strong ability to work well in a team setting and take direction from sequence leads and the art director and director as necessary. They must set aside their own feelings and be able to accept critical feedback and input from others regarding their work.

Unions and Associations
Membership in The Animation Guild, Local 839, of the IATSE is beneficial in securing guaranteed wages and benefits from signatory studios as well as other union support.

Tips for Entry
1. In high school, develop your artistic and technical skills by taking art and design, computer science, and video production classes.

2. Learn as much as you can about building models of characters or objects using available 2-D and 3-D paint programs.

3. Constantly immerse yourself in the process of making art. Read every book and tutorial you can find, and watch how-to videos to continue to learn and improve.

4. Put together a solid demo reel that demonstrates your ability to create and paint characters, objects, and environments for computer animation and post your demo on online CG forums and communities where industry professionals get together to obtain feedback on their work and network.

PERFORMING

VOICEOVER ACTOR

CAREER PROFILE

Duties: Create vocal characterizations for animated characters in film, television, and other animated productions

Alternate Title(s): Voice Artist; Voiceover Artist

Salary Range: $15,000 to $45,000 or more

Employment Prospects: Fair to Poor

Advancement Prospects: Fair

Best Geographical Location(s): Los Angeles

Prerequisites:

    Education and Training—High school diploma with additional training in voice acting

    Experience—Experience is not as important as having tremendous skill and talent to do convincing character voices; some prior acting experience helpful

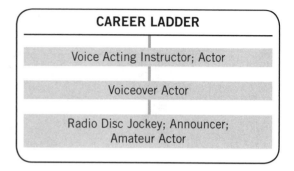

Special Skills and Personality Traits—Articulate; imaginative; creative; talented; acting ability; voice resonance and projection

Position Description

Ever since Mickey Mouse whistled in the first-released synchronized cartoon in 1928, Walt Disney's *Steamboat Willie,* Voiceover Actors have been inventing voices for a plethora of characters that cavort across movie theater and television screens delivering classic performances, memorable character dialogue, and taglines that have been imbedded in American culture.

Animation is one of the few businesses in which people can make money simply by using their voices. Many Voiceover Actors pull in a regular income working on cartoons; their faces may not be immediately recognizable, but their voices are. "I tell people I was a class clown and now I get paid for it," notes the widely known Voiceover Actor Tom Kane.

Voiceover Actors create characterizations in cartoons and performances that make the characters believable to audiences watching them. Casting animated productions is no different than casting commercials. Casting calls go out to various talent agencies that represent Voiceover Actors. Agents usually receive a drawing or sketch of the character the studio wants to cast—a smart-alecky bunny or a slow-moving, slow-talking tortoise. They use this drawing to dispatch actors under their representation to auditions. Sometimes characters are created with a specific actor in mind; in these cases, casting calls are not necessary.

Most voices for animated characters are actually recorded before a single stitch of animation is made.

The voices are subsequently synced up with the character animation. Recording the voices of the characters often involves multiple sessions. On animated feature films, actors do "scratch" recordings early on in the process, from which an animatic (a story reel) is produced. Anamatics are sometimes made from thousands of storyboard drawings in rough form, which the director edits and reviews. Afterward, the actors individually record their lines of dialogue—rarely are they ever together recording their lines in the same session—often requiring multiple takes. The dialogue is then meshed with the animation by the editor, who may combine different pieces of dialogue from different takes and sessions to create a single scene.

On television animation productions, recording sessions are handled differently. During a normal cartoon recording session, the producer, director, and entire voice cast all gather—usually a regular cast of around four to five actors and other supporting actors, if any—to review the script and record their dialogue, which is usually preceded in the script by narrative cues. Often, bedlam prevails when "a group of creative, fertile minds gather together in one tiny recording studio," according to the longtime Voiceover Artist Gary Owens, who has done voice work in more than 3,000 individual cartoon episodes during his career.

Normally, the director gives each Voiceover Actor individual instructions before recording his or her dialogue, such as, "Now make it very loud this time, because you're supposed to be over a canyon," or "You're over a vat of molten lava, and you're yelling at them."

Recording voices in cartoons is similar to acting in a live-action film or television show. The biggest difference is that cartoon characters rely on the voices of actors to convey the actions and emotions they demonstrate on screen. In addition, in animation, there is less time to record lines (recording sessions usually last no more than a few hours), and lines tend to be shorter so the action moves faster.

Television cartoon series, however, may require recording episodes back-to-back on the same day, depending on the producer and the budget. Nonetheless, the prospect of breathing life into new and original characters is something that never gets old.

Voiceover Actors perform under many different working conditions and for many different personalities. Some producers offer guidance and direction; others expect Voiceover Actors to perform flawlessly from the start or offer minimal suggestions for improvement. Work assignments range in length from one day to a few months, so work hours are irregular.

Salaries

Salaries for Voiceover Actors can range from nothing to $1,000,000. Factors that affect salaries for a Voiceover Actors include quantity of work and reputation in the industry.

A session fee for recording a SAG or AFTRA cartoon is $800; it takes anywhere from three to four hours to record. The payment is applied against the first airing, so actors do not make residuals on the first broadcast. The more the broadcast runs, the more Voiceover Actors get paid residuals, based on a sliding union scale. Lead Voiceover Actors on SAG-sanctioned television cartoon series may make from $15,000 to $18,000 a season just to record the episodes. Additional compensation is possible from overall reruns of the original episodes: on cable networks, another $20,000; on major broadcast networks, another $30,000 to $40,000. Income can double or triple if the actor is working on more than one series at a time, but most work on only one series at a time.

Voiceover Actors hired to do "legacy" characters, such as Bugs Bunny, Daffy Duck, Porky Pig, and Mickey Mouse, can make a substantially larger amount. Studios usually pay these actors double or triple scale. According to Kane, "It's hard to really [hold out with] a studio, as there may be three or four other guys out there who can do a Bugs Bunny, and they'll just replace you."

In other rare situations, run-of-the-mill civilian Voiceover Artists have made "celebrity money," as is the case with the Voiceover Artists of television's longest-running animated sitcom, *The Simpsons*. Each Voiceover Artist on this show is paid six figures per episode, a first in television history.

Employment Prospects

Employment prospects for Voiceover Actors are only fair, as many cartoons are being made in Canada. In addition, a lot of voiceover work in the United States is nonunion, which is a problem for SAG Voiceover Actors.

To become a successful Voiceover Actor, there is really only one place to live and work: Los Angeles, where most film and television animation is produced and animation talent agents are located. Doing this work requires dedication and diligence, as finding voice jobs involves constantly going on casting calls, doing readings (with dozens of other people often reading for the same part), finding agents (if you do not have one), and other time-consuming tasks that more often result in rejection than success. It is important for those seeking work to not be too discouraged by rejection and to never give up.

Most experienced Voiceover Actors do not depend on doing cartoon voices as their sole means of income. Instead, they diversify and juggle work in many other media, including radio, commercials, television broadcasting, and even bit acting parts on stage in local theater productions or in a television show or motion picture.

Advancement Prospects

For most Voiceover Actors, advancement simply means working more. There is no direct line of progression for this position. Most simply use their skills and experience to do other things throughout their voice acting careers, as mentioned above, while continuing to make voice acting as one part of their overall career. Others use their talents and experience to teach voice acting, either at small core workshops or at schools dedicated to voice acting.

Education and Training

Voiceover Actors do not need a college education. College theater, however, can help hone acting skills. Workshops and seminars at voice acting schools for animated cartoons, commercials, and announcing are helpful in acquiring the necessary skills to work in the industry. In addition, acting coaches and teachers can be assets.

Experience, Skills, and Personality Traits

Cartoon voiceover acting is talent-based; experience is not required. Voiceover Actors must be creative, extroverted, and fearless. They require excellent acting and improvisational skills that combine elements of standup comedy and mimicry. They must have the ability to do unique and exciting voices, realistic voices, and parodies of other voices. They should be funny and unafraid to fail in front of a group of people. Furthermore, Voiceover Actors must be able to take direction and perform in a collaborative setting.

Unions and Associations

Voiceover Actors, like most film and television actors, are covered under two major national unions: the American Federation of Television and Radio Artists (AFTRA), which has 32 locals in the United States, and the Screen Actors Guild (SAG), which covers film actors and, in some cases, television actors. Some actors belong to both unions. Both offer an assortment of benefits, including set wages and health and pension plans, for their members.

Tips for Entry

1. Develop your voice so you sound natural, not like someone doing impressions of voices. Also, develop the quality and range of your voice so it is distinctive. Do not copy others. Create your own niche.

2. Enroll in voice acting classes taught by professionals in the business. Learn proper vocal techniques used by many successful voice actors—everything from creating the right sound and pitch to enunciating and projecting your voice—so you can compete professionally.

3. Find sample cartoon scripts online by searching "cartoon scripts." Pick passages of dialogue you like, and read them aloud. Practice until you get a feel for the material and how you want to say it.

4. Develop a two-and-a-half to three-minute CD demo that features a wide range of short cuts of your best character voices, from superheroes to damsels in distress. Do not do more than you can handle. Avoid using common-sounding voices, and make sure your demo is of high quality. Nothing will turn off an agent more than if the overall sound of your demo is amateurish.

5. Compile a list of talent agents who represent voiceover talent. Listings of agents are available online through the Screen Actors Guild and the American Federation of Television and Radio Artists. One of the best places to find talent agents on the Web is Voicebank.net. Also, compile a list of casting directors who specifically cast animation, and send your demo with a cover letter directly to them.

6. Develop a thick skin and tenacity, and stay confident in yourself and your abilities. You must learn to accept rejection and not take it personally. Understand that acting is a totally subjective business and that you will never please every casting director. However, apply constructive criticism wisely and where needed if you are serious about enjoying a career using your voice. Keep plugging, and keep trying. You only need one "yes" to jumpstart your career!

PRODUCING

EXECUTIVE PRODUCER

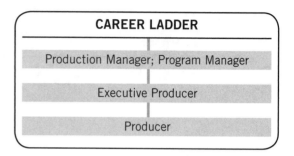
Position Description

In the world of film and television animation, Executive Producers are the point men of productions. They are primarily responsible for getting a production made and are actively involved in its major phases: green light, preproduction, and postproduction. Besides often conceiving or developing the concept for an animated film, television program, or other production, they are in charge of formulating the rationale or reason for the project, determining its format, and getting it financed, fully packaged, and made. They are also responsible for overseeing promotional efforts of the project.

Major film and television animation studios and television networks employ Executive Producers. They also work for independent production companies that produce original animated features, original programming for network or cable broadcast and first-run syndication, and projects for direct-to-video markets. Some Executive Producers are also owners and operators of their own production companies. Those employed by networks are in charge of supervising all aspects of productions as well as developing concepts for shows geared toward the network's target audience. Some Executive Producers are artist-producers; others are more like senior managers and business executives who, in addition to their significant contributions to the production process, have a personal financial interest in it aside from obtaining the financing and maintaining

business relationships with the financiers, distributors, marketers, and broadcasters and/or studios.

Executive Producers bring their particular expertise in the areas of creativity and project management to the table. They oversee and manage the production staff, which, when including all animators, writers, and production people on a major animation series such as *The Simpsons,* can number as many as 100. Executive Producers sometimes work on multiple projects at the same time. They analyze and review the scope and requirements of a project and give critical feedback and input to the animation staff. Executive Producers help identify, recruit, and hire critical talent for the production, including producers, directors, writers, and actors. They also interact and negotiate with talent and agents in addition to coordinating rights and clearances with the legal department.

According to the Executive Producer Van Partible, the creator of *Johnny Bravo,* the Executive Producer oversees the hiring and direction of the staff and puts his or her "stamp on the execution" of everything from story and design to sound and color. The Executive Producer can be as involved as he or she wants, depending on his or her capabilities. For example, if the Executive Producer is a writer, he or she probably won't be heavily involved in design aspects of the production.

In such an important role, the work can be especially meaningful. "I love watching an idea go from inception to revealing itself on film," Partible added. "I wanted to be able to tell stories and make sure they were told the way I saw them in my head. The only way I could do that was to see the film through from beginning to end."

Some Executive Producers make the leap from live-action to animation. For example, David Mirkin joined *The Simpsons* first as a consulting producer and then Executive Producer. One major difference: For a live-action comedy series such as *Newhart,* he had to manage about five episodes in production at one time; for *The Simpsons,* sometimes that number was seven, eight, or nine episodes in his head at one time. Also, executive producing an animated television series is very time consuming. For *The Simpsons,* Mirkin spent a year and half producing two seasons—or 24 episodes—at once, which he described as "kind of a nightmare," unlike live-action television, which takes half that time to produce eight episodes for a single season.

As Mirkin once explained, "No matter which type of show you're doing, you are working with episodes in different stages of development. The difference is in live action, you pretty much do an entire episode from start to finish in about two months maximum, and really the intense part is all within one month, so you really have a real quick feeling of completion. Whereas *The Simpsons* and animation like *The Simpsons* feels much more like a feature film."

Executive Producers strive to produce productions that are imaginatively and technically unique, as was the case with Cartoon Network's animated series *Stars Wars: The Clone Wars.* The legendary *Star Wars* and series Executive Producer George Lucas decided to do the series only if he could do something "really unique with computer-generated animation, and also tell great stories." Lucas's role as Executive Producer was that of a "mentor" of the project to ensure consistency. During story conferences, he would work through several story ideas and work with the writers to adapt them to *Star Wars* style. He also worked with the creative talent to bring them "up to speed" so they were thinking more like feature filmmakers.

Executive Producers do not have standard nine to five workdays. Hours can be quite long, depending on the demands of the production. The work is mainly office based.

Salaries

Salaries for Executive Producers vary depending on experience and the assets they bring to the production. The salary for this position, according to multiple industry sources, ranges from close to $60,000 to as much as $300,000 a year. More experienced Executive Producers with more diverse skill sets command higher salaries.

Executive Producers who are members of The Animation Guild, Local 839, of the IATSE are paid the same wages as producers. According to a June 2010 wage survey of its members, the weekly salary ranges for Executive Producers was $1,825 to $2,812.50, with a median of $2,500 per week. Conversely, the starting salary for journeyman Executive Producers as last reported in the guild's March 2009 wage survey was $1,754.84 per week based on a 40-hour work week. In prime-time animated television series, which are covered by the Writers Guild of America, titles and compensation are handled differently. Experienced writers who serve as producers and Executive Producers are paid differently than their executive counterparts. Unfortunately, the guild's applicable rates for these professionals are not published.

Employment Prospects

Employment opportunities for Executive Producers in the animation industry are generally poor, especially for those who are new to the industry. Because of the high cost of producing feature-length and television animation, major-market animation studios tend to prefer those with significant experience and a proven track record. Studio executives are paid to make the studio money. To make the best possible product, they hire the people who have the best track record and therefore the best chance of making a successful product. That being said, it is not impossible for talented and ambitious individuals to break into the industry as Executive Producers.

Most Executive Producers have risen up the ranks from producer after having produced a string of hit films and top-rated shows. In some cases, highly talented and skilled individuals who hold or sell exclusive rights to a project have been hired to be Executive Producers as part of an established studio team.

For those serious about becoming an Executive Producer, the best way to build a career is to start at the bottom as a production assistant on any film or television production. This position provides valuable experience and the chance to exhibit expertise and reliability. Production assistants also have the opportunity to connect with potential mentors and network with others in the industry. Personal connections can prove to be important, as people tend to prefer to work with professionals they know and trust.

By showing your talent to peers or even the Executive Producer when it comes time to staff a production, you are in a good position to receive work. As you gain more experience and become more involved in the production process, you will acquire managerial and delegation skills, which are important for Executive Producers.

Advancement Prospects

Except for the especially talented few, the prospects for advancement from Executive Producer to production manager and program manager are only fair. Individuals elevated to these positions usually have a proven track record and strong business and managerial skills. Some elect to form their own companies or join others to produce and develop original offerings for first-run syndication and cable networks. Others seek these positions within other studios or independent production firms.

Education and Training

A formal education is not necessarily required to become an Executive Producer. While some Executive Producers working in the industry have undergraduate degrees, MBA's, or MFA's in animation, no undergraduate or graduate program in animation exists for would-be producers. The only specific requirements for this position are managerial skills and knowledge of animation mechanics, animation production, and story. "Whether you learn it from the ground up on a formal animation production or create your own film and learn it the hard way, there are many road maps to get to be an Executive Producer. A formal education helps round out a person and prepare them for life but is not necessary," Partible said.

Experience, Skills, and Personality Traits

Three to five years of experience as a film or television producer is required. Executive Producers need thorough practical knowledge of all aspects of producing a film or television program and an understanding of modern film, television, and animation production processes and technologies.

Even though many Executive Producers also demonstrate creative talent in developing concepts and ideas for timely and original animation productions,

they largely serve in a leadership and managerial capacity. As a result, they must exhibit strong analytical, organizational, and project-management skills. Executive Producers must have a sound business sense in supervising all major phases of a project—green light, preproduction, and postproduction—and accurately estimating costs to create realistic budgets. They need to be good communicators and must know how to set priorities and deadlines, track and allocate resources, provide critical feedback, and effectively address and meet the needs of the support team, producers, and project as a whole. Additionally, as Partible, now an Executive Producer for Cartoon Network Asia, stated, "A person needs to really live life so that they can bring their own life experiences to the characters and motivations in their films. Whether you simply observe and experience life or study psychology and sociology, you need to really know why life is so complicated in order to communicate life through . . . characters."

Unions and Associations

While there are no specific unions or professional associations that represent Executive Producers, many in the animation industry belong to The Animation Guild, Local 839, of the IATSE, as well as the Producers Guild of America, the National Academy of Television Arts and Sciences, and the National Association of Television Program Executives as a way to network, find out about job openings, and exchange ideas with fellow producers and their peers.

Tips for Entry

1. If you pursue an undergraduate degree, enroll in business and finance courses, as you will need skills in these fields as an Executive Producer.
2. Pursue a job in the industry as a production assistant. Target the companies you want to work for, and, if necessary, apply for anything and everything, whether it is working in the mailroom or at the receptionist's desk, to start. After you are hired, you will have full access and first crack at other jobs that open up at the company.
3. Network as much as possible with professionals in the industry.

PRODUCER

CAREER PROFILE

Duties: Create ideas for and steer development of film and television animation productions

Alternate Title(s): Co-Producer; Producer-Director; Writer-Producer

Salary Range: $100,000 to $200,000

Employment Prospects: Good

Advancement Prospects: Excellent

Best Geographical Location(s): Los Angeles, New York, San Francisco

Prerequisites:

Education and Training—Undergraduate degree in animation, film, television, or equivalent; extensive background in animation

Experience—Three to five years of experience as an associate producer or director with thorough practical knowledge of animation production

Special Skills and Personality Traits—Business and financial acuity; creativity; detail-driven; communication and interpersonal skills; leadership and organizational abilities; problem-solving skills; understanding of film and television animation production and technology

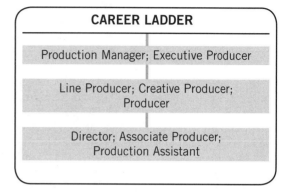

CAREER LADDER

Production Manager; Executive Producer

Line Producer; Creative Producer; Producer

Director; Associate Producer; Production Assistant

Position Description

Behind every animated full-length feature film or television series, skilled professionals coordinate and supervise the creative, budgetary, logistical, and technical aspects of the production. These professionals are known as Producers.

Producers are surrounded by a wealth of talent—directors, writers, animators, artists, and technicians—using their expertise to entertain and enthrall audiences around the world. Whether for the big or small screen, the role of the Producer is essentially the same. Producers initiate and oversee the entire process of the production, controlling matters such as budgets and scheduling, personnel, and distribution.

In their work on animated movies, Producers work side by side with the executive producer and director and are closely involved in the project's development from its earliest stage. The process of developing an animated feature film is intense and happens in one of two ways. In the first way, the Producer and the studio's creative team develop the idea for the film internally. The blockbuster hit *Ice Age* (2002), for example, was developed by a small team at 20th Century Fox. In the second way, a story is pitched and optioned for development. *Despicable Me* (2010) evolved out of this type of scenario.

In developing the production, Producers oversee the development and design of the characters and then the story, as shaped by a team of scriptwriters, and then every phase of production thereafter, from animation to completion. Throughout the process, Producers maintain the production budget and schedule. They convene with the director and department heads to determine the allocation of internal staff and staffing needs, if applicable. They calculate and forecast costs on a regular basis to maintain financial oversight and review actual costs with the executive producer throughout the project. In handling budgeting and scheduling of the production, they regularly review and resolve any conflicting issues related to budget expenditures and scheduling of the project. Producers may also view dailies and work in progress before conducting a final review of the production.

Television animation Producers are usually hand-picked by the executive producer to supervise a single animated program, episode, or series. Producers in charge of a whole series are usually known as supervising producers. Producers are actively involved in selecting scripts, casting voice actors and the needed production and technical crew, and planning and executing the production.

A network television series may staff two to three Producers, each with different responsibilities and working at different levels, depending on the complexity and size of the project. Within the structure of some programs, Producers may have a greater hand in steering the creative direction of the show, developing ideas and determining its specific approach and format. In this role, they may attend creative and production meetings; review loglines, treatments, and scripts; and participate in all areas of creative development, from script to final delivery. Other Producers may be solely concerned with the creative aspects or focus only on the logistics of the production. On most prime-time network cartoon series, some Producers focus nearly exclusively on the numerous creative elements of the production, while other Producers or staff members are delegated the tasks of handling logistics. In this environment, many Producers also act as writers; in this role, they are able to shape the program's characters and storylines in collaboration with other writers.

Working conditions for Producers vary widely. On the whole, their schedule is not a standard 40-hour workweek. They mostly work in a controlled and structured indoor environment. The work is often hectic and demanding, and the hours can be very long.

Salaries

In the film and television animation industries, earnings for Producers depend largely on the studio and production. According to various industry sources, salaries range from a low of $100,000 to a high of $200,000 or more. Larger studios pay much more for experienced Producers who have worked on financially successful movies and television shows.

In a salary survey conducted by The Animation Guild, Local 839, of the IATSE in June 2010, the going rates, as opposed to collective bargaining agreement minimums, for Producers ranged from $1,825 to $2,812.50 per week. Producers in the middle bracket took home an average of $2,500 a week, while journeyman Producers (according to figures last reported by the guild in March 2009) took in a minimum of $1,764.84 a week.

Employment Prospects

Employment opportunities for Producers are excellent. Savvy and experienced candidates with extensive backgrounds in animation have a greater chance of employment.

Producers work on a variety of productions, including animated features, television series, television specials, and direct-to-video productions, produced by major-market motion picture and television animation studios and independent production companies. The frequency of turnover and openings in these environments is fairly low, as many Producers are satisfied and therefore remain with the same employer for years until either they take on a similar role with another studio or company or branch out and work independently. According to AnimationMentor.com, the demand for Producers is expected to grow, coinciding with the future expansion and need for film and television animation in markets in the United States and abroad.

One of the best ways to get a job producing animation is to start small. While many ambitious graduates yearn to produce animated features and short subjects at giant studios the minute they graduate, beginning a producing career at smaller studios, known for faster production schedules of short projects such as commercials, is arguably the way to go. It is also easier to advance through the ranks working in a small studio.

Others rise up in the industry from the ranks of animators to become associate producers. On a feature film, associate producers are often responsible for producing the animation sequences and visual effects side of the film, if any. In television animation, they are directly responsible for the day-to-day aspects of the production, except for budgeting and scheduling. Both are a great training ground for becoming a Producer.

As Jeffrey Varab, who worked almost 30 years as a supervising animator and animator for Amblin/Universal Pictures, Industrial Light & Magic, Walt Disney Feature Animation, and Sony Pictures Animation before becoming a consultant, writer, director, and Producer, stated, "Truly experienced producers, those who have grown through the animation process and fully understand every aspect of the production pipeline, are a rare asset that puts such experienced applicants at the top of prospects. Fundamentally, experience and success in the films worked on define the value and prospects of securing and building a successful career."

Advancement Prospects

As previously stated, many Producers are content with their careers. However, others advance to become creative producers and line producers. These positions entail more direct involvement with budgeting and scheduling and greater overall responsibility. Some aspire instead for much higher positions, such as executive producer or production manager, either at large film and television animation studios or small to mid-sized independent production companies.

Education and Training

Most employers require a Producer to have an undergraduate degree in animation, film, television, or the equivalent with a broad animation background. Courses in the techniques and methods of animation and filmmaking are especially useful. Besides obtaining an education and training at schools, many have worked their way up from the lowest rung to the top after gaining needed experience along the way. Personal apprenticeships and mentorships are also useful for gaining experience, knowledge, and expertise.

Experience, Skills, and Personality Traits

In order to effectively handle the responsibilities of the job, Producers need a minimum of three to five years of experience as an associate producer or director coupled with thorough practical knowledge of animation production, including 2-D, Flash, stop-motion, and CG animation processes.

Producers require a strong familiarity with all stages of animation development, from original conception to final editing, and project and budget management. Producers must be creative and highly organized, with a proven ability to focus on priorities, solve problems, and juggle multiple tasks under tight schedules and deadlines. They must demonstrate solid business skills and industry judgment to proactively and constructively define clear outcomes and address and solve complex problems.

In addition to a passion for animation, Producers must enjoy working with creative people and have the ability to judge the quality of entertainment. They must have excellent leadership skills and written and verbal communication skills to lead a team of artists, writers, and directors through the production process.

Unions and Associations

Membership in The Animation Guild, Local 839, of the IATSE, which "fought long and hard for many years and, to a great extent very successfully, to establish healthy industry standards, as well as benefits," according to Varab, is useful for networking and enhancing your skills through educational seminars and other resources specific to the animation industry. While there is no specific union that represents Producers, joining the Producers Guild of America may be of some value, as it offers forums for members who work in the film and television industry.

Tips for Entry

1. Obtain a solid liberal arts education with a specific focus on animation and animation production.
2. To improve your business and financial acuity, enroll in business and finance courses.
3. Look for opportunities to study or mentor under experienced professionals at studios or production companies that are currently making the type of animated films or shows you would like to work on.

TECHNICAL PRODUCTION

CAMERA

CAMERA OPERATOR AND CAMERA STAGING ARTIST

CAREER PROFILE

Duties: Responsible for setup and operation of a film camera for animation

Alternate Title(s): Rostrum Cameraman; CG Camera Operator; Cinematographer

Salary Range: $12,000 to $80,000

Employment Prospects: Good

Advancement Prospects: Fair

Best Geographical Location(s): Chicago, Los Angeles, Portland, San Francisco, Seattle, New York

Prerequisites:

Education and Training—Two-year college degree or certificate

Experience—Some experience in film and television production, preferably as a production assistant

CAREER LADDER

Audio/Video Engineer; Floor Manager; Lighting Director

Camera Operator; Camera Staging Artist

Engineering Technician; Production Assistant

Special Skills and Personality Traits—Creative; technically knowledgeable; versatile; physical reflexes

Position Description

Camera Operators are the technical wizards behind the camera in animated productions. There are different kinds of Camera Operators, including rostrum cameramen on 2-D traditional cel animation, camera and staging artists on 3-D computer animation, directors of photography on stop-motion animation, and CG camera operators on motion-capture productions. They are responsible for filming or digitally shooting the actual finished animation, thereby creating the illusion of realistic actions and movements of characters or objects against vivid 2-D or 3-D backdrops. The practices they employ are similar to those used by early pioneer animators to create stop-framed animated films, only far more advanced.

For cel-animated films and television programs, Camera Operators use a special 35-millimeter camera on a setup called a rostrum to photograph each cel of animation in sequence. First they place the background drawing on a horizontal easel and then put translucent drawn and painted cel over the background. They are held in position by two sets of pegs (bottom and top) above and below the artwork. Covering them with a plate of glass, with the camera suspended and mounted to the column of the animation stand directly over them, they photograph a single frame, creating a composite image on film. They then

repeat the process using the next drawing and background in sequence.

Such a complex piece of engineering has been made easier by the introduction of computers and stepper motors, but it still requires tremendous patience and skill. Camera Operators precisely track in or out of a scene, moving the camera up and down the column with relative ease to create the illusion of the artwork getting bigger or smaller; they also move and rotate the artwork in position on the animation table for added visual impact. While filming each shot, they also apply many of the same camera techniques as do live-action cameramen—regulating the focus, exposure, and aperture and using various lenses, filters, and camera settings—to achieve the desired movement, effects, and lighting in a scene as specified by the director or director of photography. The editor constructs the finished cut of the film from the Camera Operators' various filmed shots or scenes, doing most editing with the aid of digital technology on computers.

For 2-D digital animation, Camera Operators use what is known as a virtual rostrum after the animation is layered in its place using popular ink-and-paint software programs, such as Animo and Lightwave. This allows them to move the camera freely in its space. Then, while pointed straight down at the artwork, they can film from different angles or directions whatever is in front of them.

In the 3-D digital animation world, Camera Operators employ skills and knowledge of major 3-D animation systems, such as Maya, MotionBuilder, 3-D Studio MAX, and an understanding of film language and camera terminology, framing, and movement to create and stage animation. On CG or computer-animated productions, Camera Staging Artists create sequences of shots through the application of traditional filmmaking principles in 3-D using 3-D animation software. Their work involves establishing character blocking (framing the shot), camera positioning, and camera movement in programs such as MotionBuilder, from previsualization (layouts) and blocking to final execution of each shot. They likewise generate ideas and contribute to the creative direction of the project.

On stop-motion animated productions, the director of photography, working alongside the director and supervising a team of cinematographers, designs and executes the filming of 3-D puppets or models using sophisticated mechanical rigs to make them move one movement and one frame at a time. Motion control operators use a motion control rig system to handle technically challenging moves and those that involve special effects.

On motion-capture computer-generated films, Camera Operators are charged with both creation of camera animation from scratch and working with camera motion-data capture on motion-capture shots, editing motion-capture data from motion-capture shots, and exporting them to the animation team. They handle technical setups of shots for production departments in the animation pipeline. Sony Pictures Imageworks invented a system dubbed "Wheels," whereby a Camera Operator films shots of CG characters animated with motion-capture data using a standard camera system altered to give the operator a view of the "virtual" characters.

Most film and television Camera Operators, regardless of their title, are employed by mid- to large-sized studios and small, independent studios. In most situations, they frame and shoot each sequence, meeting the specifications as dictated by the director or director of photography. For low-budget productions, only one operator is usually used; for larger-budgeted productions, usually two. On animated features, the duration of employment is anywhere from 12 to 15 months; on video games, Camera Operators are usually contracted, and jobs last up to 10 months.

Salaries

Earnings for Camera Operators are difficult to pin down. However, according to the U.S. Bureau of Labor Statistics' (BLS) *Occupational Outlook Handbook, 2010–11 Edition,* median annual earnings as of May 2008 for television, video, and motion picture Camera Operators were $41,670. The middle 50 percent earned between $29,020 and $59,970 annually. The lowest 10 percent earned $10.44 per hour, or $21,710 yearly, and the highest 10 percent earned an average of $39.19 an hour, or $79,440 annually. Beginning Camera Operators working in traditional animation can expect to earn between $16,000 and $40,000 yearly.

Earnings for freelance or self-employed Camera Operators vary as well, with most incurring additional expenses due to purchasing, owning, and maintaining their own equipment and accessories. For members of the International Cinematographers Guild (ICG), the minimum daily wage is $385.15. Weekly, wages range from $1,856.95 to $1,903.37 if the terms of employment are week-to-week or four consecutive weeks; for the International Alliance of Theatrical Stage Employees (IATSE), the weekly minimum salary for video cameramen starts at $1,416.

Employment Prospects

Employment prospects for this position are good. According to the BLS, employment of Camera Operators and editors is expected to grow faster than average—by 11 percent—between 2008 and 2018. As the motion picture industry expands, demand for Camera Operators will expand as well. Individuals with the most experience and advanced computer skills are expected to have the best opportunities. Camera Operators will also see increases in employment in the areas of made-for-Internet film broadcasts, including music videos, and Internet video games. Usually, Camera Operators in the film and television industries are hired based on the recommendations of animation professionals, such as producers, directors of photography, and camera assistants from previous projects or places of employment or through interviews with the producer. A good professional reputation often can make a difference. Besides working as production assistants to break into the business, many Camera Operators start their careers working for television stations or production facilities in small markets to gain experience.

Advancement Prospects

Career advancement for Camera Operators depends largely on experience. Individuals with the most experience and advanced computer skills have the best opportunity to advance to positions with major studios and commercial production companies. Some have gone on to become directors of photography for movie studios, advertising agencies, or television programs, or teach at technical schools, film schools, or universities.

Education and Training

A minimum requirement is an associate's degree from an accredited two-year college, certificate from a vocational school, or related on-the-job experience. Usually one or two years of training involving both on-the-job experience and informal training with experienced workers are needed. Often, apprenticeship programs associated with the field meet this requirement. As part of their required curriculum, film schools also provide training on different artistic aspects of filmmaking for undergraduates who want to pursue this profession.

Core course work in camera operations and videography, including basic courses that cover the use of equipment, processes, and techniques, can be completed at many universities, community colleges, and private trade and technical schools. A good understanding of computer technology and 2-D and 3-D animation systems is essential.

Experience, Skills, and Personality Traits

Usually, those who enter the field already have considerable experience working in film or on television cartoon productions, often starting as production assistants to learn how film and video production works before working their way up. Therefore, previous work-related experience, skill, or knowledge is required for this occupation. An understanding of photography and processes of animation and filmmaking is essential.

Furthermore, Camera Operators require good eyesight, artistic ability, and hand-eye coordination and patience, accuracy, and attention to detail in their work. They must have a solid understanding of camera operation and maintenance and 2-D and/or 3-D systems for computer animation and motion capture ideally on a television or film production. They must have good communication skills (written and oral), with the ability to work independently and with a team in high-pressure situations for extended periods of time.

Unions and Associations

The International Alliance of Theatrical Stage Employees (IATSE), the International Cinematographer Guild (ICG), the National Association of Broadcast Employees and Technicians, AFL-CIO (NABET), and the International Brotherhood of Electrical Workers (IBEW) represent most commercial film and television Camera Operators. Most unions offer a full range of benefits to members, including set wages and health and pension plans.

Tips for Entry

1. Enroll in courses in film history, and study how veteran and experienced Camera Operators in the field have used optical technology in the past to create different visual images on film and on television besides the use of 2-D and 3-D systems and applications used in creating digital or computer animation.

2. In school, sign up and volunteer to work without pay in exchange for work experience on student films and nonunion productions, including music videos and commercials, or seek part-time employment at local television stations, to broaden your experience.

3. Start out working for a motion picture camera rental company to learn more about the different kinds of equipment used by Camera Operators and meet those working in the industry, including members of camera crews, on films and television productions.

4. Accept any job with a television station or production house to gain firsthand experience working behind the camera while making valuable contacts in the industry to advance your career.

5. Subscribe to computer graphics and videographic newsletters and magazines to stay up-to-date on the latest news and developments in the industry and job classifieds in your area.

EDITING

EDITOR

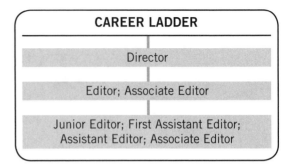

Position Description

Animation Editors have one of the most misunderstood jobs in the industry. Known as "cutters" in the business, they are the ones who effectively shape and hook every element and scene together in animated films and television shows, from start to finish. Editors seamlessly manipulate the plot, score, sound, and animation into a continuous and enjoyable whole after carefully reviewing miles of footage and turning the idea into an entertaining and compelling story.

There is a big difference between editing live-action film and editing animation. In making live-action films, the movie is shot first, and Editors then edit everything together afterward. On animated features, Editors are involved during all stages of production. As the long-time Pixar film Editor Lee Unkrich once explained, "The best analogy I could come up with is that editing an animated film is like building a sand castle, one grain at a time." Thousands of different pieces are assembled. Editors have to focus on innumerable details while keeping an eye on the big picture and how the movie is playing as a whole.

During preproduction, Editors work with the story team to help shape the plot, invent the characters, and decide on the look and style of the film—the kind of input few live-action editors ever get to realize. Early on in the production, after the story artists produce comic-book style panels of individual sequences in storyboard form from the written script to help visualize the story, Editors pair these hand-drawn scenes often from first, second, third, or more drafts with "scratch recordings," or temporary voice tracks of the character dialogue, into an edited "story reel" and "working document" to judge the flow, pace, and timing of a scene and what needs improvement. When a specific shot is not gelling and getting the laughs intended, Editors will ask the story artist to produce a new set of drawings to fix the issue as well as make any suggestions that will radically improve the flow, continuity, or pacing of the shot or scene. A well-done story reel provides a nearly completed experience that only improves when the film is animated.

After the director approves the story reels, the animation and 3-D environments enter the layout stage, and the voice cast records dialogue. It is the responsibility of Editors to wed the audio to the animated images using digital nonlinear editing systems, such as Avid, making further adjustments as needed. Often, what they create on film is taken from 20 or more takes of any given line as performed by each actor during the recording session to pace the scene. This can include combining many little pieces of dialogue and words or syllables from different takes and from multiple recording sessions, often recorded months apart, into a single scene. Editors have some control over the shape of the actors' performances, which is virtually impossible in live-action productions.

In addition to editing the vocal performances, Editors also edit sound effects around a scene to provide context. This takes considerable time to accomplish, but it helps keep the audience engrossed when they watch the finished film. Editors sometimes take music from existing movie soundtracks in a scene, and sometimes original music is used. The music in the finished film is sometimes different from what was originally used in the editing process. When combined together with dialogue and sound effects, if all goes well, the scene will end up in the finished film.

Whether doing live-action or animation, Editors have the same main responsibility at the end: to manage the narrative structure and flow of the film and converge the sound and visuals to create an engaging experience for the audience. By the animating and final rendering phase of a computer-animated feature, editing is usually mostly completed, as this is one of the most involved processes in melding everything together. However, even at this late stage, Editors have been known to make changes, though costly, if it is something that is critical to a scene.

Editors perform much of the same work in editing television animation. Reporting to the producer, they work on an Avid editing system from storyboard drawings and build an animatic, or story reel, by combining storyboard drawings in sequence with voice tracks of the dialogue. Editors then consult with the director. They spend more time on creative aspects of the show before the actual edit with the director in the editing room and "fine tune the edit until it looks good," explained Joe Elwood, a live-action and animation editor. This process includes checking shots for color, consistency, and errors before the producer signs off on it.

Afterward, the project goes into production to have the various characters, shots, and scenes animated and then cut back into a final edit after the show is complete. The hours are long (an average of 60 hours per week), the work environment can be very hectic at times, but it is also stimulating and "very creative because you are doing a show starting from scratch," Elwood added. Editors must often work on more than one project at a time.

Salaries

Many variables contribute to wages and salaries, including union affiliation, the overall budget, whether the project is for film or television, and whether the production is studio-affiliated or independent. As reported by *The Princeton Review,* Editors make an average starting salary of $26,780. After five years, they draw an average salary of $38,720 and, after 10 to 15 years, an average of $55,300 a year. On animated feature films, according to the Motion Picture Editors Guild, Local 700, of the IATSE's most recent wage scales, apprentice animation Editors are guaranteed wages of $30.05 an hour, or $1,202.20 per week; assistant animation editors, $32.66 per hour, or $1,306.44 per week; and feature animation editors, $40.62 an hour, or $1,624.84 a week for a minimum eight-hour day shift and 40-hour workweek. On animated television shows, depending on the project and union participation, an assistant editor can expect to make from $10 to $35 an hour, an animation/animatic editor from $20 to $45 an hour, and a supervising picture editor from $45 to $80 per hour. Freelancer editors can earn the same but without job security or benefits. "Experienced, competent people usually make more money," said Craig Paulsen, an editor on Warner Bros. Animation's *The Looney Tunes Show* and previously Nickelodeon's *Back at the Barnyard* and other cartoon series.

Employment Prospects

Job opportunities for Editors, given the current state of the economy, are poor to fair. Too many good and talented people are out of work, and prospects look dim, though that could very well change in the future. According to Elwood, there is less money available, and Editors are now working without assistants or graphic support at some smaller, lower-budget places; others also work as their own producers (these Editors are referred to as "Preditors" in the industry).

However, the present economic condition throughout the industry does not mean you cannot get a job. Hard work and a willingness to learn as much as possible in any job you can get will pay off, according to Paulsen.

Most career opportunities for Editors continue to be found in major cities such as Los Angeles and New York, where most major cartoon studios are located and most animated films and television programs are produced. Being in one of these cities is a huge plus. There is more pressure for top performance at the studios, and they seem to be less patient with beginners.

Finding work as an Editor in the industry usually depends on "who you know, what you know, and luck," according to Paulsen, but when you step into a job, you really have to know that job. Individuals must be ready when the opportunity presents itself.

A typical cartoon production employs two Editors, but this depends on the budget, complexity, and whether produced for film or television. The length of employment also varies dramatically and is based on the duration of the production. To gain entry, many Editors suggest starting at the lower end of the scale as a production assistant to learn about the ins and outs of film and television animation production. From there, one can become a post coordinator, then assistant editor, and eventually Editor.

It takes four to 10 years of on-the-job training, making the right connections, and building up a significant portfolio of work for an Editor to be able to start his or her own editing service, which is common in some cases.

Advancement Prospects

Advancement prospects for Editors are mostly fair to due the current employment picture throughout the film and television industry and nation as a whole. Some advance to become directors and sound editors, but more often it is the other way around. Others elect to remain in their current specialty positions, while some move toward taking on greater responsibility and better compensation if they can find it elsewhere, such as live-action editing. Some individuals leave the business altogether and go into video promotion and sales, film equipment sales, and editing equipment sales and development.

Education and Training

Most major studios and postproduction houses require a bachelor's degree in radio, television, cinema or film, multimedia and broadcast, or an equivalent. Editors require extensive academic and professional experience. Programs and curricula vary from school to school, but course work often includes basic editing and commercial editing combined with training opportunities available to work as interns on film or television productions while in graduate school. Once out of school, Editors usually work in the production field for little money, paying their dues until they become more established. According to Paulsen, "It helps to have a degree because it shows discipline." He possesses a master's in film, but it did not secure a job for him on its own.

Experience, Skills, and Personality Traits

Experience is critical because editing in animation can be complicated. Most studios and production companies require five years or more of experience in editing, usually as an assistant editor, with extensive knowledge of film and television animation production processes and digital nonlinear editing systems. Editors need strong storytelling, composition, and timing abilities. They must have patience and very good computer skills, including knowledge of file management, folder structure, and basic troubleshooting and maintenance. They must also be familiar with the tools and various software it takes to be an Editor, such as Avid, Final Cut Pro, Photoshop, and After Effects, with the ability to organize and reorganize shots to tell the story in different ways. As a result, they must be highly organized and logical in their approach. They need to have strong creative and visual and auditory skills, be good communicators, and possess good manual dexterity.

Time-management skills are also critical to success for Editors. "You have to be able to manage your edit suite [and] keep people focused on the task at hand," Elwood related. The process is a tough juggling act of many varying tasks and issues.

Unions and Associations

Editors must belong to a union to get editing jobs at most film and television animation studios and production houses. Film Editors are members of the Motion Picture Editors Guild, Local 700, of the IATSE, while television Editors join the National Association of Broadcast Employees and Technicians, AFL-CIO (NABET). Each of these unions provides many benefits to its members, including set wages and health and pension plans. In addition, some Editors find it worthwhile to become a member of the Association of Independent Video and Filmmakers (AIVF) for employment and networking purposes.

Tips for Entry

1. Keep close tabs on the industry and evolving technology. Read trade and industry publications and postings in newsgroups and forums by industry professionals.
2. Land a production assistant job, and hang around the editing department to learn as much as you can about the trade.
3. Gain practical experience working on productions and postproduction.

PRODUCTION MANAGEMENT

PRODUCTION ASSISTANT

CAREER PROFILE

Duties: Assist in production of animation for film and television

Alternate Title(s): None

Salary Range: $24,000 to $33,000

Employment Prospects: Good

Advancement Prospects: Good

Best Geographical Location(s): Los Angeles, San Francisco, New York

Prerequisites:

  Education and Training—High school diploma; college degree in film or television production preferable

  Experience—A film, television, or theater background or related work experience at a film and television school recommended

  Special Skills and Personality Traits—Ability to take orders and follow directions; cooperative; dependable; initiative; organizational abilities; willing to put in long hours; computer and word-processing skills

CAREER LADDER

Production Secretary; Production Coordinator

Production Assistant; Production Runner

Intern

Position Description

Production Assistants, or PAs, are entry-level workers. They work on both live-action and animated film and television productions, doing just about anything and everything to assist with all aspects of the production. Their duties depend on the budget of the production and how the duties of the position are defined on a particular project.

This position involves doing a lot of grunt work, but it can be very educational. At most studios and production houses, Production Assistants come up the ranks as apprentices, helping out where needed. They act as chief communication liaisons between key staff members, including producers, directors, production managers, production coordinators, camera operators, assistant directors, and associate producers. They gain firsthand experience in the production of a broad mix of entertainment requiring animation, including feature films, television programs, specials, documentaries, and commercials.

Generally, Production Assistants take their directions from the production manager, who assigns them specific projects and assignments to complete in a timely and efficient manner. They may report both to the assistant director and production manager. Typically, the work they carry out on an animated film or television production is confined to the studio, where they help plan, schedule, and coordinate the daily operation of the production department. Such duties can include preparing and distributing daily filming schedules and notifying crew members of important script changes and production arrangements. They also keep records of production shot sheets, which are used by the continuity staff during postproduction to detail the timing of various program or production segments. They also provide assistance in researching, developing, coordinating, and finalizing scripts and maintaining files and records. Files they collect and keep on hand can include on-air talent releases, personnel worksheets, photos, and other visual materials. They assist in casting and scheduling and in the control room or studio on an as-needed basis.

Their work often involves typing memos, data entry, documents, and schedules as well as photocopying and scanning. Assistants may also be responsible for keeping complete and accurate records of petty cash expenses, a supply of petty cash, and expense reports. Production Assistants occasionally assist the personal needs of the producer and director.

Kristen Drewski, who served as a production coordinator on Blue Sky Studios' 3-D computer-animated features *Ice Age: Dawn of the Dinosaurs* (2009) and *Rio* (2011), handled many such duties when she was a Production Assistant and was usually the first animation-specific employee at work in the morning. One of her main responsibilities was to organize a list of shots, or "dailies," and check with animators to see if they had any to add to the list. She loaded the shots/clips into "Sweatbox" and played and reviewed them each morning while a Production Assistant or another production coordinator took notes. Afterward, she input the notes, including notations made by the director, into an online database for tracking purposes. She was also responsible for camera and rigging ticketing when either a camera was needed or a rig broke down during production. The bulk of her duties consisted of scheduling and keeping track of all appointments for the series supervising animators. Drewski either called other PAs and rescheduled or tried to schedule an appointment a supervisor had requested. She was sometimes required to attend appointments and meetings to take notes.

Finally, Drewski handled assorted other tasks that differed from day to day and needed to get done within a very limited amount of time. Time was the greatest challenge every day. Fast-paced and physically demanding, the job required extended periods of sitting and standing, hand-eye coordination, and manual dexterity to complete her tasks effectively.

Production Assistants are vital cogs in the production pipeline. They work long hours—beyond the usual 40 hours a week—to keep the project on schedule and to keep things moving in an orderly flow.

Salaries

Income for Production Assistants is moderate compared to other animation positions in the industry. According to multiple industry sources, salaries for Production Assistants on animated motion pictures and television shows range from $24,000 to $29,000, depending on factors such as experience and qualifications. In some markets, salaries can be as high as $33,000 a year.

Employment Prospects

Employment opportunities for Production Assistants in the animated motion picture and television field are fair. Openings occasionally occur at major-market film and television studios and postproduction houses, including commercial television and cable networks and local television stations. In major markets, competition is stiff, as there are usually far more applicants than available positions. The best way to enter the business is through internship programs offered in connection with film or trade schools with ties to

the industry. Sometimes people working as runners advance to become Production Assistants.

Advancement Prospects

Opportunities for Production Assistants to advance in their careers are only fair. Much depends on particular circumstances, on-the-job performance, reputation, skills, and unique opportunities within each studio. "At our particular studio, people seemed to stay in their positions for a lengthy period of time," Drewski stated, but other studios offer more opportunities for faster growth.

Most Production Assistants use the position as a stepping-stone to advance to higher-level positions on the production side of animation, moving up the next rung to production coordinator or production secretary and eventually into such leadership roles as production supervisor. Others forge their way into becoming producers. Most Production Assistants end up trying to become producers. However, depending on career goals, Production Assistants can take any career path as long as they take the necessary steps and fulfill experience and skill requirements.

Education and Training

Many Production Assistants have undergraduate degrees in various subjects, but an undergraduate degree is generally not required. It is useful to complete short-term courses in business and production at a film or trade school. Graduates of vocational or trade schools who complete animation, computer, film, or media courses can gain experience in production and will find it easier to gain a foothold in the industry.

Experience, Skills, and Personality Traits

Because Production Assistant is an entry-level position, minimal experience is required. Production Assistants must, however, have some working knowledge of animation or how studios operate. They need to have good computer skills and knowledge of software such as Adobe Photoshop and related applications.

Production Assistants must be bright, responsive communicators and be able to think and learn quickly. Since they juggle many tasks daily, they must have good organizational skills and be good at prioritizing and multitasking to ensure that the project's needs are completed on time. Production Assistants should be proactive, diligent, and able to anticipate the needs of the production. They must have strong interpersonal skills and the ability to interface with many different personalities on the job.

Because of the high volume of paperwork and record keeping they handle, Production Assistants must be numerate, literate, and capable of taking accurate notes. As providers of much-needed administrative and back-up support to the production team, good typing and computer skills are needed. In certain situations, Production Assistants must possess a valid driver's license and their own to car to run authorized errands upon request.

Unions and Associations

Presently, no unions exist that specifically represent Production Assistants in motion pictures and television. However, at some major-market television stations representation is offered by the National Association of Broadcast Employees and Technicians AFL-CIO (NABET). States such as Arizona and California offer professional organizations—the Arizona Production Association (APA) and the Production Assistants Association (PAA), respectively—for production professionals that are beneficial for networking and improving job opportunities and working conditions.

Tips for Entry

1. While in high school, apply for an internship at your local television station to gain practical knowledge of production processes. Most likely, you will function in the role of a Production Assistant.

2. In high school or college, volunteer and accept production jobs of any kind working on your school's theater productions or campus television station.

3. Work as a Production Assistant on a nonunion student and independent film in your area to beef up your résumé.

4. Join entertainment job Web sites such as Animation World News (http://www.awn.com), FilmStaff.com, and ProductionHUB.com. They feature updated film and television production job listings daily, as well as jobs on commercials, music videos, and more. Create a profile of yourself, and apply for openings.

PRODUCTION COORDINATOR

CAREER PROFILE

Duties: Coordinate workflow and provide administrative, clerical, and office management support for an animated motion picture or television production department

Alternate Title(s): Production Office Coordinator; Production Secretary

Salary Range: $35,000 to $50,000

Employment Prospects: Good

Advancement Prospects: Good

Best Geographical Location(s): Los Angeles, New York, San Francisco

Prerequisites:

Education and Training—High school diploma and/or some technical or vocational training in animation and/or film and television production required; a bachelor's degree in film, art, theater, communications, or related field generally preferred

Experience—Minimum of two years or more of experience in film or television production, preferably in animation

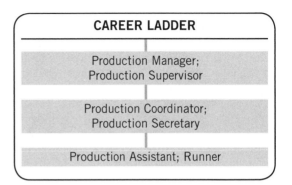

CAREER LADDER

Production Manager; Production Supervisor

Production Coordinator; Production Secretary

Production Assistant; Runner

Special Skills and Personality Traits—Motivated; detail-oriented; organizational and time-management skills; written and verbal communication skills; filing and paper-management skills; computer and word processing skills

Position Description

When it comes to the smooth and timely operation of an animated film or television production, Production Coordinators take center stage. They serve as an important liaison between all relevant members of a production and assist in the management of the production process from pre- to postproduction by effectively prioritizing, organizing, and managing the workflow and scheduling and coordinating the day-to-day workings of the production.

Production Coordinators are assigned to a specific department or group of departments and become an integral part of the management structure of that team, working directly with the line producer, producer, and production manager and providing support to other supervisors and artists. During preproduction, they are responsible for setting up and running the production office according to the guidelines set by the production manager. Their job is entirely office-based, and they typically perform a variety of important duties. They essentially run the production department and define, set up, and manage the production schedule. They coordinate all preproduction materials for ship-

ping; this involves obtaining approvals; organizing, labeling, and copying assorted materials; and maintaining and distributing artwork and storyboards needed for pitches during preproduction. They deliver required printed and recorded media to the director for slugging (timing the storyboards with the dialogue) or animatics (developing the story reel), schedule track readings of the audio recordings, prepare sheets for track readings, gather needed materials for sheet timing and for checking, and collect material for the checker.

Production Coordinators prepare and distribute production schedules, cast and crew lists, and copies of scripts as needed and facilitate communication between all departments. This includes communicating and adjusting production schedules with the production staff as needed. Furthermore, they develop and maintain systems for monitoring work in process and flow of production of assigned productions, set up files, and keep a log of start and completion dates. They label materials clearly and neatly with all necessary information. Production Coordinators also provide administrative and back-up support to the production team, which includes typing memos, documents, schedules, detailed reports, meeting notes, and notifications; photocopying; doing computer data entry and filing; preparing routine correspondence, including responding to internal and outside production faxes and e-mails; and answering phones in a timely manner.

After the start of production, Production Coordinators produce and distribute any new versions of the script after revisions or changes are made. They initiate regular contact with the artists or animators and flag potential problems and delays for the production manager and the line producer. They complete all design breakdowns of the animation and monitor animation and comp files arriving from overseas studios and distribute them to the appropriate animators. They track progress of all shots as they progress through the production pipeline and coordinate shots and wrangle artists for dailies. They anticipate and communicate any issues that arise to the producer and line producer, such as manpower issues or scheduling conflicts. They monitor distribution of production materials to broadcast networks and/or various film processing laboratories and communicate the status of deliveries to relevant parties on the production, finding ways to assist and ensure targets are met. As production draws to a close, Production Coordinators assist the production manager in closing accounts with suppliers, returning surplus stock, completing any loose ends, and storing office files safely so information can be easily accessed by key personnel if needed in the future.

Because they are responsible for the day-to-day operation of the production office, Production Coordinators typically work long hours, particularly in the final week before the start of principal photography. Depending on the size and scope of the production, they may supervise and delegate certain tasks assigned to them to one or more assistant production coordinators or production runners.

Salaries

Salaries for Production Coordinators at most major studios and animation companies are higher than salaries for Production Assistants. According to industry sources, entry-level salaries range from $45 to $75 per hour and from $35,000 to $50,000 a year.

Employment Prospects

Employment opportunities for Production Coordinators are only fair, as competition is extremely intense. Positions usually go to only the most qualified candidates. The expansion and growth, however, of the animation industry, including the ongoing and continuous demand for feature-length productions and new

and original television programming to fill the daily, nighttime, and weekly schedules of cable networks, will result in further opportunities in the future. One of the overriding issues currently undermining growth and prosperity is the national economy, with many studios cutting back personnel and hiring only as positions need to be filled, and often on a temporary basis. Savvy and talented individuals who take initiative and have solid reputations and contacts in the industry in all likelihood have a greater chance of finding employment over someone less experienced and without an inside-the-industry advantage.

Most Production Coordinators first become production runners, an entry-level job that exposes them to the many different aspects of a production. Usually, they progress up the ladder to production assistant and assistant production coordinator and with experience move up to Production Coordinator.

Advancement Prospects

Advancement prospects for Production Coordinators are fair. With demonstrable leadership and management skills, some individuals may successfully make the jump to Production Supervisor; others scout for similar positions at other studios and production companies. Only the especially talented and skilled few obtain the elevated staff positions of production supervisor and production manager at major film or television animation studios and production facilities.

Education and Training

No specific degree is currently offered for this career path. Most studios and production houses require at least a high school education and some post–high school technical or vocational training in animation and/or film and television production; in other cases, a bachelor's degree in film, art, theater, communications, or a related field is preferred. Course work in animation, film, television, and theater production as well as administrative, office, and secretarial skills are useful. Computer training in the use of software applications, including Microsoft Word, Excel, PowerPoint, and Outlook, in a work setting is highly recommended.

Experience, Skills, and Personality Traits

The role of Production Coordinator can be stressful and intense, especially during the last week of preproduction. To perform this job successfully, Production Coordinators must display a high level of initiative and flexibility and a positive attitude. It helps to have a charming and friendly personality to make the difficult times of production fun. Production Coordinators need to be hard working, driven, dynamic, dependable, patient, efficient, and cool and calm under pressure. They need to be fast learners who adapt quickly and have the ability to work independently with minimal supervision. They must establish priorities and multitask effectively, going "above and beyond" what is demanded of them in a high-pressure, fast-paced production environment.

Competent Production Coordinators understand the process of animation, the different phases of production, and the creative side of the business and always put the needs of the production and others first. Possessing excellent communication skills, they keep everyone in the loop throughout the production process. If there are any issues that arise, they must promptly tackle and resolve them.

Often employers require other specific production skills, such as experience in creating production schedules and reports and effectively managing work within a department to meet predetermined goals. As a result, Production Coordinators need excellent secretarial, word processing, and file management skills. They should be able to use project management software, including FileMaker Pro.

Studios prefer team players with the ability to perceive and solve problems and provide ideas and solutions to producers that allow departmental work to stay on schedule. They also want those who can work effectively with diverse personalities and working styles. A current driver's license and clean driving record is another requirement.

Unions and Associations

At the present time, no unions or professional organizations represent Production Coordinators in the animation and film and television industries. Some with experience elect to join the International Alliance of Theatrical Stage Employees (IATSE), the union of professional stagehands, motion picture technicians, and allied crafts originally founded in 1893, for networking opportunities and other benefits, including set wages and pay scales and health and pension plans.

Tips for Entry

1. While in school, take business and computer courses to acquire administrative, office management, computing, and secretarial skills.
2. Apply for internships, or volunteer to work unpaid at a local television station or production facility to gain practical experience.
3. Find part-time work while completing your education to gain real-world office and administrative experience.

PRODUCTION MANAGER

Duties: Find innovative and creative ways to make sure the production schedule moves forward

Alternate Title(s): None

Salary Range: $50,000 to $100,000 or more

Employment Prospects: Fair to Good

Advancement Prospects: Good

Best Geographical Location(s): Los Angeles, New York, San Francisco

Prerequisites:

Education and Training—A bachelor's degree in communications and film studies preferred

Experience—10 years of film and television experience, preferably in animation

Special Skills and Personality Traits—Administrative and management skills; patience; diplomacy; accounting, budgeting, and scheduling skills; organizational and time-management abilities; judgment; computer literacy; communication skills; thorough knowledge of film and television animation production

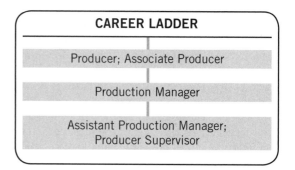

CAREER LADDER

Producer; Associate Producer

Production Manager

Assistant Production Manager; Producer Supervisor

Position Description

On any animation production on which they serve, Production Managers are like air traffic controllers: Their job is to track, coordinate, and juggle many different jobs and emergencies at once and make sure the production runs smoothly and on time.

As administrators and supervisors, Production Managers essentially run the production and are in charge of all organizational aspects of production scheduling and budgeting, managing the day-to-day details of their department and the production as a whole. Managing a small staff of production coordinators and production assistants, they produce results by determining the best allocation of labor resources, tracking production scheduling and costs and making any necessary "on-the-fly" adjustments to the process. Possessing strong work ethics, astute business minds, and organizational abilities, these dynamic and self-motivated individuals are most effective when they gain the trust of people around them and react calmly to stressful situations as they occur and are flexible enough to make necessary adjustments.

"This is a fast-paced environment that changes constantly and a production manager must be able to handle the change," stated the longtime animation Production Manager Christina DeSilva Rowell, most recently a Production Manager on *Despicable Me* (2010).

During preproduction, Production Managers closely interface with the producer, line producer, and first assistant director to break down the script page by page and to develop a provisional schedule. Afterward, they usually consult with various department heads to estimate the cost of materials needed and assist in the preparation of draft budgets. After the preliminary budget has been approved, Production Managers may assist the producers in interviewing and selecting crews and suppliers, negotiating wages and conditions of employment, and ensuring compliance with all regulations and codes of practice. Furthermore, Production Managers may negotiate, approve, and arrange the rental or purchase of all production materials, equipment, and supplies.

Once the project enters production, Production Managers shift gears to ensure that all bills are paid and to delegate tasks to their production coordinator and production assistants as needed. They monitor and control production expenditures and the progress of the production; oversee necessary production paperwork, including call sheets and daily progress reports; and ensure that the production schedule and departmental budgets are on target. Additionally, they routinely sign and authorize any purchase orders and prepare weekly cost reports, usually with the help of the production accountant or accounting department. Likewise, they make changes to the schedule or budget as required and communicate such changes to relevant personnel. After the production wraps, the Production Manager handles closing out any required paperwork, including the receipt of all final invoices and issuing payment for services provided.

Throughout the course of the production, Production Managers have busy, hectic schedules. They attend meetings and make rounds and reviews with the producer, director, and other department heads, usually accompanied by their production coordinator or production assistant to take notes. Afterward, Production Managers follow up on the things that need to be done and assign items to members of the production staff, give them deadlines, and follow up with them as needed.

For Rowell, while working as a Production Manager at smaller, independent studios, her day started the moment she woke up. "Because I was working with overseas studios [in] conflicting time zones, it was beneficial for me to be able to start my day early and end my day late," she explained. "Checking e-mail from home, in the car, and while at work was normally how the day progressed. I would try to work out all the issues between myself and whatever party was involved, come up with a solution, then present both the issue and the solution to my producers as quickly as possible."

Striking a balance between work and personal life is a challenge, as the job is very demanding. It is not uncommon for Production Managers to work 12- to 16-hour days, not including their daily commute. The role of Production Manager has its upsides—the ability to take on great responsibility and fulfill the needs of the production while working in a creative, team-oriented environment, according to Rowell.

Salaries

There is no set minimum or maximum salary for Production Managers. Salaries are based on budget, scope of the project, experience, and what a person can negotiate. On the low end, Rowell noted, salaries start at around $50,000 per year. For feature animation, Production Managers' salaries generally start at around $100,000 a year and, as salaried employees, no overtime is awarded. In addition to feature animation, Production Manager work within various branches of the animation industry—TV/episodical series, direct-to-DVD projects, CG projects, 3-D stereoscopic (a technique that creates or enhances the illusion of depth) projects, etc.—and each as a result of different variables has a different set of salary ranges. As Rowell stated, "The higher the budget is of the project, usually the higher the salary. So, a Production Manager on a six-month

direct-to-DVD will generally have a lower yearly salary than a Production Manager working a few years at a feature animation studio."

In addition, salary ranges differ by geographical location. For example, the San Francisco bay area pays less than Los Angeles. Coupled with all of this is the fact that salaries for production are also based on experience. A union does not manage Production Managers, so the salary determinations are relatively subjective.

Employment Prospects

At the moment, employment prospects for Production Managers are fair to good due to the current economic climate in the United States and many companies opening sister studios overseas in places such as India, Singapore, and Hong Kong, where the labor pool is larger and cheaper. As Rowell explained, "Because companies are hesitant to hire, if they are looking for a production manager, they are going to their existing employees to promote from within rather than hire an outside person."

Furthermore, in the United States, there are far more people available to work than positions, but studios have started turning the corner and hiring again. Most studios tend to hire those who have strong reputations in the industry. Unless hired for a full-time position, length of employment can depend on the project and studio.

Most Production Managers begin their careers at the bottom rung as production assistants, gaining hands-on experience at a studio or production company in all aspects of animation production. Others start off as producers' assistants, a role usually tied to a desk and one that is not as team-oriented as production assistant.

Rowell believes working your way up the ladder is the best preparation you can have for becoming a Production Manager. By "learning the ropes" from the ground up, you gain the necessary skills to not only do the job, she said, but anticipate the problems that may arise. From this vantage point, you can also learn from multiple mentors and see what works and does not work as a management style.

Advancement Prospects

Most successful Production Managers move on to higher-level production posts, including associate producer and producer. Many factors impact how quickly you advance in your career. According to Rowell, "Once you are established within a company and have proven to be an asset to the team, the prospects for advancing to the next level are good. The size and growth potential of the company may determine how fast one can advance. Usually the smaller companies—where people tend to wear more than one hat—have a better potential for rapid advancement, rather than a big company where there are many people in line for that one spot." The best opportunities are in bigger cities, and chances for advancement improve when working in the areas where the jobs are offered.

Education and Training

A bachelor's degree in communications and film studies is generally preferred.

During high school, students should take courses in art, art history, broadcast communications (if offered), computer applications, computer/graphic arts, English literature, photography, and theater arts. In college, communication arts majors are usually required to complete course work in broadcasting, media graphics, multimedia journalism, and visual communications. Film studies curriculums usually cover the study of film history, film concepts, script analysis, acting principles, directing, and techniques in film editing as well as business management and marketing. In addition, other course work that proves helpful includes accounting, economics, English, finance, psychology, and sociology.

Experience, Skills, and Personality Traits

For a position as business-oriented as this, individuals who seek to become Production Managers require a host of administrative skills. Difficult times during production call for Production Managers to have "extreme patience and diplomacy, and employers are looking for people that can manage these situations well," Rowell said. "In general, employers want to hire people who are strong and easy to deal with."

Successful Production Managers must have budgeting and scheduling skills. They must know how to establish a working relationship with the production's accountant in order to anticipate and provide for changes.

Production Managers must have superb planning, organizational, follow-through, and time-management abilities. As Rowell offered, "Producers need to be able to rely on their Production Manager on every task given. Production Managers are expected to know the status of every department, have a resolution plan for potential problems, and relay this information to their superiors in a clear, concise manner."

In addition, Production Managers must have exceptional communication skills in dealing with all members of the production team. They must be experienced in knowing how to communicate in all situations, whether in an important meeting with the director/producer, with a studio executive, or while giving directions to the production team.

Production Managers require technical proficiency in budgeting and accounting, scheduling, and word-processing software to work effectively in today's technology-driven world. Furthermore, a Production Manager must have a thorough understanding of the technical processes involved in animation production.

Production Managers also need a working knowledge of relevant union and broadcast regulations and agreements, necessary licenses and clearances to obtain, and any other workplace and production regulations and requirements.

Unions and Associations

There are no unions that expressly represent Production Managers. While joining certain organizations is beneficial for artists, for production people having affiliation is not necessary. Most Production Managers instead choose to join online networking sites, such as LinkedIn, to maximize visibility.

Organizations such as the Visual Effects Society (VES) are useful for networking purposes. However, to become a member, applicants require sponsorship from two existing members.

Tips for Entry

1. Gain as much experience as you can working in the industry. The more companies you are exposed to and people you meet, the better.
2. Network with people you know. Let them know you are looking for a position. Many positions are filled via word of mouth.
3. Have a good résumé that is concise and easy for a hiring manager to read. Remember that most hiring managers have limited time to read your résumé, so refrain from being verbose, and have a good layout that is easy on the eye. Also, save a copy as a PDF file so you can e-mail it easily and not worry about formatting issues between computer platforms (i.e., Mac vs. Windows).
4. Check studio and company Web sites, and submit résumés online, but also introduce yourself to company recruiters via professional social networking sites such as LinkedIn. You can search for "recruiter" by studio (e.g., "DreamWorks," "Nickelodeon," etc.).

SOUND

SOUND EDITOR

Duties: Cull and synchronize vocal and special effect sounds during postproduction in creating the final soundtrack of an animated film or television production

Alternate Title(s): Sound Effects Editor; Dialogue Editor; Music Editor; Foley Editor; ADR Editor

Salary Range: $41.21 per hour ($2,410.92+ per week)

Employment Prospects: Poor

Advancement Prospects: Fair

Best Geographical Location(s): Los Angeles, New York, San Francisco

Prerequisites:

Education and Training—High school diploma; undergraduate degree from film school preferred

Experience—A minimum of four years of experience, including two years assisting in sound editing

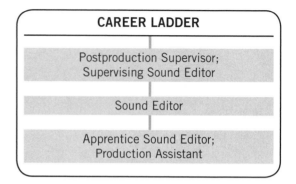

CAREER LADDER

Postproduction Supervisor; Supervising Sound Editor

Sound Editor

Apprentice Sound Editor; Production Assistant

Special Skills and Personality Traits—Creative and technically astute; personable; adaptable; good listener; organized; time-management skills; able to handle stressful situations; computer literate

Position Description

On all animated productions, the soundtrack, which includes dialogue and sound effects, accompanies the action and reinforces the direction, tone, and pacing of the story. Sound Editors assemble and synchronize the character dialogue and special sound effects in creating the finished soundtrack of the production.

For decades, Sound Editors have helped make sound an important element in films and animation, masterfully combining voice recordings, character dialogue, sound effects, and musical scores with tremendous precision and skill, from Bugs Bunny's classic "Eh, what's up, doc?" to the realistic sound of frogs croaking and bamboo crackling on fire, and everything in between.

Today, Sound Editors work as part of in-house studio sound editing teams or for independent sound facilities contracted to perform this service. On most film and television animation productions, one Sound Editor usually supervises a team of Sound Editors. Each editor is designated to handle a specific area of editing, such as dialogue (dialogue editors), sound effects (FX editors) and ADR (automatic dialogue replacement editors). Before commencing the actual sound editing, Sound Editors meet with the director, who briefs them on the general style of the production and all aspects of the soundtrack. They edit the sound based on the director's requirements along with recommen-

dations they approve. They also reference notes from their session with the director that indicate time codes of all sounds that are required, including special sound effects and Foley sounds, any revoicing or changes in the characters' performances on the soundtrack, and where music is underscored more predominantly. The supervising Sound Editor oversees looping sessions (in which actors or voice-over artists redo and rerecord lines of dialogue that need improving or changing) and additional audio special effects as needed. In addition, Sound Editors work with the music editor/composer to bridge the sounds with the musical soundtrack in the final mixing.

Almost always, the character dialogue is recorded at the beginning of production—known as preproduction—using a digital audio workstation (DAW). Dialogue editors, sometimes on staff at the animation studio, breakdown the dialogue from the recording session. They log and label the sound files and begin assembly of the normal-pause dialogue (*normal pause* is a term for having seven to 10 frames between each line of dialogue) for the EMR (edited master reel). This will be the first rough edit, or radio-play, of the program before it goes to animatic (done by animatic editors, who are usually film editors). The animatic audio will be the final, timed version of the show before it leaves for final animation. This tends to be the reference for the first cut of the picture when it returns for postproduction.

Once the final film or television production is cut down, locked, and approved, a cut of the production is sent to the studio sound department or audio-post facility during the final stage, called postproduction, for final sound design and mix, which is when the work for Sound Editors really begins. Sound supervisors or lead editors spot (mix in sounds or sound effects) or mix the show with the director and make all applicable notes for anything specific they will want in the show. "Things that are not always obvious to the editor," stated Eric Freeman, a Sound Editor on various animated television series. "Sounds like doors, atmospheres, cars, and punches usually need not be spotted."

Afterward, the supervising editor gets cuts of the production and notes to the sound team. A half-hour animated show usually staffs one to three Sound Editors. The sound effects editor (FX editor) creates and designs all the nondialogue and nonmusic portions of the film or show. Unlike a live-action production, there is no audio reference or "production sound"; the entire soundtrack has to be created from scratch. So FX editors need to add atmospheric sounds such as birds, traffic, wind, room tones, dogs barking, airplanes passing overhead, and others. They also add sounds for every action on screen: doors opening and closing, a car passing by, buildings exploding, a hand touching a face, and much more. According to Freeman, "FX editors are often called sound designers since they are 'designing' very specific or out-of-this-world sounds."

FX editors have many tools at their disposal that they use throughout the process, including DAWs, samplers, synthesizers, software plug-ins, and field recorders for capturing their own sound effects, to name a few. Depending on the budget of the project, FX editors will also edit the Foley. "Foley is the process of performing and recording sound effects to picture in real-time," Freeman explained. "The most common types of Foley performed are footsteps and cloth movements."

Dialogue editors edit the original EMR (since this is when the dialogue is at its best quality) to match the final cut of the production. This will involve resynching dialogue to match picture and organizing the lines of dialogue on the audio tracks to be in the most efficient layout for the final mix. As Freeman stated, "The dialogue editor will remove any clicks and pops that can be caused by the actor's mouth. They will also 'smooth' out the cuts between lines to make reads sound more natural."

The dialogue editor often labels the audio to give the audio mixer an easy reference of what line is where in the dialogue. The music editor, who sometimes is also the composer, will edit the composed music to best match the emotion and timing of the picture. Many times, music tends to be the driving audio force in animation. When a composer is not available or not provided for in the budget, a music editor will be brought in to pull music from licensed music libraries and create the musical soundtrack.

When it comes to sound editing, time constraints are the biggest source of stress. "Everything needs to be done yesterday, and the budgets are continually shrinking. Every producer/director wants an epic soundtrack," Freeman said.

According to Freeman, "one of the best parts of the job is helping to tell the story with an even greater depth that having only visuals cannot provide. . . . Adding sound truly brings another dimension to the story, one that can give the project additional, more intense, and sometimes signature moments in the production."

Examples of brilliant sound editing can be found throughout animation history, from famous musical gags made from orchestral accents like pizzicato violins for tiptoeing and wacky zips, slides, whistles, bonks, and splats to vocalized grunts, clicks, and gulps to the gleeful high-pitched squeals of characters such as SpongeBob SquarePants. As a result, many productions are remembered today as much for their contributions to sound and sound effects as they are for their visual artistry.

It is not unusual for Sound Editors to work more than eight hours a day or more than 40 hours a week, especially when they have to meet a deadline. The job entails repetitive use of the eyes, hands, and wrists and long hours spent in front of sound editing and mixing equipment, which can be physically and mentally draining at times.

Salaries

Salaries for Sound Editors vary based on whether the production is union or nonunion. Primetime animated shows such as *The Simpsons* and *Family Guy* pay top dollar, as they use union facilities for their sound work. Sound Editors on such shows make union scale, approximately $41.21 per hour or $2,410.92 per week, as set by the Motion Picture Editors Guild, Local 700, of the IATSE. On smaller-budgeted shows, salaries range from less than scale all the way up to union scale. Some studios may pay $300 per reel (a reel is approximately 10 minutes) or an hourly wage anywhere from $15 to $45 per hour. "It all depends on the deal the audio facility has worked out with the production company," Freeman explained. "However, since animation budgets are usually the weakest in the industry," the lower end of the pay range is probably more accurate.

Employment Prospects

Despite tremendous growth in the film and television industries, with sound technicians needed to work on small-, medium-, and large-scale productions, job prospects for Sound Editors in the animation industry are extremely poor. Animation is a niche part of entertainment, and many facilities are trying to keep the crews they have. There are many out-of-work Sound Editors. Most editors that have jobs do not leave their positions.

One reason for the drop-off in employment, particularly in the Los Angeles area, where most major film and television animation is produced, is that there are only a few facilities in the Los Angeles area that specialize in animation, and the odds of them adding to an existing crew are slim to none—unless there is a supervising editor who is already part of an established program and is looking for a new studio to set up shop. Since the cost of owning a DAW has come down so much, editors can work from home. This causes many facilities to not even keep a staff of editors. They simply hire freelancers.

The path to becoming a Sound Editor can take years. One reason is that sound facilities do not have time to train new employees to work in a specific style. On the other hand, if an intern or an assistant is reliable, available, and knowledgeable, then advancement is possible.

Most sound facilities start beginners as interns or studio assistants for very little money, doing such menial work as running errands, cleaning rooms, getting lunch, and answering calls. From there, they often move on to help in the machine room making dubs of videos, converting files, labeling media, and getting elements to editors and mixers, gaining more practical experience. After about two years—some studios take more time, some take less—a supervisor may ask interns or office assistants to help by editing some background effects, or loading dialogue reels, or editing Foley, but, again, this comes after some time of proving themselves to be efficient, reliable, and capable of working independently. After years of honing their skills, making the supervisors look good, and keeping the clients happy, they may be tapped to supervise a show.

Advancement Prospects

Sounds Editors have a few options for advancement in the area of sound editing or postproduction management, mostly to supervisory positions such as a supervising sound editor and postproduction supervisor, but attaining them can be difficult because of stiff competition.

The best way to work your way up the ladder is by working for a smaller, boutique, or mid-size postproduction company. It is very difficult, but not impossible, to advance in a major studio.

Education and Training

There is not a specific educational degree required to become a Sound Editor. A high school diploma with some training at a film or trade school or a degree from a solid film school is helpful. Otherwise, if you want a college degree, a concentration in liberal arts that focuses on creative rather than technical skills is more beneficial.

Freeman attended one of the specialized audio schools in the country and successfully completed their program before landing work in the industry. Training covered the basics regarding studio protocol, signal flow, electronics, recording, mixing, and mastering, and the greatest education was the hands-on experience. He also got to intern and assist at real studios.

Experience, Skills, and Personality Traits

A minimum of four years of experience, including two years assisting in sound editing, is generally needed to become a Sound Editor. However, experience requirements depend on the studio's needs and the person's skills and attitude, according to Freeman.

Whether working in film or television animation, Sound Editors require knowledge of computers, audio mixing consoles, digital audio workstations, audio recording techniques, sound theory, and concepts of analog and digital audio techniques. They must be creative, well organized, and good listeners, not to mention team players able to deliver what the director wants.

Sound Editors need to be personable. Most of the time their supervisor deals with the clients, but if a client meets with one of the editors and is offended or otherwise put off, the entire project can be compromised. Freeman has seen it happen, and it is not good for anyone involved.

Sound Editors must have good time-management skills, possess a high tolerance for stressful situations, and be able to put in the time required to complete the work at hand.

Unions and Associations

Membership in the Motion Picture Editors Guild, Local 700, of the IATSE is not required to work on most television animation productions. A certain amount of paid, nonunion hours are needed along with a steep initiation fee and quarterly dues thereafter to join. Some high-profile shows, such as *The Simpsons,* are union shows, but most of the animated shows from Disney, Cartoon Network, and Nickelodeon do not require a union audio facility to do the work. The advantage of joining the union is being able to work on both union and nonunion shows. On union-sanctioned productions, Sound Editors are paid union wages and receive benefits, including health and pension plans.

After gaining some experience in the industry, others belong to Motion Picture Sound Editors (MPSE), the largest independent peer group for Sound Editors in the nation, for networking purposes. Online professional networking resources, such as LinkedIn, are also useful.

Tips for Entry

1. After high school or college, find work as a production assistant to gain industry experience.
2. Seek work at a music or sound studio to acquire practical experience in sound recording and sound editing.
3. Accept any job you can find working on a post-production sound crew to learn more about sound editing, and develop contacts and relationships with more experienced industry professionals to move your career forward.

SPECIAL EFFECTS

MODELER

CAREER PROFILE

Duties: Design and build the basic skeletons and shapes of all 3-D character and environmental models that support art and story concepts in computer animated commercials, films, television productions, and games

Alternate Title(s): 3-D Computer Modeler; Character Modeler; Model Designer

Salary Range: $35,000 to $110,000 or more

Employment Prospects: Poor to Good

Advancement Prospects: Fair to Good

Best Geographical Location(s): Los Angeles, New York, San Francisco

Prerequisites:

Education and Training—A two-year college degree in digital art and animation

Experience—Minimum of three years working on high-profile projects

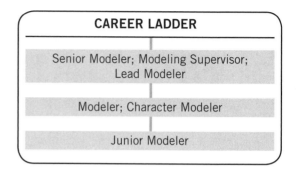

CAREER LADDER

Senior Modeler; Modeling Supervisor; Lead Modeler

Modeler; Character Modeler

Junior Modeler

Special Skills and Personality Traits—Creative; eye for detail; perfectionist; diligent; efficient; hard working; team player; listener; positive attitude; communication skills; understanding of the production pipeline, particularly texturing, rigging, and animation; sculpting and visual effects skills

Position Description

When it comes to creating genuinely realistic computer models needed for computer-generated imagery (CGI) or computer-animated productions and games, Modelers make everything possible. Working hand-in-hand with the art department from approved designs and conceptual drawings developed by the art director, raw scan data of complex objects and poses, and reference research material, they create and build 3-D computer models, from full-bodied characters to other scene assets, for film and television animation. Modelers use computers to create characters, environments, and props. Much of the process consists of working back and forth with the art director to achieve "the desired look," noted the DreamWorks Animation Modeler Charles Ellison.

Sometimes Modelers render a character design on paper first and sculpt the model from the paper design, then build them on a computer, starting with a wire frame on the computer screen. With their keen eye for form and motion, they employ a basic understanding of physical motion, weight, balance, texture, and form along with technical tools, such as programming languages and scripts, and principles of basic matrix mathematics and linear algebra to design and build their models.

Heeding the directions of their supervisors, Modelers create accurate and reliable models that adhere to the requirements of the production designer or art director. The entire process of model building is meticulous and complex and requires tremendous artistic and technical skills and patience. For example, during the making of Jerry Seinfeld's *Bee Movie,* DreamWorks Animation Modelers, working hand-in-hand with designers, handled the Herculean assignment of creating 39 locations for 43 sequences, including almost as many sublocations. In total, 150 New York City buildings, tree-topped Central Park, and Pasadena's rose-laden Rose Parade, all designed from the bees' point of view, were rendered in 3-D computer animation. As Douglas Cooper, the visual effects supervisor at DreamWorks Animation, noted, "Very early on in this movie, Jerry [Seinfeld] made it clear that he wanted the audience to see the world the characters live in, not just the stage."

In instances like these, Modelers build intricately detailed models and environments from snapshots taken of the environments and create the basic shapes first in animation software, such as Maya, before handing them over to effects artists. 3-D artwork is created afterward from those models. Other times, Modelers quickly generate models in rough form and assemble them all in one set to review the entire scene with the production designers and art director before taking the models further.

To enable layout artists to more easily compose shots, character modelers and riggers are usually charged with the responsibility of making characters scalable so animators can change their sizes dynamically from shot to shot or within a shot. At peak production, members of the modeling department can spend seven to 10 hours a week working hands on with character designers, the production designer, and the art directors. Usually, the Modelers, 3-D animators, and technical directors all work together in building the models. Once they have finished the models, they hand them over to riggers, who are responsible for rigging, or setting up, the models to be animated. It is then left up to the animators to computer animate them before texture artists apply needed surfacing and texturing. Afterward, technical directors handle the lighting and rendering, with lighters adding tone and depth to the animation's onscreen appearance during filming. On big-budget productions, Modelers are required to work with riggers, texture artists, and lighters. On smaller-scale productions, however, they often take on the added responsibility of rigging, building textures, and creating lighting.

As their skills further develop, most Modelers specialize in varied areas of model design and creation, including characters, objects, environments, or special effects. Modelers work in casual officelike settings. Their schedules are project based. They can work 40 hours or more per week to meet the demands of the production. Their job requires them to sit behind a computer for long periods of time and repeatedly use their hands, eyes, and wrists to create 3-D models.

Salaries

Industrywide, as reported by various sources, annual salaries range from $35,000 for a beginner to $110,000 or more for more experienced Modelers. According to the last reported member wage survey of The Animation Guild, Local 839, of the IATSE, Modelers, listed as model designers, earn a starting salary of $1,150.00, with a high of $2,517.50 and median of $1,800, a week. Experienced journeymen Modelers draw $1,534 weekly. On the other hand, freelance Modelers can make up to $500 or more a day. Hourly wages for work on theatrical films can range from $35 to $50. Some studios pay overtime.

Employment Prospects

Despite the large amount of films, games, and commercials being made and more and more productions requiring CG animation and digital assets, prospects for hiring are poor to good. There are far more aspiring Modelers than open positions. Employment prospects depend to a great extent upon the growth of the industry you choose—for example, films or games.

Other than cases in which companies require three years of experience on high-profile projects, the career route for a Modeler starts at the lowest level of the studio production chain, where individuals combine both modeling and texturing skills on the job. Most of these individuals mainly model characters, while others focus on designing hard-surface assets. At bigger studios, they split up the job into both specialties. Being skilled in character modeling and texturing and surfacing will lead to more opportunities. In some cases, studios recruit talented Modelers after they graduate from professional animation and art schools; others hire only seasoned industry veterans. Trainees sometimes can work their way into the position by displaying a level of modeling talent and skill.

The number of Modelers on a project depends on its size and scope; a major feature film, for example, will employ from 10 to 20 Modelers, and smaller productions usually hire one or two. Employment on a major film can last from six months to a year; on smaller commercial freelance projects from one week to one month at a time or longer if extended.

In an environment so extremely competitive, breaking into the industry can be difficult at times. Most employers, as noted earlier, look for Modelers with production experience, but no amount of experience or education can substitute for a fantastic demo reel. Exceptional portfolios can even outweigh lack of experience.

Location can impact employment prospects. Opportunities are greater in major urban areas in the United States and Canada, including Los Angeles, San Francisco, and Vancouver, and overseas in London, Australia, and New Zealand. Work opportunities are generally more plentiful at bigger studios and for freelancers.

Persistence is very important in securing employment. According to Modeler Thomas Kernan, it is vital to "Never give up. Keep working hard on your personal work and strive to find a job. Send your work out constantly. Build a network of artists or employers. Stay up to date on the industry trends. Attend visual effects conventions like ACM SIGGRAPH. . . . It can be rough in the beginning, but once you are in, finding jobs and networking will become easier."

Advancement Prospects

Potential for advancement is fair to good. Ultimately, advancement depends on the individual and the opportunities within a chosen industry. With hard work, most Modelers with excellent artistic skills advance to higher-paying jobs, including model lead, model supervisor, and even CG and visual effects supervisor, or positions in other disciplines, such as rigging, texturing, technical direction, and animation.

Speed, quality, efficiency, good leadership, supervisory abilities, and organization skills are keys to advancement. Individuals can fast-track their careers by producing high-quality work in a fast and timely manner. Modelers who demonstrate leadership and a full understanding of the modeling process on the job are more likely to move into lead or supervisory roles.

Advancement can depend on location and "where the work is being done," according to Kernan. With its plethora of studios and production houses, Los Angeles currently offers great chances for advancement. Many other states and cities where creative studios are opening up shop, such as Austin, Texas, home to a growing number of video game companies, also offer opportunities for advancement.

A good reputation and a track record of achievements and recognition among peers can also help. "This industry is small. Everyone knows everyone. If your work is amazing, it will definitely get around and people will remember it," Kernan stated. "Networking is key in this industry. On the flip side, if you have a bad attitude or arrogant personality that will get around" and hurt your chances for advancement.

Experience also impacts chances for promotion and advancement. Employers like to see that you are well rounded. Having a high-profile project on your résumé will definitely help.

Education and Training

A minimum of a two-year college degree or a diploma from a recognized animation or art school in digital arts and animation is usually required. In some cases, degrees in several other disciplines also qualify, including computer animation, computer graphics, industrial design, sculpture, and others. Comparable professional experience sometimes can outweigh the academic qualifications provided the candidate has a strong track record that demonstrates talent and skill needed for the job. Life drawing and experience in sculpting or traditional model building can also be a plus.

Individuals should become proficient in the use of one or more 3-D software programs, such as Soft Image 3-D XSI and Maya, as well as Adobe Photoshop and Zbrush. Candidates must also have a working knowledge of character and environmental modeling. Acquiring additional training to stay current on rel-

evant software also gives Modelers a definitive advantage throughout their career. Staying current with industry trends is a plus. However, as Ellison noted, no amount of experience or education can substitute for a fantastic demo reel with great examples of your work.

Experience, Skills, and Personality Traits

At least three years of experience on large-scale productions is required. The best Modelers have a background in basic anatomy, fine arts, and architecture, some training in industrial or mechanical design, and an understanding of machinery, balance, gearing, materials science, and other elements of physical engineering. More important, they should possess good drawing skills, including the use of light and shadow, and a strong sense of scale, form, weight, and volume, with the ability to design and create models in a range of styles. Modelers should also have a sense of what is possible and the amount of detail appropriate in model building.

On the job, Modelers should be able to work with a minimum amount of supervision and have a capacity to function as a team leader. They should show a willingness to take direction and address comments and changes made by their supervisor. Besides following procedures and requirements of a particular studio or production, they need to deliver their work on schedule and under pressure, so organization and time-management skills are essential.

Unions and Associations

For guaranteed wages and employment benefits, membership in The Animation Guild, Local 839, of the IATSE in Burbank, California, is beneficial. Many visual effects practitioners in the industry, including Modelers, are members of the Visual Effects Society (VES), the only organization that represents the full breadth of visual effects professionals in all areas of entertainment. The Encino-based organization offers numerous benefits and resources to its members, along with events and group gatherings. Other Modelers join ACM SIGGRAPH, a global nonprofit volunteer organization, which offers year-round programs for computer graphics professionals.

Tips for Entry

1. Decide what area of modeling you want to pursue—motion picture or game animation—as in the games industry, for example, smaller companies usually staff generic 3-D modelers and break the position into character and environment

modelers, so identifying your area of specialization is important.

2. Develop an understanding of underlying principles, styles, and methods in modeling, design, and creating dimensional models.

3. Learn, apply, and improve your modeling skills and your familiarity with traditional and industry-standard software tools. Design, develop, and create your own character models using design software to showcase your talent and skill level. Include your best work in your portfolio.

4. Network, network, network! Attend industry conferences, participate in online forums, and confer with other professionals to obtain feedback and guidance in pursuit of landing that first job and advancing in your career.

RIGGER AND RIGGING ARTIST

Duties: Conceptualize and build skeletal structures, animation controls, mechanical devices, and surface simulations of modeled and textured 3-D computer-generated and stop-motion characters or objects

Alternate Title(s): Character Technical Director; Technical Artist; Setup Artist

Salary Range: $14,412 to $22,800 (animation); $60,000 to $80,000 or more (gaming)

Employment Prospects: Good

Advancement Prospects: Fair to Good

Best Geographical Location(s): Los Angeles, New York, Portland, San Francisco, Seattle

Prerequisites:

    Education and Training—Degree in animation, computer graphics, visual effects, or related field from an art or animation school

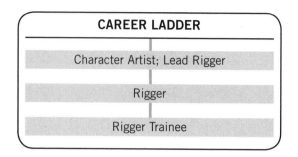

CAREER LADDER

Character Artist; Lead Rigger

Rigger

Rigger Trainee

    Experience—At least one to three years of experience rigging characters in film, television, or game environment

    Special Skills and Personality Traits—Artistic; technically savvy; motivated; deadline-driven; understanding of anatomy, muscular structure, joints, and movement; attention to detail; organization, communication, and interpersonal skills

Position Description

In preparing computer-animated characters for final rendering, Riggers, also called rigging artists, are responsible for creating a moving skeleton or structure that features working parts and joints that enables animators to animate in a realistic fashion. As a member of a studio's special effects department, or character, or technical art department, Riggers often work as part of a large group working on the same production. The art of rigging (setting up the characters to be animated) is important in maintaining the cohesive organic movement and look during the animation process; without it, animators would be unable to make 3-D models or characters move fluidly at all.

Working closely with the computer graphics lead, animation lead, and lead Rigger—usually one per production—to develop the most suitable rigging solutions, Riggers create high-quality animation rigs for characters, props, and objects. They employ computer-driven tools and techniques to design and implement rigs in a production. Riggers have a firm grasp of animal and human anatomy and know how to make rigs of real-life models that perform a wide range of movements.

Using 3-D software packages such as Maya or software that is proprietary to a given studio, Riggers first build and set up a complete body skeleton to create a character model. They assemble and place joints in appropriate locations for realistic movement and configure the axes of rotation of joints for a natural range of motion. Once the skeleton is in place, they work on rigging the model, setting up controls that enable the animator to facilitate appropriate actions and movements. After binding the character's skeleton to its skin or polygon mesh, Riggers test the joints, the joint rotation, and movements of the skeleton and finalize the character, binding and weighting their model and putting it in dramatic poses. They then export the rig to a computer with the tools in place for animation and rendering. In a game environment, the rigs they create and export for high-profile games for Xbox 360, PS3, and PC markets must work in a game setup and bring the models to life in the game engine. The rigging work Riggers do is extremely complex, as the movements they define can affect each model's external appearance and surface. The rigging therefore must be pipeline-friendly for texturing, lighting, and rendering. If it is not, there could be problems with delivering the project before the deadline.

Riggers are likely to have regular meetings with the animation directors and animators to facilitate workflow. Also, as part of their responsibility, they may test and implement new rigging approaches to improve animator interaction, deformations, and geometric components of the models to be rigged, adhering to the needs of the production.

"The creative environment of production and solving technical problems so that the best possible aesthetics can be achieved are two attractive things about the job," stated Brad Clark, an award-winning artist and animator and a cofounder of Rigging Dojo, an online school providing personal and customized character rigging and technical art education. "Animation on a computer is really limited by what the rig can do, so the constant push to make a better rig or instrument for animators to create with makes for a challenging and rewarding job."

Stop-motion animation Riggers design and build rigs or mechanical devices to support the puppets or props that stop-motion animators manipulate. One standard method employed in today's digital age is for Riggers to attach a rig or wire to guide the puppet or prop in the shot and then remove it with a computer program in postproduction. For the stop-motion animated feature *Coraline,* Rigging Artists had to rig a multitude of puppets jumping from every direction. As LAIKA studios animator Bartek Prusiewicz told *Oregon Film,* "I had 30 mice to animate and half of them were flying around, making me dizzy. The riggers came in, assessed the situation and promptly built rigs that made the animation manageable. I could not have portrayed what mice do without the amazing rigging crew."

Riggers expend a large amount of effort in putting rigs in, and the VFX department puts a lot of effort into taking them out. The Academy Award–winning visual effects supervisor and cameraman Brian Van't Hul once explained, ". . . the end product allows an animator to create realistic movement and a great performance for a character. . . . The riggers are the invisible hands that help the animator defy gravity and physics resulting in an artistic ballet for the audience."

Riggers usually work as part of a large group that focuses on the same project. The job requires prolonged periods of sitting and standing, hand-eye coordination, and repetitive movement of the hands and wrists. Riggers commonly work more than 40 hours a week to meet project deadlines.

Salaries

Salary information for Riggers is hard to find because there is little standardization across the industry, as titles and job descriptions vary not only from industry to industry (film, broadcast, and gaming) but also from company to company. Salaries for film and television animation Riggers, as set by The Animation Guild,

Local 839, of the IATSE start at $2,105.26 and increase to a high of $2,707.50 per month. The median salary for the position, including nonunion shops, is $2,120. For journey-level Riggers, pay is slightly below the median, at $1,596.64 per month.

The average salary for full-time Riggers and Rigging Artists in the gaming industry is $60,000 to $80,000 or more per year. The typical monthly starting salary is from $1,800 to $2,000 per month. With three to five years of experience, it is not uncommon in the gaming industry for Riggers to earn from $4,000 to $5,000 and after six years or more $7,000 per month. A lead Rigger can potentially earn around $9,000 per month.

Freelance rates for Riggers in the gaming industry are around $80 to $130 per hour, depending on the complexity of the work and the type of project. Companies often require a cost per rig or per character; under this arrangement, the artist has to guess how long it will take to rig the character, then bid it at a fixed price based on an agreed-upon hourly rate.

Employment Prospects

Given the emphasis on computer-animated content creation and higher-quality and large-scale projects, according to multiple reports on hiring trends in the industry, opportunities for Riggers across the film, television, and games animation industries are mostly good. "There is a decent sized demand across all industries for talented Riggers," stated the character Rigger/technical artist and Rigging Rojo cofounder Chad Moore. "The job can be more stable between projects while other positions like animators are hired as needed and let go after a project is done."

Typically, up to two Riggers are employed per production. Depending on the type of production, duration of employment for freelancers is from three to 12 months.

Advancement Prospects

As the role of Riggers in production is often so varied, advancement opportunities are generally good. However, experience is really important. As Riggers accumulate years of experience, they often pursue one of two career paths: artistic or managerial.

The more artistically inclined often move up the ranks as character artists. Eventually, they advance to higher-level positions, directing the work of others as character directors and art directors. Riggers with managerial aspirations advance to become lead riggers, which requires around five years of experience. Individuals with seven to 10 years of hands-on supervisory experience can be elevated to studio managers and producers.

Riggers have also been known to move laterally to other production positions if they so desire, such as animator or 3-D artist (modeling and texturing), and to production fields such as project management. Others become technical directors.

Education and Training

A degree in animation, computer graphics, visual effects, or related field from an art or animation school is sufficient to become a Rigger. Most programs offer courses and in-house production training in basic animation, auto rigging, camera manipulation, character modeling, character walk cycles, facial rigging and/or deformations, lighting, mechanical rigging, rendering techniques and file formats, scripting (MEL, Python, and pyMel), skeleton design, rigging and skinning, set modeling, skinning, setup and rigging for motion capture editing, texturing, tool creation, and UV mapping of characters or objects. Undergraduates also develop a good sense of motion and fluidity in their work and an in-depth understanding of rigging tools, including Autodesk Maya, which is essential. Animation classes are important so Riggers can understand and anticipate what animators will need.

Like other jobs in the entertainment industry, often the educational degree is less important than having strong work to show in a demo reel. "A strong reel and previous production experience on shipped games or movies is really what gets people jobs," Clark remarked. "While education is important, it is often not the main focus when studios are looking to hire."

Experience, Skills, and Personality Traits

Most employers require professional experience of rigging characters in a film, television, or game environment based on the level of the position. Generally, junior Riggers require up to one year of experience. A staff Rigger needs one to three years of experience, and a senior Rigger three to five.

Riggers must be highly motivated, adaptable, organized, and artistically and technically creative. They require art skills and an understanding of the process of animation—both how to animate and the vocabulary used by animators. They must have a strong sense of movement and an understanding of how muscular structure and joints interact. They must have the ability to accurately interpret 3-D layouts, analyze 3-D form, and predict and solve complex problems in a 3-D space. They must show initiative in carrying out tasks to meet intended deadlines and production schedules. In order to teach and explain in clear language how tools or rigs work, Riggers require strong oral and written communication skills. They must be able to stay cool under pressure and solve complex and technical problems. They have to be able to successfully work with animators, artists, programmers, and producers with various backgrounds and personality types.

Unions and Associations

Riggers who work in the animation industry are members of The Animation Guild, Local 839, of the IATSE, which provides guaranteed wages and union support to Rigging Artists and visual effects artists. An additional organization worthy of joining is ACM SIGGRAPH (http://www.siggraph.org/), which hosts conferences at which new technologies are shown that often directly apply to rigging characters for film. In the gaming world, the International Game Developers Association (http://www.igda.org/) is a professional society for video and computer game developers and artists worldwide. In addition, there are a number of user groups for individual software companies that are helpful for networking and learning and sharing techniques.

Tips for Entry

1. Develop good problem-solving skills; learn how to simplify and abstract problems to their simplest components. Use modular techniques (creating scripts that automate repetitive work or building "helper files" that you can load into a scene to connect things).
2. Develop an understanding of underlying principles, guidelines, and methods of artistic anatomy and basic mathematics.
3. Learn, apply, and improve your rigging skills and your use of traditional and industry-standard software tools. Design, develop, and create your own character rigs and script tools using design software. Design characters similar to the kinds of creatures currently featured in motion picture and game animation. Include your best work in your portfolio.
4. Network by attending industry conferences, participating in online forums, and conferring with other professionals to obtain feedback and guidance in pursuit of landing your first job or advancing in your career.

VISUAL EFFECTS

COMPOSITOR

Duties: Construct the final images of animation composed of layers of previously created material

Alternate Title(s): None

Salary Range: $27,514 to $97,458

Employment Prospects: Good

Advancement Prospects: Good

Best Geographical Location(s): Los Angeles, New York, San Francisco

Prerequisites:

Education and Training—Two-year college degree in animation, film, or visual effects

Experience—A minimum of two years of experience at a small studio or production facility

CAREER LADDER

Visual Effects Supervisor; Compositing Supervisor

Compositor

Matte Painter; Digital Painter

Special Skills and Personality Traits—Energetic; self-starter; analytical, organizational, and creative skills; disciplined; deadline oriented; resourceful; communicator

Position Description

Compositors are behind-the-scenes artistic and technical wizards who raise the level of film and television productions, animated and otherwise, to seemingly impossible new creative heights while enhancing the overall mood, atmosphere, and entertainment value for audiences. Their work runs the gamut from blending filmed elements to adding fire in a fireplace to blending green-screen footage into background and digital environments. At the end of the production process, Compositors blend various elements into a seamless whole.

Compositing is a highly technical approach used in both 2-D and 3-D animation to do something as simple as add animation to a background, break down character animation in a scene into different layers, or blend more complex various media into a single film frame. Compositors work in most areas of animation and postproduction and are generally the last to be hired and let go once the production is finished. Employed at major studios and postproduction houses (at some postproduction companies, technical directors may do their own compositing), they require relevant artistic skills and technical skills. They use expensive computer hardware and software and desktop technology, including many animation software packages, for basic and advanced compositing. Their job is equivalent to that of a sound mixer or a recording engineer in that they seamlessly weave different pieces together so they all make sense. Generally, their work falls into two

categories: character animation and multiple-image compositing.

With character animation, Compositors break down the character or object into separate layers. They can composite an infinite number of layers without experiencing major problems with dust, color deterioration, or inconsistent coloring between the different layers. For example, they could composite four layers of character animation. The layers could consist of two individually drawn parts that move—the head and arms—and two others that do not move at all composited into a single frame. Only the parts that move are redrawn for each frame, thus economizing the work required of the animators.

Using the same digital compositing techniques, Compositors tackle bigger and more complicated tasks when it comes to compositing many different images in films that incorporate live-action and animation. In this case, they manipulate and layer various materials provided to them, such as 3-D animation, live-action film, photographs, illustrations, graphic artwork, and special effects one on top of the other. They marry these multiple elements into one final, integrated image that looks as if it were shot all at once with the same camera. For example, in a major live-action/animated feature, Compositors may bring together such image elements as a background plate of live-action photography, blue/green screens, CGI characters and objects, miniature models, and matte paintings in the same environment. The complexities of their work often involve making corrections in camera movements, depths-of-field, lighting, shadows, color (grading and matching), contrast, distances between objects, composition, animation, and more to enhance the final image that ends up on the screen.

Although a career in this field can be rewarding, Compositors typically work long hours, and the work is highly demanding. At their busiest times, they often work 10-hour days and overtime as necessary to meet approaching production deadlines. Typically, when the project reaches the Compositor, the production is in its final stages, but their work is not quick. Sometimes they can spend many weeks compositing just 15 seconds of film or video because the work can involve considerable experimentation, rendering, tweaking, adjustments of colors and lighting, and more to get the right look. As the longtime digital Compositor John Lafauce, Jr., warns, "It can really take a big chunk of time out of your life [and it is] important to go into it for the right reasons. Do it because you're passionate about it."

Salaries

Most digital effects companies are nonunion, and therefore their rates of pay can vary. Pay for Compositors is often determined by certain factors—the type of job, experience, location, industry (e.g., film, games, industrial design, etc.), job requirements, and production budget. According to Payscale.com, salaries for Compositors with one to four years of experience range from $27,514 to $51,395. Individuals with five to nine years of experience draw a salary of $68,784 to $97,458. According to the June 2010 member wage survey of The Animation Guild, Local 839, of the IATSE, union wages for 2-D Compositors started at $1,000 weekly. The median salary was $1,600 and topped out at $2,800 thereafter. 3-D Compositors, on the other hand, made a minimum of $1,768.42 to a high of $2,800 (an average of $1,936.84) a week. Compositors with journeyman status earned $1,135.08 (2-D) and $1,428.96 (3-D) per week.

Employment Prospects

In some cases, Compositors work their way up to the position within the compositing department from bottom-rung artists. Many start as digital painters or matte painters before advancing to become Compositors. In other cases, those who acquire an understanding of compositing and computer programming and relevant experience can become Compositors. Higher-paying jobs are in greater abundance in larger markets in the United States, including Los Angeles, New York, and San Francisco, and overseas, including London.

These markets feature high concentrations of film and animation studios and special effects and postproduction facilities.

Many Compositors work as freelancers, working a couple of months at a time with time off in between. One stumbling block, however, is if the studio or facility they work for hits a slow period. In this case, freelance Compositors can be laid off, so it can be useful to have other opportunities lined up. To land your first job, it is important to network with others in the industry and build up a foundation of contacts that can potentially help you get your foot in the door.

Advancement Prospects

With appropriate talent and skills, Compositors often can advance to higher-level staff positions at studios and postproduction facilities. They can go on to become sequence heads, senior compositors, or compositing supervisors. In other cases, Compositors have advanced to become visual effects supervisors.

Education and Training

A degree from a two-year college or art and animation school in animation, design, illustration, fine arts, painting, drawing, photography, or computer animation is required.

Students are advised to attend well-established schools with solid reputations and curricula that include practical training in high-end digital effects compositing and a faculty of instructors with industry experience.

An understanding of how movies are made and what goes into making them is definitely important. Therefore, as part of the overall curriculum, many undergraduates study filmmaking and take courses in lighting, cinematography, and camera work. "Understand everything that goes into a film because the goal in my mind, as a Compositor, is to make the effects look like they're really there," said the compositor Scott Metagr. "To do that it helps to have a complete understanding of how movies work and how things should look."

Since Compositors make their living creating believable effects, technical knowledge is important. Computer graphics course work that provides hands-on experience with software used in the industry, such as After Effects for animation or Apple Shake or Eveon Digital Fusion for feature films, is beneficial. Make sure the school has a computer lab and offers lab time for students to collaborate with their fellow students on a real production. This will encourage the development of skills essential to finding work and creating a dynamic demo reel to win over potential employers after graduating.

According to the Compositor Michael Derrossett, Compositors do not have to be "a total computer geek" to succeed in the profession. Instead, they require a "fair understanding of some technical aspects. . . . You have to understand how film relates to video and how video relates to film because they run at different speeds. Each medium has different characteristics so there is some math that you have to do and you have to be aware of resolution."

Experience, Skills, and Personality Traits

A minimum of two years of professional experience is required. A demo or show reel that demonstrates honed artistic talent and technical skill is essential, as are good references.

Compositors need the artistic talent to make critical judgments, the technical skills to make practical decisions, and the analytic ability to recognize and solve problems as they arise. They must have extensive knowledge of current compositing software, such as After Effects and Shake, and various other paint programs, including Adobe Photoshop, used throughout the industry. They require a strong understanding of the processes of 3-D and 3-D animation production and a knack and passion for painting, photography, and other 3-D fine arts. Compositors also should have an eye for composition, color, lighting, shadow, and other related techniques for compositing different art forms. Since their work requires a minimum of supervision, Compositors should be highly motivated, methodical, and thorough. Good communication skills and the ability to interface well with other colleagues are helpful.

Perhaps the most important skills they must possess are resourcefulness and an ability to problem solve. Often, Compositors are assigned image elements that do not easily fit together. Thus, they must be able to effectively arrange and adjust elements presented in different resolutions or formats.

Unions and Associations

No national union exists for Compositors. However, for those working on both coasts, membership in The Animation Guild, Local 839, in Burbank, California, and Local 843 in Orlando, Florida, both of the IATSE, are very helpful in securing union wages and other union support and for networking with other professionals in the business. Many visual effects professionals belong to one of the most prominent trade organizations in the field, the Visual Effects Society (VES), the only organization that represents the full breadth of visual effects practitioners. With more than 1,500 members in 17 countries, the group offers a multitude of domestic and international programs and events to educate its members.

Tips for Entry

1. In school, gain practical experience and working knowledge under a faculty of instructors with experience in the field.
2. Pursue internships or apprenticeships through school or by networking with professionals on industry Web sites.
3. Produce an outstanding demo reel, even if it consists of only a few well-executed composited shots if that is all you have. Make sure the reel demonstrates your talent. Break down and explain the work you did on each shot, and include thumbnail stills that are easy for recruiters to understand.
4. Develop a good work reputation, and be passionate in your work.
5. Read up and stay current on the latest technological trends and developments in the industry.

LIGHTER

CAREER PROFILE

Duties: Light, render, and composite elements of an animation into a final shot

Alternate Title(s): Lighter/Compositor; Lighting Artist; Lighting Technical Animator; Lighting and Compositing Artist

Salary Range: $60,000 to $120,000

Employment Prospects: Fair to Good

Advancement Prospects: Good

Best Geographical Location(s): Australia, London, Los Angeles, San Francisco, Vancouver

Prerequisites:

Education and Training—Undergraduate degree in art, computer animation, computer science, fine arts, illustration, graphic design, or equivalent experience

Experience—Two years or more of production experience using 3-D lighting and compositing packages

Special Skills and Personality Traits—Creative; flexible; dedicated; pleasant personality; visual acuity; technical skills; detail-oriented; communication and time-management skills; ability to manage large number of files; ability to work long hours

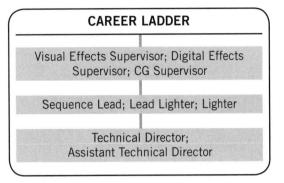

CAREER LADDER

Visual Effects Supervisor; Digital Effects Supervisor; CG Supervisor

Sequence Lead; Lead Lighter; Lighter

Technical Director; Assistant Technical Director

Position Description

On screen, 3-D images are bright, vivid, and realistic, and it takes many elements to bring a single shot to life. In computer-animated productions, the person responsible for finessing the lighting, rendering, and compositing of all the elements into a final shot is the Lighter.

In preparing all the visual pieces to be composited in individual scenes throughout a production, Lighters assemble all the incoming data—models, looks, animation, and effects. This includes making lighting adjustments, creating light rigs and adjusting lighting in those files, rendering (or processing) the levels of lighting, and using appropriate compositing software to create a "composite tree" that combines the rendered levels and adjusts the final composite until it meets the desired vision of the director, art directors, and sequence leads.

Lighters work mostly for studios and visual effects production houses. They report to a lead lighter, usually one per team, who, in some cases, lends only technical support, while the sequence supervisor makes artistic comments with respect to Lighters' work.

Lighters complete their work in three stages: lighting, rendering, and compositing. During the lighting phase, using powerful computing software, they take the wire frame from animation and apply surface materials, which are usually created by a separate department. "The greatest challenges are achieving the desired look of the shot while maximizing the efficiency of the rendering process," according to the DreamWorks Animation lighting and compositing artist Brock Stearn.

Afterward, the Lighter lights the scene in a 3-D software package such as Maya. This technical task involves placing lights, setting the intensities, the fall-off, and the color, and setting up any reflections in surfaces or refraction through surfaces, such as glass. "Often the material values are changed," according to the DreamWorks Animation senior lighter/compositor Wallace Colvard, "in order to achieve the correct look."

Next, during the rendering stage, Lighters send the file to render at the "render farm," a cluster of powerful computers built to produce computer-generated imagery (CGI) to create the finished color frames of the animation.

Then, for the final stage, using a software package such as Shake, Lighters create a composite of the rendered images, backgrounds, and any effects created by the effects department. Various members of the production team then review this composite before it is presented to the director for final approval. If the director provides notes of changes or revisions, Lighters address them. This process continues until the director approves of the finished product.

Lighters are constantly tasked with balancing a heavy load of technical skills with an equally heavy load of artistic skills. While other departments in the production pipeline may lean more to one side or another of that balance, lighting is always in the middle. Stearn thinks this is one of the things that makes being a Lighter a very attractive job, as it keeps both sides of the brain sharp and requires being able to communicate in both artistic terms and technical terms to various members of the production pipeline.

Most Lighters usually work in offices with rooms and cubicles or a group pod with workstations. The atmosphere tends to be more relaxed than more conservative corporate offices. Despite the creative nature of the work and the pleasant office atmosphere, the job is challenging. Besides technical issues, Lighters face extreme pressure in producing their work under difficult time constraints and having their work criticized by many people.

Salaries

Salaries vary by studio. The standard weekly salary for a Lighter, as set by The Animation Guild, Local 839, of the IATSE is $1,072.56. Based on skill level and experience, salaries can reach a mid-range of $1,672.73 and a maximum of $2,200 per week. On the other hand, journey-level Lighters earn slightly less than the median, $1,596.64. Depending on reputation and efficiency, Lighters can move up to the ranks to senior Lighter/composition, a position that draws about $2,000 to $2,500 a week. Conversely, lead Lighters make from $2,200 to $3,300 a week. Most companies pay overtime. Outside the United States, however, overtime rules change.

"Union shops usually have better benefits, but not always better pay. Some shops pay only an hourly rate and no special overtime rate. Some shops pay a weekly wage whether there is overtime or not," Colvard related. "Union shops have limitations on the number of consecutive days you can work and will usually pay double time and a half on the sixth day and double time for the seventh day and beyond."

In some instances, freelance Lighters make more, but most jobs are "contract run-of-picture." At DreamWorks Animation, for example, this usually means three pictures with a six-month probation period during employment. Sometimes, if a studio is in a "crunch," it will hire Lighters at a higher rate for a shorter period of time.

Employment Prospects

Job prospects for Lighters are only fair to good in Los Angeles, where most major animation studios are located, and good overall in other parts of the country.

Lighting is now the largest department in the production pipeline. Due to greater needs, more Lighters are being hired than ever, according to Stearn.

In today's new business model, though most studios require at least two years of experience for the positions, many Lighters are hired straight out of school at low salaries through apprentice or outreach programs; others are hired as production assistants. However, because lighting is such an expensive part of the pipeline, more lighting jobs are being outsourced to other countries and other cheap-labor work environments. The Walt Disney Feature Animation senior Lighter Quentin Frost has worked at every major house in southern California. According to Frost, the stability for raising a family or planning a stable future is "hideous," as staff positions continue to disappear in favor of freelance or project-for-hire positions.

According to Colvard, most companies have set up branches in less expensive locations such as India, Singapore, and right-to-work states such as New Mexico, or in countries including Canada, that give large incentives to production facilities.

The payoff in your career comes from starting "small" by working at small companies, where you may wear other "hats" than lighting. It gets your foot in the door. The second and third gigs are easier, but after you land a job at one of the top companies such as DreamWorks, Disney, or Pixar, you are, as lighting technical director Chris Jolly noted, "golden" at that point and can go anywhere you want.

In seeking employment, it is important to have a strong demo reel and be aware of the level of quality of your competition. Have something interesting on your reel that will stand out among the sea of student work out there. Plus, network and work it from every angle. Visit Web searchable career and job Web sites, such as ACM SIGGRAPH (http://www.siggraph.org/jobs/), CreativeHeads.net (www.creativeheads.net), and VDX Pro (http://www/vfxpro.com), and, if you are interested in doing lighting for video games, and Gamasutra (http://jobs.gamasutra.com/).

To increase your chances of being hired, most professional Lighters suggest researching the company you are applying for, what its needs are, and what its requirements are. A bit of research, according to Stearn, will make an applicant stand out further than people who blindly submit their work to every company.

Advancement Prospects

Advancement prospects for talented Lighters can be good, but individuals must be talented and dedicated. If you are a talented staff employee are willing to work very long hours, and can survive the politics, advancement can be fairly rapid. Unless you want to seek a more managerial and less artistic path, however, upward mobility is poor.

Some Lighters take their specialized knowledge and advance into such leadership roles as lead lighters and sequence leads. Others prefer to advance into the management areas of postproduction, such as CG supervisor, digital effects supervisor, and visual effects supervisor. According to Stearn, "There are not that many VFX supervisor jobs out there, but the prospects for advancing to that position are definitely good when coming from a lighting and compositing background."

As Jolly stated, "If you are driven to work long hours, you can move up from lighting TD to lead lighter fairly easily if there is nobody ahead of you."

In Colvard's opinion, the best ways to maximize chances for advancement include working hard, developing relationships with supervisors, and encouraging trust in group situations. Chances for advancement improve when working in major markets that feature film and television animation studios and effects and postproduction houses. Colvard believes there are more opportunities in larger studios because there are simply more positions to be filled. At large studios, you are at the heart of the industry, and there is more of a chance of meeting a superior who will recommend you. Smaller studios also have a habit of hiring for a single project, so you do not get as much of a chance to show your worth.

Education and Training

An undergraduate degree in art, computer animation, computer science, fine arts, illustration, graphic design, or equivalent experience is often required, though the educational requirements for this position vary. Most people have at least a bachelor's degree. Some people come in from the technical side and progress; others come from the art side and learn the technical.

To work in visual effects, gaining practical experience in creating visual images is necessary. Therefore, training should focus on acquiring such needed skills as drawing and painting and creating 2-D and 3-D images using common tools, such as Photoshop, After Effects, Maya, 3-DMax, Nuke, and others. Classes in set lighting or photography are also recommended. According to Stearn, "The information you learn from taking classes on set lighting or photography is directly related to digital lighting in visual effects."

Experience, Skills, and Personality Traits

Lighters need to have two years or more of production experience with 3-D lighting and compositing. Lighters must have a strong visual sense and an instinct for what a shot should look like. They must have a solid understanding of the principles of lighting, compositing, and three-point lighting. They must have in-depth knowledge of professional-level compositing systems, such as Shake, 3-D software packages, of 3-D rendering programs, preferably Renderman, and of UNIX and/or LINUX systems. This includes "The ability to take core concepts and use them across software," Frost stated, "because all houses have their own propriety software packages, each different from the next."

Because they encounter many complex technical problems on the job, Lighters need to be good problem solvers with good debugging skills. They need to take direction well, work well in a group situation, be open to learning new things, and be able to handle working long hours as necessary. To deal with colleagues in a deadline-driven environment, Lighters must have good time-management and communication skills.

Unions and Associations

Most Lighters are members of the Visual Effects Society, an organization made up of visual effects professionals. Some also belong to The Animation Guild, Local 839, of the IATSE, which offers health and pension plans and sets wages and pay scales. ACM SIG-GAPH, which has many local chapters, has online forums and provides opportunities for meeting others in the industry.

Tips for Entry

1. Develop your artistic and technical skills in creating visual images. Take software courses relevant to this line of work. Often instructors will recommend students for jobs.

2. Join organizations, such as ACM SIGGRAPH, and be aggressively sociable. This will also help you develop the social skills you need for the job.

3. Talk to friends and acquaintances in the industry, and try to get introduced to supervisors and recruiters.

4. Contact employment recruiters, and visit industry Web sites, including vfxpro.com and creativeheads.net, in seeking employment.

TECHNICAL DIRECTOR

CAREER PROFILE

Duties: Supervise the technical aspects of computer animation and visual effects in an animated production

Alternate Title(s): Character Technical Director; Creature Technical Director; Cloth Technical Director; Effects Technical Director; Generalist Technical Director; Hair/Cloth Technical Director; Lighting Technical Director; Look Technical Director; Match Move Technical Director; Pipeline Technical Director; Shading Technical Director

Salary Range: $40,000 to $100,000 or more

Employment Prospects: Fair

Advancement Prospects: Good

Best Geographical Location(s): Los Angeles, New York, San Francisco

Prerequisites:

Education and Training—Bachelor's degree in computer science, engineering, or equivalent

Experience—Production experience in computer animation, visual effects, or game industry,

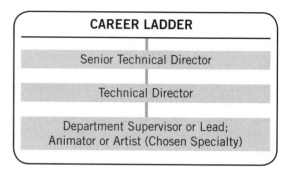

including programming and 3-D animation systems experience

Special Skills and Personality Traits—Understanding of animation production and engineering processes; creative and technical skills; leadership abilities; communication skills; computer and programming literacy

Position Description

The Technical Director, or TD, is usually a senior technical person with the highest level of competence in a specific technical field. 3-D computer animation studios and visual effects production companies as well as film and television studios employ these professionals. Typically, the Technical Director is a mix of artist and programmer, responsible for many technical aspects of modeling, texture-mapping, and lighting the characters and scenes in the production; for any needed special effects; and for complex simulation tasks and setup of how data is passed from one stage in the production to the next.

"Basically, the TD is the person who everyone turns to for an answer when difficulties arise in getting complex 3-D animation work completed," according to the CG supervisor Andrew Chapman. "TDs are expected to have an intimate knowledge of all the software being used, and be able to come up with solutions as problems arise."

Technical Directors demonstrate a delicate balance of artistic sensibilities, technical savvy, and programming skills. Most have the technical know-how to write scripts in various scripting languages, such as MEL, Perl, or Python, to script and program specific char-

acters or shots or speed up work or solve a problem in animating and rendering the production.

The title *TD* actually refers to several different positions whose responsibilities vary from studio to studio. A character technical director—sometimes called a rigger, puppeteer, physiquer, or technical animator—is responsible for constructing 3-D character rigs and animation interfaces and establishing muscle, skin, hair, fur, and clothing behaviors.

A lighting technical director—otherwise known as a lighter or lighting animator—uses light to illuminate and accentuate the mood and emotion of a 3-D scene, and a shader technical director adds the surface to the models and prepares them to be painted by texture artists or painters.

Individual technical directors on some productions are tasked with cloth, hair, effects, and modeling. Others, called pipeline technical directors, develop the architecture that links all of the departments together. Depending on the structure of the studio or company, sometimes Technical Directors also handle modeling work in the earlier stages of the production, compositing and effects animation, and particles, dynamics, and procedural animation as well.

Effects technical directors help create the effects with in-house software and third-party software such as Maya. Their job in this case is to produce a staggering number of effects—hundreds and hundreds of shots—in tandem with a team of 15 to 20 people and to make the effects look as good as possible with the resources available. Their work is broken into two phases: research and development (R&D) and shot work. Usually, the effects technical director and his team first storyboard the effects to see how they are going to be used and how they would act in the intended sequences of the film. Technical Directors use real-world references to create effects, a standard practice in the industry.

Some Technical Directors do a little bit of everything and are referred to as generalist TDs. There are advantages to being a generalist. For example, a generalist can both create and shade a model, using certain tricks in the modeling stage because he or she already knows how it will be shaded.

Approval of the shots is a three-step process. Once they are completed, the Technical Director sends them to his immediate supervisor to review. When the supervisor thinks the shots are ready, the art directors review them. Once they approve the shots, they then move on to the director for final approval.

Technical Directors work closely with the director, producer, CGI supervisors, animators, modelers, lighters, riggers, renderers, production engineers, and other TDs in developing and producing 3-D animation, graphics, and effects. They either establish a method using existing tools or software or develop and write new tools to get the job done. The work they perform is highly technical, tedious, and complex, yet highly gratifying in the end.

At DreamWorks Animation SKG in Glendale, California, the Technical Director Jacob Melvin, who has worked on such computer-animated films as *Kung Fu Panda* (2008) and *How to Train Your Dragon* (2010), writes codes and designs tools for computer animation. On a big-budget motion picture, he works with a team of 50 or more animators as one of two or three Technical Directors. Many times, animators try to do things they have never done before, creating problems as a result. His job is to "fix those issues so the movie can be made, on time and within budget" and may entail rewriting an old code, building a new software tool, or creating a graphical user interface that allows an animator to work more expeditiously.

Technical Directors work somewhere in the neighborhood of 40 to 60 hours a week. Hours vary, especially during a production's "crunch time," the period when the production is in its final stages.

Salaries

Salaries for less-experienced Technical Directors, according to multiple industry sources, range from a low of $40,000 to $60,000, with an average of $66,720. Experienced Technical Directors earn much higher salaries—between $70,000 and $100,000 or more. Wages for Technical Directors, as reported by The Animation Guild, Local 839, of the IATSE in its annual member survey in June 2010 were as low as $1,156.21 and as a high $2,880 per week. The average for the position was $2,000 a week, while journey Technical Directors drew a minimum of $1,596.64 weekly.

Employment Prospects

Competition for Technical Directors is stiff, so employment opportunities are only fair. Most major studios typically employ five or more Technical Directors, whereas smaller studios may have only two or three on staff. Production and postproduction companies also use Technical Directors but generally hire only seasoned professionals with solid credentials. Individuals seeking animation Technical Director positions generally have come up the ranks as department supervisors and leads or as animators and artists in their chosen specialty.

Advancement Prospects

Advancement prospects for Technical Directors are mostly good. Technical Directors usually advance up the ladder to senior level positions, such as senior technical directors, in their respective fields, or work to become directors, production managers, and producers. However, it is not uncommon for Technical Directors to take jobs with a more artistic bent outside of technical directing at other studios or production companies. In other cases, Technical Directors pursue an artistic path in freelance or advisory roles.

Education and Training

Minimum educational requirements for this position are a bachelor's degree in computer science, engineering, or the equivalent. Schools that have a strong art curriculum are recommended. Most studios accept either a bachelor's or master's in related disciplines. Based on the U.S. Bureau of Labor Statistics' survey of employees 25 to 44 years old, 74 percent of all producers and directors, including Technical Directors, have a bachelor's degree or higher. It is useful for candidates to have completed courses in 3-D computer animation, computer programming, and engineering, including some training in animation, modeling, lighting, and rendering using propriety or third-party software packages, such as Maya and others.

After graduating, it is recommend that aspiring Technical Directors enroll in Walt Disney Animation Studios Talent Development Program or a similar program for a three- or six-month paid position. This program has start dates in January and June of each year. In these positions, individuals apply skills in a real-world studio environment under the guidance of a studio mentor.

Experience, Skills, and Personality Traits

Most Technical Directors require a minimum of five years or more experience in computer animation, visual effects, or games production in one or more specialties, including character rigging, modeling, particle effects, lighting, rendering, and research and development. They must have experience with computer animation and 3-D animation systems and tool integration into existing or new pipelines. They must have strong troubleshooting and programming skills and proficiency in C, C++, Object Oriented Programming, Python, and/or Perl. To successfully function as part of a team, Technical Directors must have good communication skills and the ability to establish and execute priorities.

Unions and Associations

Technical Directors in film and television animation belong to The Animation Guild, Local 839, of the IATSE to work on both union and nonunion productions. Most Technical Directors hold memberships in ACM SIGGRAPH, a leading not-for-profit organization for animators, artists, engineers, technical directors, and computer graphics professionals. The organization offers meetings, events, and opportunities for networking. Another organization some find beneficial is the Visual Effects Society (VES), the only organization that represents the full spectrum of visual effects professionals in all areas of the entertainment industry.

Tips for Entry

1. If you are more interested in the technical side of the profession, take courses to earn a technical degree, such as computer science. If you are more artistic, then get a fine arts degree. Or, if you enjoy both, incorporate both into your schooling.

2. Learn the processes of drawing, painting, and 3-D animation. Read and absorb everything you can find about your particular area of interest, whether it is digital compositing, texturing modeling, or lighting and rendering.

3. After graduating, enroll in Walt Disney Animation Studios Talent Development Program or a similar program.

4. Start working in a creative position where your technical skills will soon be noticed and appreciated and vice versa if you start off in a purely technical role. Work under a mentor so you can learn what is relevant to becoming a Technical Director in your field.

VISUAL EFFECTS ARTIST

Duties: Create a myriad of visual effects using animation, live action, photography, backgrounds, and other environments for a film, television production, or video game

Alternate Title(s): Digital Effects Artist

Salary Range: $30,000 to $50,000 or more

Employment Prospects: Fair to Good

Advancement Prospects: Fair to Good

Best Geographical Location(s): Los Angeles, New York, San Francisco

Prerequisites:

Education and Training—Associate's degree in film, graphic arts, photography, or television minimum requirement; bachelor's degree in these fields preferred

Experience—Work experience as a special effects apprentice or member of a special team on film or television productions or video games

Special Skills and Personality Traits—Creativity; artistic sense; visualization skills; communication skills; management skills

Position Description

Movies, television shows, commercials, and video games depend more and more on visual effects, and some are largely driven by visual effects. Hundreds or thousands of extras and costly and extravagant sets are no longer necessary. Instead, Visual Effects Artists can create them on a computer with the click of a mouse. Working with an amazing array of technology, Visual Effects Artists are the people who make the impossible possible.

Depending on the operation and structure of the company, or industry, Visual Effects Artists work as part of a team and often collaborate with other artists, animators, programmers, and technical and production staff. They often combine live-action footage with computer-generated imagery. Sometimes, environments are combinations of real places and paintings or digital paints. The work Visual Effects Artists create is layered and stacked when it is composited in order to create vividly realistic environments.

"I've painted in clouds, trees, mountains, and such in order to recreate whole live environments," explains the Visual Effects Artist Cecile Marie Tecson. "For example, I've worked on car commercials from Mercedes to BMWs where we would have to cut the cars out of their real scenes and put them in a completely different location. This can be difficult at times because the camera may circle the car and it takes a lot of technique to try and cut out every detail needed to place it into a different environment. Also, when you watch car commercials, you don't see the cameras that are reflected through on the sides of the cars. Part of our work is removing anything from cameras to truck rigs holding those cameras. It takes a lot of work for a simple car commercial."

Visual Effects Artists, usually employed by major studios and visual effects houses or postproduction companies, creatively render characters and environments using many forms of 3-D animation and specialized computer and design programs, seamlessly placing, positioning, manipulating, and blending them in juxtaposition with other elements or backgrounds in a scene. The effects they create are known as "post effects" because they are done near the end of the production, after the animation has been created or the film has been shot.

In movies, Visual Effects Artists walk a delicate tightrope between art and real life, producing digital visual and animation effects ranging from the human-looking skin of the reverse-aging Benjamin Button to the facial expressions of characters in *Avatar* (2009). A visual effects supervisor oversees integrating the effects into the production during postproduction, when footage of real actors and the Visual Effects Artists' digital creations and that of other artists are blended into a single environment.

Visual Effects Artists work long hours—anywhere from 10 to 12 per day—with long periods of time spent behind a computer. The work requires intense hand-eye coordination and repeated use of the hands and wrists. Unless regularly employed by a company, work is on a project basis; in these cases, Visual Effects Artists have to search for work once each project is complete, which can be stressful. For many, the challenges and excitement of the job make it worthwhile.

Salaries

Salaries for Visual Effects Artists vary based on level of experience, location, and size of the company. According to industry sources, new hires make from $30,000 to $50,000 or more, while the overall average salary for this position is about $43,500. Experienced Visual Effects Artists generally command salaries at the higher end of the salary range, depending on their years of experience and record of accomplishments.

Employment Prospects

With the constant use of special effects in both live-action and animated features, current prospects for employment as Visual Effects Artists are mostly good. Job offerings most often occur in effects or postproduction houses that specialize in the production of special effects in the entertainment industry. Some enter the field as apprentices or trainees, which can lead to becoming assistant visual effects artists and eventually full-fledged Visual Effects Artists.

Advancement Prospects

With the long-term emphasis on visual effects creation expected to increase exponentially in the future, opportunities for advancement are mostly good. Based on the level of artistic and technical skills, Visual Effects Artists embark on one of two career paths: artistic or managerial. Typically, artistic-driven Visual Effects Artists are elevated to lead visual effects positions and eventually lighting directors. More managerially geared Visual Effects Artists are elevated from lead visual effects positions to visual effects supervisors, and then to either studio managers or producers.

Education and Training

Educational requirements for Visual Effects Artist vary depending on the particular industry—whether film and television or games. The minimum requirement is an associate's degree in computer animation, computer graphics, visual arts, or other related field. Sometimes a bachelor's degree in one of the above fields is required. An educational background provided by an animation, film, or trade school with a strong program in visual arts or visual effects is recommended. Programs usually cover computer sciences, programming, graphic design, and visual effects. Knowledge of computer animation software is an asset. Schools such as The Gnomon School of Visual Effects are the best places to build your skills since instructors are all working professionals who teach courses and share techniques and ideas. Most schools offer job placement services to graduates.

Experience, Skills, and Personality Traits

Visual Effects Artists require a combination of visual creativity and technical acuity. Consequently, they must have solid creative and technical abilities and strong art and animation skills relevant to visual effects, including design, composition, timing, weight, arcs, and overlapping action. To make successful, realistic effects, Visual Effects Artists must have an eye for what looks natural and believable and a flair for creating sensational effects. They must able to create both photorealistic and nonphotorealistic visual effects. Experience with CG effects systems such as Maya, Houdini, and 3-D Studio Max is a plus.

Visual Effects Artists must be meticulous and organized in their approach, with excellent follow-through abilities. They must possess good communication and problem-solving skills to work as part of a team. Finally, they must have the dedication and poise necessary to work long hours under intense pressure.

Unions and Associations

Most Visual Effects Artists are members of the Visual Effects Society (www.visualeffectssociety.com), which provides resources and opportunities to network with other industry professionals, including online forums. Others additionally join the CGSociety (www.cgsociety.org), the most respected global organization for creative digital artists, which offers a range of services to connect, inform, educate, promote, and celebrate achievement and innovation of members and digital art itself.

Tips for Entry

1. Study the visual arts, and immerse yourself in the world of digital art. Learn the basics of photography, as Visual Effects Artists need this ability to tell a story visually.

2. Enroll in a trade or film school with a program in visual effects to learn the necessary tools.

3. While you are in school, intern at a visual effects house or studio. While most internships are unpaid, you will gain needed skills working alongside professionals and make contacts that will aid you in your job search.

4. Network and surround yourself with like-minded people who aspire to do or are already doing what you want in the industry. Join organizations such as the Visual Effects Society (VES), which features events and a job board of potential employment opportunities.

VISUAL EFFECTS (VFX) SUPERVISOR

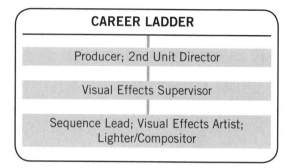
Position Description

Thanks to the rise of computer technology, larger-than-life visual effects have changed the face of filmmaking while captivating audiences of all ages around the globe. Leading the teams responsible for such fantastical flights of fancy are Visual Effects Supervisors.

Visual Effects Supervisors are responsible for helping directors fulfill their creative vision through their oversight of the entire production and the establishment of an effective workflow so the production is delivered on time and on budget. Working with leads and department supervisors, Visual Effects Supervisors define the creative and technical approach to production and oversee a team of visual effects artists and effects animators to create visual effects and animation and do visual clean-up work. Working with the director and art director, they manage lighting, visual effects, and rendering so they are on track creatively and technically; ensure that texturing and techniques are created in a way that flows through the production pipeline efficiently; work with the CG supervisor to identify areas of research and development required; evaluate artists schedules so they are realistic and achievable; and manage the day-to-day running of the

visual effects team. On a regular basis, they meet with all members of the team to ensure the director's, production designer's, and art director's vision is being met.

Largely employed at effects studios, Visual Effects Supervisors have left an indelible mark on the animation and film industry through their creativity and craftsmanship. They have successfully overcome obstacles with sheer talent and ingenuity, producing awe-inspiring moments in live-action films. Effects achieved include mammalian facial expressions, behavioral changes, and body language. Similarly, Visual Effects Supervisors and artists have provided the same success by putting their 3-D tools to work in computer-animated movies.

Visual Effects Supervisors are usually either more technically or more artistically inclined. With high-pressure deadlines and little flexibility in their schedules, they often work through the night to deliver a project on time. There is no union representation to regulate hours or working conditions. Under their supervision, capable artists employ a combination of propriety and high-end digital tools and powerful computers to design and animate characters that convey realistic emotions, actions, and movements that are endearing and form an emotional bond with audiences. Typically, as part of the process, Visual Effects Supervisors interface with other department heads charged with completing various tasks, from building CG models to rendering desired effects. For the effects in *Pirates of the Caribbean: Dead Man's Chest* (2006), for example, the Visual Effects Supervisor and his department teamed up with 13 modelers to sculpt the fishy characters, layout artists to produce 3-D layouts, and matchmovers (who insert computer animation or graphics into live-action footage) to build the digital representation of the set and location environments using photographs, which entailed 1,100 visual effects shots, 600 of them animation, in the final film. Under the oversight of Visual Effects Supervisors, in 20th Century Fox's live-action film *Fantastic Four* (2005), effects teams from a dozen studios crafted 885 visual effects shots with the help of computer animation that spanned more than half the movie.

"The best part of the role is the technical challenges presented in helping to deliver upon an artistic vision. It's very exciting to partner up with a group of talented people who are passionate about their work, nothing but great things come out of such efforts," stated the longtime VFX supervisor Gregory Yepes, who principally supervised visual effects in live-action films. "Most people I know in this industry are in it because they love it, not necessarily because it would be the most practical way to make a living. This passion is a great recipe for not only doing great work, but also coming up with new and clever ways to do the work faster and better. I learn something new about my job everyday and that makes it very exciting."

With no union representation to regulate hours and working conditions, deadlines are tight and rarely flexible. Workdays for Visual Effects Supervisors can be unusually long—as much as 10 hours a day—and a typical workweek of a minimum of 50 hours is not uncommon to deliver a project on time.

Salaries

Salaries vary according to a number of various factors, including experience, location, size of company, and budgets. According to the Visual Effects Society, junior Visual Effects Supervisors can earn an average of $2,500 a week. Salaries for top-of-the-line supervisors range from $140,000 to $220,000 a year, with the high end possibly pushed more with "more awards and accolades under your belt," Yepes related.

Employment Prospects

Although job opportunities for visual effects artists are plentiful, opportunities for Visual Effects Supervisors are only fair. Much depends on the level of experience and the amount of openings at any given company. However, as the industry continues to globalize, more opportunities will emerge abroad for individuals who seek to break into this position.

Individuals who seek to become Visual Effects Supervisors rise up from various artistic and technical positions, including matte painter, lighter or lighting artist, compositor, visual effects artist, and art director.

Advancement Prospects

Advancement prospects for Visual Effects Supervisors are only fair. Remaining within the role of Visual Effects Supervisor can be a fruitful career, and supervisors can improve on their skill sets and advance through pay raises. After advancing to the position of Visual Effects Supervisor at an effects company, some make a lateral move to supervisor at major effects or animation studios, an area with many fewer openings that is often tough to break into. As Yepes explained, "Developing that type of relationship and trust with the studio as your client will take years to develop, but that is a very logical path to take."

Some Visual Effects Supervisors choose to pursue second-unit directing positions on live-action films. However, second-unit directing is not mutually exclusive with visual effects supervising, and most experienced supervisors will do both. "Very few have made a successful transition to directing, but that's not entirely out of the question," Yepes added. "You could say the role of a VFX Supervisor is a culmination similar to being a director of photography, there isn't a lot of room for advancement into different roles, but there is a lot of opportunity to keep developing and increasing your skill set within the role."

Education and Training

Most animation and effects studios and companies require at least a college degree in animation, computer graphics, computer science, engineering, film, or a related field. The ideal field of study would be a major in art and technology with a minor in film, animation, or cinematography. "The order in which those things are studied is not always crucial," according to Yepes, "but the role of visual effects supervisor will require knowledge of both. Some supervisors come from an M.F.A. and pick up the technical skills along the way."

Experience, Skills, and Personality Traits

To become a Visual Effects Supervisor, most companies require at least 10 years of experience in visual effects; some require less, but the minimum is usually seven years. Specifically, experience as a CG lighting artist, compositor, matte painter, or art director is an asset.

One of the most important personal traits for Visual Effects Supervisors is the ability to think critically about exploring new ways of doing things. To successfully guide their subordinates and delegate responsibility, they must have excellent leadership, management, and social skills. A sense of the elements of storytelling and a strong working knowledge of 3-D software packages and pipelines are important.

Unions and Associations

Most Visual Effects Supervisors are affiliated with the Visual Effects Society, which provides in-depth information, panels, and online forums and other resources to help members advance in the industry. Other annual industry events, such as ACM SIGGRAPH, one of the largest trade conventions for computer graphics professionals, and FMX, a specialty conference for animators, filmmakers, and visual effects professionals, are also helpful for networking purposes.

Tips for Entry

1. Become computer literate. Take classes in computer graphics and computer animation. Study methods and processes of computer-generated animation, including how to make real-life models, surfaces, texturing, lighting, and shadowing.

2. Learn how visual effects and effects animation are made by reading tutorials, books, and magazines devoted to the subject.

3. Keep up to date with new tools and approaches in the field.

4. Be open-mind about where you work. As the industry continues to globalize, many more opportunities will evolve, including opportunities abroad.

5. Accept any position with a postproduction and effects facility working either as an effects animator, lighter, compositor, matte painter, or visual effects artist—anything to learn the process of putting visual effects together, and make vital contacts in the industry.

WRITING

SCRIPT SUPERVISOR

Duties: Responsible for managing and overseeing the creative and technical elements of the story and script through all stages of an animated film or television production

Alternate Title(s): None

Salary Range: $40,000 to $80,000

Employment Prospects: Fair

Advancement Prospects: Fair

Best Geographical Location(s): Greenwich, Connecticut, Los Angeles, Portland, Oregon, San Francisco

Prerequisites:

Education and Training—A bachelor's degree in animation, film, English, creative writing, or communications

Experience—Two years of experience as a production assistant or production coordinator on a completed animated film or television show

CAREER LADDER

Production Manager; Director

Script Supervisor

Script Production Assistant; Script Coordinator

Special Skills and Personality Traits—Creative; flexible; detail-oriented; management and organizational skills; computer literate; knowledge of word processing, script creation, and project management software; understanding of animation and filmmaking pipelines

Position Description

Writing an animated motion picture or television series is a multilayered process. From concept to screen, most full-length animated films takes from two to three years to produce, and it can take up to nine months to create an entire season of television episodes. Script Supervisors coordinate and contribute to the various creative aspects of the story and script to ensure that the project stays on track and meets the desired vision.

"You need to be able to balance working for micro and macro managers," stated the former Blue Sky Studios Script Supervisor Brett Hoffman, now a script/recording supervisor for Illumination Entertainment. "You need to prove you can process scripts in a fast and efficient manner for distribution and are able to track all of the lines throughout a production."

Working in the story department of a studio, Script Supervisors usually manage a small staff of people, including storyboard artists and a production assistant, also known as a script production assistant. In their role, Script Supervisors oversee all statistics, storyboards, and scripts between the story, editorial, and animation departments throughout the production. They are responsible for tracking all written materials

generated during the making of the film, including all versions and revisions of the script, treatments, pitch materials, and character descriptions.

During preproduction, Script Supervisors review story portfolios and interview artists to determine who to hire. They build a consensus between the directors, producers, and production management on action steps required for creative goals and schedules. To this end, they create tracking databases for story assignments that lead up to executive meetings. They compile reference materials for writers and field any questions they have about the story.

Acting as editorial managers, Script Supervisors attend all story, script, editorial, and brainstorming meetings to suggest creative solutions and guide discussion. They participate in all writing sessions with lead actors to help rewrite dialogue for production recording. They write character descriptions for casting and marketing references. They analyze character and story arcs in scripted material for consistency, making recommendations to the film's directors, producers, and executives. To generate ideas, Script Supervisors review archived scripts, recorded material, and story pitches for possible story ideas. They also work with the story and legal departments throughout the entire film production to track script revisions in order to help determine writers' credits.

Besides supervising the editorial side of the production, Script Supervisors manage and create scripts, called "recording scripts," for the director, actors, and staff for every recording session. Prior to these sessions, in which the actors record their characters' dialogue, they collaborate with directors and executive producers to determine how to communicate script changes and other production changes to each actor. They must also decide how to organize and distribute scripts to and from multiple writers. They attend all scratch recordings—initial recordings done with the cast, used to create a rough cut of animation from storyboards and character voices known as an "animatics" or story reels—and production recording sessions. They track selected audio tracks and ad-libs and slate and log all sessions when editorial is busy or unavailable. They also conform scripts to executive meeting reels and approved storyboards derived from scratch recordings and spot-check the scripts and reels for all dialogue (spoken and visual) that may require legal clearance.

Working conditions for Script Supervisors vary from project to project. The hours they work are at times unpredictable—eight or more on a given day. Most Script Supervisors work in structured, officelike settings and spend large amounts of time sitting at a desk or workspace in front of a computer. The position requires hand-eye coordination and repetitive movements.

Salaries
According to various industry sources, salaries for Script Supervisors on animated features range from around $40,000 to $80,000; weekly salaries average from $770 to $1,500. Studio size and talent can impact salaries. Of the major animation studios, Pixar pays on the low side of the scale. "It really comes down to what you bring to the table," Hoffman said.

Employment Prospects
While more and more animated productions are being made, most major animation film studios generally employ only one Script Supervisor—sometimes with story and editorial coordinators sharing the Script Supervisor's duties. Thus, prospects for employment are only fair.

Depending on the studio, most Script Supervisors are usually not contracted, with a few exceptions such as DreamWorks Animation, which contracts its Script Supervisors, with assignments typically lasting two years or however long it takes to complete the production. Many take the route of becoming production

assistants first and thus are able to interact with the people who would possibly promote them to Script Supervisor. The best places for employment, like most other positions in animation, are in Los Angeles and San Francisco as well as Portland, Oregon and Greenwich, Connecticut. The bulk of the jobs are in California due to the high concentration of animation studios there.

Otherwise, getting hired for the position is hard if you have not already done this kind of work before. Usually, time Script Supervisors have to work up through a company to get the job. The position entails a tremendous amount of responsibility, and management prefers people that they already know and trust.

Advancement Prospects
Many Script Supervisors stay in their positions, as, unlike other industry management roles, there is no direct path for advancement. Thus, prospects for advancement are only fair.

Script Supervisors who are good at their jobs can possibly advance to assistant production manager, production manager, and department supervisor in the editorial department of a studio because "the position is very high profile," Hoffman said. "While you might only have a PA or coordinator under you, you work directly with the producers and directors and are in many high-level meetings most other managers don't get to attend."

Making the leap to a creative position is much more difficult, especially without drawing or animation skills. Sometimes Script Supervisors can successfully make the leap to become writers, but this is rare.

While chances for advancement improve when working in major markets, the skills Script Supervisors learn and how well they apply them, combined with their dedication and ambition, play an important factor in advancing to other high-level jobs. "Each production is a different beast," according to Hoffman. "The personalities and workflow of producers and directors can vary greatly depending on the show, and it all comes down to them feeling comfortable with you and your skill level."

As with most positions in the entertainment arts, a Script Supervisor's reputation is very important. Few studios hire or promote someone to or from this position without them proving themselves and receiving recognition from their peers.

Education and Training
For this position, a bachelor's of fine arts or bachelor's of science in animation, film, English, creative writing,

or communications is sufficient. As Hoffman enumerated, majoring in film or English helps because then you have at least gotten some exposure to creative writing. Part of the job is rewriting the script to match what is in the storyboards or editorial reels, so being able to write helps. A thorough working knowledge of the filmmaking process is also helpful.

Experience, Skills, and Personality Traits

Script Supervisors generally start out as production assistants before moving up to production coordinators. At least two years of experience as a production assistant or production coordinator, having completed a full film, is required. Script Supervisors require superb creative writings skills to be able to describe what's happening in storyboards in a clear, concise way. They must be able to use word processing, script creation, and project management software such as Final Draft, Microsoft Excel, and Microsoft Word. They must be detail-oriented and able to track notes and lines and understand shorthand given in notes from meetings.

Script Supervisors also must be tactful and mindful of competing interests, as sometimes directors, producers, and writers want different things. They require tremendous flexibility, as the job requires long hours and the ability to be ready at a moment's notice, including holidays. Great communication skills and time management skills are an asset, as the job requires getting answers from extremely busy people in a pressure-packed environment.

Furthermore, Script Supervisors must be trustworthy and able to keep closely guarded story information private, even from friends at the same company.

New script drafts come out all the time, and sometimes management wants to keep changes from the crew until they are approved in order to keep them focused and on schedule. Script Supervisors must be able to work professionally with acting talent.

Unions and Associations

Currently, there are no unions for animation Script Supervisors. However, for most network live-action films and series, membership in the International Alliance of Theatrical Stage Employees (IATSE) is required and helpful for working on nonunion productions.

Tips for Entry

1. Read as many books on film and screenwriting as you can get yours hands on. Recommended are Robert McKee's *Story*, Christopher Vogel's *A Writer's Journey*, Bruce Block's *A Visual Story*, Linda Seger's *Advanced Screenwriting*, Syd Field's *Screenwriting*, David Mamet's *On Writing*, and Sidney Lumet's *Making Movies*.

2. Start working as a production assistant or as a live-action development assistant, working closely with scripts.

3. Hone your writing and note-taking skills.

4. Make friends with the managers/supervisors of the front-end departments. Learn when it is appropriate to speak in meetings and when it is better to keep quiet and take notes.

5. Look for jobs at Showbizjobs.net, Showbizdata.com, and Variety.com.

6. Sign up for LinkedIn to get connected with people in the industry.

STORY EDITOR

CAREER PROFILE

Duties: Generate and/or approve all episode storylines; hire and oversee freelance scriptwriters; develop characters, stories, and dialogue; edit and finalize all premises; outline and script for studio and network approval of an animated television show

Alternate Title(s): Executive Story Editor

Salary Range: $3,000 to $15,000 per half hour

Employment Prospects: Poor to Fair

Advancement Prospects: Fair

Best Geographical Location(s): Los Angeles, New York, San Francisco

Prerequisites:

Education and Training—None; undergraduate degree in film, theater, English, journalism or related field helpful

Experience—Experience is measured less in years and more in terms of scripts, particularly the quality and speed of editing and delivery

Special Skills and Personality Traits—Creativity; speed; efficiency; subjective thinking; detail-oriented; organized; time-management skills; team player

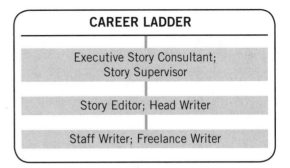

CAREER LADDER

Executive Story Consultant; Story Supervisor

Story Editor; Head Writer

Staff Writer; Freelance Writer

Position Description

While writers craft the scripts for an animated television series for network or cable television, Story Editors are responsible for the script process. Writers may story-edit themselves, or a producer may story-edit their scripts, but Story Editors make sure the scripts have a consistent tone, that they are the right length and that they are clearly understood for the actors, artists, and crew to bring to life and meet the show's overall guidelines.

The amount of rewriting Story Editors do is directly proportional to how "in sync" the writer is with the story editor, according to Greg Weisman, a supervising Story Editor. When someone gives him a script that needs a lot of work, Weisman does a major rewrite. If he is given a script that does not need a lot of work, he will do as little as he has to in order to shape it up.

Story Editors usually oversee the show's team of writers. Credit for the show's success often is split among the writing team. The most fruitful Story Editor–writer relationships are those that are in perfect sync with each other. The Story Editor serves as an extra set of eyes that provides additional ideas to make a story better. When the effort of mutual compromise does not exist between the Story Editor and writers, the result is nothing of interest in the story.

Under immense pressure and driven by tight production deadlines, the Story Editor's work is "a juggling act," a constant stream of nonstop deadlines—premises, outlines, first draft scripts, second draft scripts, final draft scripts—all running concurrently as you try to finalize a script per week to meet voice record dates. This can go on "for 13, 26 or even 52 scripts in a row with little to no break," notes the animation veteran Marty Isenberg, a Story Editor since 1996 on various animated series.

When not actually editing or writing premises, outlines, or scripts, Story Editors are busy coordinating with their freelancers and attending voice recording sessions and production meetings. "You are usually beholden to an executive producer," Isenberg stated, "although in some instances, you may end up running the whole show in conjunction with the supervising director/producer."

Most Story Editors, like Isenberg, generally prefer to develop stories by starting with a basic season arc—a map of the overall arc of 13 to 26 episodes. Then Story Editors meet with a writer or writers to break the story or several stories at once. The writer then delivers three to five premises mapping out the basics of the story. Isenberg will give verbal notes to the writer, who will revise the appropriate premise or premises.

Afterward, Story Editors do their edits on the writers' second draft and submit it to the studio and network for their review and notes. According to Isenberg, once Story Editors receive the notes, assuming no revised draft is required, they review the notes with the writers and have them create an outline (a more detailed, scene-by-scene breakdown of the story), including the act breaks and often some preliminary dialogue.

Isenberg usually has the writer(s) provide him two drafts. He then edits the second draft and submits it to the studio and network for another round of review or notes. Then the writer will go to the script phase based on those notes, again providing two drafts, which Isenberg will then edit.

Ideally, after that, the Story Editor submits the edited script to the studio and network. Any notes received are then the Story Editor's responsibility to implement. On any given week, Story Editors will likely deal with multiple scripts, all at different stages in the process. To make voice record deadlines on a consistent basis, Story Editors must simultaneously feed a minimum of one premise, one outline, and one script into the pipeline every week. It can be difficult to keep track of the details of multiple active scripts. Story Editors may also be responsible for reviewing storyboards, animatics (a show reel of the story), and rough cut animation at various stages, which means they may be dealing with all 13 or 26 stories at one time during some stages of production.

In a sense, Story Editors serve as middlemen between writers and executives from production companies and networks. The work Story Editors perform is a delicate balance between politics and diplomacy. As the Emmy Award–winning Story Editor Dean Stefan explained, "For example, you are sometimes saddled with writers that you would not necessarily pick yourself, because the network wants you to use them." In these cases, Story Editors might have to accept working with a less-than-ideal writer and that they will probably have to do a lot of the writing themselves.

Another challenge of the job is dealing with freelance writers. Good freelancers are often very busy, so often Story Editors are trying to accommodate them and their schedules. At the same time, Story Editors must also meet their own deadlines. Meeting deadlines is the most difficult and rewarding part of the job, as Story Editors are ultimately responsible for each and every premise, outline, script, and deadline. It is a seven-day-a-week job in most cases.

In the end, Story Editors find that the creative latitude the position offers is rewarding. Stefan likes "being able to shape the direction and tone of a series." He likes making up stories and getting paid for it. He likes being able to use all sides of his brain and creativity—being visual, being funny, being imaginative. He also likes the lifestyle—the deadlines are "insane," but he is really his own boss in terms of how he spends his days.

Salaries

Story Editors usually negotiate contracts before they start work, arranging fees and delivery deadlines for each stage of the process. The nature of their roles vary depending on whether they are engaged on a freelance basis or if they are working in-house for a studio or production company. Union jobs generally pay better than nonunion jobs, as do jobs at larger studios, such as Walt Disney, which are more likely to have more money to spend on their writing budgets.

On a per-episode basis, based on industry sources, Story Editors make anywhere from $3,000 to $15,000 per half hour, but compensation tends to hover in the $8,000 to $10,000 range. More experienced Story Editors receive higher salaries.

Freelancers are paid on a per-script basis. Payment is usually broken into a three-step process—a third paid upon delivery of an approved outline, a third for the first draft, and final third upon receipt of a revised draft.

While the pay as an animation Story Editor is very good compared to most jobs, it is not very good in comparison to most TV writing jobs. The position is not covered by the Writers Guild of America, and thus, as a rule, there are no residuals in animation as opposed to live action. Script fees are also lower compared to live action. So even if you are good, you have to work 10 times as hard as live-action series Story Editors to make a comparable living. Since Story Editors are not paid residuals, even if you have 10 good years, there are no revenue streams coming in off of previous work.

Stefan notes that Story Editors who are good at animation writing may work a lot, but their deadlines will overlap, and, if they extended themselves too far, they may end up doing a less than stellar job on one assignment or another. As he added, "Some writers are more adept than others at taking on multiple assignments projects at once." Thus, it is important to recognize your abilities and limits. If you do a poor job, an employer will remember it and will not hire you again.

Employment Prospects

With the role of Story Editor among the most critical to the story process, prospects for employment vary and depend on your level of experience and "who you are," Isenberg said. Generally, only about a handful of animation writers are considered worthy of being Story Editors. If you are one of these talented few, you have a good chance of becoming a Story Editor.

There are many qualified, experienced editors competing for "a relatively small number" of jobs, according to Michael Yank. In addition, it is often the case that when a show is picked up, the producers will already have writers in mind for the project, so it can be difficult to get your foot in the door at this stage.

Yank senses that opportunities for Story Editors are both "more and fewer." On one hand, there are more cable channels and shows in general. On the other hand, shows may have smaller writing budgets than they once had to keep costs low. However, all shows do need writers, so there are jobs to be had. Talent is definitely important, as in all fields, but luck plays a role too—one cannot underestimate the importance of being in the right place at the right time.

To work as a Story Editor, you have to be where the production is, especially if you are just starting out. This means the best geographical locations are places such as Los Angeles and to a lesser extent New York, Toronto, and Vancouver. It is possible to secure work from elsewhere via phone and Internet, but it helps to be able to meet face to face with an employer on short notice.

Most productions usually employ only one Story Editor, but if the order is large or the production schedule is tight, there could be up to two, three, or possibly four Story Editors on a show. For freelance Story Editors, the duration of employment usually lasts the script production season—typically 20 to 25 weeks for every 13 episodes.

The trajectory of writers who becoming Story Editors is different in most cases. The career ladder is not clearly defined, other than freelance writer to staff writer to Story Editor. However, many begin as an assistant, either at a studio or network. According to Isenberg, once you get a writing assignment, it is a matter of developing a reputation as a good and reliable writer. It is a small community, and Story Editors tend to recommend the good writers to one another. Once you have a couple of scripts on your résumé, it is fairly easy to get an agent. From there, it is a matter of getting to know the development people at the studios and networks, either through pitch meetings, meet-and-greets, and/or other networking opportunities, all of which can lead to potential development assignments. The writer who does the development is likely to get first crack at story editing the series if it sells.

Working as a writer's assistant is a good stepping-stone to becoming a writer. Writer's assistants work closely with writers, taking notes and handling the formatting of the script. Working as a production assistant in some cases could lead to an opportunity to become a writer's assistant.

Yank advises those who have their hearts set on becoming a Story Editors to write as much as possible. Also, seek as many different avenues into the industry as possible. Stick with it and you will find an opening.

Even for experienced writers, however, connections are very important. The best strategy is to put yourself in front of the people who do the hiring as much as possible, according to Isenberg. Many writers get their start as script coordinators, productions assistants, or assistants to development executives.

Advancement Prospects

Advancement prospects for Story Editors are relatively good. With experience, Story Editors can advance to become executive story consultants, producers, and executive producers. To advance, Story Editors must hone their writing skills and develop and increase their artistic skills. Those who are able only to write will have fewer opportunities for promotions.

One step Story Editors can take is to create and sell an original show. This is a difficult task, but the rewards are bountiful. According to Isenberg, there is that rare individual who earns a full-time staff producer/Story Editor position with a studio, but beyond that, there really is no advancement.

Story Editors who are especially fast, efficient, and easy to get along with have a stronger likelihood of advancing, especially at smaller studios, where there is less competition. As Isenberg noted, if you are willing to work very hard and not be paid a lot, there are probably many smaller studios and lower-budget productions that would be willing to take a chance with you.

Reputation is also important. If the right producers and executives like the quality of your work and you personally, you have a much higher chance for advancement. "Having your name attached to a hit show or hot studio doesn't hurt either," Isenberg added.

Having the right contacts can also make a difference. Established Story Editors usually have a large network of professional contacts, which can be valuable in securing new jobs and more advanced positions in the industry.

Education and Training

There is no specific educational or training requirement for this position. However, an undergraduate degree in film, radio, television, or writing is helpful, especially in landing an entry-level position as a writer's assistant, which might in turn lead to an opportunity to become a writer and eventually a Story Editor.

To develop and hone writing and editing skills, a basic and broad-based liberal arts education is an asset. Most undergraduate curricula require completing specific courses in composition, playwriting, and writing as well as film and television production. Many colleges and trade schools offer short courses in scriptwriting and animation writing.

As part of any education, undergraduates should learn how to self-edit, proofread, take others' notes for revisions, and read extensively—both classic as well as modern books, more than industry trades and newspapers, according to Weisman. He also suggests they watch contemporary and classic films and "look at the history of these mediums."

Stefan recommends taking a workshop at a reputable school that offers writing classes, for example, UCLA Extension. You will meet other writers who may go on to become good contacts, and sometimes the professors are working professionals who can become mentors and give you advice.

Experience, Skills, and Personality Traits

No specific amount of experience is needed. Story editors generally have had success as writers on films or television shows and have a firm grasp of the technical and practical aspects of animation filmmaking. According to Yank, producers might look for someone with experience working on a project similar to their current one. For example, if they are hiring for an action show for kids, they might look for candidates who have written on other kids' action shows in the past.

First and foremost, Story Editors must be creative and have a keen grasp of all aspects of scriptwriting, including tone, genre, style, character, plot, action, and dialogue and understand various stages of development, including loglines (a short pitch on the story), premises (concept that drives the plot), synopses (a brief summary of the story), beat-outlines (an outline of major dramatic moments), step-outlines (brief details of every scene), treatments (a vivid scene-by-scene narrative of the story), and rough drafts. They should also have a keen understanding of the use of the dramatist's tools—comic irony, suspense, mystery, and

dramatic tension—as they work within the confines of an animated story or setting. Story Editors must have strong time-management skills, as there are a million things to do, and Story Editors often juggle multiple scripts at different stages of development.

Story Editors must be extremely patient, resilient, and have a strong work ethic. They must have exceptional interpersonal and communication abilities to successfully liaise and interact with producers, network executives, and other animation professionals.

Unions and Associations

Story Editors can belong to two unions: The Animation Guild, Local 839, of the IATSE, and the Writers Guild of America, which represents many animation writers as well as film and television writers. According to Isenberg, "Most animation writing is still covered by The Animation Guild, which pays no residuals. In the last ten years or so, most of primetime animation has managed to get covered under the Writers Guild, which pays residuals." A major benefit of joining the Writers Guild is that it offers an Animation Writers Caucus, which is open to any writer with a production animation credit of 30 minutes or more, along with good benefits, information on contracts and working conditions, and networking opportunities. However, the union covers very few animated shows, mostly those in primetime. Writers do not need to join unless they have been hired on a show covered by a particular union.

Tips for Entry

1. Pursue as many avenues as possible. Apply for assistant positions or internships, join writing groups, search online listings—do whatever you can to meet people who might be looking to hire writers in the future.
2. Keep writing scripts. The more you write, the better you will become. Keep trying to improve.
3. Never miss an opportunity to show and tell someone what you do, especially if you think it is good.
4. If possible, self-promote by posting your writing online, or find a way to have it produced and post videos online. You never know who might read or watch it.

WRITER

CAREER PROFILE

Duties: Write and develop original scripts and screenplays for animated television series, specials, films, and direct-to-video productions

Alternate Title(s): Scriptwriter; Screenwriter

Salary Range: $1,534.64 to $9,600 per week (television animation); $15,000 to $800,000 or more (per screenplay)

Employment Prospects: Fair to Good

Advancement Prospects: Poor

Best Geographical Location(s): Los Angeles, New York, San Francisco

Prerequisites:

Education and Training—Undergraduate degree in English or screenwriting with an understanding of animation and filmmaking

CAREER LADDER

Producer

Head Writer; Story Editor

Staff Writer; Freelance Writer

Experience—Some television or film writing helpful

Special Skills and Personality Traits—Creativity; imagination; friendly; flexible; story sense and storytelling abilities; work ethic; computer literate; typing skills; proficient in script-writing software

Position Description

Animated feature films and television shows would be nothing without the creative storylines and dialogue generated by scriptwriters and screenwriters, or Writers.

The community of animation Writers is a relatively small, friendly, and supportive group. Some write fantastic screenplays for big-budget features. Others toil as staff writers on primetime or cable network television cartoon series. Many work in studio offices or freelance at home or in offices of their own choosing. A significant portion of their time is spent networking with other writers, executives, and others to find out where people are hiring and then asking relevant people to read samples of their work in the hope of being hired.

The creative process itself varies. On an animated television series, most Writers report to a story editor, who oversees, reviews, and edits multiple pieces they create—from premise to rough and revised drafts—requiring approval of the studio and network for which the show is produced. Day-to-day duties vary depending on the show and how the individual story editor likes to work. Some producers may be involved and have specific ideas for stories. Sometimes the head writer will have the Writers go off and write their scripts by themselves, while others prefer a more collaborative approach, with all the writers getting together in a "writer's room."

Television animation Writers start by "breaking" a story, under the direction of the show runner. This consists of writing out the beats (or major dramatic story elements) on index cards and posting them on a wall or table. Using index cards is a good tool, as it helps them see where the story beats should fall, something story editors use to lay out an entire season. Over the course of the season, Writers will meet with other writers or as a group to break down the stories and then sit down to develop and flesh out the episodic story. Other times, the process will involve interaction between the Writer and the story editor in person, by e-mail, or over the phone. On some shows, Writers have to develop a list of story ideas, from which the story editor(s) will ask them to flesh out or expand one or two so they can be pitched to the producers and studio.

Following the idea's approval, Writers are assigned to write a premise, usually three to four pages in length that takes a few days to a week to complete, or will alternately turn in a "beat sheet" to the story editor. When the premise is approved, Writers have a week or two to pen an eight- to 14-page outline (for a 22-minute episode); different time frames apply to 11-minute episodes.

After the approval of the outline, Writers forge ahead in writing the script, which may include more than one draft. Writers usually have two weeks in which to write the first draft of the script and a week or so to do rewrites until approved by the executive producer and the network. Multiple rewrites often follow after writing the first draft, so Writers should never get too attached to "any particular idea or pitch," explained the Writer Michael Yank. "Entire scripts may be thrown out far into the process."

Writers are also often involved in all the other steps of the production, giving notes on storyboards, animatics, and animation. Seeing the story told in each of these formats usually spurs new ideas, and this way the episode is essentially being rewritten all the way up to the final cut.

The process on staff-written shows is slightly different. The original Writer will get notes from the show runner and then a gag room, consisting of approximately four Writers who will take a "joke pass" on the outline, in which they pitch potential jokes and joke areas for the writer to reference when he or she writes the script.

The original Writer usually gets two weeks to write the first draft, and then the entire staff gathers and does a rewrite, punching it up and making needed story changes. That becomes the table draft, which is read by the actors for the Writers, animators, and studio and network executives, according to the Writer Brian Scully. After the table read, Writers fix jokes and story points that need improvement, and then the actors record that script. The animators then create storyboards for the episode. They get notes on that and create an "animatic" (a video story reel), which is a black and white, roughly animated version of the script.

The producers then screen the animatic for the Writers, animators, and guests so they can see what works and make changes. The new version then goes back to the animators, who create a less rough color version, again screen that, and make final fixes and cuts before it goes out for final animation. From the beginning of the writing process to the final product, it can take about nine months to create an episode.

Feature film Writers, or screenwriters, are brought in during preproduction after the director initially reviews the screenplay. In some cases, Writers may have written a treatment that is optioned by the producing studio to develop into a screenplay, either by the same Writer or by enlisting other established Writers to do the job. Then story artists usually craft a storyboard, the first visual representation of the screenplay, after which the director may request specific tweaks to the story artist's storyboard and to the screenplay itself. Often, the director will have a story reel, or animatic, made, culling together thousands of individual storyboarded sequences with scratch recordings of the actors' voices

for the director to review, at which time the director may have the Writer or Writers revise the screenplay yet again. It is not uncommon for a screenplay to go through multiple drafts—after conception, during pre-visualization, before or after recording sessions, up to completion of the production itself—before the animation is photographed, cut, printed, and released in final form.

According to the longtime animation Writer Andrew Robison, the upside of the job is getting "paid to make up stuff for heroes and villains to do to each other." In addition, it is a thrill to write dialogue and sit in on recording sessions in which talented actors get together in a studio and "say dialogue I wrote. I'm a big hit with boys 7 to 37 years of age," said Robison.

Animation Writers juggle multiple deadlines and must handle many competing demands. They work long, erratic hours in diverse workplaces that are generally comfortable and well equipped. The hours for Writers on a cartoon series are project based. Freelancers set their own hours but devote the necessary time to meet assigned deadlines. Writers spend extended periods using a computer and keyboard, resulting in eyestrain, fatigue, and back pain in some cases. Freelancers work under similar conditions in home-based offices.

Salaries

Compared to the compensation for live-action television and film Writers, the pay for animation Writers is meager. Two unions set wages for Writers: The Animation Guild, Local 839, of the IATSE, and the Writers Guild of America (WGA). The Animation Guild covers "daytime" animation, while the WGA covers mostly primetime animation shows. Based on The Animation Guild's June 2010 member wage survey, the minimum salary for a staff Writer is $1,700.00 a week. The median to maximum salary ranges is from $2,500 to $6,100 per week. Journey-level staff writers draw a minimum weekly salary of $1,596.64.

Per The Animation Guild's most recent wage scales, wages vary for Writers who both write and storyboard a production. For writing a four- to seven-minute television or theatrical cartoon short, Writers are paid $835.06 for a synopsis and outline and $1,994.91 for a teleplay or screenplay. For storyboard only, they can earn $1,091.54. For cartoon short subjects up to 15 minutes long, they are paid $842.64 (synopsis and outline), $1,402.32 (storyboard only), and $2,748.39 (teleplay or screenplay). For half-hour theatrical or television cartoons, wages are as follows: $1,499.01 (synopsis and outline), $2,662.94 (storyboard only), and $5,267.66 (teleplay or screenplay). Additional rates apply for theatrical or television cartoons an hour or more in length: $2,230.80 (synopsis and outline), $3,971.96 (storyboard only), and $7,924.11 (teleplay or screenplay). Rates are substantially lower for beginning animation writers: for a half-hour subject (television or theatrical): $1,381.37 (synopsis and outline) and $4,854.25 (teleplay or screenplay); for one hour or longer: $2,045.69 (synopsis and outline) and $7,266.59 (teleplay or screenplay).

Unit rates (rates based on the length of the production), according to the guild's annual member wage survey, overall were much higher. For four- to seven-minute scripts, earnings ranged from $2,400 to $3,000; for seven to 15 minutes, $2,000 to $7,200; and for a 30-minute show outline, $1,759 and up. For a 30-minute episodic script (syndicated), the payout was $6,500 and up; for a 30-minute episodic script (cable), $6,500 to $7,000; for a 30-minute script, $7,000 to $10,000; for a one-hour special script, $10,154.91 (journey minimum) to $39,000; and for a series bible (a document that maps out the production's characters, settings, stories, and other elements), $5,000 to $12,500.

Animated feature Writers earned comparably more than their television counterparts in 2009. For a theatrical feature script polish, they earned a minimum of $4,000; for a first draft direct-to-video script, a minimum of $12,000; for a first draft theatrical feature script, a minimum of $95,000; for a direct-to-video feature script, a minimum of $38,000; and for a theatrical feature screenplay, from $64,000 to $640,000.

Writers who work on primetime animated television shows, such as *The Simpsons* and *Family Guy,* covered by the Writer's Guild, make anywhere from $850 to several thousand a week. Specific minimums depend on the position. More experienced Writers are given titles such as story editor, executive story editor, executive story consultant, coproducer, producer, and coexecutive producer and are paid applicable guild rates in these instances.

In all other cases, Writers are paid according to agreed-upon wages under the union's most recent collective bargaining agreement. From May 1, 2010, to May 2, 2011, minimums for Writers writing for network television animation were, for programs 15 minutes or less, for story, $4,165; for teleplay, $10,115; and for story and teleplay, $12,513. For programs 30 minutes or less, guild minimums were, for story, $7,634; for teleplay, $16,424; and for story and teleplay, $22,900. For programs 60 minutes or less, applied rates were, for story, $13,439; for teleplay, $22,158; and for story and teleplay, $33,681. For programs lasting 90 minutes or less, applied rates were, for story, $17,956; for teleplay, $31,927; and for story and teleplay, $47,388.

Writers of animation screenplays had significantly higher payouts. The going rates for original feature screenplays, including treatment, were $62,642 to $117,602; for nonoriginal feature screenplays, $54,814 to $101,936; for original feature screenplays, including treatment, or sale/purchase of original screenplay, $42,088 to $86,156; and for nonoriginal feature screenplays, excluding treatment, or sale/purchase of nonoriginal screenplay, $34,251 to $70,489. Additional compensation for story and screenplay was $7,837 to $15,667; for story or treatment, $28,382 to $47,000; for first draft screenplay, with or without option for final draft screenplay (nonoriginal), $24,668 to $47,000; for final draft screenplay, $16,440 to $31,334; for rewrite of screenplay, $20,554 to $31,334; and for polish of screenplay, $10,283 to $15,667.

There is no salary per se for freelance Writers. They can make anywhere from $1,500 to $7,000 per script, depending on a host of factors, such as the length of episode, whether union or nonunion, and whether they perform all writing duties for that episode (i.e., being hired to write the outline but not the script or vice-versa). Freelance Writers work on a job-for-hire basis and are paid piecemeal. For a 22-minute episode, Robison was paid as little as $1,500 for a job and as much as $7,500. There is often room for negotiating higher wages.

Writing for animation is a cyclical and speculative business. As a result, Writers may face extended periods of unemployment. Writers may have eight to nine months of working steadily, for example, followed by periods as long as six months or more when no writing jobs materialize. Because of this, Writers may want to have another source of income in case writing jobs dry up for a long period of time.

Employment Prospects

Industrywide, prospects of obtaining work as a Writer with an animation studio are fair to good, depending on location and experience. The odds of breaking into daytime animation writing are similar to those for breaking into primetime animation writing. Some 96 percent of animation writers live in Los Angeles or its outlying regions. Only a few well-established animation Writers who live elsewhere work consistently. Freelancers can also work on writing comic books, video games, novels, and other screenplays, but if you want to be a staff Writer, you most likely have to live in Los Angeles.

The number of Writers hired for an animated television series depends on the project and on the story editor. One current cartoon series has one story editor and four staff Writers; another has one story editor, one staff

Writer, and five freelance Writers who operate in rotation; and a third has two story editors and 10 freelance Writers.

Duration of employment for animation Writers varies dramatically. Staff Writers contracted to work on a series work as long as nine months during the course of a season. Freelancer work is completely unpredictable unless you work on one of those shows with a small number of freelancers given a number of episodes; in these situations, you can reasonably predict how many episodes you will be given to write. Robison has had many jobs where he completed the script, was paid, and then received a contract a couple of months later based on his good work.

Because there is no entry-level job in the animation industry that directly leads to becoming a Writer, one viable way of breaking into the business is by working as a producer's assistant, as it puts you in the office where scripts are coming in, being processed, and are turned around. It also gives you the opportunity to read every idea, premise, outline, and script draft and to get to learn the show you are working on as well as anyone—so that if you get an opportunity to write a script, you are ready.

Generally, becoming an animation Writer is very difficult. Scully advises up-and-coming Writers to learn the craft of funny storytelling and how to create characters that are multidimensional and unique. Some people have gotten writing assignments straight out of film school and have become brilliant Writers, but such instances are rare. Robison spent years as a development executive for film and television while writing on the side before he landed his first professional assignment. Even then, it took a few seasons to hone his skills to the point at which people put him on a "short list" for hiring.

Your best bet at getting your first writing job is to have a friend in a position to hire you. You may secure an agent with a strong writing sample, but many agencies do not want to make the effort or take the time to work with a beginning Writer.

Advancement Prospects

Career advancement for animation Writers and scriptwriters as a whole is extremely limited, and thus opportunities are poor. After years of toiling as Writers, some become staff writers or head writers ("where you actually do get a weekly salary," Robison said) on an animated television series. These positions are currently quite uncommon, but they do exist here and there.

Securing more advanced positions is dependent on the relationships Writers are able to build with producers and story editors and their skill at breaking stories and helping move things forward in the production. Some talented Writers with excellent credits and stature move up to become story editors in charge of Writers and scripts and of giving the show a consistent tone. There is a pool of talent that all the companies first go to for story editing, so it can be difficult to advance to this position.

For shows under the aegis of the Writers Guild of America, more experienced Writers are elevated to roles of executive story editor and executive story consultant. Still, some with a strong industry standing elect to become producers or directors, especially if they have enjoyed success as executive producers of a program or series they developed, pitched, and sold. Overall, however, most continue to write for their own or other animated programs as well as animated features, direct-to-video productions, and short subjects.

Advancing in your career as an animation Writer depends on many variables—personal connections, luck, and reputation. However, the main ingredients for enhancing your chances are writing good scripts, turning them in on time, and always being available when an opportunity presents itself.

Education and Training

An undergraduate degree in English or screenwriting is useful. Getting a degree in screenwriting is important, as in most programs you not only learn the craft but how to hit deadlines. It is not uncommon, however, for Writers to have degrees in other fields.

Specific courses in composition, playwriting, and scriptwriting are beneficial, but students need to keep in mind that animation writing requires a slightly different skill set than live-action, as Writers are frequently asked to place the "camera" in the script, so obtaining additional training in the art and methods of animation scriptwriting is recommended. Otherwise, the only real prerequisite is the ability to write good scripts for different types of shows.

Experience, Skills, and Personality Traits

Most animation Writers have honed their craft in one form or another after starting at an early age and continuing to write every single day. Therefore, it is useful for individuals to master the myriad techniques and specifics of writing for animation.

The key ingredients that Writers have to demonstrate are a feverish imagination to dream up ideas, a strong sense of logic to keep those ideas grounded in the story you have to tell, and flexibility to know when your ideas aren't working and you have to reverse course.

Thus, Writers must have a strong work ethic with the ability to execute and hand in their assignments, whether it involves writing a three-page premise, a 12-page outline, or 35-page television script, on time. You have to be flexible and easygoing enough to handle criticism that you may not agree with.

Writers must also have excellent computer and typing skills, but the most important quality is the ability to write a good script, including a sense of drama and the ability to tell a story in other characters' voices.

Unions and Associations

Regular, full-time Writers or freelance Writers in the animation industry often are members of the Writers Guild of America (WGA) West and The Animation Guild, Local 839, of the IATSE, both of which represent Writers for bargaining purposes and provide educational and training opportunities. Union membership is required for Writers to work in the industry on union-signatory productions. Another benefit of joining the WGA West is its Animation Writers Caucus, which, founded in 1994, sponsors many events during the year, including monthly meetings and networking opportunities. Joining these organizations can help introduce you to other writers and professionals in the animation industry.

Tips for Entry

1. In high school, start educating yourself. Sit and analyze shows on the air. Watch as many shows as you can. Pay attention to how the elements of shows are assembled—the flow of dialogue, how long time passes before the picture changes to a new shot, and the timing of how high an animated ball bounces onscreen.

2. If you want to write, track down animation scripts and their completed counterparts. See how what is on the page translated to the screen, what was cut, and what dialogue was changed. You can start educating yourself this way right now, until the opportunity to educate yourself on the job comes along.

3. "Doing" is the greatest teacher. Start writing a scene every day for a sample, or "spec," script for an episode of your favorite show, in addition to writing live-action drama shows, sitcoms, pilots, or movie scripts, to learn and hone your skills. You never know who is going to like your work and ask for a writing sample or what they are going to want to see.

4. Attend social events where you are likely to meet animation Writers, including comic conventions.

5. Find an agency that specializes in animation, and make sure the agency accepts new clients without referrals. For a list of agents, visit the Web site of the Writers Guild of America, and click on their *List of Agents* link. For the best way to find animation agents, call the WGA (323-951-4000) and ask them to mail you a copy of their latest Directory of Animation Writers, issued by the Animation Writers Caucus. It lists more than 300 WGA members and their agents, including the agents' names and telephone numbers.

APPENDIXES

I. Animation Schools and Educational Institutions

II. Major Trade Periodicals, Newsletters, and Other Publications

III. Industry and Trade Associations, Guilds, and Unions

IV. Recommended Animation Industry Web Sites

V. U.S. Film, Television, Game, and Web Animation Companies

APPENDIX I
ANIMATION SCHOOLS AND EDUCATIONAL INSTITUTIONS

Listed below are animation schools, colleges, and universities with established curricula that offer certificated and degreed programs in animation and related disciplines. Excluded are noncertified and nondegreed workshops. For additional information and to view complete listings of all animation schools regardless of their qualifications, visit the complete Animation School Database at AWN (Animation World News) at http://schools.awn.com/. Schools are searchable and viewable by name and by location.

ALABAMA

Twilight Studios
Imaging & Animation
201 Ivy Brook Trail
Pelham, AL 35124
Phone: (205) 335-3782
E-mail: rush@twilight-studios.com
http://www.twilight-studios.com
Degrees: Certificate
Academic Areas: Animation History/Theory, Computer Animation/Digital Art, Experimental Animation, Multimedia/Games, Web Graphics/Design, Workshops, Online Courses, Kids' Programs, Private Training

ARIZONA

The Art Center Design College
Animation Graphics
2525 N. Country Club Road
Tucson, AZ 85716
Phone: (800) 825-8753
Fax: (520) 325-5535
E-mail: inquire@theartcenter.edu
http://www.theartcenter.edu
Degrees: A.A., B.A., B.S., B.F.A.
Academic Areas: Character Animation, Experimental Animation, Computer Animation/Digital Art, Graphic Design, Multimedia/Games, Web Graphics/Design, Web Animation, Animation History/Theory

The Art Institute of Phoenix
2233 W. Dunlap Avenue
Phoenix, AZ 85021
Phone: (800) 474-2479
Fax: (602) 216-0439
E-mail: aipxadm@aii.edu
http://www.aipx.edu
Degrees: A.A., B.A., B.S., B.F.A.
Academic Areas: Character Animation, Computer Animation/Digital Art, Graphic Design, Multimedia/Games, Web Graphics/Design, Web Animation, Workshops, Online Courses

Collins College
Animation Department
1140 S. Priest Drive
Tempe, AZ 85281
Phone: (800) 876-7070
Fax: (480) 902-0663
E-mail: info@collinscollege.edu
http://www.collinscollege.edu
Degrees: A.A., B.A., B.S., B.F.A.
Academic Areas: Character Animation, Computer Animation, Digital Art

University of Advancing Technology
2625 W. Baseline Road
Tempe, AZ 85283-1056
Phone: (877) UAT-GEEK
Fax: (602) 383-8222
E-mail: admissions@uat.edu
http://www.uat.edu
Degrees: B.A., B.S., B.F.A.

Academic Areas: Character Animation, Computer Animation/Digital Art, Graphic Design, Multimedia/Games, Web Graphics/Design, Web Animation, Distance Learning, Online Courses

ARKANSAS

Henderson State University
1100 Henderson Street
Arkadelphia, AR 71999-0001
Phone: (870) 230-5000
Fax: (870) 230-5144
http://www.hsu.edu
Degrees: B.A., B.S., B.F.A.
Academic Areas: Computer Animation/Digital Art, Fine Art, Graphic Design, Web Graphics/Design

John Brown University
Digital Media Arts
2000 W. University
Siloam Springs, AR 72761
Phone: (479) 524-9500
http://digital.jbu.edu
Degrees: B.A., B.S., B.F.A.
Academic Areas: Character Animation, Computer Animation/Digital Art, Multimedia/Games, Web Animation

CALIFORNIA

3-D Exchange Courseware
P.O. Box 51

Byron, CA 94514
Phone: (661) 245-2240
Fax: (661) 245-2218
E-mail: info@3dexchange.com
http://www.3dexchange.com
Degrees: Certificate
Academic Areas: Character Animation, Experimental Animation, Computer Animation/Digital Art, Multimedia/Games, Web Graphics/Design, Web Animation, Animation History/Theory, Distance Learning, Online Courses, Kids' Programs, Private Training, Vocational Training

Abram Friedman Occupational Center

Friedman 3-D
570 W. Avenue 26
Suite 300
Los Angeles, CA 90065
Phone: (323) 227-4776
Fax: (323) 227-8775
E-mail: afoc@friedman3d.com
http://www.studioarts.tv/no_frame/friedman3d.html
Degrees: Certificate
Academic Areas: Character Animation, Experimental Animation, Computer Animation/Digital Art, Graphic Design, Multimedia/Games, Animation History/Theory, Distance Learning, Vocational Training

Academy of Digital Animation

Cerro Coso Community College
3000 College Heights Boulevard
Ridgecrest, CA 93555
Phone: (760) 384-6100
Fax: (760) 375-4776
E-mail: recruit@cerrocoso.edu
http://www.coyote3d.com
Degrees: Certificate, A.A.
Other: multiple certificates, software application certifications
Academic Areas: Character Animation, Experimental Animation, Computer Animation/Digital Art, Fine

Art, Multimedia/Games, Web Graphics/Design, Web Animation, Animation History/Theory, Distance Learning, Online Courses

American Animation Institute

1105 N. Hollywood Way
Burbank, CA 91505-2528
Phone: (818) 845-7000
E-mail: lyn@mpsc839.org
http://animationguild.org/education/
Academic Areas: Character Animation, Fine Art, Performance Animation, Workshops, Vocational Training

The Animation Academy

3407 W. Olive Avenue
2nd Floor
Burbank, CA 91505-4616
Phone: (818) 848-6590
E-mail: info@theanimationacademy.com
http://www.theanimationacademy.com
Degrees: Certificate
Academic Areas: Character Animation, Web Graphics/Design, Web Animation, Workshops, Kids' Programs, Vocational Training

Animation Mentor

The Online Animation School
1400 65th Street
Suite 250
Emeryville, CA 94608
Phone: (510) 450-7200
Fax: (510) 450-7272
E-mail: info@animationmentor.com
http://www.AnimationMentor.com
Degrees: Certificate
Academic Areas: Character Animation, Computer Animation/Digital Art, Distance Learning, Online Courses

The Art Institute of California—Los Angeles

Career Services
2900 31st Street

Santa Monica, CA 90405
Phone: (310) 752-4700
Fax: (310) 314-6005
E-mail: weichbrj@aii.edu
http://www.aicala.artinstitutes.edu
Degrees: A.A., B.A., B.S., B.F.A.
Academic Areas: Cartooning, Character Animation, Experimental Animation, Computer Animation/Digital Art, Graphic Design, Multimedia/Games, Web Graphics/Design, Web Animation, Performance Animation, Animation History/Theory, Workshops, Online Courses

The Art Institute of California—Orange County

Media Arts and Animation
3601 W. Sunflower Avenue
Santa Ana, CA 92704
Phone: (714) 830-0200
Fax: (702) 556-8937
http://www.aicaoc.aii.edu
Degrees: B.A., B.S., B.F.A.
Academic Areas: Cartooning, Character Animation, Experimental Animation, Computer Animation/Digital Art, Graphic Design, Multimedia/Games, Web Graphics/Design, Web Animation, Performance Animation, Online Courses

The Art Institute of California—San Diego

7650 Mission Valley Road
San Diego, CA 92108
Phone: (858) 598-1399
Fax: (619) 291-3206
http://www.aicasd.artinstitutes.edu
Degrees: B.A., B.S., B.F.A.
Academic Areas: Computer Animation/Digital Art, Graphic Design, Multimedia/Games, Web Graphics/Design, Online Courses

Associates in Art

5211 Kester Avenue
Sherman Oaks, CA 91411
Phone: (818) 986-1050

Fax: (818) 986-6363
E-mail: enroll@associatesinart.com
http://www.associatesinart.com
Degrees: Certificate
Academic Areas: Character Animation, Experimental Animation, Computer Animation/Digital Art, Fine Art

Aten Works

3-D/3-D Animation
3979 Freedom Circle
Suite 210
Santa Clara, CA 95054
E-mail: media@atenworks.com
http://www.atenworks.com
Degrees: Certificate
Academic Areas: Cartooning, Character Animation, Computer Animation/Digital Art, Web Animation

Biola University

Admissions Department
13800 Biola Avenue
La Mirada, CA 90639-0001
Phone: (800) OK-BIOLA
http://www.biola.edu
Degrees: Certificate, B.A., B.S., B.F.A., M.A., M.S., M.F.A.
Academic Areas: Computer Animation/Digital Art, Fine Art, Graphic Design, Multimedia/Games, Web Graphics/Design

Brooks College Long Beach

Animation, Multimedia
4825 E. Pacific Coast Highway
Long Beach, CA 90804
Phone: (562) 597-6611
E-mail: jhobbs@brookscollege.edu
http://www.brookscollege.edu
Degrees: A.A.
Academic Areas: Cartooning, Character Animation, Experimental Animation, Computer Animation/Digital Art, Fine Art, Graphic Design, Multimedia/Games, Web Graphics/Design, Web Animation, Performance

Animation, Animation History/Theory, Workshops, Private Training, Vocational Training

Brooks Institute of Photography

Admissions
801 Alston Road
Santa Barbara, CA 93108
Phone: (805) 966-3888
Fax: (805) 565-1386
E-mail: admissions@brooks.edu
http://www.brooks.edu
Degrees: A.A., B.A., B.S., B.F.A., M.A., M.S., M.F.A.
Academic Areas: Computer Animation/Digital Art, Graphic Design, Web Graphics/Design, Workshops

Butte Community College

Multimedia Studies
3536 Butte Campus Drive
Oroville, CA 95965
Phone: (530) 895-2511
E-mail: audio_geek@yahoo.com
http://www.butte.edu/
Degrees: A.A.
Academic Areas: Character Animation, Computer Animation/Digital Art, Graphic Design, Multimedia/Games, Web Graphics/Design, Web Animation, Animation History/Theory, Vocational Training

California College of Arts and Crafts

1111 Eighth Street
San Francisco, CA 94107-2247
Phone: (800) 447-1ART
Fax: (415) 703-9539
E-mail: enroll@ccac-art.edu
http://www.ccac-art.edu
Degrees: M.A., M.S., M.F.A.
Academic Areas: Animation, Graphic Design, Illustration, Painting/Drawing, Visual Studies

California Institute of Creative Arts (CICA)

672 S. La Fayette Park Place, 41

Los Angeles, CA 90057
Phone: (213) 384-8814
E-mail: info@calinstitute.com
http://www.calinstitute.com
Degrees: Certificate
Academic Areas: Cartooning, Character Animation, Experimental Animation, Computer Animation/Digital Art, Fine Art, Graphic Design, Multimedia/Games, Voice Acting, Performance Animation, Animation History/Theory, Workshops, Distance Learning, Online Courses, Kids' Programs, Private Training, Vocational Training

California Institute of the Arts

School of Film/Video
24700 McBean Parkway
Valencia, CA 91355-2397
Phone: (661) 255-1050
Fax: (661) 253-7824
E-mail: admiss@calarts.edu
http://www.calarts.edu
Degrees: Certificate, B.A., B.S., B.F.A., M.A., M.S., M.F.A.
Academic Areas: Character Animation, Experimental Animation, Computer Animation/Digital Art

California State University, Chico

Computer Graphics Lab
Normal Avenue
Chico, CA 95929-0005
Phone: (530) 898-4421
Fax: (530) 898-5369
E-mail: rvertolli@csuchico.edu
http://www.csuchico.edu/
Degrees: B.A., B.S., B.F.A., M.A., M.S., M.F.A.
Academic Areas: Computer Animation/Digital Art, Fine Art, Graphic Design, Multimedia/Games, Distance Learning

California State University, Fullerton

Entertainment Art and Animation
Visual Arts Department

P.O. Box 6850
Fullerton, CA 92834-6850
Phone: (714) 278-3471
Fax: (714) 278-2390
E-mail: dlamb@fullerton.edu
http://www.fullerton.edu
Degrees: B.A./B.S./B.F.A., M.A./
M.S./M.F.A.
Academic Areas: Character
Animation, Experimental
Animation, Computer
Animation/Digital Art, Fine Art,
Animation History/Theory

California State University, Long Beach

Advanced Media Production
1250 Bellflower Boulevard
Long Beach, CA 90840
Phone: (562) 985-5471
Fax: (562) 985-5292
E-mail: art@csulb.edu
http://www.amp.csulb.edu
Degrees: Certificate, B.A., B.S.,
B.F.A., M.A., M.S., M.F.A.
Academic Areas: Computer
Animation/Digital Art, Graphic
Design, Animation History/
Theory, Distance Learning,
Online Courses

California State University, Northridge

Art Department
18111 Nordhoff Street
Northridge, CA 91330-8300
Phone: (818) 677-2242
Fax: (818) 677-3046
E-mail: art.dept@csun.edu
http://www.csun.edu/animation
Degrees: B.A., B.S., B.F.A.
Academic Areas: Character
Animation, Computer
Animation/Digital Art, Fine Art,
Graphic Design, Multimedia/
Games, Web Graphics/Design

California State University Summer Arts

401 Golden Shore
6th Floor
Long Beach, CA 90802
Phone: (562) 951-4060

Fax: (562) 951-4982
E-mail: summerarts@calstate.edu
http://www.csusummerarts.org
Degrees: Undergraduate or
graduate credit
Academic Areas: Character
Animation, Computer
Animation/Digital Art, Web
Animation, Animation History/
Theory, Workshops

Caltech Graphics Group

Computer Science Department
350 Beckman Institute
MS 350-74
California Institute of Technology
Pasadena, CA 91125
Phone: (626) 395-3104
Fax: (626) 584-5917
E-mail: david@cacr.caltech.edu
http://www.gg.caltech.edu
Degrees: Doctorate/Other
Postgraduate
Academic Areas: Computer
Animation/Digital Art

Central County Regional Occupational Program

Animation
250 S. Yorba Street
Orange, CA 92869
Phone: (714) 997-6066
Fax: (714) 997-6035
E-mail: ehansbury@orangeusd.k12.
ca.us
http://www.orangeusd.k12.ca.us/
rop/
Degrees: Certificate
Academic Areas: Animation
History/Theory, Character
Animation, Computer
Animation/Digital Art,
Experimental Animation, Fine
Art, Performance Animation,
Web Animation

Chapman University

Cecil B. DeMille School of Film and
Television
One University Drive
Orange, CA 92866
Phone: (714) 997-6765
Fax: (714) 997-6700

E-mail: ftvinfo@chapman.edu
http://ftv.chapman.edu
Degrees: B.A., B.S., B.F.A., M.A.,
M.S., M.F.A.
Academic Areas: Experimental
Animation, Computer
Animation/Digital Art, Fine Art,
Graphic Design, Multimedia/
Games, Animation History/
Theory

Cogswell Polytechnical College

Admission Department
1175 Bordeaux Drive
Sunnyvale, CA 94089
Phone: (800) 264-7955
Fax: (408) 747-0764
E-mail: admin@cogswell.edu
http://www.cogswell.edu
Degrees: B.A., B.S., B.F.A.
Academic Areas: Cartooning,
Character Animation,
Experimental Animation,
Computer Animation/
Digital Art, Fine Art, Graphic
Design, Multimedia/Games,
Web Graphics/Design, Web
Animation, Voice Acting,
Performance Animation,
Animation History/Theory

College of the Canyons

Animation
26455 Rockwell Canyon Road
Santa Clarita, CA 91355
Phone: (661) 362-5039
Fax: (661) 259-8302
E-mail: sheila.sofian@canyons.edu
http://www.canyons.edu/
departments/dat/animation/
index.html
Degrees: Certificate, A.A.
Academic Areas: Character
Animation, Computer
Animation/Digital Art, Fine Art,
Graphic Design, Multimedia/
Games, Web Graphics/Design,
Web Animation, Vocational
Training

De Anza College

Creative Arts Division
21250 Stevens Creek Boulevard

Cupertino, CA 95014
Phone: (408) 864-8832
Fax: (408) 864-8492
E-mail: zl04009@fhda.edu
http://www.deanza.fhda.edu/
    creativearts/
Degrees: Certificate, A.A.
Academic Areas: Character
    Animation, Experimental
    Animation, Computer
    Animation/Digital Art, Fine Art,
    Animation History/Theory

DH Institute of Media Arts (DHIMA)
5657 Wilshire Boulevard
Suite 470
Los Angeles, CA 90036
Phone: (323) 904-1135
Fax: (323) 904-1162
E-mail: info@dhima.com
http://www.dhima.com
Degrees: Certificate
Other: Demo reel
Academic Areas: Character Anima-
    tion, Experimental Animation,
    Computer Animation/Digital
    Art, Fine Art, Multimedia/
    Games, Web Graphics/Design,
    Web Animation, Animation
    History/Theory, Workshops,
    Vocational Training

Drew College Preparatory School
2901 California Street
San Francisco, CA 94115
Phone: (415) 409-DREW
Fax: (415) 346-0720
E-mail: todd_barringer@hotmail.
    com
http://www.drewschool.org
Degrees: Diploma
Academic Areas: Character
    Animation, Computer
    Animation/Digital Art, Fine Art,
    Kids' Programs

Earthlight Pictures Animation Training—Santa Monica
Auxiliary Service—Crossroads
    School
1714 21st Street

Santa Monica, CA 90404
Phone: (805) 563-1242
E-mail: JT@earthlightpictures.com
http://www.earthlightpictures.com
Degrees: Certificate
Academic Areas: Cartooning,
    Character Animation,
    Experimental Animation,
    Computer Animation/Digital
    Art, Fine Art, Workshops,
    Distance Learning, Kids'
    Programs, Private Training,
    Vocational Training

East Los Angeles College
Art
1301 Avenida Cesar Chavez
Monterey Park, CA 91754-6099
Phone: (323) 415-5348
Fax: (323) 260-8173
E-mail: cdmoreno@pacbell.net
http://elacart.bizland.com
Degrees: Certificate, A.A.
Academic Areas: Cartooning,
    Character Animation,
    Experimental Animation,
    Computer Animation/
    Digital Art, Fine Art, Graphic
    Design, Multimedia/Games,
    Web Graphics/Design, Web
    Animation, Animation History/
    Theory, Vocational Training

Fairfax Magnet Center for Visual Arts
7850 Melrose Avenue
Los Angeles, CA 90046
Phone: (323) 651-5200, ext. 233
E-mail: artmagnet@lausd.k12.ca.us
http://www.lausd.k12.ca.us/Fairfax_
    Magnet_HS/
Degrees: High School Diploma
Academic Areas: Fine Art, Graphic
    Design

FIDM
Interactive Multimedia/Graphic
    Design
919 S. Grand Avenue
Los Angeles, CA 90015
Phone: (213) 624-1200
E-mail: info@fidm.com
http://www.fidm.com

Degrees: A.A., Post-Degree
    Advanced Programs
Academic Areas: Computer
    Animation/Digital Art,
    Graphic Design, Multimedia/
    Games, Web Graphics/Design,
    Workshops, Vocational Training

Glendale Community College
Animation
1500 N. Verdugo Road
Glendale, CA 91208-2894
Phone: (818) 240-1000, ext. 5815
E-mail: rdickes@glendale.edu
http://www.glendale.edu
Degrees: Certificate, A.A.
Academic Areas: Character
    Animation, Computer
    Animation/Digital Art,
    Web Graphics/Design, Web
    Animation, Workshops,
    Vocational Training

Gnomon Inc.
School of Visual Effects for Film,
    Television, and Games
Television Center
1015 N. Cahuenga Boulevard
Suite 5430i
Hollywood, CA 90038
Phone: (323) 466-6663
Fax: (323) 466-6710
E-mail: admin@gnomon3d.com
http://www.gnomon3d.com
Degrees: Certificate
Academic Areas: Character
    Animation, Computer
    Animation/Digital Art,
    Multimedia/Games, Web
    Graphics/Design, Web
    Animation, Animation History/
    Theory, Workshops, Online
    Courses, Private Training

Hilltop High School/Sweetwater Unified High School District
Animation
555 Claire Avenue
Chula Vista, CA 91910
Phone: (619) 691-5640
Fax: (619) 425-3284
http://hth.sweetwaterschools.org/
    default.aspx

Laurus College

75 Higuera Street, #110
San Luis Obispo, CA 93401
Phone: (805) 267-1690
E-mail: www.lauruscollege.com
http://www.lauruscollege.com
Degrees: Certificate
Academic Areas: Character
Animation, Experimental
Animation, Computer
Animation/Digital Art, Graphic
Design, Multimedia/Games,
Animation History/Theory,
Vocational Training

Learning Tree University

Chatsworth Campus
20920 Knapp Street
Chatsworth, CA 91311-5906
Phone: (818) 882-5599
Fax: (818) 341-0707
E-mail: ltu@ltu.org
http://www.ltu.org
Degrees: Certificate
Academic Areas: 3-D Animation
& Special Effects, Character
Animation, Computer
Animation/Digital Art, Fine
Art, Graphic Design/Visual
Communications, Web
Graphics/Web Site Design,
Distance Learning

Los Angeles City College

Cinema-Television Department
855 N. Vermont Avenue
Los Angeles, CA 90029
Phone: (323) 953-4545
Fax: (323) 953-4505
E-mail: obernvg@email.lacc.cc.ca.us
http://citywww.lacc.cc.ca.us/
academic/depar
Degrees: Certificate, A.A.
Academic Areas: Character
Animation, Computer
Animation/Digital Art

Loyola Marymount University

School of Film and Television
One LMU Drive, MC 8230
Los Angeles, CA 90045-8347
Phone: (310) 338-3033
Fax: (310) 338-3030
E-mail: aclenden@lmumail.lmu.edu
http://www.lmu.edu/filmschool
Degrees: B.A., B.S., B.F.A.
Academic Areas: Character
Animation, Experimental
Animation, Computer
Animation/Digital Art, Graphic
Design, Multimedia/Games,
Web Animation, Animation
History/Theory

Media Code

Division of AEC Technologies, Inc.
2165-D Francisco Boulevard
San Rafael, CA 94901
Phone: (415) 453-9293
Fax: (415) 454-0229
E-mail: chris@aectech.com
http://www.aectech.com
Degrees: Certificate
Academic Areas: Character
Animation, Computer
Animation/Digital Art,
Multimedia/Games

Mission College

Graphic Design Area
3000 Mission College Boulevard
Santa Clara, CA 95054-1897
Phone: (408) 988-2200
Fax: (408) 567-2892
E-mail: tanesha_gipson@wvmccd.
cc.ca.us
http://www.missioncollege.org
Degrees: Certificate, A.A.
Academic Areas: Computer
Animation/Digital Art, Fine Art,
Graphic Design, Multimedia/
Games

Montecito Fine Arts College of Design

Animation
524 S. First Avenue
Arcadia, CA 91006
Phone: (626) 447-1499
Fax: (626) 446-6012
E-mail: information@
montecitofinearts.com
http://www.montecitofinearts.com
Degrees: Certificate
Academic Areas: Graphic Design,
Industrial/Product Design, Web

Design, 3-D Animation, Interior
Design, Architectural Drafting,
Desktop Publishing

Motion Ocean

810 Orange Grove Avenue
Unit 5
South Pasadena, CA 91030-2423
Phone: (626) 403-6407
E-mail: garymck@pacbell.net
http://www.motion-ocean.com
Degrees: Certificate
Academic Areas: Fine Art, Graphic
Design, Workshops, Private
Training

Mt. Carmel High School

Animation/ROP
9550 Mt. Carmel Road
San Diego, CA 92129-2799
Phone: (858) 484-1180, ext. 3227
Fax: (760) 789-7152
E-mail: ltfoot@sdcoe.k12.ca.us
http://powayusd.sdcoe.k12.ca.us/
artonline/mchsart/Animation/
animindex.html
Degrees: Certificate
Academic Areas: Character
Animation, Experimental
Animation, Computer
Animation/Digital Art, Fine Art,
Voice Acting

Mt. San Antonio College

Animation/Digital Media
1100 N. Grand Avenue
Walnut, CA 91789
Phone: (909) 594-5611, ext. 4565
Fax: (909) 468-4067
http://www.mtsac.edu/
Degrees: Certificate, A.A.
Academic Areas: Character
Animation, Computer
Animation/Digital Art, Fine
Art, Multimedia/Games,
Web Graphics/Design, Web
Animation

Mt. San Jacinto College

Multimedia
28237 La Piedra Road
Menifee, CA 92584
Phone: (951) 672-6752

Fax: (951) 672-7915
E-mail: jevan@msjc.edu
http://multimedia.msjc.edu/
animation/
Degrees: Certificate, A.A.
Academic Areas: Character
Animation, Computer
Animation/Digital Art, Graphic
Design, Multimedia/Games,
Web Graphics/Design, Web
Animation, Animation History/
Theory, Online Courses,
Vocational Training

Orange Coast College

Film/Video Department
2701 Fairview Road
P.O. Box 5005
Costa Mesa, CA 92628-5005
Phone: (714) 432-5629
Fax: (714) 432-5072
E-mail: occfvd@cccd.edu
http://www.occ.cccd.edu
Degrees: Certificate, A.A.
Academic Areas: Computer
Animation/Digital Art,
Multimedia/Game

Otis College of Art & Design

9045 Lincoln Boulevard
Los Angeles, CA 90045
Phone: (800) 527-OTIS
Fax: (310) 665-6821
E-mail: otisart@otisart.edu
http://www.otis.edu/http://www.
otis.edu/
Degrees: B.A., B.S., B.F.A., M.A.,
M.S., M.F.A.
Academic Areas: Computer
Animation/Digital Art, Fine Art,
Graphic Design

The Pixelyard

Game Art
3950 Sorrento Valley Boulevard
San Diego, CA 92121
Phone: (858) 427-1616
Fax: (866) 741-8349
E-mail: info@thepixelyard.com
http://www.thepixelyard.com/
Degrees: Certificate
Academic Areas: Computer
Animation/Digital Art,

Multimedia/Games, Workshops,
Private Training, Vocational
Training

Rowland High School

Animation/L.P.V.-R.O.P.
2000 S. Otterbein Avenue
Rowland Heights, CA 91748
Phone: (818) 965-3448
Fax: (818) 810-4859
http://rhs.rowlandschools.org/
Degrees: Diploma
Academic Areas: Character
Animation, Distance Learning,
Kids' Programs

San Francisco Art Institute

Advanced Technology Center
800 Chestnut Street
San Francisco, CA 94133
Phone: (415) 771-7020
Fax: (415) 749-4590
E-mail: admissions@sfai.edu
http://www.sfai.edu/
Degrees: B.A., B.S., B.F.A., M.A.,
M.S., M.F.A.
Academic Areas: Computer
Animation/Digital Art, Graphic
Design, Multimedia/Games

San Francisco State University

Department of Cinema
1600 Holloway Avenue
San Francisco, CA 94132
Phone: (415) 338-1629
E-mail: cinedept@sfsu.edu
http://www.cinema.sfsu.edu/
Degrees: B.A., B.S., B.F.A., M.A.,
M.S., M.F.A.
Academic Areas: Character
Animation, Computer
Animation/Digital Art, Fine Art,
Distance Learning

San Francisco State University

Multimedia Studies Program
Downtown Center
425 Market Street
2nd Floor
San Francisco, CA 94105
Phone: (415) 405-7700
Fax: (415) 405-7760
E-mail: msp@sfsu.edu

http://msp.sfsu.edu
Degrees: Certificate
Academic Areas: Computer
Animation/Digital Art,
Graphic Design, Multimedia/
Games, Web Graphics/Design,
Web Animation, Workshops,
Distance Learning, Vocational
Training

San Jose State University

Animation/Illustration
School of Art and Design
One Washington Square
San Jose, CA 95192-0089
Phone: (408) 924-4346
Fax: (408) 924-4326
E-mail: dwijas@email.sjsu.edu
http://ad.sjsu.edu/programs/
animationillust.html
Degrees: B.A., B.S., B.F.A., M.A.,
M.S., M.F.A.
Academic Areas: Character
Animation, Computer
Animation/Digital Art

Santa Barbara City College

Multimedia Arts and Technologies
722 Cliff Drive
Santa Barbara, CA 93109-2394
Phone: (805) 965-0581
Fax: (805) 963-7222
http://www.sbcc.net
Degrees: Certificate
Academic Areas: Computer
Animation/Digital Art, Distance
Learning, Online Courses

Santa Monica College, Academy of Entertainment & Technology

Entertainment & Technology
1660 Stewart Street
Santa Monica, CA 90404
Phone: (310) 434-3700
Fax: (310) 434-3768
E-mail: academy_info@smc.edu
http://academy.smc.edu
Degrees: Certificate, A.A.
Academic Areas: Character
Animation, Computer
Animation/Digital Art, Graphic
Design, Multimedia/Games,

Web Graphics/Design, Web
Animation, Animation History/
Theory, Distance Learning,
Online Courses, Vocational
Training

Studio Arts, Ltd.

Animation and Visual Effects
570 W. Avenue 26
Suite 425
Los Angeles, CA 90065
Phone: (323) 227-8776
Fax: (323) 227-8775
E-mail: admin@studioarts.tv
http://www.studioarts.tv
Degrees: Certificate
Academic Areas: Character
Animation, Computer
Animation/Digital Art, Graphic
Design, Multimedia/Games,
Web Graphics/Design, Web
Animation, Performance
Animation, Workshops,
Distance Learning, Online
Courses, Kids' Programs,
Private Training, Vocational
Training

Technology Development Center

5200 Valentine Road
Ventura, CA 93003
Phone: (805) 676-7310
E-mail: tdcinfo@vace.com
http://www.vace.com/
Degrees: Certificate
Academic Areas: Character
Animation, Experimental
Animation, Computer
Animation/Digital Art, Graphic
Design, Multimedia/Games,
Vocational Training

Thinksmart

FX 3-D & 3-D Animation,
Production & Post Production
Works, Software & Web
Programming
508 S. Barrington Avenue
Suite 2
Los Angeles, CA 90049
Phone: (310) 440-0209
http://www.thinksmartfx.com

Degrees: Certificate, A.A.,
Diploma, B.A., B.S., B.F.A.,
M.A., M.S., M.F.A., Doctorate/
Other Postgraduate
Academic Areas: Graphic Design,
Performance Animation

UCLA Animation Workshop

Department of Film & TV
P.O. Box 951622
Los Angeles, CA 90095-1622
Phone: (310) 206-8441
Fax: (310) 825-3383
E-mail: UCLAnimation@hotmail.
com
http://animation.filmtv.ucla.edu
Degrees: M.A., M.S., M.F.A.
Academic Areas: Character
Animation, Experimental
Animation, Computer
Animation/Digital Art,
Animation History/Theory

UCLA Extension

Entertainment Studies and
Performing Arts
10995 LeConte Avenue
Suite 437
Los Angeles, CA 90024
Phone: (310) 825-9064
Fax: (310) 206-7435
E-mail: entertainmentstudies@
uclaextension.edu
http://www.uclaextension.edu/
entertainmentstudies
Degrees: Certificate
Academic Areas: Character
Animation, Computer
Animation/Digital Art, Fine Art,
Graphic Design, Multimedia/
Games, Web Graphics/Design,
Web Animation, Voice Acting,
Performance Animation,
Workshops, Distance Learning,
Online Courses, Private
Training, Vocational Training

UCLA Extension Visual Arts

Art Studio/Computer Graphics
10995 Le Conte Avenue
Room 414
Los Angeles, CA 90024
Phone: (310) 206-1422

Fax: (310) 206-7382
E-mail: visualarts@uclaextension.org
http://www.uclaextension.org/
visualarts
Degrees: Certificate
Academic Areas: Computer
Animation/Digital Art, Fine Art,
Graphic Design, Multimedia/
Games, Web Graphics/Design,
Web Animation, Animation
History/Theory, Workshops,
Vocational Training

University Extended Education—Cal State Fullerton

Business, Arts and Social Sciences
2600 E. Nutwood Avenue
Suite 770
Fullerton, CA 92831
Phone: (714) 278-2611
Fax: (714) 278-5445
E-mail: lgarcia@fullerton.edu
http://www.takethelead.fullerton.
edu
Degrees: Certificate
Other: Stand-alone classes
Academic Areas: Computer
Animation/Digital Art, Graphic
Design, Web Graphics/Design,
Web Animation, Workshops

University of California at Berkeley

Computer Science Division
387 Soda Hall
Suite 1776
Berkeley, CA 94720-5800
Phone: (510) 642-1042
Fax: (510) 642-5775
E-mail: csoffice@cs.berkeley.edu
http://www.cs.berkeley.edu
Degrees: B.A., B.S., B.F.A.
Academic Areas: Computer
Animation/Digital Art

University of Southern California

School of Cinema & TV
850 W. 34th Street
LPB 202
Los Angeles, CA 90089
Phone: (213) 740-3986

E-mail: admissions@cinema.usc.edu
http://www.usc.edu
Degrees: M.A., M.S., M.F.A.
Academic Areas: Experimental
Animation, Computer
Animation/Digital Art

Victor Valley College

Digital Animation
18422 Bear Valley Road
Victorville, CA 92392
Phone: (760) 245-4271, ext. 2732
E-mail: nelles@vvc.edu
http://www.vvc.edu/academic/
media_arts/index.htm
Degrees: Certificate
Academic Areas: Character
Animation, Computer
Animation/Digital Art, Graphic
Design, Multimedia/Games,
Web Graphics/Design, Web
Animation, Animation History/
Theory

Video Symphony

Lightwave 3-D VFX
731 N. Hollywood Way
Burbank, CA 91505
Phone: (818) 557-7200
Fax: (818) 845-1951
E-mail: info@videosymphony.com
http://www.videosymphony.com
Degrees: Certificate
Academic Areas: Computer
Animation/Digital Art, Graphic
Design, Multimedia/Games,
Web Graphics/Design, Web
Animation, Private Training,
Vocational Training

Woodbury University

7500 Glenoaks Boulevard
Burbank, CA 91510-7846
Phone: (800) 784-9663
Fax: (818) 504-9320
E-mail: info@woodbury.edu
http://www.woodbury.edu
Degrees: B.A., B.S., B.F.A.
Academic Areas: Character
Animation, Computer
Animation/Digital Art, Fine Art,
Graphic Design, Multimedia/
Games, Web Graphics/Design

COLORADO

101 Voice Overs

P.O. Box 272441
Fort Collins, CO 80527
Phone: (970) 223-3659
E-mail: student@anthonyreece.com
http://www.anthonyreece.com/
reece/vo101.html
Degrees: Certificate
Academic Areas: Voice Acting,
Workshops, Distance Learning,
Online Courses, Kids' Programs,
Private Training, Vocational
Training

The Art Institute of Colorado

Media Arts & Animation
1200 Lincoln Street
Denver, CO 80203
Phone: (303) 837-0825
Fax: (303) 860-8520
E-mail: muehlj@aii.edu
http://www.aic.aii.edu
Degrees: B.A., B.S., B.F.A.
Academic Areas: Experimental
Animation, Computer
Animation/Digital Art, Graphic
Design, Multimedia/Games,
Web Graphics/Design, Web
Animation, Animation History/
Theory, Online Courses

Digital-Evolutions—Smoky Hill High School

Digital Media Studies
16100 E. Smoky Hill Road
Aurora, CO 80015
Phone: (720) 886-5300
E-mail: dcornell2@
cherrycreekschools.org
http://www.Digital-Evolutions.org
Degrees: Certificate, Diploma
Academic Areas: Cartooning,
Character Animation,
Experimental Animation,
Computer Animation/
Digital Art, Fine Art, Graphic
Design, Multimedia/Games,
Web Graphics/Design, Web
Animation, Workshops, Kids'
Programs

Red Rocks Community College

Multimedia Graphics Design
13300 W. 6th Avenue
Lakewood, CO 80288
Phone: (303) 914-6600
Fax: (303) 914-6409
http://www.rrcc.cccoes.edu/
academic/multimediacenter/
http://www.rrcc.cccoes. edu/
multimedia
Degrees: A.A.
Academic Areas: Character
Animation, Computer
Animation/Digital Art, Fine Art,
Graphic Design, Multimedia/
Games, Web Graphics/Design,
Web Animation

Rocky Mountain College of Art & Design

6875 E. Evans Avenue
Denver, CO 80224
Phone: (800) 888-ARTS
Fax: (303) 759-4970
E-mail: admissions@rmcad.edu
http://www.rmcad.edu
Degrees: B.A., B.S., B.F.A.
Academic Areas: Cartooning,
Character Animation,
Experimental Animation,
Computer Animation/
Digital Art, Fine Art, Graphic
Design, Multimedia/Games,
Web Graphics/Design, Web
Animation, Performance
Animation, Animation History/
Theory, Workshops, Kids'
Programs

University of Colorado at Denver, Digital Animation Center

College of Arts and Media
Campus Box 177
P.O. Box 173364
Denver, CO 80217-3364
Phone: (303) 556-6217
E-mail: howard.cook@cudenver.
edu
http://www.cu3d.org
Degrees: B.A., B.S., B.F.A.

Academic Areas: Character Animation, Experimental Animation, Computer Animation/Digital Art, Fine Art, Performance Animation

CONNECTICUT

Guy Gilchrist's Cartoonist's Academy
448 Main Street
Winsted, CT 06098
Phone: (860) 738-8822
Fax: (860) 379-9617
E-mail: info@
gilchristcartoonacademy.com
http://www.
gilchristcartoonacademy.com
Degrees: Certificate
Academic Areas: Cartooning, Character Animation

Middlesex Community College
Arts & Media Department
100 Training Hill Road
Middletown, CT 06457
Phone: (860) 343-5800
Fax: (860) 343-5819
http://www.mxcc.commnet.edu
Degrees: Certificate, A.A.
Academic Areas: Computer Animation/Digital Art, Graphic Design, Multimedia/ Games, Web Graphics/Design, Workshops, Online Courses

DISTRICT OF COLUMBIA

Future Media Concepts—DC
818 18th Street, NW
Washington, DC 20006
Phone: (202) 429-9700
http://www.fmctraining.com
Degrees: Certificate
Academic Areas: Character Animation, Experimental Animation, Computer Animation/Digital Art, Graphic Design, Multimedia/ Games, Web Graphics/Design, Performance Animation, Workshops

Howard University
Fine Arts–Electronic Studio
2455 6th Street, NW
Washington, DC 20059
Phone: (202) 806-7047
Fax: (202) 806-9258
E-mail: visualarts@howard.edu
http://art.howard.edu
Degrees: B.A., B.S., B.F.A., M.A., M.S., M.F.A.
Academic Areas: Computer Animation/Digital Art, Fine Art, Graphic Design

FLORIDA

Ai Institute Miami International University of Art and Design
1501 Biscayne Boulevard
Suite 100
Miami, FL 33132
Phone: (800) 225-9023
Fax: (305) 374-5933
http://www.artinstitutes.edu/miami
Degrees: B.A., B.S., B.F.A., M.A., M.S., M.F.A.
Academic Areas: Character Animation, Experimental Animation, Computer Animation/Digital Art, Fine Art, Graphic Design, Multimedia/ Games, Performance Animation, Animation History/Theory

Animation & Design @ CBT
School of Art & Design
8991 SW 107 Avenue 200
Miami, FL 33176
Phone: (305) 225-5228
E-mail: admissions@cbt.edu
http://www.cbt.edu
Degrees: Certificate, A.A., Diploma
Academic Areas: Character Animation, Experimental Animation, Computer Animation/Digital Art, Graphic Design, Multimedia/ Games, Web Graphics/Design, Web Animation, Workshops, Distance Learning, Online Courses

The Art Institute of Fort Lauderdale
1799 SE 17th Street
Fort Lauderdale, FL 33309
Phone: (954) 463-3000
Fax: (954) 525-2602
E-mail: murphyr@aii.edu
http://www.aifl.edu
Degrees: A.A., B.A., B.S., B.F.A.
Academic Areas: Character Animation, Computer Animation/Digital Art, Fine Art, Graphic Design, Multimedia/ Games, Performance Animation, Animation History/Theory

The Art Institute of Tampa
Parkside at Tampa Bay Park
4401 N. Himes Avenue
Suite 150
Tampa, FL 33614-7001
Phone: (866) 703-3277
Fax: (813) 873-2171
E-mail: aitainformation@aii.edu
http://www.AiTA.artinstitutes.edu
Degrees: A.A., B.A., B.S., B.F.A.
Academic Areas: Character Animation, Computer Animation/Digital Art, Graphic Design, Multimedia/Games, Web Graphics/Design, Web Animation, Vocational Training

College of Business & Technology
Graphic Design
8991 SW 107 Avenue
Suite 200
Miami, FL 33176
Phone: (305) 273-4499
E-mail: pablo@cbt.edu
http://www.cbt.edu
Degrees: Certificate, A.A., Diploma
Academic Areas: Character Animation, Experimental Animation, Computer Animation/Digital Art, Graphic Design, Multimedia/ Games, Web Graphics/Design, Web Animation, Workshops, Distance Learning, Online Courses, Private Training, Vocational Training

DAVE School—Digital Animation & Visual Effects School
Universal Studios Florida
2000 Universal Studios Plaza
Suite 200
Orlando, FL 32819
Phone: (407) 224-3283
E-mail: admissions@daveschool.com
http://www.daveschool.com/
Academic Areas: Character Animation, Computer Animation/Digital Art

Digital Media Arts College
Admissions
3785 N. Federal Highway
Boca Raton, FL 33431
Phone: (866) 255-DMAC
Fax: (561) 391-2480
E-mail: admissions@dmac-edu.org
http://www.dmac-edu.org
Degrees: B.A., B.S., B.F.A., M.A., M.S., M.F.A.
Academic Areas: Character Animation, Experimental Animation, Computer Animation/Digital Art, Graphic Design, Multimedia/Games, Web Graphics/Design, Web Animation, Private Training

Florida Atlantic University
Center for Electronic Communication
Askew Tower
111 Las Olas Boulevard
Fort Lauderdale, FL 33301
Phone: (954) 762-5618
Fax: (954) 762-5658
E-mail: newmand@laureate.cec.fau.edu
http://www.animasters.com
Degrees: B.A., B.S., B.F.A., M.A., M.S., M.F.A.
Academic Areas: Character Animation, Experimental Animation, Computer Animation/Digital Art, Fine Art, Graphic Design, Multimedia/Games, Web Graphics/Design, Web Animation, Voice Acting, Animation History/Theory,

Distance Learning, Online Courses, Private Training, Vocational Training

Forest Hill Community High School
Computer Graphics and Animation/Art
6901 Parker Avenue
West Palm Beach, FL 33405
Phone: (561) 540-2462
Fax: (561) 540-2440
E-mail: animart@netzero.net
http://www.animatorman.com
Degrees: Diploma
Academic Areas: Cartooning, Character Animation, Experimental Animation, Fine Art, Graphic Design, Multimedia/Games, Web Graphics/Design, Web Animation, Voice Acting, Performance Animation, Workshops

Full Sail University
Full Sail, Inc.
3300 University Boulevard
Winter Park, FL 32792
Phone: (407) 679-0100
Fax: (407) 678-0070
E-mail: admissions@fullsail.com
http://www.fullsail.edu
Degrees: B.A., B.S., B.F.A., M.A., M.S., M.F.A.
Academic Areas: Character Animation, Experimental Animation, Computer Animation/Digital Art, Fine Art, Graphic Design, Multimedia/Games, Web Graphics/Design, Web Animation, Animation History/Theory

Future Media Concepts—Miami
5201 Blue Lagoon Drive
8th Floor
Miami, FL 33126
Phone: (305) 629-3018
http://www.fmctraining.com
Degrees: Certificate
Academic Areas: Experimental Animation, Computer

Animation/Digital Art, Graphic Design, Multimedia/Games, Web Graphics/Design, Web Animation, Performance Animation, Workshops

International Academy of Design & Technology
5225 Memorial Highway
Tampa, FL 33634
Phone: (800) 222-3369
Fax: (813) 881-0008
E-mail: leads@academy.edu
http://www.academy.edu
Degrees: B.A., B.S., B.F.A.
Academic Areas: Character Animation, Computer Animation/Digital Art, Graphic Design, Multimedia/Games, Web Graphics/Design, Animation History/Theory

Maya Training Center
Training
P.O. Box 172906
Tampa, FL 33672
Phone: (888) 275-2849
Fax: (813) 221-6715
E-mail: info@MayaTraining.com
http://www.MayaTraining.com
Degrees: Certificate
Other: Alias Certified Training
Academic Areas: Cartooning, Character Animation, Experimental Animation, Computer Animation/ Digital Art, Fine Art, Graphic Design, Multimedia/Games, Web Graphics/Design, Web Animation, Workshops, Distance Learning, Online Courses, Kids' Programs, Private Training, Vocational Training

Miami Digital Arts
5701 Sunset Drive
Suite 212
Miami, FL 33143
Phone: (786) 277-4614
E-mail: email@3dtrainer.com
http://miamidigitalarts.com
Other: Autodesk Certification

Academic Areas: Character Animation, Experimental Animation, Computer Animation/Digital Art, Graphic Design, Workshops, Online Courses, Kids' Programs, Private Training, Vocational Training

M.I.A. Training Center
P.O. Box 172906
Tampa, FL 33602
Phone: (888) 275-2849
E-mail: info@mayatraining.com
http://www.animationtraining.com
Degrees: Certificate
Other: Alias Certification, Autodesk Certification
Academic Areas: Cartooning, Character Animation, Experimental Animation, Computer Animation/ Digital Art, Graphic Design, Multimedia/Games, Web Graphics/Design, Web Animation, Voice Acting, Performance Animation, Workshops, Distance Learning, Online Courses, Kids' Programs, Private Training, Vocational Training

Planet Digital, Inc.
Education
1413 Haven Drive
Orlando, FL 32803
Phone: (407) 896-7326
Fax: (407) 896-2561
E-mail: training@planetdigital.com
http://training.planetdigital.com
Degrees: Certificate
Academic Areas: Character Animation, Experimental Animation, Computer Animation/Digital Art, Graphic Design, Multimedia/Games, Web Graphics/Design, Web Animation, Animation History/ Theory, Workshops, Private Training, Vocational Training

Planet Digital Training Center
17 N. Summerlin Avenue
Suite 200

Orlando, FL 32801
Phone: (407) 896-7326
E-mail: training.planetdigital.com
http://www.planetdigital.com
Degrees: Certificate
Academic Areas: Character Animation, Computer Animation/Digital Art, Multimedia/Games, Web Graphics/Design, Web Animation

Project Firefly Animation Studios
Education
1000 Universal Studios Boulevard
Building 22A
Orlando, FL 32819
Phone: (407) 224-6730
E-mail: education@projectfirefly. com
http://www.projectfirefly.com
Other: Workshops
Academic Areas: Character Animation, Computer Animation/Digital Art, Web Animation, Workshops

Ringling School of Art and Design
Computer Animation
2700 N. Tamiami Trail
Sarasota, FL 34234-5895
Phone: (800) 255-7695
Fax: (941) 359-7517
E-mail: admissions@ringling.edu
http://www.ringling.edu
Degrees: B.A., B.S., B.F.A., B.F.A. in Computer Animation
Academic Areas: Computer Animation/Digital Art

Surrealistic Producing Effects
4270 Aloma Avenue
Suite 124, PMB 14B
Winter Park, FL 32792
Phone: (407) 529-8210
E-mail: customerservice@speffects. com
http://www.speffects.com
Degrees: Certificate
Academic Areas: Character Animation, Computer

Animation/Digital Art, Workshops, Distance Learning, Online Courses, Private Training

GEORGIA

The Art Institute of Atlanta
6600 Peachtree Dunwoody Road
100 Embassy Row
Atlanta, GA 30328
Phone: (800) 275-4242
Fax: (770) 394-0008
E-mail: aiaadm@aii.edu
http://www.aia.artinstitutes.edu
Degrees: A.A., B.A., B.S., B.F.A.
Academic Areas: Computer Animation/Digital Art, Graphic Design, Multimedia/ Games, Web Graphics/Design, Workshops

Atlanta College of Art
Woodruff Arts Center
1280 Peachtree Street, NE
Atlanta, GA 30309
Phone: (800) 832-2104
E-mail: acainfo@woodruffcenter.org
http://www.aca.edu
Degrees: B.A., B.S., B.F.A.
Academic Areas: Character Animation, Computer Animation/Digital Art, Graphic Design, Multimedia/Games

Savannah College of Art and Design
P.O. Box 2072
Savannah, GA 31402-2072
Phone: (800) 869-7223
Fax: (912) 525-5986
E-mail: admission@scad.edu
http://www.scad.edu
Degrees: Certificate, B.A., B.S., B.F.A., M.A., M.S., M.F.A.
Academic Areas: Cartooning, Character Animation, Experimental Animation, Computer Animation/ Digital Art, Fine Art, Graphic Design, Multimedia/Games, Web Graphics/Design, Web Animation, Workshops, Distance Learning, Online Courses

Southern Polytechnic State University
1100 S. Marietta Parkway
Marietta, GA 30060-2896
Phone: (770) 528-7200
Fax: (770) 528-7292
E-mail: admissions@spsu.edu
http://www.spsu.edu
Degrees: Certificate, A.A., B.A.,
B.S., B.F.A., M.A., M.S., M.F.A.
Academic Areas: Distance
Learning, Online Courses

University of Georgia
Lamar Dodd School of Art
Visual Arts Building
Athens, GA 30602-4102
Phone: (706) 542-1511
Fax: (706) 542-2080
http://www.visart.uga.edu
Degrees: B.A., B.S., B.F.A., M.A.,
M.S., M.F.A.
Academic Areas: Character
Animation, Computer
Animation/Digital Art,
Fine Art, Graphic Design,
Multimedia/Games, Voice
Acting, Performance
Animation, Animation History/
Theory

HAWAII

Kapiolani Community College
Arts & Humanities
4303 Diamond Head Road
Honolulu, HI 96816
Phone: (808) 734-9000
Degrees: A.A.
Academic Areas: Character
Animation, Computer
Animation/Digital Art, Fine Art,
Graphic Design, Multimedia/
Games, Web Graphics/Design,
Web Animation

University of Hawaii
Academy for Creative Media
2550 Campus Road
Crawford 312
Honolulu, HI 96822
Phone: (808) 956-7736
Fax: (808) 956-6662

Degrees: B.A., B.S., B.F.A.
Academic Areas: Character
Animation, Computer
Animation/Digital Art,
Multimedia/Games,
Performance Animation

ILLINOIS

Columbia College Chicago
Film and Video Department
600 S. Michigan Avenue
Chicago, IL 60605
Phone: (312) 663-1600
Fax: (312) 344-8044
E-mail: byoung@colum.edu
http://www.colum.edu
Degrees: B.A., B.S., B.F.A.
Academic Areas: Character
Animation, Experimental
Animation, Computer
Animation/Digital Art, Fine Art,
Graphic Design, Multimedia/
Games, Animation History/
Theory, Online Courses, Kids'
Programs

DePaul University
Animation Program
243 S. Wabash Avenue
Chicago, IL 60604
Phone: (312) 362-8381
E-mail: cti@cti.depaul.edu
http://GameDev.DePaul.edu
Degrees: B.A., B.S., B.F.A., M.A.,
M.S., M.F.A.
Academic Areas: Character
Animation, Experimental
Animation, Computer
Animation/Digital Art,
Multimedia/Games, Web
Graphics/Design, Web
Animation, Performance
Animation, Animation History/
Theory

Flashpoint, The Academy of Media Arts and Sciences
Visual Effects and Animation, Film,
Game Design, Recording Arts
28 N. Clark Street
Chicago, IL 60602
Phone: (312) 332-0707

Fax: (312) 633-0707
Degrees: Certificate
Academic Areas: Character
Animation, Computer
Animation/Digital Art,
Performance Animation,
Animation History/Theory,
Workshops, Vocational
Training

Harper College
1200 W. Algonquin Road
Palatine, IL 60067-7398
Phone: (847) 925-6000
E-mail: tech@harper.cc.il.us
http://www.harper.cc.il.us
Degrees: Certificate, A.A.
Academic Areas: Computer
Animation/Digital Art, Graphic
Design, Web Graphics/Design,
Vocational Training

The Illinois Institute of Art at Chicago
350 N. Orleans Street
Suite 136
Chicago, IL 60654-1593
Phone: (800) 351-3450
Fax: (312) 280-3528
http://www.ilia.aii.edu
Degrees: Certificate, B.A., B.S.,
B.F.A.
Academic Areas: Character
Animation, Computer
Animation/Digital Art, Fine Art,
Graphic Design, Multimedia/
Games, Animation History/
Theory

The Illinois Institute of Art at Schaumburg
1000 Plaza Drive
Schaumburg, IL 60173-5070
Phone: (800) 314-3450
Fax: (847) 619-3064
http://www.ilia.aii.edu
Degrees: B.A., B.S., B.F.A.
Academic Areas: Character
Animation, Computer
Animation/Digital Art, Fine Art,
Graphic Design, Multimedia/
Games, Animation History/
Theory

Moraine Valley Community College
10900 S. 88th Avenue
T-Building
Palos Hills, IL 60465-0937
Phone: (708) 974-4300
E-mail: moraine@morainevalley.edu
http://www.morainevalley.edu
Degrees: Certificate, A.A.
Academic Areas: Computer Animation/Digital Art, Web Graphics/Design

Northwestern University
Department of Radio/Television/Film
1920 Campus Drive
Annie May Swift Hall
Room 212
Evanston, IL 60208
Phone: (847) 491-7315
Fax: (847) 467-2389
E-mail: rtvfinfo@northwestern.edu
http://www.rtvf.nwu.edu
Degrees: B.A., B.S., B.F.A., M.A., M.S., M.F.A., Doctorate/Other Postgraduate
Academic Areas: Character Animation, Computer Animation/Digital Art, Multimedia/Games

Oakton Community College
Graphic Design
1600 E. Golf Road
Des Plaines, IL 60016
Phone: (847) 635-1600
E-mail: webmaster@oakton.edu
http://www.oakton.edu
Degrees: A.A., Diploma
Academic Areas: Character Animation, Computer Animation/Digital Art, Fine Art, Graphic Design, Multimedia/Games, Web Graphics/Design, Web Animation, Online Courses

School of the Art Institute of Chicago
37 S. Wabash Avenue
Chicago, IL 60603
Phone: (312) 629-6100

E-mail: admiss@saic.edu
http://www.saic.edu/
Degrees: Certificate, B.A., B.S., B.F.A., M.A., M.S., M.F.A., Doctorate/Other Postgraduate
Academic Areas: Character Animation, Computer Animation/Digital Art, Fine Art, Graphic Design, Multimedia/Games

Southern Illinois University
Department of Cinema & Photography
Carbondale, IL 62901
Phone: (618) 453-2365
http://cp.siu.edu/
Academic Areas: Vocational Training

University of Illinois
School of Art and Design
408 E. Peabody Street
Champaign, IL 61820
Phone: (217) 333-0855
Fax: (217) 333-6632
Degrees: B.A., B.S., B.F.A., M.A., M.S., M.F.A.
Academic Areas: Computer Animation/Digital Art, Graphic Design, Multimedia/Games, Web Graphics/Design

University of Illinois at Chicago
School of Art and Design
106 Jefferson Hall
929 W. Harrison Street
Chicago, IL 60607-7038
Phone: (312) 996-3337
Fax: (312) 413-2333
http://www.uic.edu/aa/artd
Degrees: B.A., B.S., B.F.A., M.A., M.S., M.F.A.
Academic Areas: Computer Animation/Digital Art, Graphic Design, Multimedia/Games, Web Graphics/Design, Web Animation

VirtualONE, Inc.
11110 E. Cove Circle, #2C
Palos Hills, IL 60465
Phone: (630) 561-8987

Degrees: B.A., B.S., B.F.A.
Academic Areas: Character Animation, Graphic Design, Multimedia/Games, Workshops, Distance Learning, Online Courses, Private Training, Vocational Training

IOWA

The Franciscan University
Computer Graphics Department
400 N. Bluff Boulevard
Clinton, IA 52732
Phone: (563) 242-4023
Fax: (563) 243-6102
Degrees: B.A., B.S., B.F.A.
Academic Areas: Character Animation, Computer Animation/Digital Art, Graphic Design, Multimedia/Games, Web Graphics/Design, Web Animation, Animation History/Theory

Maharishi University of Management
Department of Fine Arts
Digital Media Program
1000 N. 4th Street
Fairfield, IA 52557
Phone: (641) 472-1110
Fax: (641) 472-1179
Degrees: B.A., B.S., B.F.A.
Academic Areas: Character Animation, Experimental Animation, Computer Animation/Digital Art, Fine Art, Graphic Design, Web Graphics/Design, Web Animation

KANSAS

Washburn University
Division of Continuing Education
1700 S.W. College Avenue
Topeka, KS 66621
Phone: (785) 231-1010, ext. 1639
Fax: (785) 231-1028
Degrees: B.A., B.S., B.F.A.
Academic Areas: Character Animation, Computer Animation/Digital Art, Fine Art, Web Animation

KENTUCKY

Louisville Technical Institute
Computer Graphic Design
3901 Atkinson Drive
Louisville, KY 40218
Phone: (800) 844-6528
Fax: (502) 456-2341
E-mail: dritz@louisvilletech.com
http://www.louisvilletech.com
Degrees: A.A.
Academic Areas: Character
Animation, Computer
Animation/Digital Art, Graphic
Design, Multimedia/Games,
Web Graphics/Design, Web
Animation

Spencerian College
Computer Graphic Design
2355 Harrodsburg Road
Lexington, KY 40504
Phone: (800) 456-3253
Fax: (859) 224-7744
http://www.spencerian.edu
Degrees: A.A.
Academic Areas: Computer
Animation/Digital Art, Graphic
Design

University of Kentucky
College of Fine Arts
202 Fine Arts Building
Lexington, KY 40506-0022
Phone: (859) 257-2727
Fax: (859) 323-1050
http://www.uky.edu/FineArts
Degrees: B.A., B.S., B.F.A., M.A.,
M.S., M.F.A.
Academic Areas: Computer
Animation/Digital Art, Fine Art,
Graphic Design, Multimedia/
Games

University of Louisville
College of Arts and Sciences
230 Gardiner Hall
Louisville, KY 40292
Phone: (800) 334-8635
Fax: (502) 852-6791
E-mail: ansinfo@gwise.louisville.
edu
http://www.louisville.edu/a-s/

Degrees: B.A., B.S., B.F.A.
Academic Areas: Graphic Design

MAINE

The International Film Workshops
Animation
P.O. Box 200
2 Central Street
Rockport, ME 04856
Phone: (207) 236-8581
Fax: (207) 236-2558
E-mail: Info@TheWorkshops.com
http://www.TheWorkshops.com
Degrees: Certificate, A.A., M.A.,
M.S., M.F.A.
Other: One-week workshops and
master classes
Academic Areas: Cartooning,
Character Animation, Computer
Animation/Digital Art, Graphic
Design, Web Animation,
Performance Animation,
Workshops, Kids' Programs,
Vocational Training

MARYLAND

Anne Arundel Community College
Communication Arts Technology
Department
101 College Parkway
Arnold, MD 21012-1895
Phone: (410) 647-7100
E-mail: webmaster@aacc.cc.md.us
http://www.aacc.cc.md.us/
Degrees: Certificate, A.A.
Academic Areas: Computer
Animation/Digital Art, Fine Art,
Web Graphics/Design, Online
Courses

Maryland Institute College of Art (MICA)
Experimental Animation
1300 Mount Royal Avenue
Baltimore, MD 21217
Phone: (410) 225-2300
Fax: (410) 669-9201
E-mail: pr@mica.edu
http://www.mica.edu/

Degrees: B.F.A, Post-Baccalaureate
Certificate in Fine Art, M.A.,
M.F.A., M.P.S.
Academic Areas: Animation;
Art History, Theory, and
Criticism; Ceramics; Drawing;
Environmental Design; Fiber;
General Fine Arts; Graphic
Design; Humanistic Studies;
Illustration; Interaction Design
and Art; Interdisciplinary
Sculpture; Painting;
Photography; Printmaking;
Video and Film Arts

UMBC Computer Certification Training Center
3108 Lord Baltimore Drive
Suite 200
Baltimore, MD 21244
Phone: (410) 594-2282
Fax: (443) 436-3014
E-mail: info@umbccctc.com
http://www.umbc.edu/cctc
Degrees: Certificate
Academic Areas: Character
Animation, Computer
Animation/Digital Art,
Vocational Training

MASSACHUSETTS

Animation Gurus
290 Turnpike Road
Suite 6
Westboro, MA 01581
Phone: (508) 340-4068
Fax: (508) 256-6553
E-mail: trishna@ssiincusa.com
http://www.animationgurus.com
Degrees: Certificate, Diploma, B.A.,
B.S., B.F.A.
Academic Areas: Cartooning,
Character Animation,
Experimental Animation,
Computer Animation/Digital
Art, Graphic Design, Web
Animation

The Art Institute of Boston at Lesley University
Office of Admissions

700 Beacon Street
Boston, MA 02215-2598
Phone: (800) 773-0494, ext. 6700
E-mail: admissions@aiboston.edu
http://www.aiboston.edu
Degrees: Certificate, Diploma,
B.A., B.S., B.F.A., M.A., M.S.,
M.F.A.
Academic Areas: Character
Animation, Experimental
Animation, Computer
Animation/Digital Art, Fine Art,
Graphic Design, Web Graphics/
Design, Web Animation,
Animation History/Theory,
Workshops

Fitchburg State College
Communications Media
160 Pearl Street
528 Mechanic Street
Fitchburg, MA 01420
Phone: (978) 665-3260
E-mail: croberts@fsc.edu
http://www.fsc.edu
Degrees: B.A., B.S., B.F.A., M.A.,
M.S., M.F.A.
Academic Areas: Multimedia/
Games

Future Media Concepts—Mass
43 Thorndike Street
Cambridge, MA 02141
Phone: (617) 621-1155
E-mail: info@fmctraining.com
http://www.fmctraining.com
Degrees: Certificate
Academic Areas: Character
Animation, Computer
Animation/Digital Art, Graphic
Design

Hampshire College
893 West Street
Amherst, MA 01002
http://www.hampshire.edu
Degrees: B.A., B.S., B.F.A.
Academic Areas: Cartooning,
Character Animation,
Experimental Animation,
Computer Animation/
Digital Art, Fine Art, Graphic
Design, Multimedia/Games,

Web Graphics/Design, Web
Animation, Voice Acting,
Performance Animation,
Animation History/Theory

Harvard University
Carpenter Center for the Arts
Visual and Environmental Studies
24 Quincy Street
Cambridge, MA 02138
Phone: (617) 495-3251
Fax: (617) 495-8197
E-mail: mlawrenc@fas.harvard.
edu
http://ves.fas.harvard.edu
Degrees: B.A., B.S., B.F.A.
Academic Areas: Character
Animation, Experimental
Animation, Computer
Animation/Digital Art, Fine Art,
Animation History/Theory

Massachusetts Institute of Technology
The MIT Media Laboratory
The Program in Media Arts and
Sciences
77 Massachusetts Avenue
Cambridge, MA 02139
Phone: (617) 253-0338
Fax: (617) 258-6264
E-mail: mas@media.mit.edu
http://www.media.mit.edu
Degrees: B.A., B.S., B.F.A., M.A.,
M.S., M.F.A., Doctorate/Other
Postgraduate
Academic Areas: Computer
Animation/Digital Art,
Multimedia/Games

Mount Ida College
Computer Animation
777 Dedham Street
Newton, MA 02459
Phone: (617) 928-4500
E-mail: jakaufman@mountida.edu
http://www.mountida.edu
Degrees: B.A., B.S., B.F.A.
Academic Areas: Character
Animation, Experimental
Animation, Computer
Animation/Digital Art,
Animation History/Theory

The New England Institute of Art
Media Arts & Animation
10 Brookline Place West
Brookline, MA 02445
Phone: (800) 903-4425
E-mail: neiaadm@aii.edu
http://www.neia.artinstitutes.edu
Degrees: B.A., B.S., B.F.A.
Academic Areas: Character
Animation, Computer
Animation/Digital Art, Graphic
Design, Web Graphics/Design,
Web Animation

Northeastern University
Department of Visual Arts
c/o Ed Andrews
239 Ryder Hall
Boston, MA 02115
Phone: (617) 373-4081
Fax: (617) 373-8535
http://www.animation.neu.edu
Degrees: B.A., B.S., B.F.A.
Academic Areas: Character
Animation, Experimental
Animation, Computer
Animation/Digital Art, Fine Art,
Graphic Design, Multimedia/
Games, Animation History/
Theory

School of the Museum of Fine Arts
Film-Making Department
230 The Fenway
Boston, MA 02115
Phone: (617) 267-6100
Fax: (617) 424-6271
E-mail: academicaffairs@smfa.edu
http://www.smfa.edu
Degrees: B.A./B.S./B.F.A., M.A./
M.S./M.F.A.
Academic Areas: Computer
Animation/Digital Art, Fine Art,
Graphic Design, Multimedia/
Games, Web Graphics/Design,
Web Animation

Springfield College
Computer College
263 Alden Street
Springfield, MA 01109

Phone: (413) 748-3930
E-mail: Ruth_West@spfldcol.edu
http://www.spfldcol.edu/cg
Degrees: B.A., B.S., B.F.A.
Academic Areas: Character
Animation, Experimental
Animation, Computer
Animation/Digital Art, Graphic
Design, Multimedia/Games,
Web Graphics/Design, Web
Animation, Animation History/
Theory

University of Massachusetts—Amherst

Art Department
Fine Arts Center East
151 Presidents Drive
Amherst, MA 01003
Phone: (413) 545-1902
Fax: (413) 545-3929
http://www.umass.edu/art/index.
html
Degrees: B.A., B.S., B.F.A., M.A.,
M.S., M.F.A.
Academic Areas: Experimental
Animation, Computer
Animation/Digital Art, Fine
Art, Web Graphics/Design, Web
Animation, Workshops

MICHIGAN

Baker College

1500 University Drive
Auburn Hills, MI 48326-2642
Phone: (888) 429-0410
Fax: (248) 340-0608
http://www.baker.edu
Degrees: Certificate, A.A., B.A.,
B.S., B.F.A.
Academic Areas: Computer
Animation/Digital Art, Graphic
Design, Web Graphics/Design

College for Creative Studies

Animation and Digital Media
201 E. Kirby Street
Detroit, MI 48202-4034
Phone: (313) 664-7400
E-mail: admissions@ccscad.edu
http://www.ccscad.edu
Degrees: B.A., B.S., B.F.A.

Academic Areas: Character
Animation, Experimental
Animation, Computer
Animation/Digital Art, Fine Art,
Graphic Design, Multimedia/
Games, Web Graphics/Design,
Web Animation, Animation
History/Theory

Ferris State University

Digital Animation and Game
Design
410 Oak Street
Big Rapids, MI 49307
Phone: (231) 591-2340
E-mail: fsugr@ferris.edu
http://cpts.ferris.edu/
Degrees: B.A., B.S., B.F.A.
Academic Areas: Computer
Animation/Digital Art,
Multimedia/Games, Workshops,
Distance Learning, Online
Courses

Grand Valley State University

School of Communications
121 Lake Superior Hall
Allendale, MI 49401
Phone: (616) 331-3668
E-mail: go2gvsu@gvsu.edu
http://www.gvsu.edu
Degrees: B.A., B.S., B.F.A., M.A.,
M.S., M.F.A.
Academic Areas: Character
Animation, Experimental
Animation

Kalamazoo Valley Community College

Center for New Media
202 N. Rose Street
P.O. Box 4070
Kalamazoo, MI 49007-4030
Phone: (269) 373-7800
E-mail: newmedia@kvcc.edu
http://www.kvcc.edu/
Degrees: Certificate, A.A., Associ-
ate's of Applied Science (AAS)
Academic Areas: Cartooning,
Character Animation, Computer
Animation/Digital Art, Fine Art,
Graphic Design, Multimedia/
Games, Web Graphics/Design,

Web Animation, Workshops,
Vocational Training

Kendall College of Art and Design

Ferris State University
17 Fountain Street
Grand Rapids, MI 49503-3102
Phone: (800) 676-2787
Fax: (616) 831-9689
E-mail: packarda@kcad.edu
http://www.kcad.edu
Degrees: B.A., B.S., B.F.A., M.A.,
M.S., M.F.A.
Academic Areas: Computer
Animation/Digital Art, Fine Art,
Graphic Design, Multimedia/
Games

Lansing Community College

Art, Design & Multimedia Program
315 N. Grand Avenue
P.O. Box 40010
Lansing, MI 48901-7210
Phone: (517) 483-1476
Fax: (517) 483-9781
E-mail: SWood2@lcc.edu
http://www.lcc.edu/vam/art/
Degrees: Certificate, A.A.
Academic Areas: Computer
Animation/Digital Art, Fine Art,
Graphic Design, Multimedia/
Games, Distance Learning,
Online Courses

MINNESOTA

Academy College

1101 E. 78th Street
Suite 100
Minneapolis, MN 55420
Phone: (952) 851-0066
Fax: (952) 851-0094
E-mail: email@academyeducation.
com
http://www.academycollege.edu
Degrees: Certificate, A.A.
Academic Areas: Character
Animation, Computer
Animation/Digital Art, Graphic
Design, Multimedia/Games,
Web Graphics/Design, Web
Animation

The Art Institutes International Minnesota

15 S. 9th Street
Minneapolis, MN 55402
Phone: (800) 777-3643
Fax: (612) 332-3934
E-mail: aimadm@aii.edu
http://www.aim.artinstitutes.edu
Degrees: A.A., B.A., B.S., B.F.A.
Academic Areas: Computer Animation/Digital Art, Graphic Design, Multimedia/Games, Web Graphics/Design, Web Animation, Online Courses

Art Instruction Schools

3400 Technology Drive
Minneapolis, MN 55418
Phone: (612) 362-5075
E-mail: info@artinstructionschools.com
http://www.artists-ais.edu
Degrees: Certificate
Academic Areas: Cartooning, Fine Art, Distance Learning

Minneapolis College of Art and Design

2501 Stevens Avenue South
Minneapolis, MN 55404
Phone: (612) 874-3760
http://www.mcad.edu
Degrees: B.A., B.S., B.F.A., M.A., M.S., M.F.A.
Academic Areas: Character Animation, Experimental Animation, Computer Animation/Digital Art, Fine Art, Graphic Design, Multimedia/Games

Minnesota School of Computer Imaging

Animation
1401 W. 76th Street
Suite 500
Richfield, MN 55423-9820
Phone: (612) 861-2000
Fax: (612) 861-5548
E-mail: pgallipo@msbcollege.com
http://www.msbcollege.edu
Degrees: Certificate, A.A.

Academic Areas: Cartooning, Character Animation, Computer Animation/Digital Art, Web Animation, Animation History/Theory, Workshops

St. Olaf College

Art Department
1520 St. Olaf Avenue
Northfield, MN 55057
Phone: (507) 646-3248
Fax: (507) 646-3332
E-mail: danielsg@stolaf.edu
http://www.stolaf.edu/depts/art
Degrees: B.A., B.S., B.F.A.
Academic Areas: Computer Animation/Digital Art, Fine Art, Graphic Design, Multimedia/Games

MISSISSIPPI

Mississippi State University

Department of Art
P.O. Box 5182
Mississippi State, MS 39762
Phone: (662) 325-2970
Fax: (662) 325-3850
E-mail: da@ra.msstate.edu
http://www.msstate.edu/dept/art
Degrees: B.A., B.S., B.F.A., M.A., M.S., M.F.A.
Academic Areas: Character Animation, Computer Animation/Digital Art, Fine Art, Graphic Design, Multimedia/Games, Animation History/Theory

MISSOURI

Kansas City Art Institute

4415 Warwick Boulevard
Kansas City, MO 64111
Phone: (800) 522-5224
Fax: (816) 802-3309
E-mail: admiss@kcai.edu
http://www.kcai.edu
Degrees: B.A., B.S., B.F.A.
Academic Areas: Cartooning, Character Animation, Experimental Animation, Computer Animation/Digital

Art, Fine Art, Web Animation, Performance Animation, Animation History/Theory, Workshops

Webster University

Animation Program
470 E. Lockwood Avenue
St. Louis, MO 63119
Phone: (314) 968-6900
E-mail: admissions@webster.edu
http://www.webster.edu
Degrees: B.A., B.S., B.F.A.
Academic Areas: Character Animation, Experimental Animation, Computer Animation/Digital Art, Fine Art, Web Graphics/Design, Web Animation, Voice Acting, Performance Animation, Animation History/Theory, Workshops

MONTANA

Montana State University—Northern

Industrial and Engineering Technology
Box 7751
Havre, MT 59501
Phone: (406) 265-4157
Fax: (406) 265-3580
E-mail: kegel@msun.edu
http://www.msun.edu
Degrees: A.A., B.A., B.S., B.F.A.
Academic Areas: Computer Animation/Digital Art, Graphic Design

NEVADA

The Art Institute of Las Vegas

2350 Corporate Circle
Henderson, Nevada 89074-7737
Phone: (702) 369-9944; Toll-free: (800) 833-2678
Fax: (702) 992-8558
http://www.artinstitutes.edu/lasvegas/
Degrees: B.S.
Academic Areas: Character Animation, Computer

Animation/Digital Art, Fine Art,
Graphic Design, Multimedia/
Games, Web Graphics/Design,
Web Animation

NEW JERSEY

The College of New Jersey
Department of Art
Holman Hall 407
P.O. Box 7718
2000 Pennington Road
Ewing, NJ 08628
Phone: (609) 771-2652
http://www.tcnj.edu/~artmain/
Degrees: B.A., B.S., B.F.A.
Academic Areas: Computer
Animation/Digital Art, Fine Art,
Graphic Design, Multimedia/
Games, Web Graphics/Design,
Web Animation

Joe Kubert School of Cartoon & Graphic Art, Inc.
Cinematic Animation
37 Myrtle Avenue
Dover, NJ 07801
Phone: (973) 361-1327
Fax: (973) 361-1844
E-mail: kubert@earthlink.net
http://www.kubertsworld.com
Degrees: Certificate, Diploma
Academic Areas: Cartooning,
Character Animation,
Experimental Animation,
Computer Animation/Digital
Art, Fine Art, Graphic Design,
Multimedia/Games, Web
Graphics/Design, Web Animation

Mercer County Community College
Arts/Communications/Technology
P.O. Box B
Trenton, NJ 08690
Phone: (609) 586-4800
Fax: (609) 586-6944
E-mail: admiss@mccc.edu
http://www.mccc.edu/~fiksy/
cgatmccc.htm
Degrees: A.A.
Academic Areas: Character
Animation, Computer

Animation/Digital Art, Fine Art,
Graphic Design, Multimedia/
Games, Web Graphics/Design,
Web Animation

Rutgers University
Department of Fine Arts
311 N. Fifth Street
Camden, NJ 08102
Phone: (609) 757-6176
Fax: (609) 757-6330
E-mail: jjg@camden.rutgers.edu
http://finearts.camden.rutgers.edu
Degrees: B.A., B.S., B.F.A.
Academic Areas: Character
Animation, Experimental
Animation, Computer
Animation/Digital Art, Fine Art,
Graphic Design, Multimedia/
Games, Animation History/
Theory

NEW MEXICO

Albuquerque TVI Community College
525 Buena Vista, SE
Albuquerque, NM 87106
Phone: (505) 224-3000
Fax: (505) 272-7969
http://www.tvi.cc.nm.us
Degrees: Certificate, A.A.
Academic Areas: Computer
Animation/Digital Art, Graphic
Design, Multimedia/Games,
Distance Learning, Vocational
Training

NEW YORK

3-D Training Institute
3 E. 28th Street
8th Floor
New York, NY 10016
Phone: (212) 967-7777, ext. 8
Fax: (212) 967-7971
E-mail: info@3dtraining.com
http://www.3dtraining.com
Degrees: Certificate
Academic Areas: Character
Animation, Computer
Animation/Digital Art,
Web Graphics/Design, Web

Animation, Workshops,
Distance Learning, Online
Courses, Private Training

Alfred State College
Computer Arts and Design
Engineering Technology Building
Alfred, NY 14802
Phone: (607) 587-4698
Fax: (607) 587-4620
E-mail: simpsora@alfredstate.edu
http://web.alfredstate.edu/ciat
Degrees: A.A.
Academic Areas: Character
Animation, Experimental
Animation, Computer
Animation/Digital Art,
Multimedia/Games, Web
Graphics/Design, Web
Animation, Animation History/
Theory, Workshops

Brooklyn College of the City University of New York
Department of Film
2900 Bedford Avenue
0314 Plaza Building
Brooklyn, NY 11210-2889
Phone: (718) 951-5664
Fax: (718) 951-4733
E-mail: film@brooklyn.cuny.edu
http://depthome.brooklyn.cuny.
edu/film/
Degrees: Certificate, B.A., B.S.,
B.F.A.
Academic Areas: Character
Animation

Cooper Union School of Art
Film/Animation
30 Cooper Square
New York, NY 10003
Phone: (212) 353-4100
E-mail: admissions@cooper.edu
http://www.cooper.edu
Degrees: Certificate, B.A., B.S.,
B.F.A.
Academic Areas: Distance
Learning

Cornell University
Office of Computing and
Information Science

4132 Upson Hall
Ithaca, NY 14853
Phone: (607) 255-9188
Fax: (607) 255-4428
E-mail: www@cs.cornell.edu
http://www.cis.cornell.edu
Degrees: B.A., B.S., B.F.A., M.A.,
M.S., M.F.A., Doctorate/Other
Postgraduate
Academic Areas: Computer
Animation/Digital Art

Croog Studios
135 W. 27th Street
7th Floor
New York, NY 10001
Phone: (212) 457-6578
E-mail: info@croogstudios.com
http://www.croogstudios.com
Degrees: Certificate
Academic Areas: Cartooning,
Character Animation, Computer
Animation/Digital Art, Web
Animation, Workshops

CyberArts
60 Park Avenue
Rochester, NY 14607
Phone: (585) 244-0425
E-mail: cyberart@frontiernet.net
http://www.cyberartsgroup.com
Degrees: Certificate
Academic Areas: Character Ani-
mation, Experimental Anima-
tion, Computer Animation/
Digital Art, Multimedia/Games,
Workshops, Private Training,
Vocational Training

Digital Film Academy
Animation
630 Ninth Avenue
Suite 901
New York, NY 10036
Phone: (212) 333-4013
Fax: (212) 333-2238
E-mail: info@digitalfilmacademy.
com
http://www.DigitalFilmAcademy.
com
Degrees: Certificate
Academic Areas: Character
Animation, Experimental

Animation, Computer
Animation/Digital Art, Graphic
Design, Web Graphics/Design,
Web Animation, Performance
Animation, Animation History/
Theory, Workshops, Online
Courses, Private Training,
Vocational Training

Future Media Concepts—NY
305 E. 47th Street
New York, NY 10017
Phone: (212) 888-6314
Fax: (212) 888-7531
E-mail: info@fmctraining
http://www.fmctraining.com
Degrees: Certificate
Academic Areas: Character Anima-
tion, Computer Animation/Digi-
tal Art, Multimedia/Games, Web
Graphics/Design, Workshops

Genesee Community College, SUNY
Information Technology
1 College Road
Batavia, NY 14020
Phone: (585) 343-0055, ext.6252
Fax: (585) 343-0433
E-mail: multimedia@genesee.edu
http://www.genesee.edu
Degrees: Certificate, A.A., A.A.S.
Academic Areas: Character
Animation, Computer
Animation/Digital Art, Graphic
Design, Multimedia/Games,
Web Graphics/Design, Web
Animation

Globix Corporation
Training Department
139 Centre Street
New York, NY 10013
Phone: (800) 4 GLOBIX
Fax: (212) 334-8615
E-mail: info@globix.com
http://www.globix.com
Degrees: Certificate
Academic Areas: Character
Animation, Experimental
Animation, Computer
Animation/Digital Art, Graphic
Design, Multimedia/Games

Katharine Gibbs School of Animation & Design
Digital Arts
320 S. Service Road
Melville, NY 11747
Phone: (631) 370-3300
Fax: (631) 293-1276
http://www.gibbsmelville.com/
Degrees: A.A.
Academic Areas: Character
Animation, Computer
Animation/Digital Art,
Fine Art, Graphic Design,
Multimedia/Games, Web
Graphics/Design, Web
Animation, Animation History/
Theory

Long Island University— Brooklyn
Media Arts
1 University Plaza
Brooklyn, NY 11201
Phone: (718) 488-1052
E-mail: claire.goodman@liu.edu
http://www.brooklyn.liu.edu/depts/
mediarts/index.html
Degrees: B.A., B.S., B.F.A., M.A.,
M.S., M.F.A.
Academic Areas: Character
Animation, Experimental
Animation, Computer
Animation/Digital Art, Fine Art,
Graphic Design, Multimedia/
Games, Web Graphics/Design,
Web Animation, Animation
History/Theory

The Mac Learning Center
19 W. 34th Street
New York, NY 10001
Phone: (212) 594-2280
Fax: (212) 594-9897
E-mail: mike10001613@yahoo.com
http://applemacintosh.com
Degrees: Certificate
Academic Areas: Character
Animation, Computer
Animation/Digital Art, Graphic
Design, Multimedia/Games,
Web Graphics/Design, Web
Animation, Private Training,
Vocational Training

Mercy College

Center for Digital Arts
Computer Arts + Design
277 Martine Avenue
White Plains, NY 10601
Phone: (914) 948-3666
E-mail: computerarts@mercy.edu
http://artdesign.mercy.edu
Degrees: B.A., B.S., B.F.A.
Academic Areas: Character Animation, Experimental Animation, Computer Animation/Digital Art, Multimedia/Games, Web Graphics/Design, Web Animation, Animation History/Theory

Mercy College Manhattan

Computer Arts + Design
66 W. 35th Street
New York, NY 10001
Phone: (914) 948-3666
E-mail: computerarts@mercy.edu
http://artdesign.mercy.edu
Degrees: B.A., B.S., B.F.A.
Academic Areas: Character Animation, Experimental Animation, Computer Animation/Digital Art, Fine Art, Multimedia/Games, Web Animation, Animation History/Theory

New York Film Academy

100 E. 17th Street
New York, NY 10003
Phone: (212) 674-4300
Fax: (212) 477-1414
http://www.nyfa.com/
Degrees: Certificate
Academic Areas: Computer Animation/Digital Art, Workshops

New York Institute of Technology

Communication Arts
1855 Broadway
New York, NY 10023
Phone: (800) 345-NYIT
E-mail: plipsky@nyit.edu
http://iris.nyit.edu/~plipsky/mgl

Degrees: B.A., B.S., B.F.A., M.A., M.S., M.F.A.
Academic Areas: Computer Animation/Digital Art, Graphic Design, Multimedia/Games, Web Graphics/Design, Web Animation, Animation History/Theory

New York University

Tisch School of the Arts
721 Broadway
8th Floor
New York, NY 10003
Phone: (212) 998-1779
Fax: (212) 995-4062
E-mail: jc7@is8.nyu.edu
http://www.nyu.edu/tisch/filmtv/
Degrees: B.A., B.S., B.F.A.
Academic Areas: Character Animation, Experimental Animation, Computer Animation/Digital Art, Multimedia/Games, Animation History/Theory

New York University—SCPS

Center for Advanced Digital Applications
11 W. 42nd Street
10th Floor, Room 1009
New York, NY 10036-8083
Phone: (212) 992-3370
Fax: (212) 992-3377
E-mail: cada@nyu.edu
http://www.scps.nyu.edu/cada
Degrees: Certificate, B.A., B.S., B.F.A., M.A., M.S., M.F.A.
Academic Areas: Character Animation, Experimental Animation, Computer Animation/Digital Art, Graphic Design, Multimedia/Games, Animation History/Theory, Workshops, Vocational Training

Parsons School of Design

66 Fifth Avenue
New York, NY 10011
Phone: (212) 229-8910
Fax: (212) 229-5648
E-mail: parsadm@newschool.edu
http://www.parsons.edu

Degrees: B.A., B.S., B.F.A., M.A., M.S., M.F.A.
Academic Areas: Character Animation, Experimental Animation, Computer Animation/Digital Art, Fine Art, Graphic Design, Multimedia/Games, Web Graphics/Design, Voice Acting

Pratt Institute

Center for Continuing and Professional Studies
144 W. 14th Street
Room 209
New York, NY 10011-7300
Phone: (212) 647-7199
Fax: (212) 367-2489
E-mail: prostudy@pratt.edu
http://www.pratt.edu
Degrees: Certificate
Other: noncredit Courses
Academic Areas: Character Animation, Computer Animation/Digital Art, Fine Art, Graphic Design, Multimedia/Games, Animation History/Theory, Workshops

Rochester Institute of Technology

School of Film & Animation
Frank E. Gannett Building
70 Lomb Memorial Drive
Rochester, NY 14623-5604
Phone: (585) 475-6175
Fax: (585) 475-7575
E-mail: sofa@rit.edu
http://www.rit.edu/~animate/
Degrees: B.A., B.S., B.F.A., M.A., M.S., M.F.A.
Academic Areas: Cartooning, Character Animation, Experimental Animation, Computer Animation/Digital Art, Multimedia/Games, Animation History/Theory, Distance Learning, Online Courses

School of the Visual Arts

209 E. 23rd Street
New York, NY 10010

Phone: (212) 592-2100
Fax: (212) 592-2116
E-mail: admissions@sva.edu
http://www.sva.edu
Degrees: B.A., B.S., B.F.A., M.A., M.S., M.F.A.
Academic Areas: Cartooning, Character Animation, Experimental Animation, Computer Animation/ Digital Art, Fine Art, Graphic Design, Multimedia/Games, Web Graphics/Design, Web Animation, Workshops

NORTH CAROLINA

North Carolina School of the Arts
School of Design and Production/ Filmmaking
1533 S. Main Street
Winston-Salem, NC 27127-2188
Phone: (336) 770-3220
Fax: (336) 770-3213
http://www.ncarts.edu
Degrees: B.A., B.S., B.F.A.
Academic Areas: Character Animation, Computer Animation/Digital Art, Fine Art, Graphic Design, Animation History/Theory

North Carolina State University
College of Design
Campus Box 7701
Raleigh, NC 27695-7701
Phone: (919) 513-1259
E-mail: lee_cherry@ncsu.edu
http://www.ncsudesign.org
Degrees: B.A., B.S., B.F.A., M.A., M.S., M.F.A., Doctorate/Other Postgraduate
Academic Areas: Cartooning, Character Animation, Experimental Animation, Computer Animation/Digital Art, Fine Art, Graphic Design, Multimedia/ Games, Web Graphics/Design, Web Animation, Animation History/Theory, Workshops, Distance Learning, Online Courses, Vocational Training

School of Communication Arts
Digital Circus
3000 Wakefield Crossing Drive
Raleigh, NC 27614
Phone: (919) 488-8500
E-mail: school@higherdigital.com
http://www.higherdigital.com
Degrees: Certificate, A.A., Diploma
Academic Areas: Computer Animation/Digital Art, Graphic Design, Web Graphics/Design

University of North Carolina
College of Arts and Sciences
P.O. Box 26170
Greensboro, NC 27402-6170
Phone: (336) 334-5000
Fax: (336) 334-5270
E-mail: pameginn@uncg.edu
http://www.uncg.edu/aas
Degrees: B.A., B.S., B.F.A.
Academic Areas: Computer Animation/Digital Art, Graphic Design

Winston-Salem State University
Fine Arts Department
601 Martin Luther King, Jr., Drive
Winston-Salem, NC 27110
Phone: (336) 750-2000
Fax: (336) 750-2522
E-mail: gamma1lab@aol.com
http://www.wssu.edu/
Degrees: B.A., B.S., B.F.A.
Academic Areas: Character Animation, Experimental Animation, Computer Animation/Digital Art, Fine Art, Graphic Design, Multimedia/ Games, Web Graphics/Design, Web Animation

OHIO

Bowling Green State University
Fine Arts
1000 Fine Arts Center
Bowling Green, OH 43403
Phone: (866) 246-6732
Fax: (419) 372-6955
E-mail: admissions@bgnet.bgsu.edu
http://www.bgsu.edu

Degrees: B.A., B.S., B.F.A., M.A., M.S., M.F.A.
Academic Areas: Character Animation, Experimental Animation, Computer Animation/Digital Art, Fine Art, Graphic Design, Multimedia/Games, Web Graphics/Design, Web Animation, Animation History/Theory

Central State University
Department of Fine and Performing Arts
1 Welsey Drive
Wilberforce, OH 45384
Phone: (937) 376-6403
E-mail: info@csu.ces.edu
http://www.centralstate.edu/
Degrees: B.A., B.S., B.F.A.
Academic Areas: Computer Animation/Digital Art, Fine Art, Graphic Design

Columbus College of Art & Design
Media Studies
107 N. 9th Street
Columbus, OH 43215
Phone: (614) 224-9101
Fax: (614) 222-4040
E-mail: admissions@ccad.edu
http://www.ccad.edu
Degrees: B.A., B.S., B.F.A.
Academic Areas: Character Animation, Experimental Animation, Computer Animation/Digital Art, Fine Art, Graphic Design, Multimedia/ Games, Web Graphics/Design, Web Animation, Animation History/Theory, Workshops

Kent State University Tuscarawas
Engineering Technology
330 University Drive, NE
New Philadelphia, OH 44663
Phone: (330) 339-3391
Fax: (330) 339-3321
E-mail: depsec@cs.kent.edu
http://www.tusc.kent.edu
Degrees: Certificate, A.A.S., B.A., B.S., B.F.A.

Academic Areas: Character Animation, Computer Animation/Digital Art, Graphic Design, Multimedia/ Games, Web Graphics/Design, Workshops, Online Courses

The Ohio State University
Digital Animation and Interactive Media (DAIM) in Design
Advanced Computing Center for the Arts & Design
1224 Kinnear Road
Columbus, OH 43212
Phone: (614) 292-3416
Fax: (614) 292-7776
E-mail: daim@accad.osu.edu
http://accad.osu.edu/daim
Degrees: M.A., M.S., M.F.A., Doctorate/Other Postgraduate
Academic Areas: Experimental Animation, Computer Animation/Digital Art, Multimedia/Games, Performance Animation, Animation History/Theory

University of Dayton
Visual Arts
300 College Park Drive
Dayton, OH 45469-1690
Phone: (937) 229-3237
E-mail: info@udayton.edu
http://www.udayton.edu/contact.html
Degrees: B.A., B.S., B.F.A.
Academic Areas: Computer Animation/Digital Art, Graphic Design, Multimedia/Games, Web Graphics/Design, Web Animation

OKLAHOMA

Northern Oklahoma College
MMDC–Advanced Animation Lab
1220 E. Grand
P.O. Box 310
Tonkawa, OK 74653
Phone: (580) 628-6777
Fax: (580) 628-6209
E-mail: bmatson@mmdclab.com
http://www.mmdclab.com

Degrees: A.A., Diploma
Academic Areas: Character Animation, Computer Animation/Digital Art, Graphic Design, Multimedia/ Games, Web Graphics/Design, Web Animation, Workshops, Distance Learning

OREGON

The Art Institute of Portland
Admissions
1122 N.W. Davis Street
Portland, OR 97209
Phone: (888) 228-6528
Fax: (503) 228-4227
E-mail: aipdadm@aii.edu
http://www.aipd.artinstitutes.edu
Degrees: A.A., B.A., B.S., B.F.A.
Academic Areas: Character Animation, Computer Animation/Digital Art, Fine Art, Graphic Design, Multimedia/ Games, Web Graphics/Design, Web Animation

Earthlight Pictures Animation Training
791 Fourth Street
Lake Oswego, OR 97034
Phone: (503) 697-7914
E-mail: JT@earthlightpictures.com
http://www.earthlightpictures.com
Degrees: Certificate
Academic Areas: Cartooning, Character Animation, Experimental Animation, Computer Animation/Digital Art, Fine Art, Animation History/Theory, Workshops, Distance Learning, Kids' Programs, Private Training, Vocational Training

Northwest Film Center
Portland Art Museum
1219 S.W. Park Avenue
Portland, OR 97205
Phone: (503) 221-1156
Fax: (503) 294-0874
E-mail: info@nwfilm.org
http://www.nwfilm.org/

Degrees: Certificate
Academic Areas: Character Animation, Experimental Animation, Computer Animation/Digital Art

Pacific Northwest College of Art
1241 N.W. Johnson Street
Portland, OR 97209
Phone: (503) 226-4391
E-mail: pncainfo@pnca.edu
http://www.pnca.edu
Degrees: Certificate, A.A., B.A., B.S., B.F.A.
Academic Areas: Character Animation, Computer Animation/Digital Art, Fine Art, Graphic Design

University of Oregon
Fine Arts Department
5232 University of Oregon
Eugene, OR 97403
Phone: (541) 346-3610
http://www.uoregon.edu/~uoanim/
Degrees: B.A., B.S., B.F.A., M.A., M.S., M.F.A.
Academic Areas: Character Animation, Computer Animation/Digital Art, Graphic Design, Multimedia/ Games, Web Graphics/Design, Animation History/Theory

PENNSYLVANIA

The Art Institute of Philadelphia
1622 Chestnut Street
Philadelphia, PA 19103
Phone: (215) 405-6408
Fax: (215) 405-6399
E-mail: aiphadm@aii.edu
http://www.aiph.aii.edu
Degrees: A.A., B.A., B.S., B.F.A.
Academic Areas: Character Animation, Experimental Animation, Computer Animation/Digital Art, Fine Art, Graphic Design, Multimedia/ Games, Web Graphics/Design, Web Animation

The Art Institute of Pittsburgh
420 Boulevard of the Allies
Pittsburgh, PA 15219
Phone: (800) 275-2470
Fax: (412) 263-3715
E-mail: admissions-aip@aii.edu
http://www.aip.aii.edu
Degrees: B.A., B.S., B.F.A.
Academic Areas: Character
Animation, Experimental
Animation, Computer
Animation/Digital Art, Fine Art,
Graphic Design, Multimedia/
Games, Web Graphics/Design,
Voice Acting, Performance
Animation, Animation History/
Theory, Online Courses

**Bradley Academy for the Visual
Arts**
Animation
1409 Williams Road
York, PA 17402
Phone: (717) 755-2300
Fax: (800) 864-7725
E-mail: info@bradleyacademy.net
http://www.artinstitutes.edu/york/
Degrees: Diploma
Academic Areas: Character
Animation, Graphic Design,
Web Graphics/Design

Carnegie-Mellon University
School of Computer Science
5000 Forbes Avenue
Pittsburgh, PA 15213
Phone: (412) 268-2565
Fax: (412) 268-5576
E-mail: jmlucas@cs.cmu.edu
http://www.cs.cmu.edu/
Degrees: B.A., B.S., B.F.A., M.A.,
M.S., M.F.A., Doctorate/Other
Postgraduate
Academic Areas: Computer
Animation/Digital Art

Douglas Education Center
130 Seventh Street
Monessen, PA 15062
Phone: (724) 684-3684
Fax: (724) 684-7463
E-mail: dec@douglas-school.com
http://www.douglas-school.com

Degrees: A.A.
Academic Areas: Character Ani-
mation, Computer Animation/
Digital Art, Graphic Design,
Multimedia/Games, Web
Graphics/Design, Web Anima-
tion, Performance Animation,
Animation History/Theory

Drexel University
Digital Media Program
College of Media Arts and Design
33rd and Market Streets
Philadelphia, PA 19104
Phone: (215) 895-2407
http://www.drexel.edu/comad/
digitalmedia
Degrees: B.A., B.S.
Academic Areas: Digital Media,
Animation, Gaming and Web
Development

DuBois Business College
One Beaver Drive
DuBois, PA 15801
Phone: (800) 692-6213
Fax: (814) 371-3974
E-mail: mainc@dbcollege.com
http://www.dbcollege.com
Degrees: A.A., Diploma
Academic Areas: Character
Animation, Experimental
Animation, Computer
Animation/Digital Art, Graphic
Design, Multimedia/Games

Duquesne University
Interactive Media
600 Forbes Avenue
Pittsburgh, PA 15282-1702
Phone: (412) 396-5772
E-mail: woytekd@duq.edu
http://mmtserver.mmt.duq.edu
Degrees: Certificate, B.A., B.S.,
B.F.A., M.A., M.S., M.F.A.
Academic Areas: Cartooning,
Character Animation, Computer
Animation/Digital Art, Graphic
Design, Multimedia/Games,
Web Graphics/Design, Web
Animation, Animation History/
Theory, Distance Learning,
Online Courses

**Edinboro University of
Pennsylvania**
Art
215 Meadville Street
Edinboro, PA 16444
Phone: (814) 732-2406
Fax: (814) 732-2414
E-mail: www.edinboro.edu
http://www.edinboro.edu
Degrees: A.A., B.A., B.S., B.F.A.,
M.A., M.S., M.F.A.
Academic Areas: Cartooning,
Character Animation,
Experimental Animation,
Computer Animation/
Digital Art, Fine Art, Graphic
Design, Multimedia/Games,
Web Graphics/Design, Web
Animation, Performance
Animation, Animation History/
Theory

Kutztown University
College of Visual and Performing
Arts
Kutztown, PA 19530
Phone: (610) 683-4500
Fax: (610) 683-4502
E-mail: morrison@kutztown.edu
http://www.kutztown.edu
Degrees: Certificate, B.A., B.S.,
B.F.A.
Academic Areas: Computer
Animation/Digital Art, Fine Art,
Graphic Design

Lycoming College
Department of Art
700 College Place
Williamsport, PA 17701
Phone: (570) 321-4026
E-mail: admissions@lycoming.edu
http://www.lycoming.edu
Degrees: B.A., B.S., B.F.A.
Academic Areas: Computer
Animation/Digital Art, Graphic
Design

Thompson Institute
Technical Department
5650 Derry Street
Harrisburg, PA 17111
Phone: (717) 901-5848

E-mail: nwindemaker@
thompsoninstitute.org
http://www.thompson.edu
Degrees: A.A.
Academic Areas: Character
Animation, Computer
Animation/Digital Art, Graphic
Design, Multimedia/Games,
Web Graphics/Design, Web
Animation, Animation History/
Theory, Vocational Training

University of the Arts
Media Arts Department
320 S. Broad Street
Philadelphia, PA 19102
Phone: (800) 616-ARTS
Fax: (215) 732-4832
http://www.uarts.edu
Degrees: B.A., B.S., B.F.A.
Academic Areas: Character
Animation, Experimental
Animation, Computer
Animation/Digital Art, Fine Art,
Graphic Design, Multimedia/
Games, Web Graphics/Design,
Web Animation, Animation
History/Theory

RHODE ISLAND

Brown University
Department of Computer Science
115 Waterman Street
Providence, RI 02912
Phone: (401) 863-7600
Fax: (401) 863-7657
E-mail: dept@cs.brown.edu
http://www.cs.brown.edu
Degrees: B.A., B.S., B.F.A., M.A.,
M.S., M.F.A., Doctorate/Other
Postgraduate
Academic Areas: Computer
Animation/Digital Art

SOUTH DAKOTA

South Dakota State University
Visual Arts
Grove Hall
P.O. Box 2802
Brookings, SD 57007
Phone: (605) 688-4103

Fax: (605) 688-6769
E-mail: diane.vanderwal@sdstate.
edu
http://www3.sdstate.edu/Academics/
CollegeOfArtsAndSciences/
VisualArts/
Degrees: Certificate, B.A., B.S.,
B.F.A.
Academic Areas: Character
Animation, Experimental
Animation, Graphic Design

TENNESSEE

East Tennessee State University
Digital Media
Niswonger Digital Media Center
2001 Millenium Place
Johnson City, TN 37604
Phone: (423) 979-3170
Fax: (423) 979 3160
E-mail: go2etsu@etsu.edu
http://avl.etsu.edu
Degrees: B.A., B.S., B.F.A., M.A.,
M.S., M.F.A.
Academic Areas: Character
Animation, Computer
Animation/Digital Art, Graphic
Design, Multimedia/Games,
Web Graphics/Design, Web
Animation

Freed-Hardeman University
School of Arts and Humanities
158 E. Main Street
Henderson, TN 38340
Phone: (800) 348-3481
Fax: (901) 989-6065
E-mail: admissions@fhu.edu
http://www.fhu.edu
Degrees: B.A., B.S., B.F.A.
Academic Areas: Computer
Animation/Digital Art, Fine Art,
Graphic Design, Multimedia/
Games

Memphis College of Art
Overton Park
1930 Poplar Avenue
Memphis, TN 38104-2764
Phone: (901) 272-5122; toll-free:
(800) 727-1088

E-mail: admissions@mca.edu
http://www.mca.edu
Degrees: B.A., B.S., B.F.A., M.A.,
M.S., M.F.A.
Academic Areas: Character
Animation, Experimental
Animation, Computer
Animation/Digital Art, Fine Art,
Graphic Design, Multimedia/
Games, Animation History/
Theory

Middle Tennessee State University
Electronic Media Communication
P.O. Box 58
Murfreesboro, TN 37132
Phone: (615) 898-2813
Fax: (615) 898-5682
http://www.mtsu.edu/~emc
Degrees: B.A., B.S., B.F.A.
Academic Areas: Character
Animation, Computer
Animation/Digital Art, Graphic
Design, Multimedia/Games,
Web Graphics/Design, Web
Animation

The Renaissance Center
Education
855 Highway 46 South
Dickson, TN 37055
Phone: (888) 700-2300
Fax: (615) 740-5618
E-mail: laura.jackson@rcenter.org
http://www.rcenter.org
Degrees: Certificate
Academic Areas: Character
Animation, Experimental
Animation, Computer
Animation/Digital Art

TEXAS

The Art Institute of Dallas
Computer Animation/Multimedia
and Web Development
8080 Park Lane
Suite 100
Dallas, TX 75231-5993
Phone: (214) 692-6541; toll-free:
(800) 275-4243
E-mail: aidadm@aii.edu

http://www.aid.aii.edu
Degrees: A.A.
Academic Areas: Character Animation, Computer Animation/Digital Art, Graphic Design, Multimedia/Games, Web Graphics/Design

The Art Institute of Houston
1900 Yorktown Street
Houston, TX 77056-4197
Phone: (713) 966-2797; toll-free: (800) 275-4244
E-mail: wrightr@aii.edu
http://www.aih.aii.edu
Degrees: A.A.
Academic Areas: Character Animation, Experimental Animation, Computer Animation/Digital Art, Graphic Design, Multimedia/Games, Web Graphics/Design

Austin Community College
Visual Communication Design
11928 Stonehollow Drive
Austin, TX 78758
Phone: (512) 223-4838
Fax: (512) 223-4444
E-mail: viscom@austin.cc.tx.us
http://www2.austin.cc.tx.us/viscom
Degrees: Certificate, A.A.
Academic Areas: Character Animation, Computer Animation/Digital Art, Graphic Design, Multimedia/Games, Web Graphics/Design, Web Animation, Online Courses

Austin School of Film
906 E. 5th Street
Suite 106
Austin, TX 78702
http://austinfilmschool.org/
Degrees: Certificate
Academic Areas: Character Animation, Experimental Animation, Computer Animation/Digital Art, Fine Art, Multimedia/Games, Performance Animation, Workshops, Kids' Programs

Garman's Visual Effects Academy
Vizy Acky
15654 Quorum Drive
Addison, TX 75001
Phone: (469) 374-9974
Fax: (469) 374-9974
E-mail: admissions@vizyacky.com
http://www.vizyacky.com
Degrees: Certificate
Academic Areas: Character Animation, Experimental Animation, Computer Animation/Digital Art, Multimedia/Games, Web Graphics/Design, Web Animation, Animation History/Theory, Workshops, Distance Learning, Online Courses, Kids' Programs, Private Training, Vocational Training

Sam Houston State University
Sam Houston Visualization Laboratory
2424 Sam Houston Avenue
Suite B8
Huntsville, TX 77341
Phone: (936) 294-3715
Fax: (936) 294-3822
E-mail: christopher@shsu.edu
http://vizlab.shsu.edu
Degrees: Certificate, B.A., B.S., B.F.A., M.A., M.S., M.F.A.
Academic Areas: Computer Animation/Digital Art, Graphic Design, Web Graphics/Design, Workshops

Texas A&M University
Visualization Laboratory
College of Architecture
A216 Langford Center
3137 TAMU
College Station, TX 77843-3137
Phone: (979) 845-3465
Fax: (979) 845-4491
E-mail: vizinfo@viz.tamu.edu
http://www-viz.tamu.edu
Degrees: M.A., M.S., M.F.A.
Other: M.S. in Visualization Science
Academic Areas: Computer Animation/Digital Art

Texas State Technical College
Digital Media Design
3801 Campus Drive
Waco, TX 76705
Phone: (800) 792-8784
E-mail: http://www.tstc.edu/
http://dmd.tstc.edu/
Degrees: A.A., 3-D-VR Advanced Certificate
Academic Areas: Character Animation, Computer Animation/Digital Art, Graphic Design, Multimedia/Games, Web Graphics/Design, Web Animation

University of Mary Hardin-Baylor
Business and Computer Information Systems
900 College Street
Belton, TX 76513
Phone: (254) 295-4520
Fax: (254) 295-5049
http://www.umhb.edu
Degrees: B.A., B.S., B.F.A.
Academic Areas: Character Animation, Computer Animation/Digital Art, Fine Art, Graphic Design, Multimedia/Games, Web Graphics/Design, Web Animation

University of Texas at Dallas
Arts and Technology
P.O. Box 830688, JO 31
Richardson, TX 73083-0688
Phone: (972) 883-4376
E-mail: beckygo@utdallas.edu
http://iiae.utdallas.edu/
Degrees: B.A., B.S., B.F.A., M.A., M.S., M.F.A., Doctorate/Other Postgraduate
Academic Areas: Cartooning, Character Animation, Experimental Animation, Computer Animation/Digital Art, Fine Art, Graphic Design, Multimedia/Games, Web Graphics/Design, Web Animation, Performance Animation, Animation History/Theory

University of the Incarnate Word
Computer Graphic Arts
4301 Broadway
Box 389
San Antonio, TX 78209
Phone: (210) 805-1209
E-mail: watkins@cgauiw.com
http://www.cgauiw.com
Degrees: B.F.A.
Academic Areas: Computer Graphic Art

UTAH

Brigham Young University
Department of Visual Arts
College of Fine Arts and Communication
C-502 HFAC
Provo, UT 84602-6402
Phone: (801) 422-4266
E-mail: ab273@byu.edu
http://www.byu.edu/visualarts/
Degrees: B.A., B.S., B.F.A., M.A., M.S., M.F.A.
Academic Areas: Character Animation, Experimental Animation, Computer Animation/Digital Art, Fine Art, Graphic Design, Multimedia/Games

Salt Lake Community College
Visual Art and Design
Redwood Road Campus
4600 S. Redwood Road
Salt Lake City, UT 84123
Phone: (801) 957-4267
Fax: (801) 957-4444
E-mail: heigerke@slcc.edu
http://www.slcc.edu/
Degrees: Certificate, A.A.
Academic Areas: Computer Animation/Digital Art, Graphic Design, Multimedia/Games

University of Utah
Department of Computer Science–Graphic Design
50 S. Central Campus Drive
Room 3190
Salt Lake City, UT 84112

Phone: (801) 581-8224
Fax: (801) 581-5843
E-mail: info@cs.utah.edu
http://www.cs.utah.edu
Degrees: B.A., B.S., B.F.A., M.A., M.S., M.F.A.
Academic Areas: Computer Animation/Digital Art, Graphic Design

University of Utah
Arts Technology Program
College of Fine Arts
375 South 1530 East
Room 250
Salt Lake City, UT 84112
Phone: (801) 581-6764
Fax: (801) 585-3066
E-mail: artstech@finearts.utah.edu
http://www.artstech.utah.edu/
Degrees: Certificate, B.A., B.S., B.F.A.
Academic Areas: Character Animation, Experimental Animation, Computer Animation/Digital Art, Multimedia/Games, Web Graphics/Design, Web Animation

VIRGINIA

The Art Institute of Washington
1820 N. Fort Myer Drive
Ames Building
Arlington, VA 22209-1802
Phone: (877) 303-3771
Fax: (703) 358-9759
http://www.aiw.artinstitutes.edu
Degrees: B.A., B.S., B.F.A., M.A., M.S., M.F.A.
Academic Areas: Character Animation, Experimental Animation, Computer Animation/Digital Art, Graphic Design, Multimedia/Games, Web Graphics/Design, Web Animation

Norfolk State University
Department of Fine Arts
700 Park Avenue

Norfolk, VA 23504
Phone: (757) 823-8396
Fax: (757) 823-8290
E-mail: admissions@nsu.edu
http://www.nsu.edu/academics/liberal/finearts/index.htm
Degrees: B.A., B.S., B.F.A.
Academic Areas: Character Animation, Computer Animation/Digital Art, Fine Art, Graphic Design, Multimedia/Games, Animation History/Theory, Online Courses

Regent University
School of Communication and the Arts
1000 Regent University Drive
Virginia Beach, VA 23464
Phone: (888) 777-7729
Fax: (757) 226-4381
E-mail: stusrv@regent.edu
http://www.regent.edu/acad/schcom/
Degrees: M.A., M.S., M.F.A., Doctorate/Other Postgraduate
Academic Areas: Character Animation, Computer Animation/Digital Art, Graphic Design, Animation History/Theory, Workshops

WASHINGTON

The Art Institute of Seattle
2323 Elliott Avenue
Seattle, WA 98121-1622
Phone: (206) 448-6600
Fax: (206) 269-0275
E-mail: aisadm@aii.edu
http://www.ais.edu
Degrees: B.A., B.S., B.F.A., M.A., M.S., M.F.A.
Academic Areas: Character Animation, Experimental Animation, Computer Animation/Digital Art, Graphic Design, Multimedia/Games, Web Graphics/Design

Bellevue Community College
Media Communication and Technology Program

300 Landerholm Circle, SE
Bellevue, WA 98007
Phone: (425) 564-1000
E-mail: bparks@bcc.ctc.edu
http://www.bcc.ctc.edu/mct
Degrees: Certificate, A.A.
Academic Areas: Character Animation, Computer Animation/Digital Art, Multimedia/Games, Web Graphics/Design, Web Animation, Animation History/Theory, Distance Learning, Online Courses

DigiPen Institute of Technology
Production Computer Animation
9931 Willows Road, NE
Redmond, WA 98052
Phone: (866) 478-5236
Fax: (425) 558-0378
E-mail: akugler@digipen.edu
http://www.digipen.edu
Degrees: B.A., B.S., B.F.A., M.A., M.S., M.F.A.
Academic Areas: Computer Animation/Digital Art, Multimedia/Games

Lake Washington Technical College
Multi-Media Design and Production
11605 132nd Avenue, NE
Kirkland, WA 98034-8506
Phone: (425) 739-8100
Fax: (425) 739-8298
E-mail: John.Gabriel@lwtc.ctc.edu
http://https://www.lwtc.ctc.edu/
Degrees: Certificate, A.A.
Academic Areas: Cartooning, Character Animation, Computer Animation/Digital Art, Multimedia/Games, Web Graphics/Design, Web Animation, Vocational Training

Mesmer Animation Labs
1116 N.W. 54th Street
Suite A
Seattle, WA 98107
Phone: (206) 782-8004

Fax: (206) 782-8101
E-mail: info@mesmer.com
http://www.mesmer.com
Degrees: Certificate
Academic Areas: Character Animation, Computer Animation/Digital Art, Multimedia/Games, Web Animation, Workshops, Distance Learning, Online Courses, Private Training

University of Washington
Department of Computer Science
Box 352350
Seattle, WA 98195-2350
Phone: (206) 616-3423
Fax: (206) 543-2969
http://www.cs.washington.edu
Degrees: B.A., B.S., B.F.A., M.A., M.S., M.F.A., Doctorate/Other Postgraduate
Academic Areas: Character Animation, Experimental Animation, Computer Animation/Digital Art, Fine Art, Graphic Design, Multimedia/Games, Performance Animation

Washington State University
Fine Arts/English/Films
Avery Hall, Room 329
Pullman, WA 99164-5020
Phone: (888) 468-6978
E-mail: admissions@wsu.edu
http://www.wsu.edu/
Degrees: B.A., B.S., B.F.A.
Academic Areas: Computer Animation/Digital Art, Graphic Design, Web Graphics/Design, Performance Animation

WEST VIRGINIA

West Virginia Wesleyan College
Communication & Dramatic Arts
59 College Avenue
Buckhannon, WV 26201
Phone: (800) 722-9933
Fax: (304) 473 8888
E-mail: oiler@wvwc.edu
http://www.wvwc.edu
Degrees: B.A., B.S., B.F.A.

Academic Areas: Computer Animation/Digital Art, Fine Art, Web Graphics/Design

WISCONSIN

Beloit College
700 College Street
Beloit, WI 53511
Phone: (608) 363-2000
E-mail: swedberg@beloit.edu
http://www.beloit.edu
Degrees: B.A., B.S., B.F.A.
Academic Areas: Computer Animation/Digital Art, Fine Art, Graphic Design

Madison Media Institute
Education
2702 Agriculture Drive
Madison, WI 53718
Phone: (800) 236-4997
Fax: (608) 442-0141
E-mail: info@madisonmedia.com
http://www.madisonmedia.com
Degrees: A.A.
Academic Areas: Computer Animation/Digital Art, Graphic Design, Web Graphics/Design, Web Animation, Distance Learning, Vocational Training

Milwaukee Area Technical College
Animation
700 W. State Street
Milwaukee, WI 53233-1443
Phone: (414) 297-7721
E-mail: Deckertw@matc.edu
http://www.matc.edu
Degrees: A.A.
Academic Areas: Character Animation, Experimental Animation, Computer Animation/Digital Art, Graphic Design, Multimedia/Games, Web Graphics/Design, Web Animation, Animation History/Theory, Kids' Programs

University of Wisconsin
716 Langdon Street
Madison, WI 53706-1481

Phone: (608) 262-3961
E-mail: onwisconsin@admissions.
wisc.edu
http://www.wisc.edu
Degrees: B.A., B.S., B.F.A., M.A.,
M.S., M.F.A.
Academic Areas: Computer
Animation/Digital Art, Graphic
Design, Multimedia/Games,
Web Graphics/Design, Web
Animation

University of Wisconsin—
Milwaukee

Peck School of the Arts
P.O. Box 413
Milwaukee, WI 53201
Phone: (414) 229-4763
Fax: (414) 229-2473
E-mail: cwalsh@uwm.edu
http://www4.uwm.edu/psoa/about/
index.html
Degrees: B.A., B.S., B.F.A., M.A.,
M.S., M.F.A.
Academic Areas: Cartooning,
Character Animation,
Experimental Animation,

Computer Animation/
Digital Art, Fine Art, Graphic
Design, Multimedia/Games,
Web Graphics/Design, Web
Animation, Voice Acting,
Performance Animation,
Animation History/Theory,
Workshops, Kids' Programs

University of Wisconsin—
Parkside

Admissions
900 Wood Road, Art Department
Kenosha, WI 53141-2000
Phone: (262) 595-2300
E-mail: robert.miller@uwp.edu
http://www.uwp.edu/departments/
art/concentrations.html
Degrees: B.A., B.S., B.F.A.
Academic Areas: Character
Animation, Experimental
Animation, Computer
Animation/Digital Art, Fine Art,
Graphic Design, Multimedia/
Games, Web Graphics/Design,
Web Animation, Animation
History/Theory

Virtual Partners Training
Center

Animation and Graphics
1920 Libal Street
Suite 10A
Green Bay, WI 54301
Phone: (920) 435-7345
E-mail: murph@virtualpartners.
com
http://www.virtualpartners.com
Degrees: Certificate
Academic Areas: Cartooning,
Character Animation,
Experimental Animation,
Computer Animation/
Digital Art, Graphic Design,
Multimedia/Games, Web
Graphics/Design, Web
Animation, Performance
Animation, Animation History/
Theory, Workshops, Distance
Learning, Online Courses, Kids'
Programs, Private Training,
Vocational Training

APPENDIX II
MAJOR TRADE PERIODICALS, NEWSLETTERS, AND OTHER PUBLICATIONS

Animation Journal
Department of Film and Video
California Institute of the Arts
2700 McBean Parkway
Valencia, CA 91355-2397
E-mail: editor@animationjournal.
com
http://www.animationjournal.com

Animation Magazine
30941 West Agoura Road
Suite 102
Westlake Village, CA 91361
Phone: (818) 991-2884
Fax: (818) 991-3773
http://www.animationmagazine.net

Animation World Magazine
6525 Sunset Boulevard
Garden Suite 10
Hollywood, CA 90028
Phone: (323) 606-4200
Fax: (323) 466-6619
E-mail: info@awn.com
http://awn.com

The Artist's Magazine
F+W Publications
4700 E. Galbraith Road
Cincinnati, OH 45236
Phone: (513) 531-2222
Fax: (513) 891-7153
http://www.artistsmagazine.com

Cartoonnews.com: The Leading Anime Site on the Web
http://cartoonnews.com/

The Comic Buyer's Guide
705 E. State Street
Iola, WI 54990-0001

Phone: (715) 445-4612
E-mail: ohso@krause.com
http://www.cbgxtra.com

The Comics Journal
7563 Lake City Way, NE
Seattle, WA 98115
Phone: (206) 524-1967
Fax: (206) 524-2104
http://www.tcj.com

Computer Graphics World
PennWell Corp.
98 Spit Brook Road
Nashua, NH 03062-5737
Phone: (603) 891-0123
Fax: (603) 891-0574
E-mail: atd@pennwell.com
http://cgw.pennnet.com/home.cfm

The Current Events Educational Magazine
375 Park Avenue
Suite 1301
New York, NY 10152
http://www.cartoonnews.com

FPS Magazine of Animation Frames Per Second
P.O. Box 46546
C.O.P. Boul. St-Jean R.P.O.
Pierrefonds, Quebec, Canada H9H 5G9
E-mail: editor@fpsmagazine.com
http://www.fpsmagazine.com

The Gag Recap and Cartoon Opportunities
P.O. Box 248
Chalfont, PA 18914

Game Developer
CMP Game Group
600 Harrison Street
6th Floor
San Francisco, CA 94107
Phone: (415) 947-6603
Fax: (415) 947-6079
http://www.gdmag.com/

The Hollywood Reporter
VNU Business Media USA
770 Broadway
New York, NY 10003
Phone: (646) 654-4500
Fax: (646) 654-5744
E-mail: bmcomm@vnuinc.com
http://www.hollywoodreporter.
com/thr/index.jsp

Interactive
5280 Publishing Inc.
1224 Speer Boulevard
Denver, CO 80204 USA
Phone: (303) 832-5280; Toll-free: (866) 271-5280
Fax: (303) 832-0470
E-mail: danb@5280pub.com
http://www.5280pub.com/

Journal of Film and Video
University of Illinois Press
3800 Barham Boulevard
Suite 305
Los Angeles, CA 90068
Phone: (323) 851-6199; Toll-free: (800) 280-7709
Fax: (323) 851-6748
E-mail: uipress@uillinois.edu;
UFVAjournal@aol.com
http://www.press.uillinois.edu/
journals/jfv.html

*Journal of Visualization and
    Computer Animation*
John Wiley & Sons, Inc.
111 River Street
Hoboken, NJ 07030-5774
Phone: (201) 748-6000
Fax: (201) 748-6088
E-mail: info@wiley.com
http://www3.interscience.wiley.
    com/a/acp/cgi-bin/jhome/5499

MacWorld
101 Communications
501 2nd Street
Suite 500
San Francisco, CA 94107-1431
Phone: (415) 243-0505
Fax: (415) 442-0766
E-mail: info@101com.com
http://www.101com.com; http://
    www.macworld.com/

Millimeter
Primedia Business Magazines &
    Media
5 Penn Plaza
13th Floor
New York, NY 10001
Phone: (212) 563-3028
Fax: (212) 563-3028
E-mail: inquiries@
    primediabusiness.com
http://digitalcontentproducer.com

Pegboard
The Animation Guild Local 839
    IATSE
1105 N. Hollywood Way
Burbank, CA 91505
Phone: (818) 845-7500
Fax: (818) 843-0300
E-mail: info@animationguild.org
http://www.animationguild.org

Slate Magazine
395 Hudson Street
4th Floor
New York, NY 10014
Phone: (212) 445-5300
E-mail: nyoffice@slate.com
http://www.slate.com

Variety
Reed Business Information
5700 Wilshire Boulevard
Suite 120
Los Angeles, CA 90036
Phone: (323) 857-6600
Fax: (323) 965-2475
http://www.variety.com

APPENDIX III
INDUSTRY AND TRADE ASSOCIATIONS, GUILDS, AND UNIONS

ACM SIGGRAPH Association for Computing Machinery
1515 Broadway
New York, NY 10036
Phone: (212) 869-7440
Fax: (212) 869-0824
http://www.SIGGRAPH.org/

Affiliated Property Craftsmen (IATSE, AFL, Local 44)
11500 Burbank Boulevard
North Hollywood, CA 91601
Phone: (818) 769-2500

Alliance of Motion Picture & Television Producers (AMPTP)
15503 Ventura Boulevard
Sherman Oaks, CA 91436
Phone: (818) 995-3600
Fax: (818) 382-1793

American Academy of Independent Film Producers
2067 S. Atlantic Avenue
Los Angeles, CA 90040
Phone: (213) 264-1422

American Association of Producers (AAP)
10850 Wilshire Boulevard
9th Floor
Los Angeles, CA 90024
Phone: (310) 446-1000
Fax: (310) 446-1600
http://www.tvproducers.com

American Cinema Editors, Inc.
100 Universal City Plaza
Building 2282, Room 234
Universal City, CA 91608
Phone: (818) 777-2900

Fax: (818) 733-5023
http:://www.ace-filmeditors.org

American Federation of Film Producers
Warner Hollywood Studios
Pickford Building
Suite 204
West Los Angeles, CA 90046
E-mail: info@filmfederation.com
http://www.filmfederation.com

American Federation of Television and Radio Artists (AFTRA)
5757 Wilshire Boulevard
Suite 900
Los Angeles, CA 90036
Phone: (323) 634-8100
Fax: (323) 634-8246
http://www.aftra.org

American Federation of Television and Radio Artists (AFTRA)
260 Madison Avenue
7th Floor
New York, NY 10016
Phone: (212) 532-0800
Fax: (212) 545-1238
http://www.aftra.org

The American Institute of Architects (AIA)
1735 New York Avenue, NW
Washington, DC 20006
Phone: (202) 626-7300
Fax: (202) 626-7547
E-mail: infocentral@aia.org
http://www.aia.org

American Institution of Graphics Artists (AIGA)
National Design Center

164 Fifth Avenue
New York, NY 10010
Phone: (212) 807-1990
Fax: (212) 807-1799
http://www.aiga.org

American Society of Cinematographers (ASC)
P.O. Box 2230
Hollywood, CA 90078
Phone: (323) 969-4333
Fax: (323) 882-6391
http://www.cinematographer.com

The Animation Guild Local 839 IATSE
1105 N. Hollywood Way
Burbank, CA 91505
E-mail: info@animationguild.org
http://www.animationguild.org

Art Directors Club of Metropolitan Washington
c/o Fuszion
901 Prince Street
Alexandria VA 22314
Phone: (703) 778-4649
E-mail: adcmw@adcmw.org
http://www.adcmw.org/

Art Directors Guild (ADG)
11969 Ventura Boulevard
2nd Floor
Studio City, CA 91604
Phone: (818) 762-9995
Fax: (818) 762-9997
E-mail: scott@artdirectors.org
http://www.artdirectors.org

ASIFA Atlanta
c/o Joe Peery
783 Mercer Street
Atlanta, GA 30312

E-mail: atlanta-@asifa.net
http://www.asifa-atlanta.com

ASIFA Canada
C.P. 5226
Ville St. Laurent, QC H4L 4Z8
Canada
E-mail: asifacanada@mail.com
http://www.awn.com/asifa-canada

ASIFA Central
c/o Deanna Morse
268 LSH School of
    Communications
Grand Valley State University
Allendale, MI 49402
E-mail: usa-central-@asifa.net
http://www.asifa.org/animate

ASIFA Colorado
Ed Desroches
6585 W. 62nd Place
Arvada, CO 80003
E-mail: colorado-@asifa.net
http://www.asifa-colorado.org

ASIFA East
David B. Levy
c/o Michael Sporn Animation
35 Bedford Street
New York, NY 10014
E-mail: dbl1973@earthlink.net
http://www.asifaeast.com

ASIFA Hollywood
Antran Manoogian
2114 W. Burbank Boulevard
Burbank, CA 91506
Phone: (818) 842-8330
Fax: (818) 842-5645
E-mail: hollywood-@asifa.net
http://www.asifa-hollywood.org
Online ASIFA archive: http://www.
    animationarchive.org

ASIFA Portland
c/o Brian Larson
Kerplunk Animation
3946 S.E. Taggart Street
Portland, OR 97202
E-mail: asifa-nw@hotmail.com
http://www.asifaportland.org

ASIFA San Francisco
Karl Cohen
478 Fredrick Street
San Francisco CA 94117
Phone: (415) 386-1004
Fax: (415) 387-2844
E-mail: sanfrancisco-@asifa.net
http://www.asifa-sf.org

Association of American
Editorial Cartoonists
3899 N. Front Street
Harrisburg, PA 17111
Phone: (717) 703-3086
Fax: (717) 703-3001
http://editorialcartoonists.com

Broadcast TV Recording
Engineers and
Communications
Technicians (IBEW, Local 45)
6255 Sunset Boulevard
Suite #721
Los Angeles, CA 90028
Phone: (323) 851-5515

Casting Society of America
606 N. Larchmont Boulevard
Suite 4-B
Los Angeles, CA 90004-1309
Phone: (323) 463-1925
Fax: (323) 462-5753
http://www.castingsociety.com

Casting Society of America
2565 Broadway
Suite 185
New York, NY 10025
Phone: (212) 868-1260 x22
http://www.castingsociety.com

Comic Art Professional Society
P.O. Box 656
Burbank, CA 91503
E-mail: info@capscentral.org
http://www.capscentral.org

Directors Guild of America
(DGA)
7920 Sunset Boulevard
Los Angeles, CA 90046
Phone: (310) 289-2000; Toll-free:
    (800) 420-4173

Fax: (310) 289-2029
E-mail: darrellh@dga.org
http://www.dga.org

Graphic Artists Guild
32 Broadway
Suite 1114
New York, NY 10004
Phone: (212) 791-3400
Fax: (212) 791-0333
E-mail: admin@gag.org
http://gag.org

Interactive Multimedia Arts &
Technologies Association
(IMAT)
Unit 6, 37 Kodiak Crescent
Downsview, Ontario M3J 3E5
Canada
Phone: (416) 233-2227
Fax: (416) 256-4391
E-mail: imat@imat.tv
http://www.imat.tv/

International Game Developers
Association (IGDA)
19 Mantua Road
Mt. Royal, NJ 08061
Phone: (856) 423-2990
Fax: (856) 423-3420
E-mail: contact-at-igda.org
http://www.igda.org/

International Photographers
Guild (Cameramen) (IATSE,
Local 659)
7715 Sunset Boulevard
Suite #300
Los Angeles, CA 90046
Phone: (213) 876-0160
http://www.cameraguild.com

International Sound
Technicians,
Cinetechnicians, Studio
Projectionists, and Video
Projection Technicians
(IATSE, MPMO, AFL, Local
695)
11331 Ventura Boulevard
Suite #201
Studio City, CA 91604
Phone: (818) 985-9204

Motion Picture Illustrators and Matte Artists (IATSE, Local 790)
13245 Riverside Drive
Suite 300A
Sherman Oaks, CA 91423
Phone: (818) 784-6555

Motion Picture Sound Editors (MPSE)
10061 Riverside Drive
PMB Box 751
Toluca Lake, CA 91602-2560
Phone: (818) 506-7731
Fax: (818) 506-7732
E-mail: mail@mpse.org
http://www.MPSE.org

National Academy of Television Arts and Sciences
111 W. 57th Street
Suite 600
New York, NY 10019
Phone: (212) 586-8424
Fax: (212) 246-8129
E-mail: info@emmyonline.tv
http://www.emmyonline.org

National Association of Broadcasters (NAB)
1771 N. Street, NW
Washington, DC 20036
Phone: (202) 429-5300
Fax: (202) 775-3520
http://www.nab.org/

National Cartoonists Society
341 N. Maitland Avenue
Suite 130
Maitland, FL 32751
Phone: (407) 647-8839

Fax: (407) 629-2502
E-mail: phil@crowsegal.com
http://www.reuben.org/news/

Producers Guild of America (PGA)
400 S. Beverly Drive
Suite 211
Beverly Hills, CA 90212
Phone: (310) 557-0807
Fax: (310) 557-0436
E-mail: info@producersguild.org
http://www.producersguild.org/

Production Assistants Association
8644 Wilshire Boulevard
Suite #202
Beverly Hills, CA 90211
Phone: (310) 659-7416
Fax: (310) 659-5838

Production Office Coordinators and Accountants Guild (IATSE, Local 717)
14724 Ventura Boulevard
Penthouse Suite
Sherman Oaks, CA 91403
Phone: (818) 906-9986

Screen Story Analysts (IATSE Local 854)
14724 Ventura Boulevard
Penthouse B
Sherman Oaks, CA 91403
Phone: (818) 784-6555

Society of American Graphic Artists (SAGA)
32 Union Square

Room 1214
New York, NY 10003
E-mail: tbaker@monmouth.edu
http://saga.monmouth.edu

Society of Motion Picture and Television Engineers (SMPTE)
3 Barker Avenue
White Plains, NY 10601
Phone: (914) 761-1100
Fax: (914) 761-3115
http://www.smpte.org

Women in Animation (WIA)
P.O. Box 17706
Encino, CA 91416
Phone: (818) 759-9596
E-mail: wia@womeninanimation.org
http://wia.animationblogspot.com

Writers Guild of America, East
555 W. 57th Street
Suite 1230
New York, NY 10019
Phone: (212) 767-7800
Fax: (212) 582-1909
E-mail: info@wgaeast.org
http://www.wgaeast.org

Writers Guild of America, West
7000 W. Third Street
Los Angeles, CA 90048
Phone: (323) 951-4000; Toll-free: (800) 548-4532
Fax: (323) 782-4800
E-mail: website@wga.org
http://www.wga.org

APPENDIX IV
RECOMMENDED ANIMATION INDUSTRY WEB SITES

EMPLOYMENT

Animation World Network Career Connections

http://careers.awn.com

This job database is searchable by keyword, job function, business type, location (city and state), and more. It offers a directory of employers of animation artists, and you can open a free "Job Seeker" account, where you can post your resume and cover letter and submit an anonymous résumé to prospective employers. The site also contains animation news and articles on the latest happenings in the industry.

EntertainmentCareers.net: Animation & Graphic Design Jobs

http://www.entertainmentcareers.net/jcat.asp?jcat=104

This site indexes animation, graphic design, and visual FX jobs nationwide. Sorted from newest to oldest, jobs are listed by date, city and state, job title, and company.

GameJobs

http://www.gamejobs.com

View new job opportunities in the interactive entertainment field on this site. Jobs are searchable by keyword, location, and job type. Visitors also can establish an online account to post résumés and submit them to potential employers.

HISTORY

The History of Animation

http://www.viz.tamu.edu/courses/viza615/97spring/history.html

This Web site provides easy-to-navigate links with information about all forms of animated entertainment—traditional animation, 3-D animation, and special effects.

Origins of American Animation, Library of Congress

http://lcweb2.loc.gov/ammem/oahtml/oahome.html

This Library of Congress site covers the development of early American animation. It offers a collection of 21 animated films and two fragments, including clay, puppet, cutout, and pen-drawn animation, created between 1900 and 1921.

JOB SEARCH

AnimationJobs.net

http://www.animationjobs.net/

Animation Nation

http://www.animationnation.com/

Animation World Network

http://jobs.awn.com

Careeronestop.org

http://wwwq.careeronestop.org

CG Jobs—CGSociety of Digital Artists

http://jobs.cgsociety.org/

Collegegrad.com

http://www.collegegrad.com

CollegeRecruiter.com

http://www.collegerecruiter.com

Creative Directory Services

http://creativedir.com

CreativeHeads.Net

http://www.creativeheads.net

NEWS

Animation World Network: Film News

http://news.awn.com/index.php3?ltype=cat&category1=Films

Publishes news related to animated films and theatrical films that use animation.

ORGANIZATIONS

Animators Unite

http://www.animatorsunite.com/data/

A not-for-profit group that provides informational and promotional services to those in the animation industry.

Association Internationale du Film d'Animation (ASIFA)

http://asifa.net/

Official site of this international animation society, founded in 1960 by many well-known animators, with information on more than 30 chapters in the United States and abroad.

CGSociety of Digital Artists

http://www.cgsociety.org/

Online community of this respected global organization for professional and nonprofessional creative artists that offers a range of services to connect, inform, educate, and promote members from all genres and related areas of digital art, computer graphics, animation, and digital visual effects.

National Cartoonists Society (NCS)

http://www.reuben.org

Web site for the world's largest and most prestigious organization of professional cartoonists, formed in 1946, featuring member news, information on how to become a cartoonist, and more.

Quickdraw Animation Society

http://www.awn.com/qas

Based in Calgary, this nonprofit, artist-run film production coop, incorporated in 1984, is dedicated to the production of independent animation and the appreciation of the art form through artistic presentations and education and outreach programs.

Women in Animation

http://www.womeninanimation.org

A professional nonprofit group established to foster the dignity, concerns, and advancement of women in any and all aspects of the art of animation, offering regional information, FAQs, discussion forums, and events for members and visitors.

WAGES AND SALARIES

Careeronestop.org Salary Information

http://www.careeronestop.org/ SalariesBenefits/Salaries Benefits.aspx

Collegegrad.com Salary Information

http://www.collegrad.com/salaries. index.shmtl

Indeed.com Salary Search

http://www.indeed.com/salary

Salary.com

http://www.salary.com

Vault.com Salaries and Compensation

http://www.vault.com/salaries.jsp

Wage Web

http://www.wageweb.com

APPENDIX V
U.S. FILM, TELEVISION, GAME, AND WEB ANIMATION COMPANIES

The following is a directory of links to thousands of employers in all fields of animation, organized by industry category and location throughout the United States and as listed in AnimationWorldNews.com's animation industry database.

ANIMATION PRODUCTION

2-D Computer Animation
http://aidb.com/index.php?ltype=list&cat=spec&spec=001&loc2=United+States&offset=0&order=loc

3-D Computer Animation
http://aidb.com/index.php?ltype=list&cat=spec&spec=002&loc2=United+States&offset=0&order=loc

3-D/Traditional
http://aidb.com/index.php?ltype=list&cat=spec&spec=007&loc2=United+States&offset=0&order=loc

Animated Object Animation
http://aidb.com/index.php?ltype=list&cat=spec&spec=003&loc2=United+States&offset=0&order=loc

Clay Animation
http://aidb.com/index.php?ltype=list&cat=spec&spec=004&loc2=United+States&offset=0&order=loc

Cut-Out Animation
http://aidb.com/index.php?ltype=list&cat=spec&spec=005&loc2=United+States&offset=0&order=loc

Digital/Visual Effects Animation
http://aidb.com/index.php?ltype=list&cat=spec&spec=006&loc2=United+States&offset=0&order=loc

Engraving on Film Animation
http://aidb.com/index.php?ltype=list&cat=spec&spec=008&loc2=United+States&offset=0&order=loc

Flash/Internet Animation
http://aidb.com/index.php?ltype=list&cat=spec&spec=010&loc2=United+States&offset=0&order=loc

Ink on Paper Animation
http://aidb.com/index.php?ltype=list&cat=spec&spec=009&loc2=United+States&offset=0&order=loc

Live-Action Animation
http://aidb.com/index.php?ltype=list&cat=spec&spec=011&loc2=United+States&offset=0&order=loc

Motion Capture
http://aidb.com/index.php?ltype=list&cat=spec&spec=021&loc2=United+States&offset=0&order=loc

Paint on Glass Animation
http://aidb.com/index.php?ltype=list&cat=spec&spec=012&loc2=United+States&offset=0&order=loc

Pastel on Paper Animation
http://aidb.com/index.php?ltype=list&cat=spec&spec=013&loc2=United+States&offset=0&order=loc

Pencil on Paper Animation
http://aidb.com/index.php?ltype=list&cat=spec&spec=014&loc2=United+States&offset=0&order=loc

Photo Animation
http://aidb.com/index.php?ltype=list&cat=spec&spec=015&loc2=United+States&offset=0&order=loc

Photocopy Animation
http://aidb.com/index.php?ltype=list&cat=spec&spec=016&loc2=United+States&offset=0&order=loc

Pixilation Animation
http://aidb.com/index.php?ltype=list&cat=spec&spec=017&loc2=United+States&offset=0&order=loc

Puppet Animation
http://aidb.com/index.php?ltype=list&cat=spec&spec=018&loc2=United+States&offset=0&order=loc

Rotoscope Animation
http://aidb.com/index.php?ltype=list&cat=spec&spec=019&loc2=United+States&offset=0&order=loc

Sand Animation

http://aidb.com/index.php?ltype=list&cat=spec&spec=020&loc2=United+States&offset=0&order=loc

CABLE/TELEVISION NETWORKS

http://aidb.com/index.php?ltype=list&cat=btype&btype=016&loc2=United+States&offset=0&order=loc

GAMES AND GAMES DEVELOPMENT

http://aidb.com/index.php?ltype=list&cat=btype&btype=015&loc2=United+States&offset=0&order=loc Multimedia/Interactive

GRAPHIC DESIGN

http://aidb.com/index.php?ltype=list&cat=btype&btype=017&loc2=United+States&offset=0&order=loc

MOTION PICTURE STUDIOS

http://aidb.com/index.php?ltype=list&cat=btype&btype=023&loc2=United+States&offset=0&order=loc

MULTIMEDIA/ INTERACTIVE DEVELOPMENT

http://aidb.com/index.php?ltype=list&cat=btype&btype=024&loc2=United+States&offset=0&order=loc

PERFORMANCE ANIMATION/MOTION CAPTURE STUDIOS

http://aidb.com/index.php?ltype=list&cat=btype&btype=026&loc2=United+States&offset=0&order=loc

POSTPRODUCTION SERVICES

http://aidb.com/index.php?ltype=list&cat=btype&btype=027&loc2=United+States&offset=0&order=loc

PREPRODUCTION SERVICES

http://aidb.com/index.php?ltype=list&cat=btype&btype=028&loc2=United+States&offset=0&order=loc

SOUND/MUSIC PRODUCTION

http://aidb.com/index.php?ltype=list&cat=btype&btype=034&loc2=United+States&offset=0&order=loc

TELEVISION STUDIOS

http://aidb.com/index.php?ltype=list&cat=btype&btype=035&loc2=United+States&offset=0&order=loc

THEME PARK/RIDE DESIGN

http://aidb.com/index.php?ltype=list&cat=btype&btype=036&loc

2=United+States&offset=0&order=loc

VISUAL EFFECTS PRODUCTION

http://aidb.com/index.php?ltype=list&cat=btype&btype=038&loc2=United+States&offset=0&order=loc

VOICE ACTING/VOICE TALENT

http://aidb.com/index.php?ltype=list&cat=btype&btype=039&loc2=United+States&offset=0&order=loc

WEB ANIMATION PRODUCTION

http://aidb.com/index.php?ltype=list&cat=btype&btype=053&loc2=United+States&offset=0&order=loc

WEB SITE DEVELOPMENT

http://aidb.com/index.php?ltype=list&cat=btype&btype=041&loc2=United+States&offset=0&order=loc

GLOSSARY

2-D Graphics Computer-generated images mostly from 2-D models, including 3-D geometric, text, and digital images, that use only two spatial coordinates: height and width (x, y)

3-D Graphics The creation, display, and manipulation of objects in three dimensions using 3-D graphics programs that employ three spatial coordinates: height, width, and depth (x, y, z). Images can be rotated and viewed from any angle in the 3-D scene, as well as scaled larger or smaller.

Animatic A movie or video reel with sound developed from a storyboard. The storyboard panel is exposed for the duration of the scene, and sometimes the characters are placed on a trajectory to indicate a motion. The camera moves are also animated. The animatic is used to determine the rhythm of a project and provide a preview of what is happening before starting the production.

Animation An illusion of movement created by a rapid display of a series of pictures or frames of animation in succession. When each image differs slightly, and the images are viewed at speeds of more than 10 images per second, the eye perceives motion.

Animation Camera A motion picture camera, often mounted on a crane over the animation, with single-frame photography and reverse capabilities

Animator An artist skilled in the technique of frame-by-frame animation to give the artwork the illusion of movement

Anime Made famous in Japan, an animation style known for its "sinister and dark feel"

Assistant Animator The artist responsible for producing drawings that fall between the extreme points (see **key frame**) of movement

Audio The added soundtrack of an animated production, including character dialogue, music, and effects

Background The background is the most distant element of a scene, usually consisting of flat pieces of artwork that serve as the setting of the animation action. Abbreviated as BG or BKG.

Blue Screening A process commonly used to blend together two or more images by placing an actor or image in front of a "blue screen." Elements in the blue screen image are replaced or composited with another image or background that contrasts the actor and action in the scene.

Breakdown In cut-out animation, the breakdown is the action of breaking a character in pieces to create a puppet with articulations. To breakdown a character, the artist cuts parts such as hands and arms from the character's model and pastes them in separate layers before fixing the joints and setting the pivots. In traditional animation, a breakdown is an animation pose generally found between two key poses. The key poses are the main poses in an animation, and the breakdowns are secondary poses that help to describe the motion and the rotation curve.

Cel A thin, flexible, transparent sheet of cellulose acetate, also known as celluloid, on which the animation is inked and painted in doing traditional hand-drawn animation before being sent to the camera. The drawings are colored or painted on the reverse side of the cel, with the outline of the drawing on the front.

Cel Animation In cel animation, also known as traditional animation, animated characters are hand-drawn and then transferred to cels, painted and placed over handmade backgrounds, and photographed one frame at a time.

CGI An acronym most commonly used for Computer-Generated Imagery used in the creation of 3-D computer animation and visual effects

Character Animation The art of creating an animated character or object with a distinct personality and unique characterization through expressions, actions, and movements either by traditional, computer-generated, Flash, or stop-motion animation

Character Design Original design for each character for an animated production drawn from multiple angles or poses in poster-style format (called a model sheet) that serves as reference for the animators

Checking The point in production in which all elements of an animated scene are checked and examined against the exposure sheet to ensure they are correct before being filmed

Clay Animation An animation technique, also known as Claymation, that involves the use of pliable clay figures that are manipulated before each exposure in stop-motion animation

Claymation A term used to describe the stop-motion animation technique using sculpted clay trademarked by Will Vinton Studios; popularized in 1988

with the studio's clay-animated creations the California Raisins.

Clean-up This process involves cleaning up any errors or inconsistencies in rough drawings used to create final drawings to be inked, painted, and shot.

Compositing This technique, performed by a compositing artist, consists of digitally merging two or more images to create a final image of a scene, combining all elements together, including animation, background, overlays, and underlays in a scene and positioning them correctly before sending the composited scene for rendering. The process includes the creation of any computer-generated effects that are required.

Computer Animation Creation of animated images entirely on computers using propriety animation design and editing software that can be output to different formats

Computer Graphic Any and all images that are digitally generated by a computer

Conceptual Storyboard A series of comic book style illustrations used to tell a story or visually present an idea for a motion picture, television program, or game. Basic visual ideas, such as the actions of the characters, the camera positions, the timing of motions, and the transitions between scenes, are usually based on the script.

Cut-out Animation The action of animating characters made out of several pieces by moving them around frame by frame. Cutout animation can either be computer generated or done traditionally using paper.

Cycle A group of images that make up an action, such as walking, repeated as a loop over time either as a series of animated drawings or a series of key frames

Dailies A daily review of animation work by the director for the purpose of critiquing the animation in progress

Dialogue The text spoken by a character

Digital Compositing A technique that involves combining digital video signals, as opposed to analog signals

Digital Painting A popular method of painting artwork using a computer

Digital Postproduction The practice of scanning, retouching, resequencing, and compositing all the various visual images and effects during postproduction

Dope Sheet Used by animators, directors, and other members of a crew to track the sequence and timing of images, dialogue, sound effects, soundtracks, and camera moves. Also known as an **Exposure Sheet.**

Editing The process of manipulating, trimming, and rearranging both the audio and visual elements of a scene into the order desired

Editor The individual responsible for deleting or adding scenes according to the instructions of the director during postproduction

Effects Animation Specialty involving creating non-character movements, such as rain, smoke, lightning, or water, in a scene

Exposure The number of cels on which a drawing appears in a scene; the longer the drawing appears, the longer the exposure must be extended over cels

Exposure Sheet (Xsheet) A sheet, also known as an Xsheet, that features several vertical columns and horizontal frames used by animators, directors, and other members of the crew to track the sequence and timing of images, dialogue, sound effects, soundtracks, and camera moves. Also known as a **Dope Sheet.**

Frame A single photographic image in a movie. For traditional animation, a second generally contains 24 frames in North America; in Europe, 25 frames.

Frame Rate The measurement of the frequency (rate) at which an imaging device produces consecutive images (called frames) that applies to computer graphics, video cameras, film cameras, and motion capture systems. Frame rate is most often expressed in frames per second (FPS) and, in progressive-scan monitors, as hertz (Hz).

Graphic Backgrounds The bottom-most layer on a Web page, usually with either a design or color that highlights the copy above. A small graphic can be tiled to create a background texture for a Web page.

Graphics The visual content prepared for a production

Inbetweener A person, usually a novice, whose primary function is to draw in-between, or transitional, drawings in traditional animation

Inbetweens The drawings that fall between the key poses or extreme points of movement to create fluid transitions between poses in traditional hand-drawn animation

Ink and Paint The process of painting and coloring the lines on final animation drawings, as in old-fashioned hand-drawn animation

Interactive Media Different types of media that allow users to control the flow of program material

Interface Design The process of using software programs to create graphical conventions, such as the shape of icons, typography, and color, as well as the sequencing of events, the available selection techniques, and the interplay of sound, text, and images

Interpolation The computer-generated motion created between two key frames

Key Frame The starting and ending points of any smooth transition

Key Pose The main drawing in an animation sequence that shows a character in an important position that defines the action or motion of the character

Layers Components superimposed in a scene to form one final image

Layouts The important step, between the storyboard and animation, of drawing backgrounds for each scene, later to be rendered by the background artist

Line of Action The direction that the action will follow; also known as the Path of Action

Lip-Sync The process of synchronizing a character's mouth to sounds in the dialogue soundtrack to create the illusion of speech

Mapping a Sequence of Images The technique whereby 2-D picture files are applied as maps to 3-D objects

Matte A black, opaque silhouette that restricts exposure for specific areas of the film

Matte Painting A photorealistic background that is often composited with a live-action foreground

Model/Color Model In animation, a model is the approved character, prop, or location design that each artist must follow for the production. A color model is the official color design that must be used to paint the animation.

Modeling The creation and placement of 3-D objects, environments, and scenes within a computer environment

Morphing A 3-D effect that takes computer-generated or scanned images and transforms them into another

Multimedia A form of communication combining text with graphics, page layout, video, audio, animation, etc.

Multiplane Camera A camera used to move, scale, and rotate any elements in an animated scene and add a 3-D depth of field to make it even more realistic

Music Editor An editor whose specialty is editing music tracks

Palette/Master Palette A grouping of colors attributed to a character or prop used throughout an entire production to create a consistent look during a production

Peg Used in traditional animation to ensure accurate registration of action of cel layers in cel animation; in digital animation, also used for more advance puppet rigging

Pose-to-Pose A technique characterized by the drawing of key frames at significant points in the action first, then refining the key drawings, and then doing the in-betweens; the process gives the creator more control and ensures the accuracy of the final result.

Postproduction The work done on a film once principal photography has been completed, including editing, developing, and printing

Preproduction Involves all the conceptualization and planning that takes place before any animation production is produced

Production The process of creating or producing a visual project, especially in the film and television industry

Production Cel The final creation in hand-drawn animation; consists of the animators' drawings transferred onto transparent acetate sheets that are painted the appropriate colors on the reverse side

Rendering In computer animation, the final stage whereby all the components are processed into a final image after the compositing process

Rigging The action of attaching the parts of character models to the others, readying them to be animated

Rotoscoping A form animation originally created by the pioneer animator Max Fleischer that involves tracing movements of objects from the frame-by-frame projection of a live-action scene or figure to create an animated sequence

Scene A shot in an animated or live-action movie or television show

Script The story as written by a scriptwriter; contains location descriptions, dialogues, time, and more from which a production starts

Sequence A series of scenes or shots that form a distinct part of the story or movie, usually connected by location or time

Sound The audio portion of a film, television, or video production that consists of the dialogue or narration, music, and sound effects

Sound Effects Additional sounds created to add specific effects heard in an animated production

Stop Motion The method of animating 3-D objects made of clay, foam, rubber, or plasticine by photographing the scenes one at a time and moving the characters or objects in small increments to create the illusion of motion

Storyboard A visual plan or visual interpretation of the screenplay represented by a series of drawings with accompanying captionlike descriptions of the action and sound, usually arranged in comic strip fashion and used to plan a film, television, or video production

Texture Mapping The process of applying a 3-D image to a 3-D object defined within a computer

Traditional Animation See **Cel Animation.**

Transition The passing from one scene to another involving transitional effects (e.g., cross-dissolve, wipe, etc.) in a film, television, or video production

Underlay In animation, part of the decor placed behind the main animation

Visual Effects The production of effects, including digital effects, stop-motion, and composited imagery (combining live-action and computer-generated imagery)

Walk Cycles A series of drawings animators routinely make for characters, creating the illusion of movement with background pans

Xsheet See **Exposure Sheet.**

SELECTED BIBLIOGRAPHY

Akanbi, Avione. "Working as an Animation Illustrator: A Career That Moves." Available online. URL: http://www.brighthub.com/arts/drawing-illustration/articles/68874.aspx. Accessed April 17, 2010.

AllArtSchools.com. "Animation Career and Education Resource Center." Available online. URL: http://www.allartschools.com/faqs/animation-schools.php. Accessed March 22, 2011.

Alvarado, Holli. E-mail interview by author. May 7, 2010.

Amoroso, Angela. "David Russell Storyboarding's Super Hero." Storyboardart.com. Available online. URL: http://www.storyboardart.com/interviews.php.

The Animation Guild Local 839. "The CBA Minimums, 2006–2009." Available Online. URL: http://www.animationguild.org/_Contract/wages_pdf/TAG_Minimums_2006–2009.pdf. Accessed March 22, 2011.

———. "Contract, 2006–2009." Available online. URL: http://www.animationguild.org/_Contract/contract_pdf/AnimationGuildCBA.pdf.

———. "Past Wage Minimums, 1995–2006." Available online. URL: http://www.animationguild.org/_Home/home_FRM1.html.

———. "The 2009 Wage Survey." Available online. URL: http://www.animationguild.org/2009WageSurveyv1.pdf.

———. "Wage Surveys, 1996–2007." Available online. URL: http://www.animationguild.org/_Home/home_FRM1.html.

Animation Mentor. "Animation Mentor Industry Report." Available online. URL: http://www.animationmentor.com/report/. Accessed March 22, 2011.

Baker, Thomas. E-mail interview by author. May 14, 2010.

Bashor, John. "Interview with Dr. Evan Smythe, DreamWorks Animation." Hoise.com. June 2006. Available online. URL: http://www.hoise.com/primeur/06/articles/weekly/AE-PR-06-06-122.html. Accessed March 22, 2011.

"Becoming a 3-D Animator: Giovanni Nakpil." AnimationArena.com. Available online. URL: http://www.animationarena.com/becoming-a-3d-animator.html. Accessed March 22, 2011.

Brinkman, Ron. *The Art and Science of Digital Compositing*. San Francisco: Morgan Kaufman, 1999.

Bureau of Labor Statistics, U.S. Department of Labor. *May 2009 National Occupational Employment and Wage Estimates*. Compiled by the U.S. Office of Personnel Management. Available online. URL: http://www.bls.gov/oes/current/oes_nat.htm#27-0000. Accessed March 22, 2011.

———. *Occupational Employment and Wages, May 2009*. "Sound Engineering Technicians." Available online. URL: http://www.bls.gov/oes/current/oes274014.htm. Accessed March 22, 2011.

———. *Occupational Outlook Handbook and Career Guide to Industries, 2010–11 Edition*. "Advertising and Public Relations." Available online. URL: http://www.bls.gov/oco/cg/cgs030.htm. Accessed March 22, 2011.

———. *Occupational Outlook Handbook and Career Guide to Industries, 2010–11 Edition*. "Announcers." Available online. URL: http://www.bls.gov/oco/ocos087.htm. Accessed March 22, 2011.

———. *Occupational Outlook Handbook and Career Guide to Industries, 2010–11 Edition*. "Broadcasting." Available online. URL: http://www.bls.gov/oco/cg/cgs017.htm. Accessed March 22, 2011.

———. *Occupational Outlook Handbook and Career Guide to Industries, 2010–11 Edition*. "Television, Video, and Motion Picture Camera Operators and Editors." Available online. URL: http://www.bls.gov/oco/ocos091.htm. Accessed March 22, 2011.

Charnov, Aharon. E-mail interview by author. June 24, 2010.

Cherry, Shavonne. E-mail interview by author. May 26, 2010.

College Board Editors. *2010 Book of Majors*. Plano, Tex.: College Board Publications, 2009.

Colvard, Wallace. E-mail interview by author. May 28, 2010.

Conrad, Gary. E-mail interview by author. July 7, 2010.

Corcoran, Matt. E-mail interview by author. June 11, 2010.

Danielle Paulet, 2-D animator, e-mail interview by author. June 13, 2010.

Dawson, Nick. "The Future of Stop-Motion: Carlos Lascano." FilminFocus.com. 6 February 2009. Available online. URL: http://www.filminfocus.com/article/the_future_of_stop_motion__carlos_lascano. Accessed May 25, 2011.

DeCastro, Cinthia. "Cecile Marie Tecson—Visual Effects Artist." AsianJournal.com. Available online. URL: http://www.asianjournal.com/galing-pinoy/59-

galing-pinoy/2300-cecile-marie-tecson-visual-eff ects-artist.html. Posted July 12, 2009.

"Dennis Presnell Interview." Kidzworld.com. Available online. URL: http://www.kidzworld.com/ article/3507-dennis-presnell-interview. Accessed March 22, 2011.

DeSilva Rowell, Christina. E-mail interview by author. May 14, 2010.

Drewski, Kristen. E-mail interview by author. June 28, 2010.

Duncan, Brendan. E-mail interview by author. May 20, 2010.

Education-Advancement.com. "Animation Design Job Outlook." Available online. URL: http://www. education-advancement.com/education-resources/ Animation-Design-Job-Outlook.htm. Accessed March 22, 2011.

Ellison, Charles. E-mail interview by author. June 28, 2010.

Elwood, Joe. E-mail interview by author. May 20, 2010.

Ettedgui, Peter. *Production Design & Art Direction.* Woburn, Mass.: Focal Press, 1999.

Falkowski, Jeremy. "Inbetweening/Cleanup." AnimationArtist.com. October 1999. Available online. URL: http://www.animationartist.com/columns/ JFalkowski/Inbetweening_Tutorial/inbetweening_ tuto rial.html

Freeman, Eric. E-mail interview by author. July 1, 2010.
———. E-mail interview by author. June 29, 2010.

"From Intern to Environment Artist: Interview with Aaron Canaday." TakeInitiaive.co.uk. Available online. URL: http://www.takeinitiative. co.uk/?p=481. Posted November 27, 2009.

Frost, Quentin. E-mail interview by author. June 15, 2010.

Gallegly, Kevin. E-mail interviews by author. June 4, 2010 and June 11, 2010.

"Game Art Interview—Josh Harvey." deviantART.com. Available online. URL: http:// news.deviantart.com/ article/80722/. Posted May 21, 2009.

Gardner, Garth. *Careers in Computer Graphics & Animation.* Fairfax, Va.: GGC, Inc., Publishing, 2001.

Gray, Milton. *Cartoon Animation: Introduction to a Career.* Northridge, Calif.: Lion Den's Publications, Inc., 1991.

GuidetoOnlineSchools.com. "Animation Careers." Available online. URL: http://www.guidetoonline schools.com/careers/animation#career_salary_out look. Accessed March 22, 2011.

Guske, Carolyn. E-mail interview by author. April 30, 2010.

Hamm, Gene. *How to Get a Job in Animation (And Keep It).* Portsmouth, N.H.: Heinemann, 2006.

Hart, John. *The Art of the Storyboard: Storyboarding for Film, TV, and Animation.* Woburn, Mass.: Focal Press, 1999.

Heller, Steven. "Giving Credits the Credit They're Due." *New York Times,* March 28, 2004.

Hoffman, Brett. E-mail interview by author. May 13, 2010.

Hooks, Ed. *Acting for Animators: A Complete Guide to Performance Animation.* Rev. ed. Portsmouth, N.H.: Heinemann, 2003.

Hooper, Jon. E-mail interview by author. July 10, 2010.

Hurst, John. E-mail interview by author. June 23, 2010.

"Interview: Inside Pixar with Neil Blevins." ThunderChunky.co.uk. Available online. URL: http://www. thunderchunky.co.uk/articles/inside-pixar-with-neil-blevins/. Posted December 12, 2004.

"Interview—Mark McDonnell." CGAdvertising.com. Available online. URL: http://www.cgadvertising. com/pages/latest-news/interview---mark-mcdon nell.php. Accessed March 22, 2011.

"Interview with 3D Character Artist from Blitz Game Studios Jose Lazaro." TutorialBoard.net. Available online. URL: http://www.tutorialboard.net/inter view-3d-character-artist-blitz-game-studios-jose-lazaro/. Accessed March 22, 2011.

Isenberg, Marty. E-mail interview by author. May 11, 2010.

Jacobsmeyer, Wendy. E-mail interview by author. June 23, 2010.

Jobstar.org. "Industry Profiles, 2010." Available online. URL: http://jobstar.org/tools/salary/index.cfm. Accessed March 22, 2011.

"JobStar: Salary Information Index." *The Wall Street Journal: Career/Journal.com.* Available online. URL: http://jobstar.org/tools/salary/index.cfm. Accessed March 22, 2011.

Jolly, Chris. E-mail interview by author. July 14, 2010.

Jones, Jason. E-mail interview by author. May 4, 2010.

"Justin Rasch Interview." Anime8StopMotion.com. Available online. URL: http://www.anim8stopmotion.com/ interview.php?id=7. Accessed March 22, 2011.

Kane, Tom. Interview by author. May 14, 2010.

Kernan, Thomas. E-mail interview by author. May 3, 2010.

Klatte, Owen. E-mail interview by author. May 21, 2010.

Knowlton, Alex. "Dream Job: Interview with Film Graphics Designer Eric Rosenberg." DesignObserver. com. Available online. URL: http://www.design observer.com/observatory/entry.html?entry=12407. Accessed January 8, 2010.

Krall, Dan. E-mail interview by author. June 24, 2010.

Kroon, Pieter. E-mail interviews by author. June 8, 2010, and June 15, 2010.

Lignan, Christian. E-mail interview by author. June 15, 2010.

LoBrutto, Vincent. *By Design: Interviews with Film Production Designers.* Westport, Conn.: Praeger, 1992.

Lord, Peter, Brian Sibley, and Nick Park. *Cracking Animation: The Aardman Book of 3-D Animation.* 3d ed. New York: Thames & Hudson, 2010.

Lu, Luis. E-mail interview by author. May 14, 2010.

Lyons, Rosanna. E-mail interview by author. May 16, 2010.

McGuckin, Gene. E-mail interview by author. May 7, 2010.

Meier, Doron A. "2D Animation: Acting and Animation." AnimationArena.com. Available online. URL: http://www.animationarena.com/2d-animation.html. Accessed March 22, 2011.

Milo, Mike. "Character Layout." MilowerkMedia.com. Available online. URL: http://www.milowerx.com/tv-animation-process/character-layout. Accessed March 22, 2011.

Nelson, Jennifer. E-mail interview by author. May 20, 2010.

Noyer, Jeremie. "The Princess and the Frog's Supervising Animator Mark Henn." AnimatedViews.com. Available online. URL: animatedviews.com/2010/the-princess-and-the-frog-supervising-animator-mark-henn-part-2-the-disney-decade. Posted January 8, 2010.

Obena, Nollan. E-mail interviews by author. June 3, 2010, and June 11, 2010.

Oehrl, Eric. "Interview with Pixar TD Kim White." *Frame by Frame.* Winter 1998. Available online. URL: http://www.asifa.org/pdf/winter98.pdf. Accessed March 22, 2011.

O'Sullivan, Celine. E-mail interview by author. May 11, 2010.

Partible, Van. E-mail interview by author. July 8, 2010.

Paulsen, Craig. E-mail interview by author. May 16, 2010.

Perry, Tekla S. "Dream Jobs 2010: Jacob Melvin, Technical Director at DreamWorks Animation." *IEEE Spectrum.* February 2010. Available online. URL: http://spectrum.ieee.org/at-work/tech-careers/dream-job-jacob-melvin. Accessed March 22, 2011.

Pignotti, Philip. E-mail interview by author. May 21, 2010.

Priebe, Ken A. *The Art of Stop-Motion Animation.* Boston: Thomson Course Technology, 2007.

"Q&A with Dick Zondag, Supervising Animator on Meet the Robinsons." FutureMovies.co.uk. Available online. URL: http://www.futuremovies.co.uk/filmmaking.asp?ID=216. Accessed March 22, 2011.

Robertson, Barbara. "Peter Sohn: Artist Profile." CGSociety. Available online. URL: http://features.cgsociety.org/story_custom.php?story_id=4996. Posted April 9, 2009.

Robinson, Andrew. E-mail interview by author. May 20, 2010.

Roman, Christian. E-mail interview by author. June 4, 2010.

Sacks, Terence J. *Opportunities in Cartooning & Animation Careers,* Rev. ed. New York: McGraw-Hill Companies, 2008.

Salary Wizard. "Salary Data from Salary.Com, Inc." Available online. URL: http://swz.salary.com/. Accessed March 22, 2011.

Satrun, Sarah. E-mail interview by author. May 15, 2010.

Shaw, Susannah. *Stop Motion: Craft Skills for Model Animation.* 2d ed. London; New York: Focal Press: 2008.

Showbiz Labor Guide, 2009/2010. 15th ed. Los Angeles: Entertainment Publishers, 2009.

Silver, Stephen. E-mail interview by author. May 3, 2010.

Sito, Tom. *Drawing the Line: The Untold Story of the Animation Unions from Bosko to Bart Simpson.* Lexington, Ky.: University Press of Kentucky, 2006.

SkillSet (Skills for Business). *Jobs in the Film Industry.* Available online. URL: http://www.skillset.org. Accessed March 22, 2011.

Sly, Randall. "Andre Medina Interview: Character Layout Artist." Blogspot.com. Available online. URL: http://andre-medina-interview.blogspot.com/. Accessed March 22, 2011.

Smith, Brian. E-mail interview by author. May 22, 2010.

"Software Engineering—Mike King." Graduating Engineering.com. Available online. URL: http://www.graduatingengineer.com/articles/20010531/Software-Engineering. Accessed May 25, 2011.

Stearn, Brock. E-mail interview by author. July 6, 2010.

Stefan, Dean. E-mail interview by author. May 21, 2010.

"3D Animator: Liem Nguyen." AnimationArena.com. Available online. URL: http://www.animationarena.com/3d-animator.html. Accessed March 22, 2011.

Tumminello, Wendy. *Exploring Storyboarding.* New York: Thomas/Delmar Learning, 2005.

"UK MOVIES: James Wood Wilson Interview." BBC.co.uk. Available online. URL: http://www.bbc.co.uk/films/ukmovies/interviews/britplayers/james_wood_wilson.shtml. Posted July 2005.

Ulene, Nancy. E-mail interview by author. May 25, 2010.

"Video Game Animator: Patrick Beaulieu." AnimationArena.com. Available online. URL: http://www.animationarena.com/video-game-animator.html. Accessed March 22, 2011.

von Riederman, Dominic. "Up Animator Jason Boose Talks About Technical Challenges." Suite101.com. Available online. URL: http://hollywood-animated-films.suite101.com/article.cfm/animator_jason_boose_on_up_interview. Posted June 22, 2009.

Walker, Adrian. "Interview with Jeff Hanna, Senior Technical Artist at Volition." Tech-Artists.org. Available online. URL: http://tech-artists.org/forum/showthread.php?t=273. Posted December 30, 2008.

———. "Interview with Jason Parks, Senior Technical Artist at Sony Online Entertainment." Tech-Artists.org. Available online. URL: http://tech-artists.org/forum/showthread.php?t=178. Posted September 26, 2008.

Warnock, Theodore. E-mail interview by author. May 13, 2010.

Webster, Chris. *Animation: The Mechanics of Motion.* Burlington, Mass.: Focal Press, 2005.

Weis, Nicolas. E-mail interview by author. June 27, 2010.

WetFeet.com. "Career Profiles, 2010." Available online. URL: http://www.wetfeet.com. Accessed March 22, 2011.

Whitaker, Harold, and John Halas. *Timing for Animation.* London: Focal Press, 1981.

"WiG Weekend: Interview with Megan Sawyer, Bethesda Softworks." GamingAngels.com. Available online. URL: http://www.gamingangels.com/2010/04/wig-weekend-interview-with-megan-sawyer-bethesda-softworks/. Posted April 11, 2010.

Williams, Nate. "Interview with Kirsten Lepore." IllustrationMUNDO.com. Available online. URL: http://www.illustrationmundo.com/wp/462. Posted February 2, 2009.

Williams, Richard. *The Animator's Survival Kit.* London: Faber & Faber, 2001.

Wolf, Rich. E-mail interview by author. May 15, 2010.

Wolff, Ellen. "Animator Davis Wrangles Golden Bots in Hellboy II." AWN.com. Available online. URL: http://www.awn.com/articles/production/animator-davis-wrangles-golden-bots-ihellboy-iii. Posted July 16, 2008.

Wyatt, Carol. E-mail interview by author. June 3, 2010.

Yank, Michael. E-mail interview by author. May 9, 2010.

INDEX

Page numbers in **boldface** indicate main articles.

ABOUT JEFF LENBURG

Jeff Lenburg is an award-winning author, celebrity biographer, and nationally acknowledged expert on animated cartoons who has spent nearly three decades researching and writing about this lively art. He has written more than 30 books, including such acclaimed histories of animation as *Who's Who in Animated Cartoons, The Great Cartoon Directors,* and four previous encyclopedias of animated cartoons. His books have been nominated for several awards, including the American Library Association's "Best Non-Fiction Award" and the Evangelical Christian Publishers Association's Gold Medallion Award for "Best Autobiography/Biography." He lives in Arizona.

ABOUT BOB KURTZ

Bob Kurtz, founder of the Burbank-based animation studio Kurtz & Friends, writes, designs, and directs entertainment films and television commercials. His work includes animation sequences. He is the recipient of numerous awards, including an Emmy for the PBS special *Roman City,* the Peabody Award for the Lily Tomlin special *Edith Ann's Christmas,* ASIFA Hollywood's Annie Award for Lifetime Achievement, and more than 250 international awards. His films are included in the permanent collections of the Museum of Modern Art, New York; the Los Angeles County Museum of Art, Los Angeles; and the ASIFA Archive, Germany. Kurtz was also formerly recognized as *Adweek's* "Animator of the Year" and as Japan's "Artist of the Year."